Photography Building Blocks

Photo Techniques

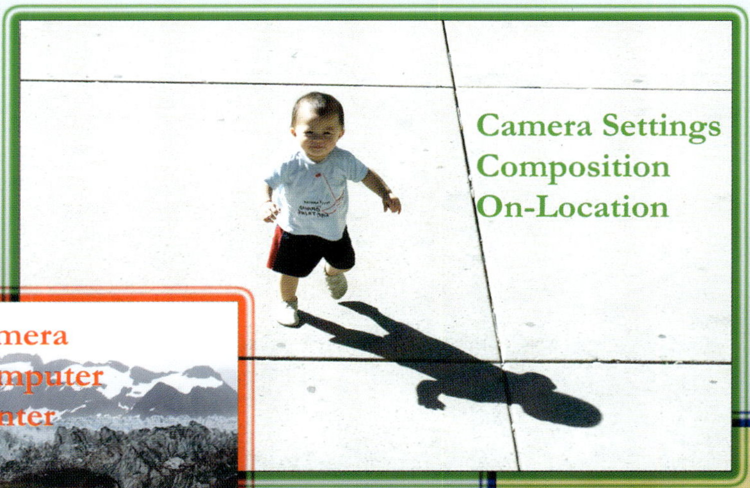

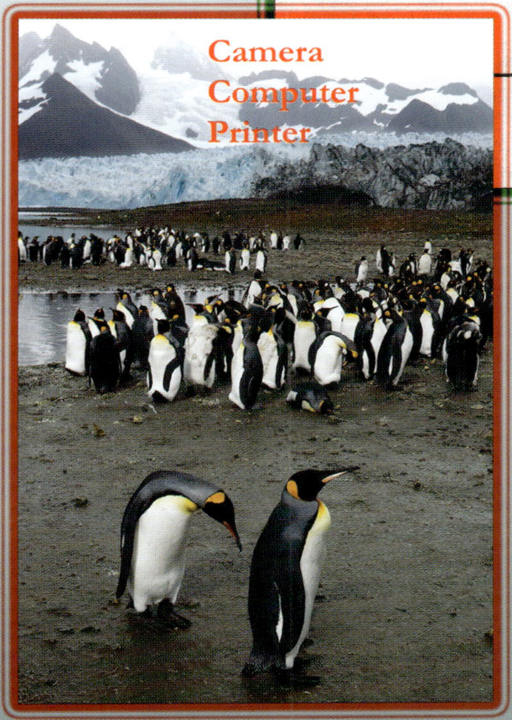

Photo Equipment

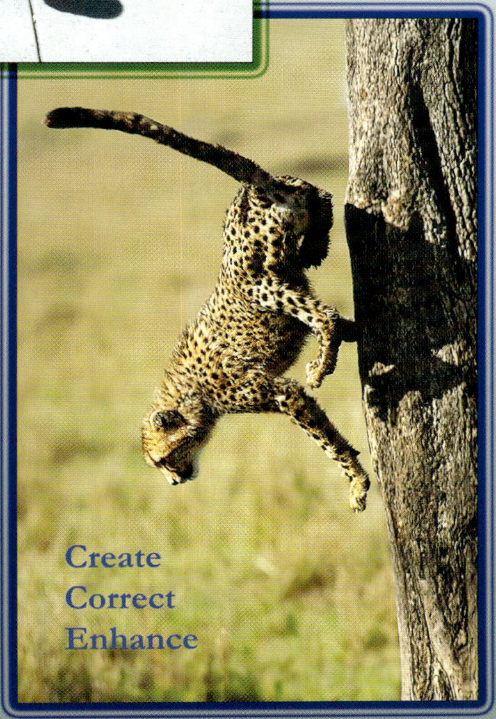

Photo Editing

Printed by

Best Deal Graphics & Printing

FIRST EDITION: August 2006

Trademarks

All terms mentioned in this book that are known to be trademarks or service marks have been appropriately capitalized. DPinstruct.com cannot attest to the accuracy of this information. Use of a term in this book should not be regarded as affecting the validity of any trademark or service mark.

Photoshop is a registered trademark of Adobe Systems, Inc.

Windows is a registered trademark of Microsoft Corp.

Warning and Disclaimer

This book is designed to provide information about cameras, photography and editing for digital photographers. Every effort has been made to make this book as complete and as accurate as possible, but no warranty of fitness is implied.

The information is provided on an as-is basis. The authors and printer shall have neither the liability nor responsibility to any person or entity with respect to any loss or damages arising from the information contained in this book or from the use of any disc, program or website that may accompany it.

Photo Images

The photos used in this book are contributed by Phil Kwan, Antony Chow and Henry Christiansen.

ISBN 0-9781800-0-3

Introduction

With current advances in cameras, computers and printers, digital images are fast becoming an essential part of the way we communicate, as widely shared as text messages and e-mails. While most digital photography books are aimed at serious amateurs and professionals, this book is instead aimed at the ***beginner and intermediate photographer***. No previous knowledge of cameras, computers or editing is assumed or required.

Digital Photography Instruction is a companion book to the website: www.dpinstruct.com. The book is designed both to stand alone and to work in conjunction with the website for those who want additional and more recently updated information. Our website contains more articles, numerous examples and continuously updated information.

Digital Photography Instruction is simply about creating better pictures. This is not a book about the theory of photography but one that will show you how to take better pictures, through precise and easy to understand examples.

This book can be used in two different ways:

1) **The Jump-in-Anywhere Approach:** Turn to any section that contains a topic you are interested in and start right there. Each topic contains comprehensive step-by-step instructions that are logical and easy to follow.
2) **The Start-to-Finish Approach:** Since chapters progress in a logical sequence from taking pictures, to digitally manipulating them, to printing and e-mailing them, you can also start at the beginning of the book and follow through each section in sequence.

Digital Photography Instruction is written in clear and easy to follow text, accompanied by pictures illustrating each technique. We use a minimum of jargon. Information on **photo techniques**, **photo editing** and **photo equipment** is broken down into multiple steps. Anyone can follow our easy step-by-step approach.

TABLE OF CONTENTS

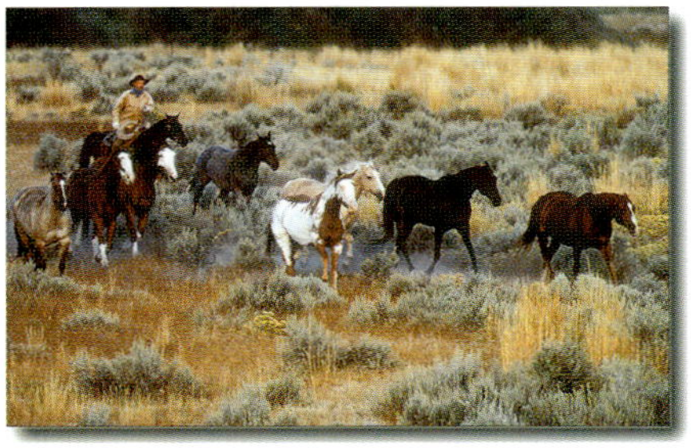

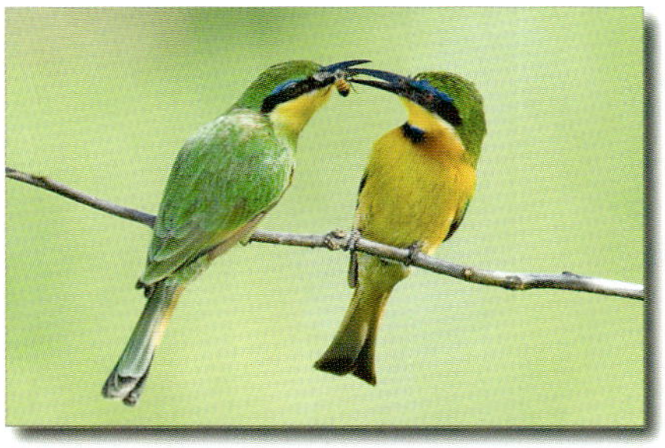

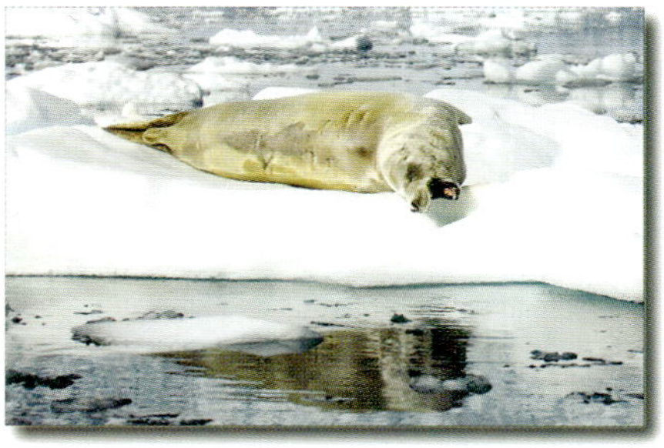

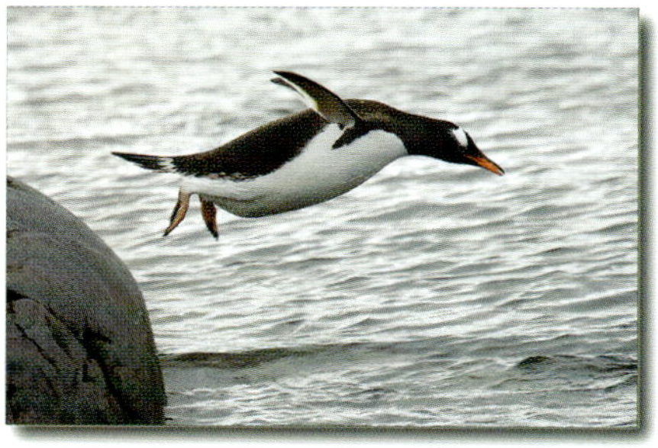

TABLE OF CONTENTS

PHOTO EDITING

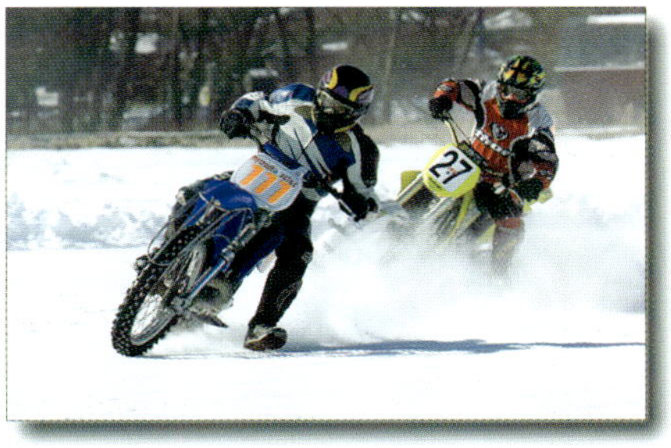

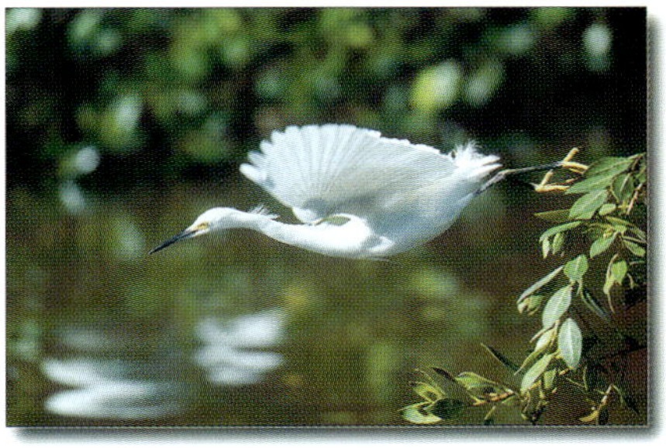

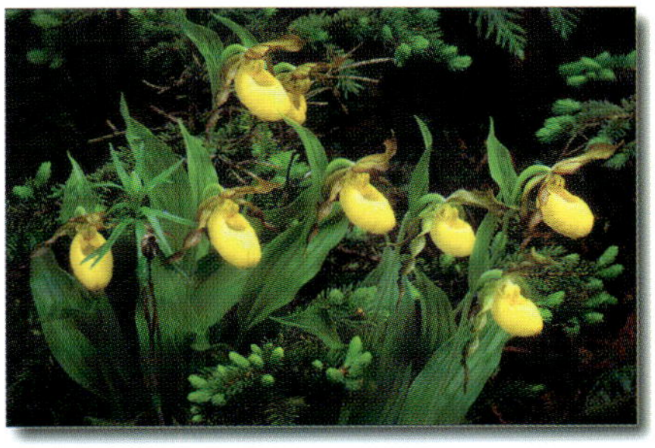

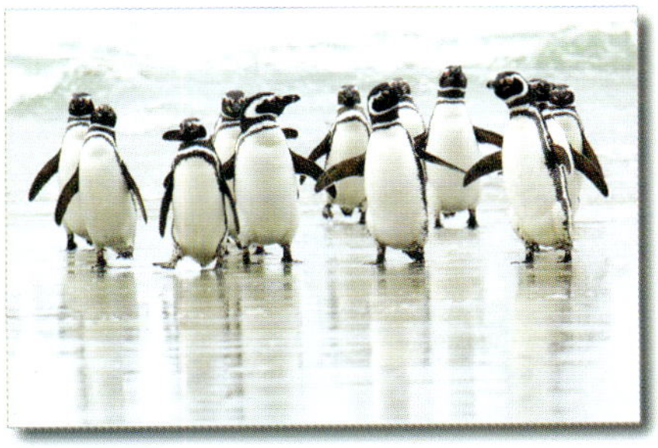

TABLE OF CONTENTS

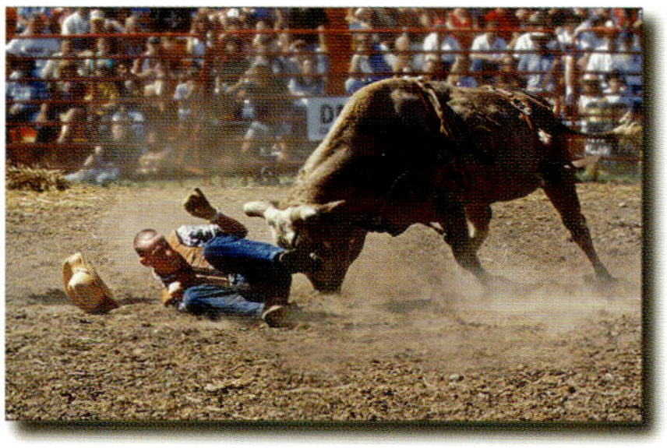

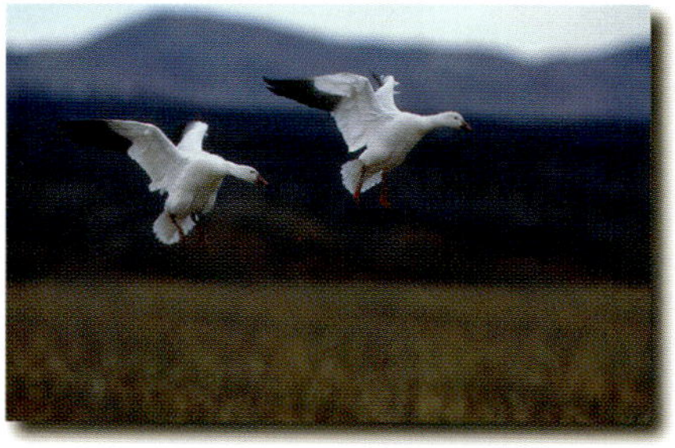

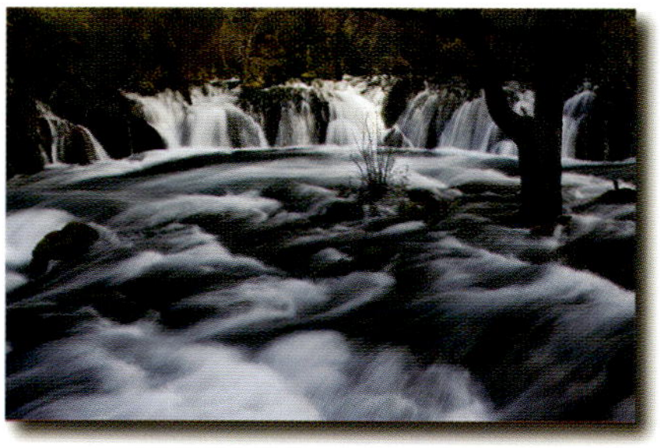

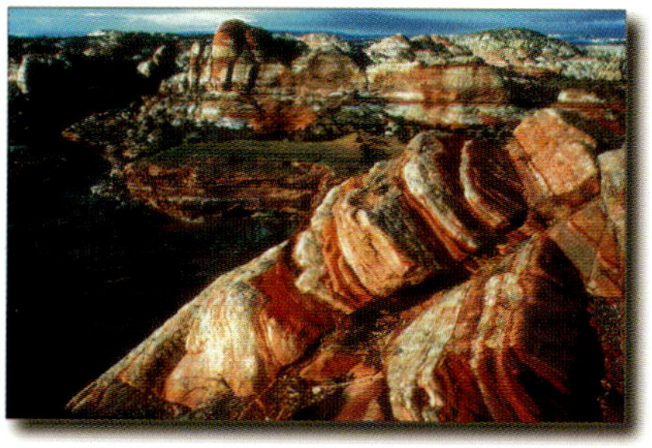

Chapter 1 START USING YOUR CAMERA

Start Using Your Camera

Most beginners arrive home with their new digital camera and do not know where to start. While essential as reference documents, camera manuals often fail when it comes to walking you through the initial steps needed to get you using your new camera. Manuals attempt to be complete and exhaustive, but they often fail to stress important aspects of camera use and do not tend to mention any issues that do not involve the camera itself.

Fortunately, the initial steps are the same for virtually every digital camera. We have organized these steps into a logical order to help you get started. We recommend that you follow these steps and use your camera manual as a reference for the specifics that relate to your camera alone.

Introduction

In this chapter, we will cover the extra accessories you will require and the initial steps you will need to take prior to turning on your camera. We will then list the most important camera controls that you should locate on your camera using the instruction manual. We will review the initial camera settings that you should make. We will then take you through the basic steps to get you taking pictures, reviewing your images and transferring them to your computer.

Step 1 – Confirm Contents

When you first open that wonderful box holding your new digital camera, you should immediately make sure you have received everything that should be in the box.

There is usually an outline in the front of the camera manual that lists the contents of the box.

Standard Contents:

1	Camera
2	Camera Strap / Lens Cap
3	Batteries / Battery Charger
4	Camera Manual – Printed / CD Version
5	Download Cable – Camera to Computer
6	Memory Card
7	Software on CD

Step 2 – Rechargeable Batteries

Non-rechargeable batteries run down much too quickly and end up costing far too much to be practical.

If your camera uses "AA" batteries and came with non-rechargeable batteries, you will need to change to a rechargeable "AA" battery system.

In this case you should purchase a "NiMH" (Nickel Metal Hydride) recharger with NiMH "AA" batteries.

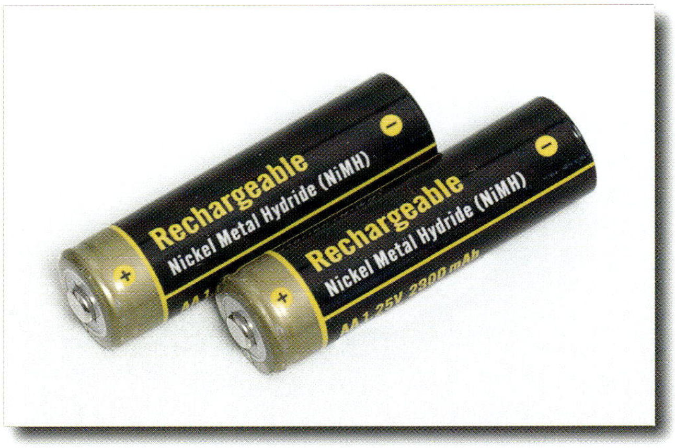

Step 3 – Get Accessories

The three basic accessories we recommend you purchase to get the most out of your camera are:

1. Extra Batteries: Batteries in digital cameras tend to work nicely for a while before suddenly running down and taking a long time to recharge. You should acquire an extra set of batteries.
2. Memory Cards: provided by the manufacturer are usually of a low capacity. You should get one or more extra cards, of the appropriate type, with a capacity of 512MB or more
3. Memory Card Readers: We recommend you use these to copy images from your cards to your computer, rather than connecting your camera directly to the computer. Get a Card Reader that matches the type of Memory Card you use.

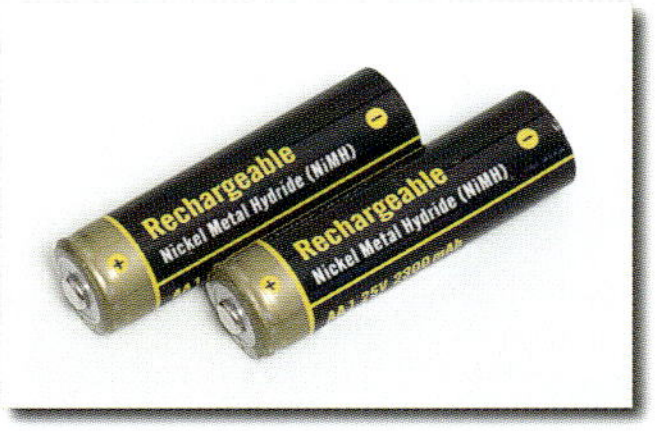

Some cameras need 2 and some 4 "AA" batteries

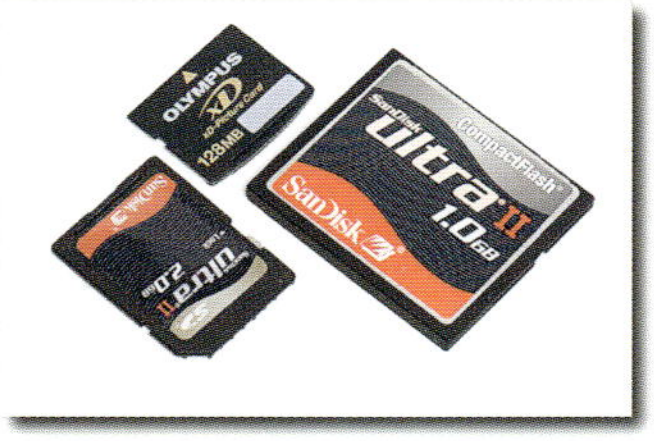

A "Secure Digital" Card, "xD" Card and a "Compact Flash" Card

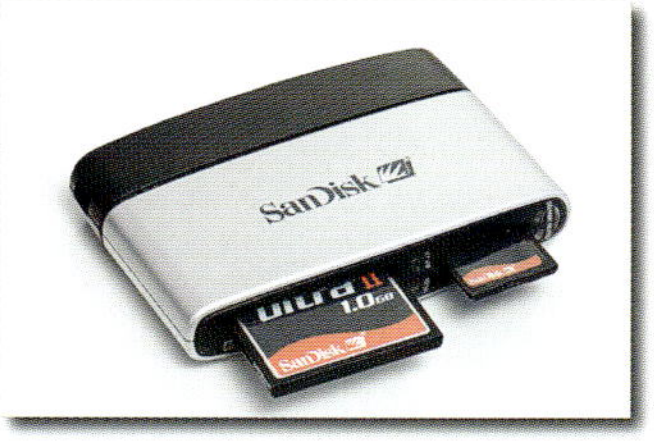

Card Reader for a "Compact Flash" Card and "Secure Digital" Card.

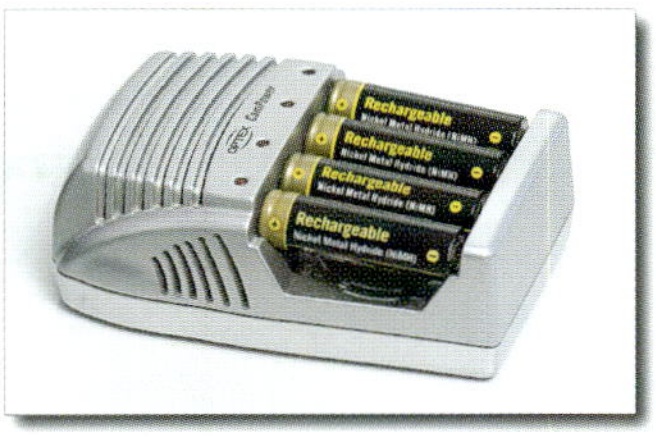

"AA" NiMH Batteries and Charger

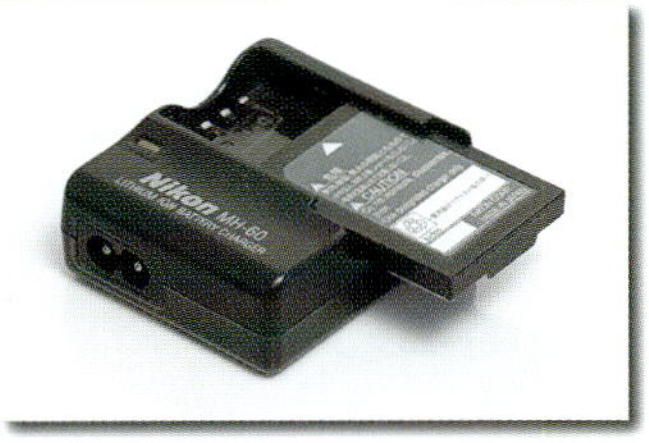

Proprietary Li-Ion Battery and Charger

Step 4 – Charge Batteries

Don't even attempt to turn your camera on until you have fully charged one complete set of batteries. When one set is charged, you can move to the next step.

Put your second set on charge to have them at the ready. Always travel with one battery set in your camera and a completely charged spare set ready for when the first set runs down.

It is considered good technique to let batteries run down completely before recharging or the batteries can start to lose their recharging capacity. Some batteries, like NiMH are more sensitive to this. Li-Ion (Lithium-Ion) batteries are less prone to losing their recharging capacity.

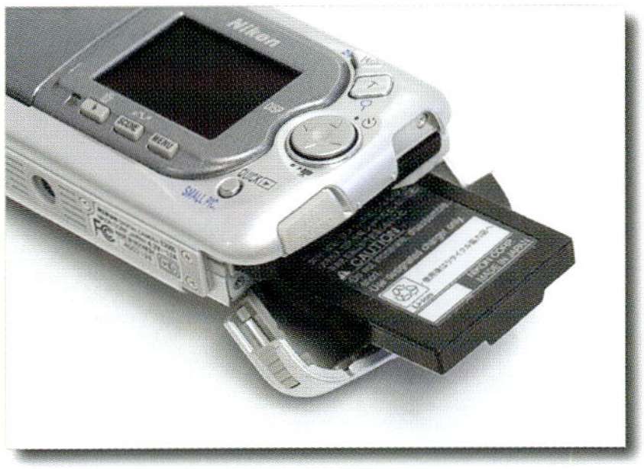

Step 5 – Insert Batteries

With the camera turned off, insert a fully charged set of batteries into your camera. Make sure the batteries are placed in the camera in the correct orientation as shown in the manual.

The orientation of the "+" and "-" ends of batteries is critical in cameras that take "AA" batteries.

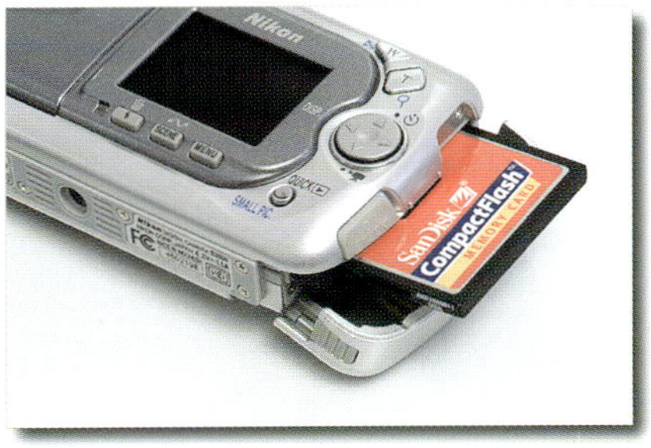

Step 6 – Insert Memory Card

With the camera turned off, insert a Memory Card in the camera. Make sure the card is placed in the camera in the appropriate slot and in the correct orientation as shown in the camera manual.

Memory cards should be placed in the camera with contacts facing in and should slide in easily when inserted correctly.

Step 7 – Camera Controls

There are many controls on a digital camera. However, there are a few essential controls that you need to know to perform basic functions. Please locate the following controls on your camera using the camera manual.

1	**On / Off Switch** – this will allow you to turn the camera on and off.
2	**Focus Control** – this engages auto focus. It's often integrated in the shutter button.
3	**The Shutter Button** – this is the button you depress when you wish to take a picture.
4	**Exposure Mode Dial** – this enables auto exposure.
5	**Play / Review Control** – to switch from taking pictures to looking at images you have already taken.
6	**Selection Dial** – this is often a rocker dial that allows you to make selections in the menus and to advance images in picture review mode.
7	**Flash Selector** – this turns the flash on and off.
8	**Zoom Lever** – this allows you to zoom from wide angle to a narrow angle telephoto view
9	**Menu Button** – this allows you to change settings in the camera.

These camera controls are shown on the Canon A700 to give you an example.

There are far more camera controls and features on most modern digital cameras. However, if you learn to operate these basic ones, you will be well on the way to taking, viewing and downloading digital images. After that, it will be time to learn more.

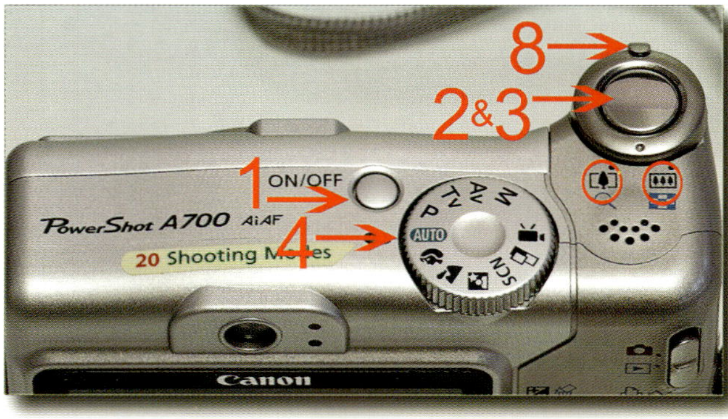

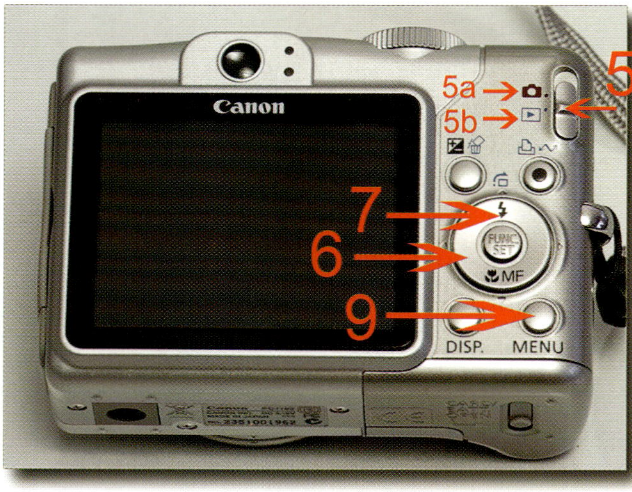

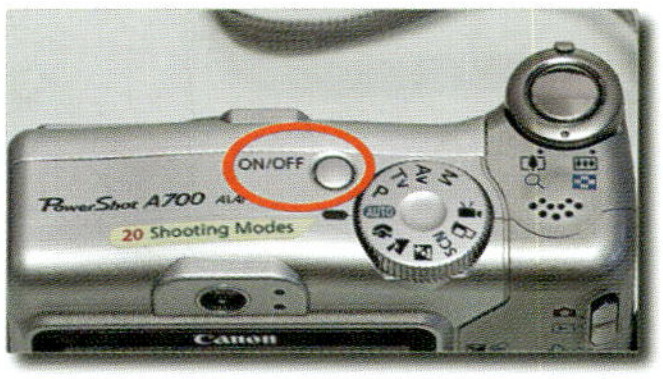

Step 8 – Turn the Camera On

With fully charged batteries and a memory card in the camera, you are finally ready to turn on your camera. Use the On/Off switch to accomplish this.

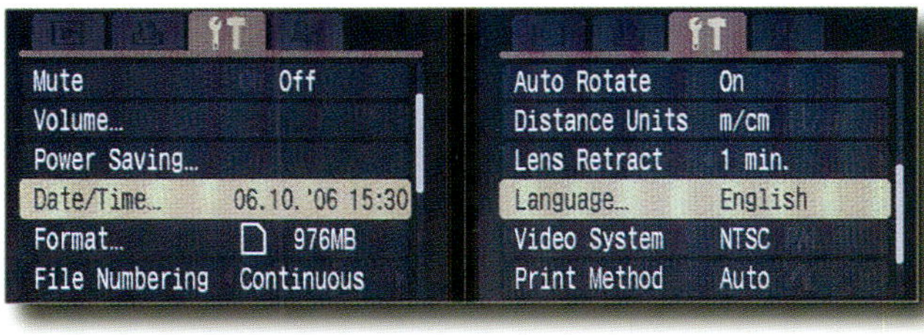

Setting the date and time in the camera will allow the camera to label every image with a time stamp for future reference.

Step 9 – First Time Settings

After you have turned it on, the camera will spring to life. The camera will request that you enter in some basic information. You can view this on the LCD screen on the back of the camera. Generally you use the "Selection Dial", which is usually a rocker switch, to enter information. This information is usually the present date and time along with the language you wish to use.

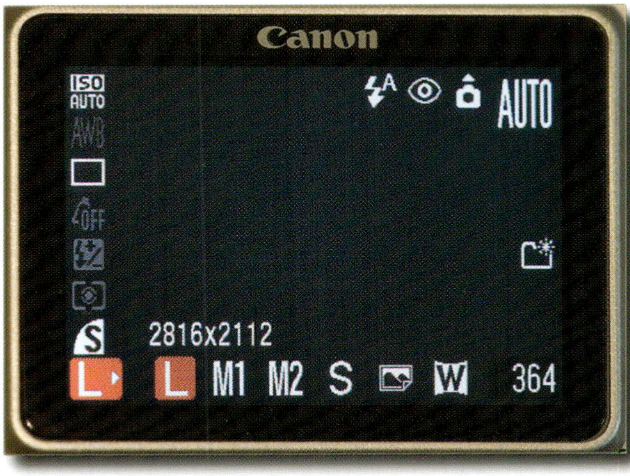

Here we have set the camera to "**L**", which is the largest "Jpeg" size. The numbers "**2816x2112**" are the pixel dimensions. You want the highest numbers in the pixel dimensions.

Step 10 – Setting File Type

It is important to set the File Type. It should be "Jpeg" and not "Tiff". Most manufacturers set their camera to "Jpeg" by default. However, some set the size to something other than the largest size. Set the File Type to the largest "Jpeg" size offered.

1. Jpeg
2. Largest Jpeg

This is usually set via the Menu Button and Selection Dial as outlined in the camera's instruction manual.

Note: Sometimes some manufacturers combine File Type and Compression into one step in the menu.

Step 11 – Setting Quality (Compression)

"Quality" and "Compression" mean the same thing. This setting refers to how much your images are going to be compressed. The more compression that occurs, the more loss of image quality. Most manufacturers default to a lower quality setting that uses more compression in order to make the camera record images more quickly, and so that more images will fit on a memory card.

We recommend that you set this to the highest quality with the least amount of compression. This is set via the Menu Button and Selection Dial as per your camera's instruction manual.

Note: Sometimes some manufacturers combine File Type and Compression into one step from the menu.

Step 12 – Image Numbering

There is yet another important setting to confirm in your camera. Many manufacturers set cameras to number pictures consecutively in the camera until you change memory cards. In this case the numbering is reset back to "1" every time a new empty Memory Card is inserted. This goes back to the days of film, when your camera's picture counter returned to "1" every time a new roll of film was inserted. This can be a problem with digital images, since you will end up with many images with the same number. We recommend you set your counter to continuous rather than to reset using your camera's menu.

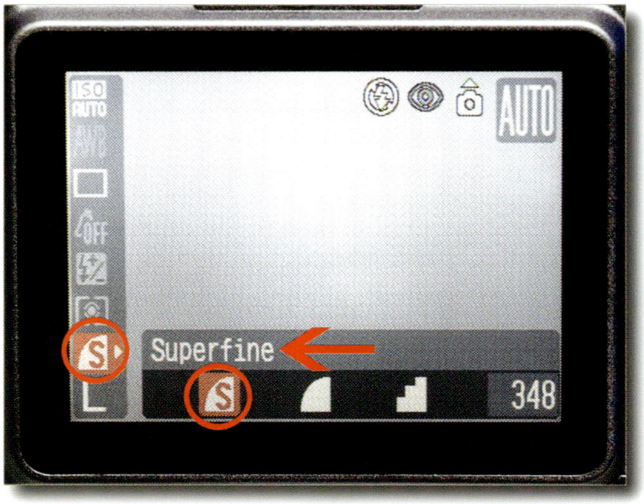

Here we have set the quality to "**S**" or "**Superfine**". This is the highest quality setting with the least amount of compression for this camera. These terms are not universal and vary from one manufacturer to the next. The number on the bottom right of the screen shows the number of images that can be taken with the setting we have chosen. Selecting the best quality will result in the fewest number of images on the card. This is what you want.

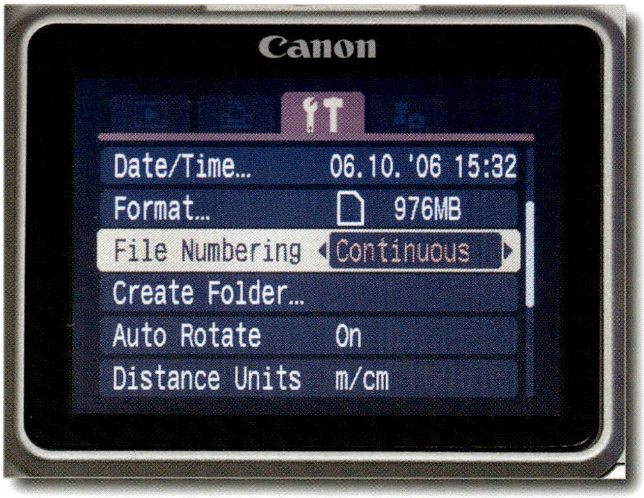

Here we have set file numbering to "**Continuous**" so that pictures will continue to be numbered consecutively, and not reset to "1" when a new memory card is inserted.

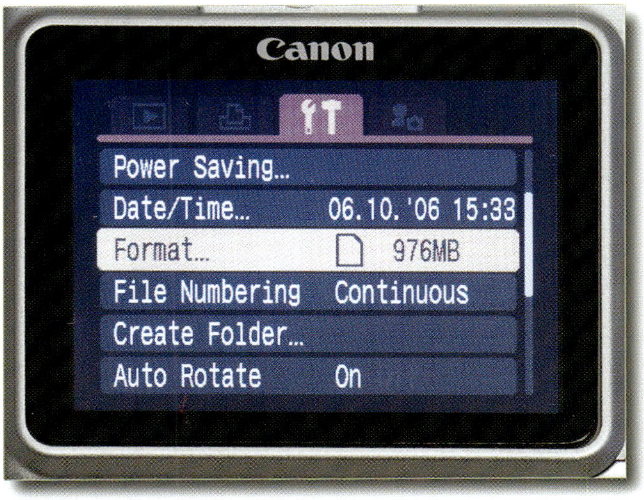

Step 13 – Format Memory Card

Memory Cards come ready to use. However, there is a danger that some will not record properly until they have been reset by your camera. This process is called "formatting". We recommend that you format every new card in your camera prior to first time use.

This is done via the Menu Button and Selection Dial according to the camera instruction manual.

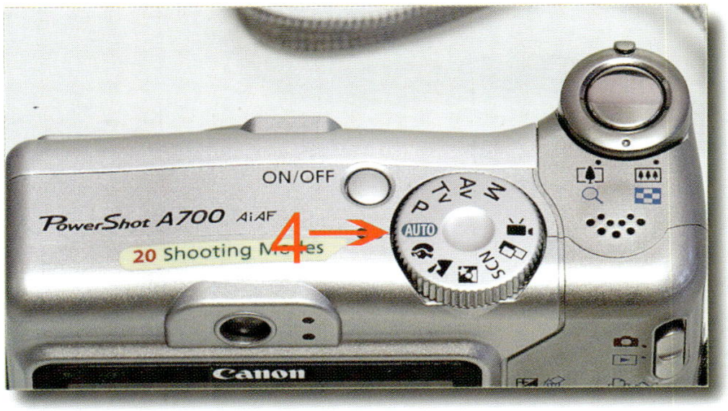

Step 14 – Set Mode Dial

The Mode Dial lets you select the Exposure Mode in which the camera will function. This can be set to Manual, Aperture Preferred, Shutter Speed Preferred, Special Scenes or Automatic.

We recommend that you set this to "Automatic" or "A" or "Auto" to begin with. You can explore the other settings at a later time.

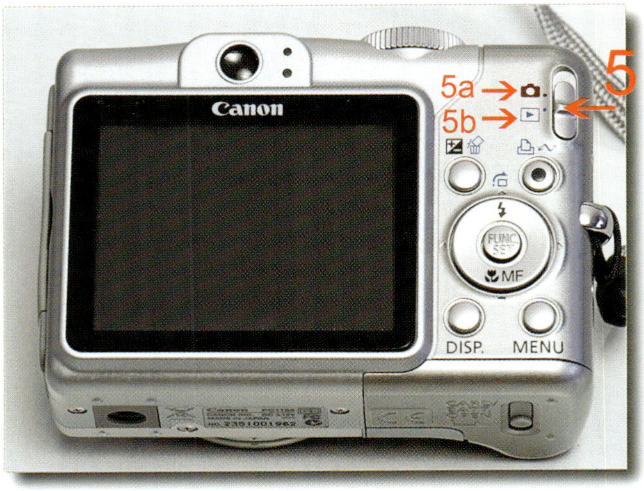

Step 15 – Shooting / Playback

Digital cameras can be set to two functional states. You are either taking pictures or you are reviewing the images that you have already taken. You must be in the right state to perform the desired function.

1. Shooting State (5a)
2. Playback State (5b)

Step 16 – Shooting State

We must take some pictures before we have anything to playback or review.

Therefore, set the camera into its "Shooting" state using the Play/Review Control.

Now you will be able to watch your future images appear live on the LCD screen on the back of the camera.

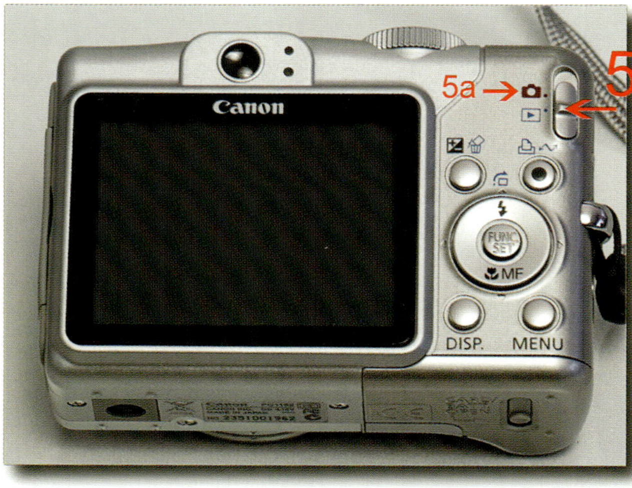

Step 17 – Using the Zoom

One of the most common functions that we use when composing pictures is the zoom. When you zoom in, the main object appears closer and larger with less surrounding background.

When you zoom out, the main object appears farther away and smaller with more surrounding background.
Use the Zoom Lever to play around with the zoom.

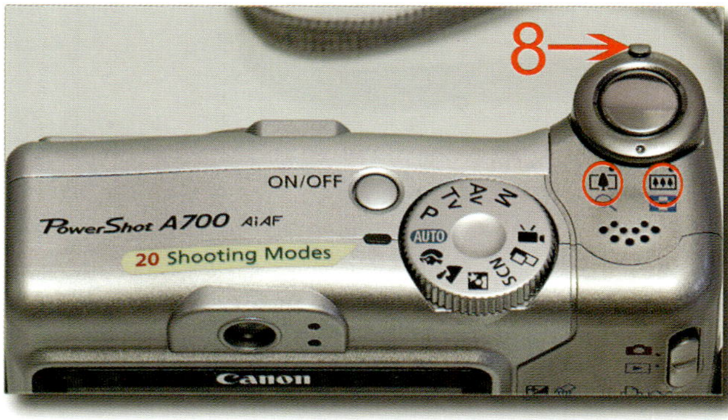

Step 18 – The Flash

The flash should be used in low light situations. Many digital cameras have low light and underexposure warnings that alert you to the need for flash. You should use the Flash Selector to turn the flash function on and off. Some cameras will function with the flash set to on at all times. In this case when there is an adequate amount of natural light, the flash intensity is reduced to give the image a fill flash which will not overpower the available light.

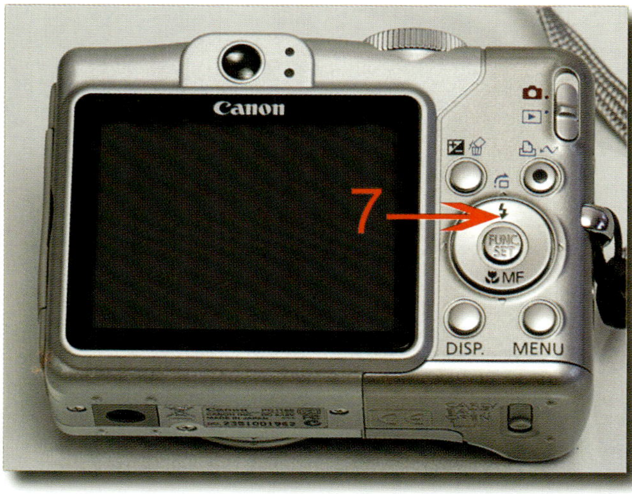

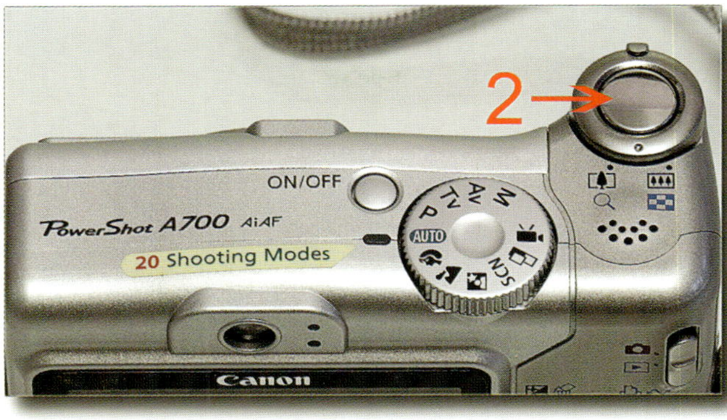

On this camera, like most, the focus and shutter are integrated onto the same control.

Step 19 – Focusing

Every digital camera has Auto Focus and comes set in Auto Focus Mode. This function is engaged by pressing the Shutter Button down halfway and holding it there.

One common mistake made by new photographers is to press down on the shutter too quickly without stopping and holding it half way. The result is that the camera will either not have a chance to focus, or will spend extra time looking for focus, and delaying the picture and possibly missing the moment.

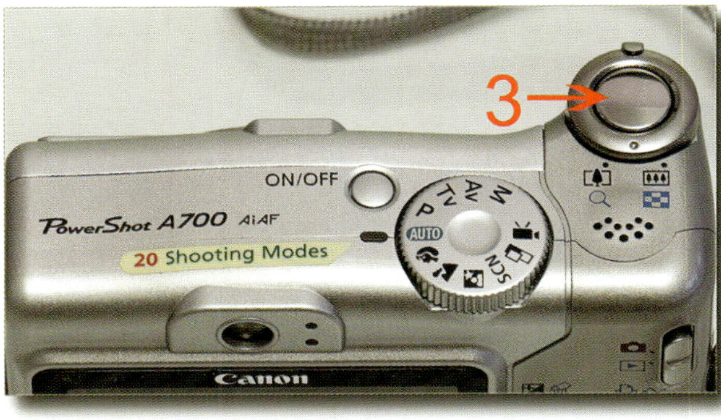

Step 20 – Taking a Shot

To actually take a picture, you press the Shutter Button down all the way.

The Shutter Button should be pressed down gently and not pushed down with force. When the Shutter Button is squeezed against the camera, instead of jabbed, there is less camera shake. The result is a sharper image.

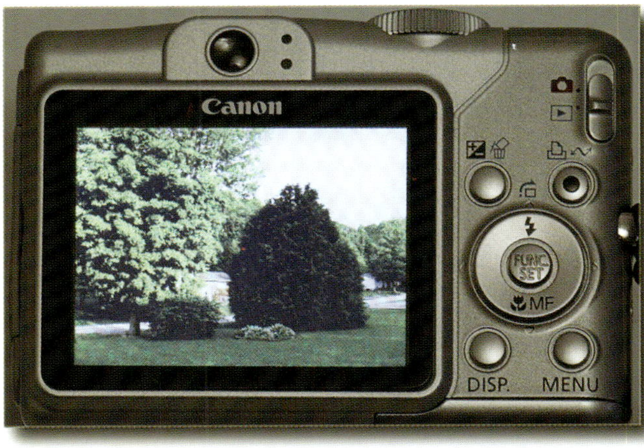

Step 21 – The Image

The image that you have just taken will appear on the LCD screen for a few seconds before your camera returns to what is in front of the lens, ready to take another shot. If the viewing time is too brief for your taste, it can be changed using the Menu Button and the Selection Dial.

Step 22 - Playback State

As mentioned earlier, digital cameras can be set to two functional states. You are either taking (or ready to take) pictures, or you are reviewing the images that you have already taken. You must be in the right state to perform the desired function.

After you have taken some shots, you will probably want to have a look at them. Therefore, set the camera into its "Playback" state using the Play/Review Control.

Remember, you cannot take any new images while in this state. You will have to set the Play/Review control to "Play" in order to return to taking pictures.

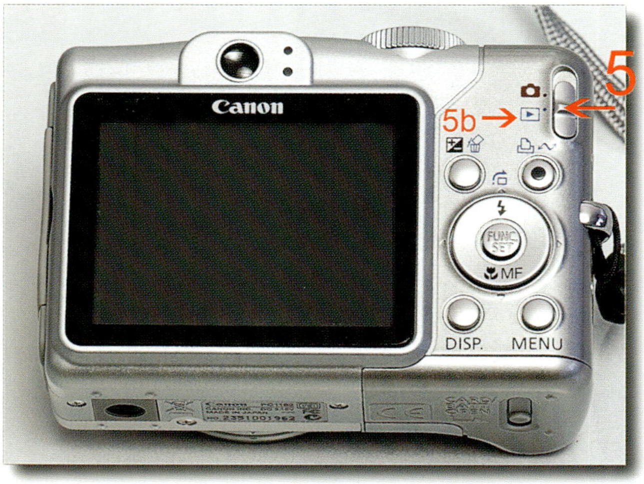

Step 23 – Reviewing Images

In the "Playback" State, you can step through all the images that are on the Memory Card.

You can also turn the camera off and change memory cards if you want to view the contents on another card. If you do so, remember to return the original card to the camera.

To view these images, use the Selection Dial. This dial tends to be a rocker dial that allows you to advance through the images when pressing the dial in one direction, while also allowing you to look at close-ups of your images when pressing it in the opposite direction.

Some cameras have a separate button which will allow you to magnify your images in the "Playback" State.

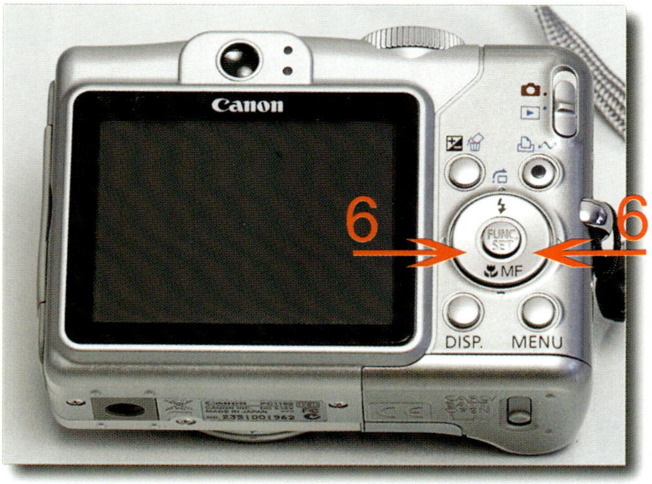

The "6" indicates the "Selection Dial" which is a rocker dial on this camera.

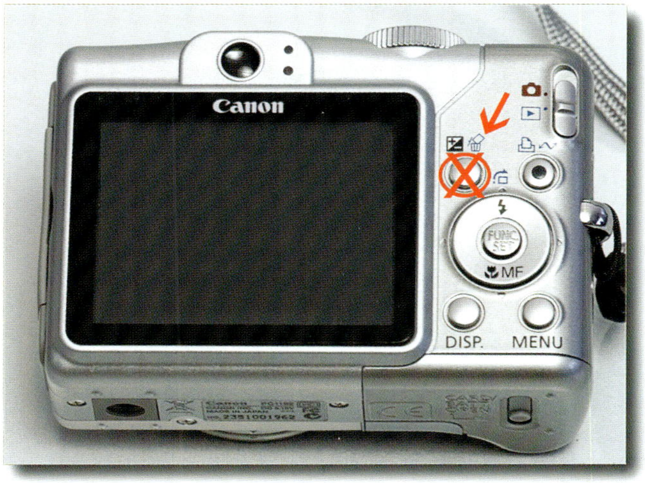

Remember to always turn your camera off before exchanging or removing Memory Cards.

Also, remember to let the camera finish processing your last image before turning the camera off.

There is usually a glowing light on the camera that is illuminated as long as the camera is still saving your last image to the Memory Card. When this light goes out, it is safe to turn the camera off and remove the Memory Card.

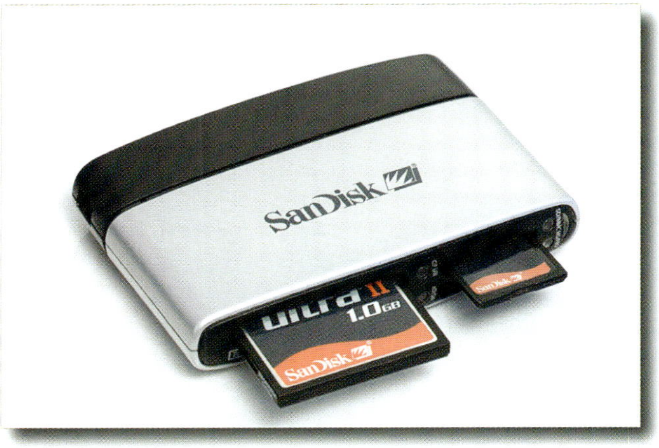

Step 24 – Filling Your Card

Eventually you will fill up your Memory Card, no matter what its capacity. It is important to realize that once the camera has finished writing pictures to the card, the card can be safely removed from the camera. The images will remain on the Memory Card. You can now insert another empty card and continue to take pictures.

With film you wasted money if you didn't finish taking each roll of film.

In digital, you don't have to fill a card in order to transfer images from the card to your computer.

We recommend that you do not erase unwanted images in your camera. It is healthier for your memory card to be erased in the computer after your images have been copied to the computer.

Erase your Memory Card by reformatting as described in Step #26.

Step 25 – Image Transfer

You will eventually want to copy your images onto your computer. This will afford you the opportunity to permanently store them on the computer's hard drive and also burn them on to CDs or DVDs for backup storage.

We recommend that you do this using a Card Reader (purchased separately) rather than by using the cable provided by the camera manufacturer. This procedure is outlined in each of the four editing chapters of this book.

Step 26 – (Re)Format Card(s)

Once you are absolutely positive that your images are stored safely in your computer's hard drive in at least one location (preferably in two, or also backed up onto a CD), you should clear your Memory Card(s) so they can be reused.

This process is called "Formatting" or "Reformatting". This is the same process you performed before using a new Memory Card (see Step 12).

This is done via the Menu Button and Selection Dial as described in your camera's instruction manual.

Note: Formatting totally erases the card and all images on the card are lost. However, this is necessary so that you can reuse the card.

As mentioned earlier, reformatting and erasing all your images at once is preferable to erasing individual images in your camera one at a time.

Cameras make formatting a little bit difficult on purpose. They make it a two or three step procedure to force you to confirm that you really want to erase and lose all the images on your card.

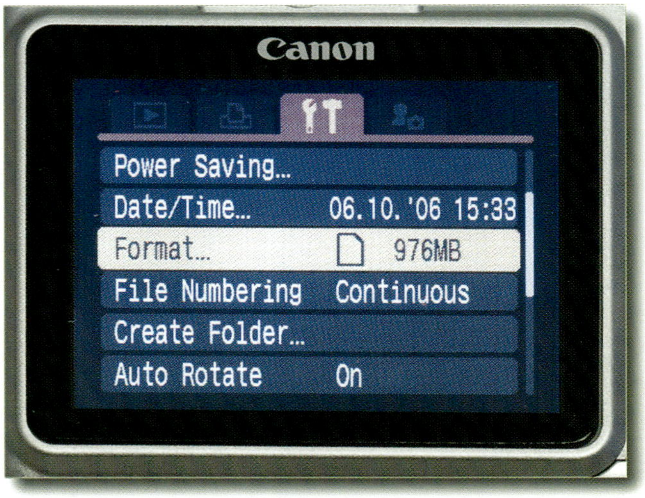

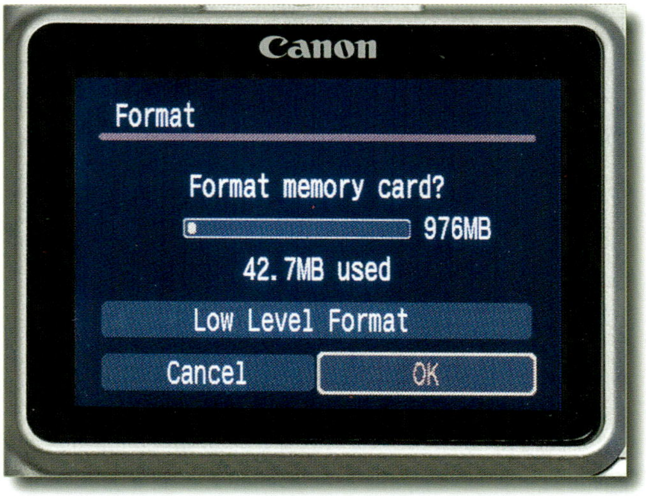

Conclusion

In this chapter, we covered the extra accessories that you will require and the initial steps you should take prior to turning on your camera. We then listed only the most important camera controls that you should locate using your camera's instruction manual. We outlined the initial camera settings you should make. We then took you through the basic steps to get you taking pictures, reviewing your images and transferring them to your computer.

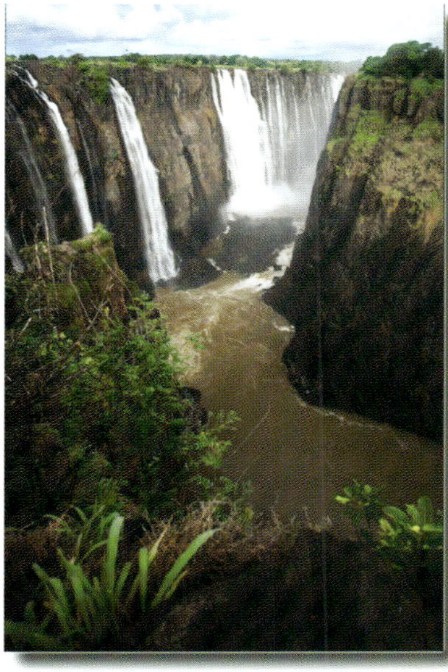
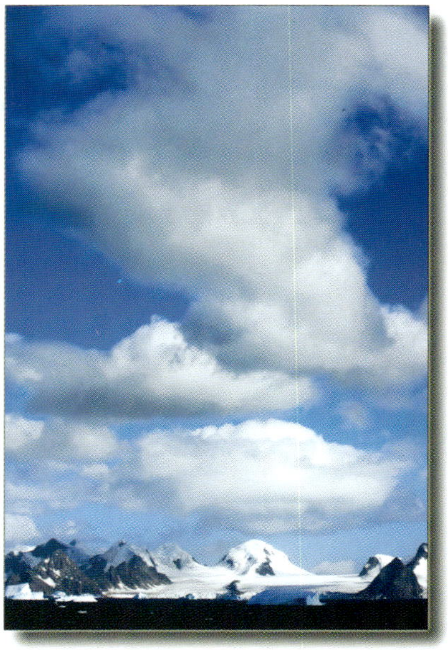
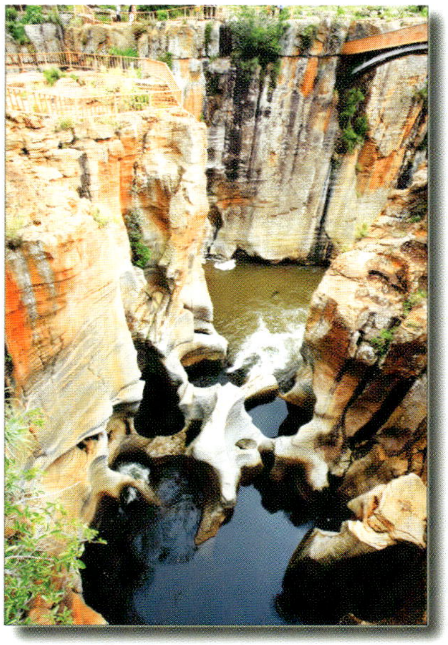
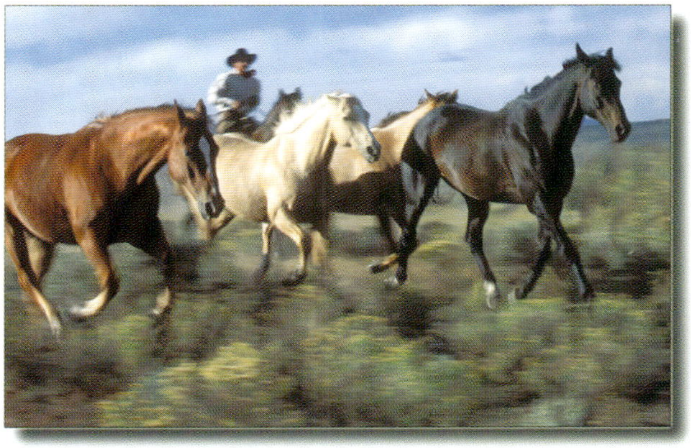
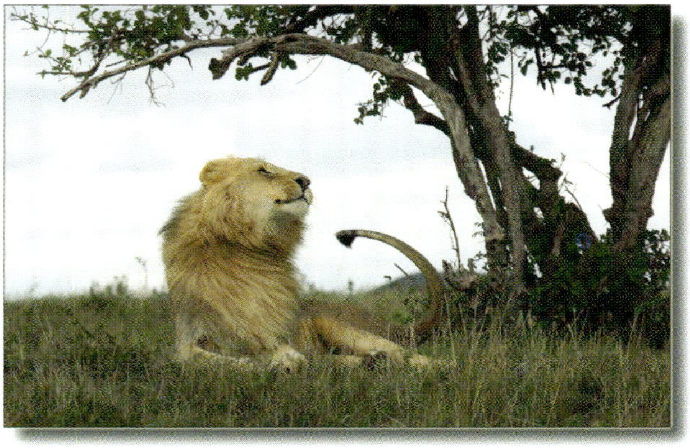
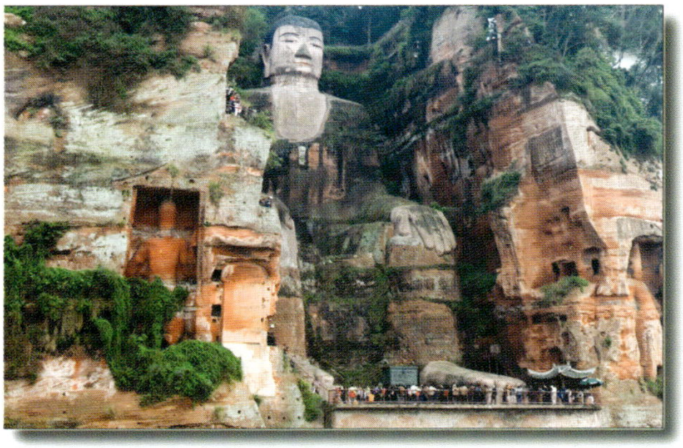
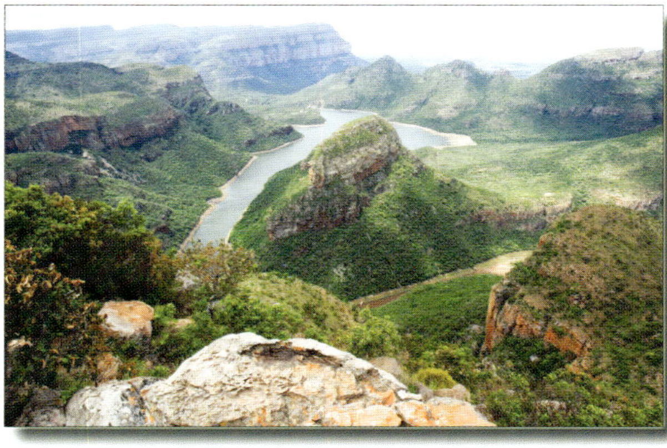

Photos by Phil Kwan

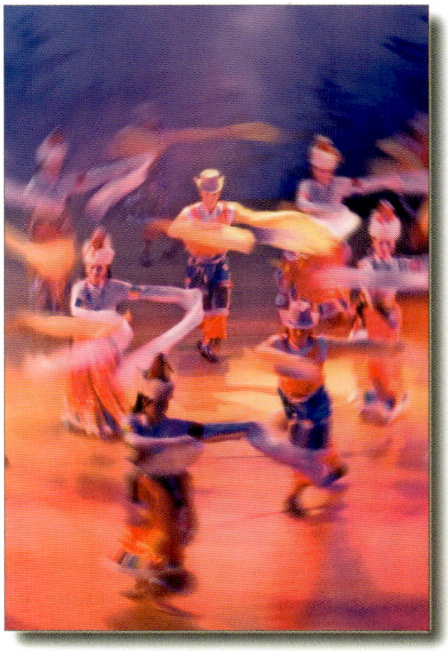
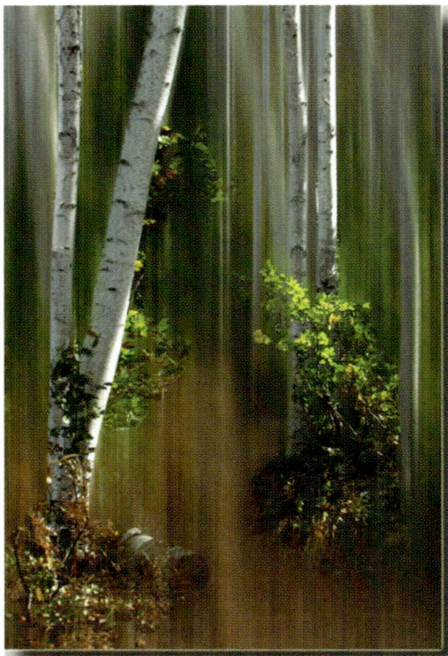
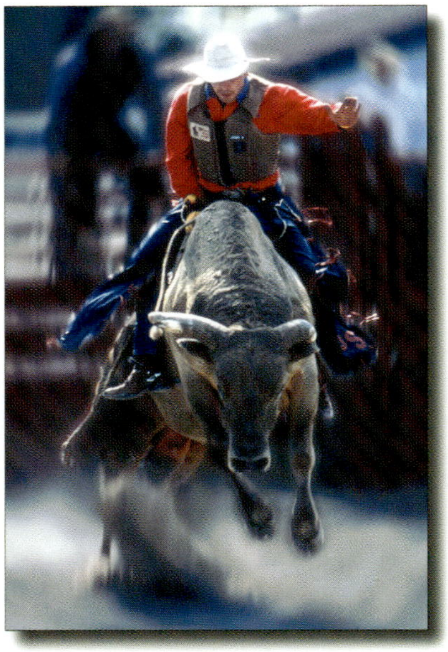
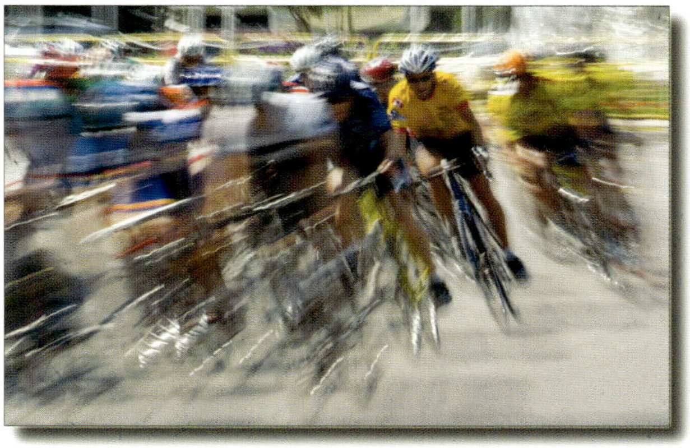
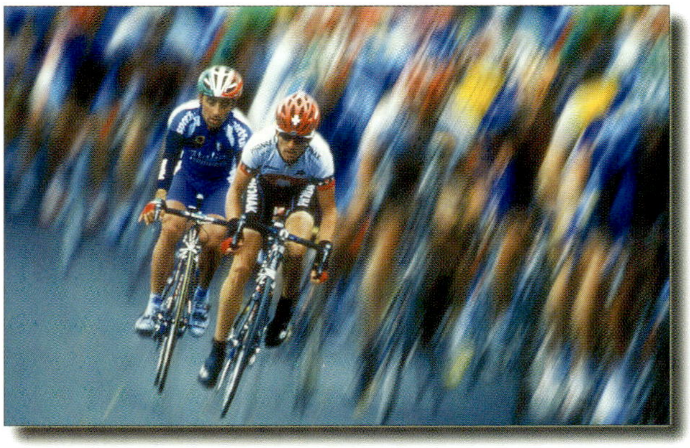
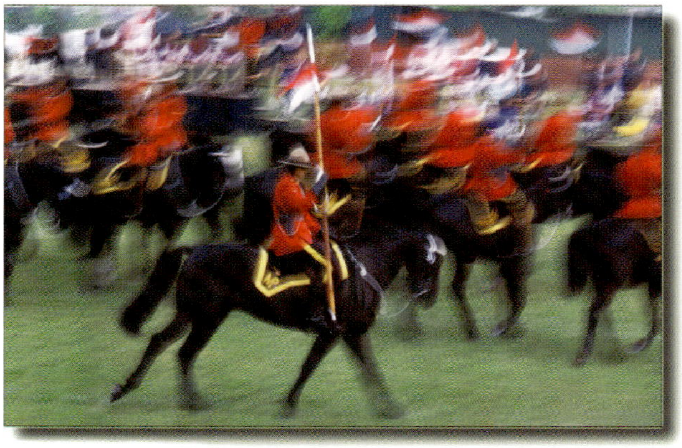
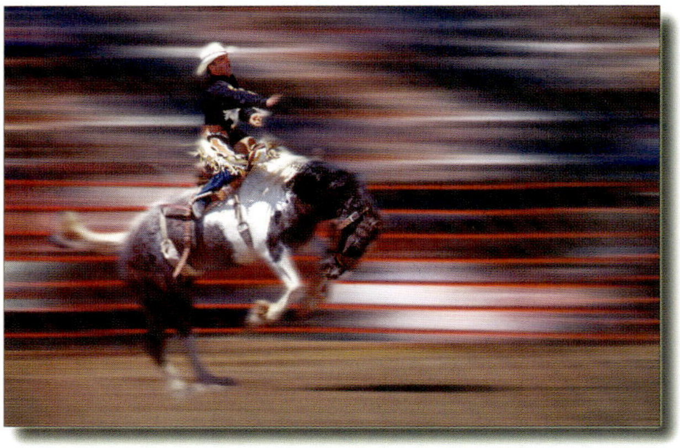

Photos by Phil Kwan

Chapter 2 CAMERA SETTINGS

Camera Settings

Understanding and learning how to take advantage of camera settings such as Auto Exposure, Exposure Compensation, Histogram, Shutter Speed, Shutter Priority, and Aperture Priority are the fundamental building blocks of photography. The following sections will illustrate how to use different camera settings to create better pictures.

Auto Exposure

In the Auto Exposure Mode your camera selects an appropriate aperture - the opening that permits light to pass into the camera (see page 42) - and shutter speed - the amount of time the shutter is allowed to remain open (see page 32) - for the scene you are photographing.

Introduction

Using your camera's Auto Exposure Mode will allow you to take acceptable pictures without having to rely on charts and tables. In Auto Exposure Mode, the camera uses its built-in light meter to choose an aperture that will expose your subject at a medium tone. It then selects a shutter speed to match that aperture. The light meter measures the amount of light reflected from the subject at which the camera is pointed, assuming that all subjects reflect 18% of the available light. In many instances, this is the easiest way to take a good picture.

Medium Tone Subjects

The fern and the tree in this photograph are both medium in tone, reflecting about 18% of light. In average light conditions and when shooting from a comfortable distance, using the Auto Exposure Mode will give you an excellent picture.

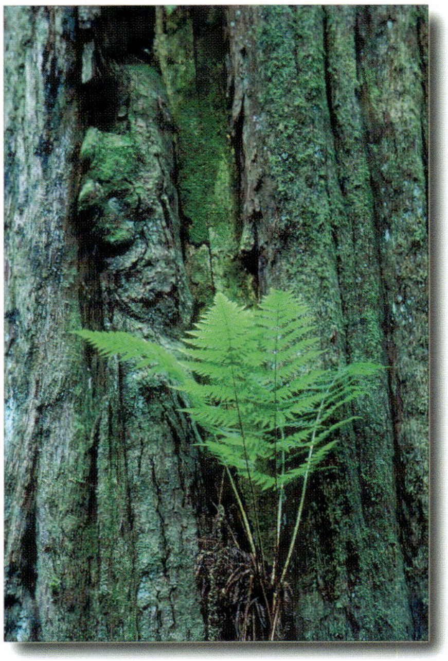

Fern and Redwood Tree (Oregon, US)

Medium Tone Scenery

This sage desert scene was shot in early morning when the light was even. Although the picture contains both white and dark brown horses, the overall tone of the composition is medium, with the subjects on average reflecting 18% of light. Again, in this situation, the Auto Exposure Mode will give you a properly exposed image.

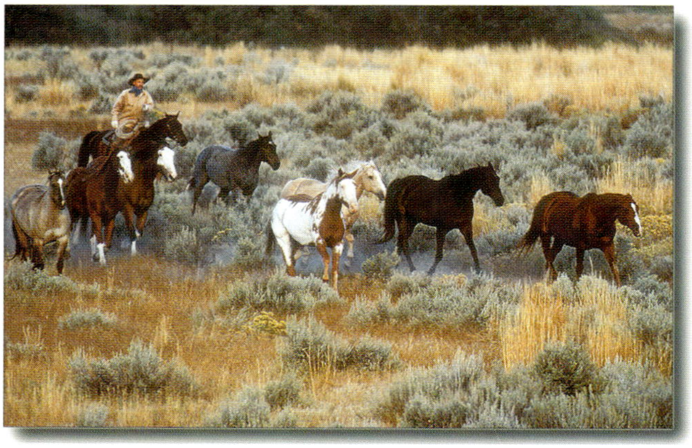

Sage Desert (Idaho, US)

Medium Tone Landscape

This coastal image is composed of many different tones: the water is light, the grass is medium and the rock is dark. However, once again, the overall tone of the landscape is medium and the Auto Exposure Mode can be used.

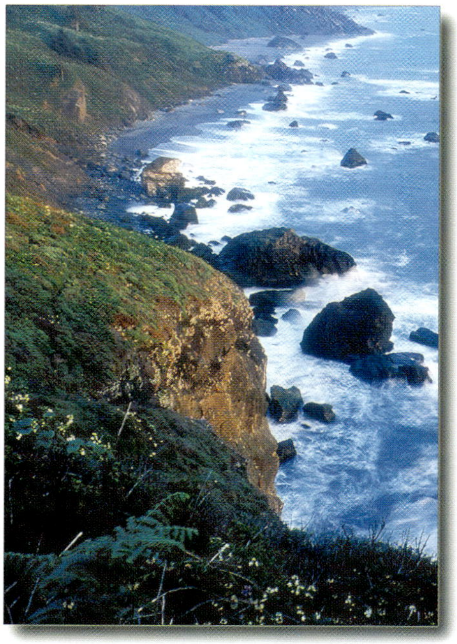

Coastal Stacks (Oregon, US)

Conclusion

When photographing medium tone subjects you can usually leave your camera in the Auto Exposure Mode, allowing it to choose an appropriate combination of aperture and shutter speed. However, learning to use your camera's exposure compensation, aperture priority and shutter speed priority options will give you more opportunities for creativity and allow you to take great pictures.

Exposure Compensation

Introduction

Exposure compensation is used to alter the camera's standard exposure settings.

In the Auto Exposure Mode, your camera will select the aperture and shutter speed needed to get a good exposure. However if your subject is not medium in tone, the Auto Exposure Mode can be fooled. In this case, you will need to use the exposure compensation dial to allow more, or less, light into your sensor. Use plus compensation for light subjects and minus compensation for dark ones. Some experimentation may be required before your pictures turn out exactly the way you want them to.

Plus	**For Light Subjects**
Minus	**For Dark Subjects**

Light Subjects – Water

As we discussed in the earlier section on auto exposure, the light meter in your camera assumes that all subjects are medium in tone and reflect 18% of the available light. However, in actuality some subjects such as water or snow reflect more light than others.

If your subject is water that either reflects a lot of sky or appears white because it is moving, using the Auto Exposure Mode will leave you with a picture that is too dark. This is called underexposure. It occurs because white subjects reflect about 36% of the available light instead of the normal average of 18%.

To achieve proper exposure in such an instance, set the exposure compensation to plus 1-2. This will allow more light to enter the camera, yielding a picture in which the white water looks white and the darker water a lighter, more natural, color.

Plus	**For Light Subjects**

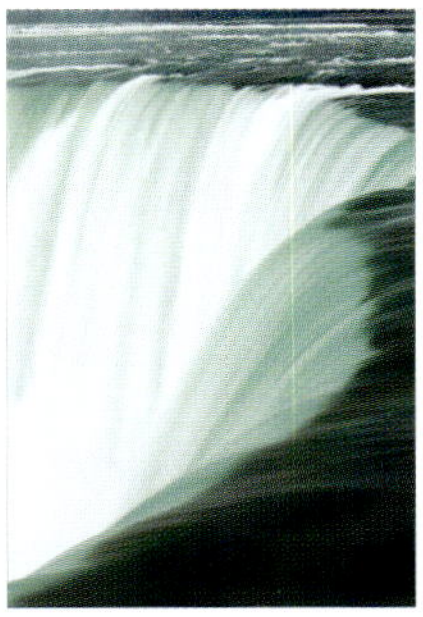

No exposure compensation (water too dark).

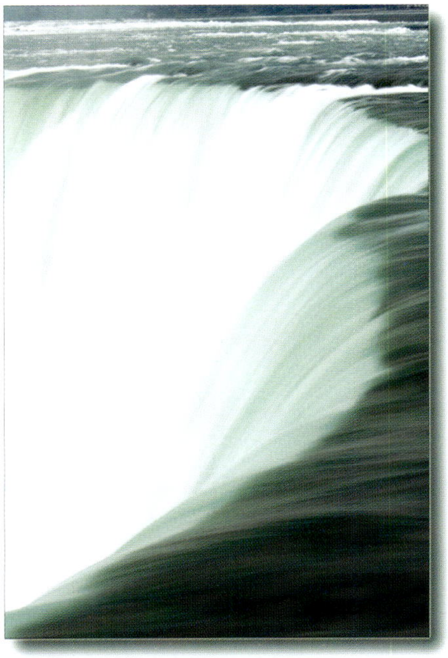

Plus 1 exposure compensation (white water).

Light Subjects - Snow

Snow is another subject that is not medium tone. If you rely on your light meter alone to govern your exposure, the white snow will appear gray.

To get proper exposure for a snow scene, dial plus 1-2 compensation to allow more light to reach your sensor. This will make the snow in your picture appear as brilliant and white as it does in nature.

Plus	**For Light Subjects**

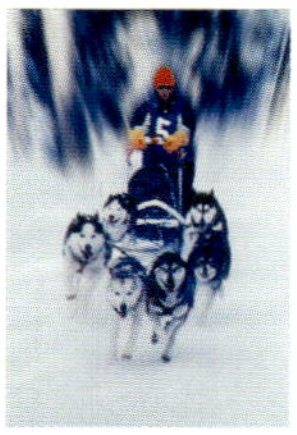

No exposure compensation (gray snow)

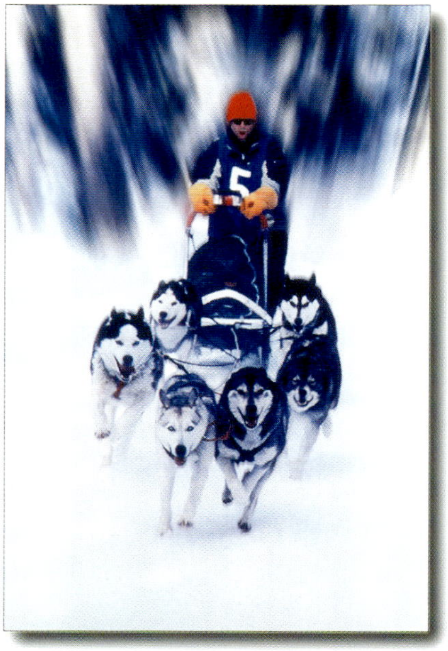

Dog Sled Race (Barrie, Canada)

Plus 1 exposure compensation (white snow).

Light Subjects - Icebergs

Icebergs are another example of subjects that are not medium tone. Without exposure compensation, an iceberg will appear gray.

In such a situation, you should dial plus 1-2 exposure compensation into your camera settings. The extra light will make the iceberg in your image look as white as it does in nature.

Plus	**For Light Subjects**

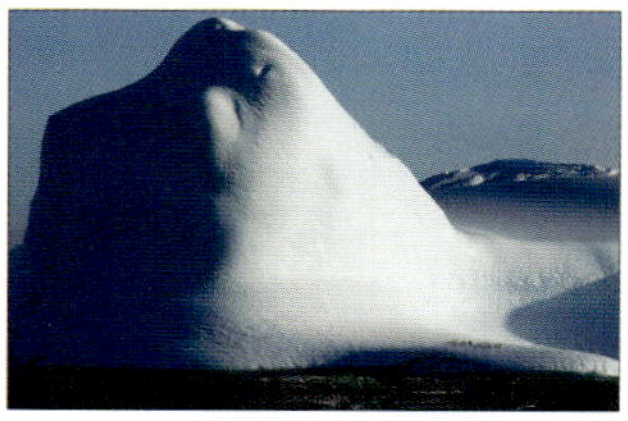

No exposure compensation (gray iceberg)

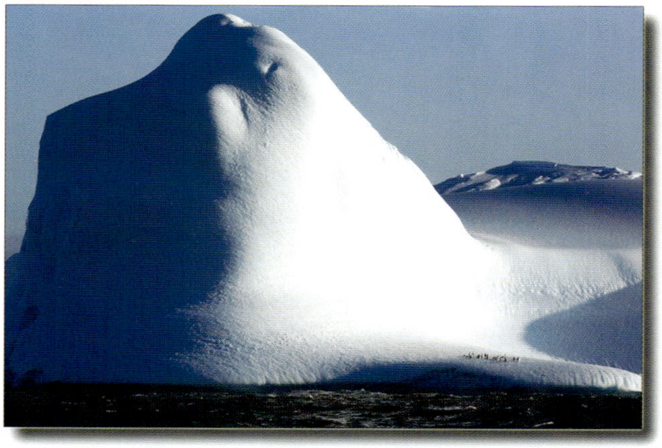

Iceberg (Antarctica) Plus 1 exposure compensation (white iceberg)

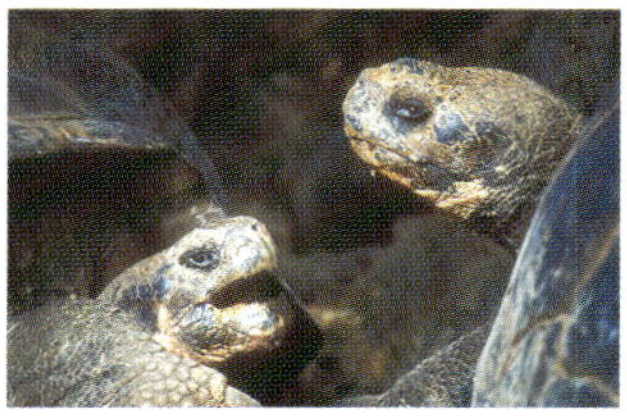

Auto exposure with no exposure compensation (tortoises too light).

Dark Subjects - Tortoises

As with light subjects, when shooting a darker subject, your camera still assumes a reflection of 18% of the available light. Because the tortoises in this picture only reflect 9% of the light, your camera will allow an amount of light into the camera that will make them appear medium gray rather than a dark brown. This is called overexposure.

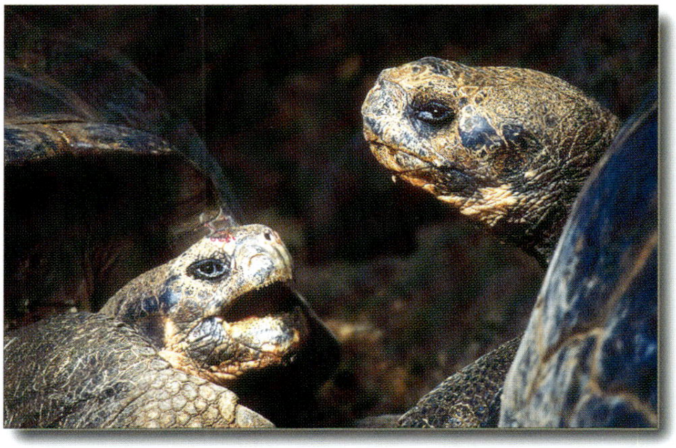

Tortoises (Galapagos Islands)

Auto exposure with minus 1 exposure compensation (dark tortoises)

To get proper exposure of a dark subject, set your exposure compensation to minus 1-2. The subject will appear darker, and in the case of these tortoises, a more natural color.

Minus	**For Dark Subjects**

For subjects that are medium in tone, use the camera settings indicated by the light meter. For subjects with a lot of white, such as moving water, snow or icebergs, use plus compensation to let in more light. For darker subjects, choose minus compensation to reduce the amount of light let into the camera.

Exposure Compensation	
Plus	**For Light Subjects**
Minus	**For Dark Subjects**

To learn how to use exposure compensation, you will need to refer to your camera manual. Every camera is unique.

Conclusion

Understanding Histograms

Although it may seem complex at first, once you know the basics of a histogram, you'll find it is one of the most useful tools you'll employ to get a good exposure.

Introduction

Most digital camera can be set to have a histogram display function located on their LCD screen on the back.

Histogram

A histogram is a graph displaying the level of brightness or tone along the horizontal axis and the amount of light at any level of brightness or tone along the vertical axis.

Note: The term "brightness" and "tone" are the same.

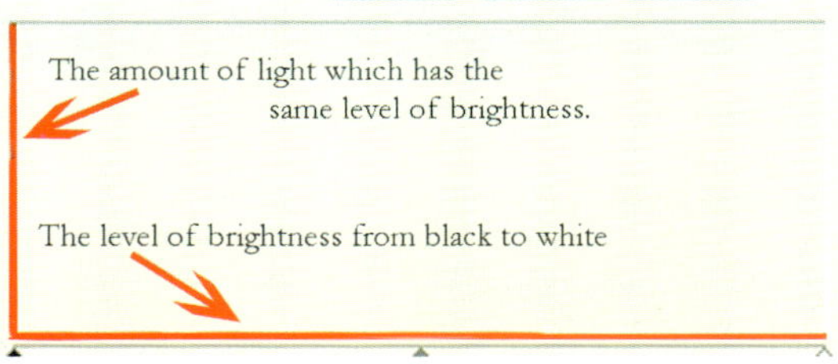

Vertical Axis

The height of the vertical line indicates the amount of light that is present at a particular level of brightness. A shorter line indicates a smaller amount and a longer line, a larger amount.

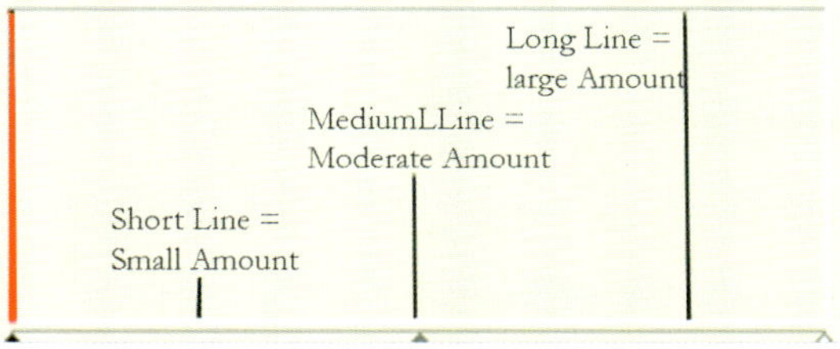

Horizontal Axis

The horizontal line tells us where each particular level of brightness in an image is located along a scale. The dark tones are located towards the left, the mid-tones in the middle and the white tones towards the right.

We can describe the horizontal line from left to right as:
1. Black gradually increasing to white.

2. Shadow turning into mid-tones turning into highlight.

3. Numeric values between 0 to 255.

4. A graded scale that runs from black to white.

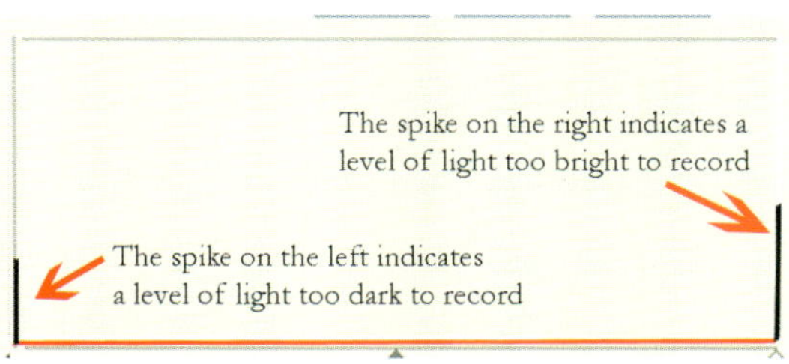

Black	Dark	Medium	Light	White
Shadow		Mid-tones		Highlight
0	64	128	192	255

These two pictures below illustrate how the level of brightness is displayed on the horizontal axis of a histogram, while the amount of light existing at that level of brightness is displayed on the vertical axis.

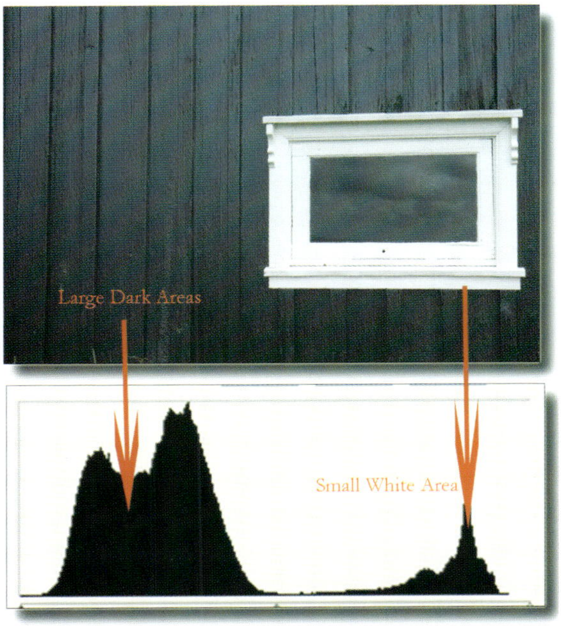

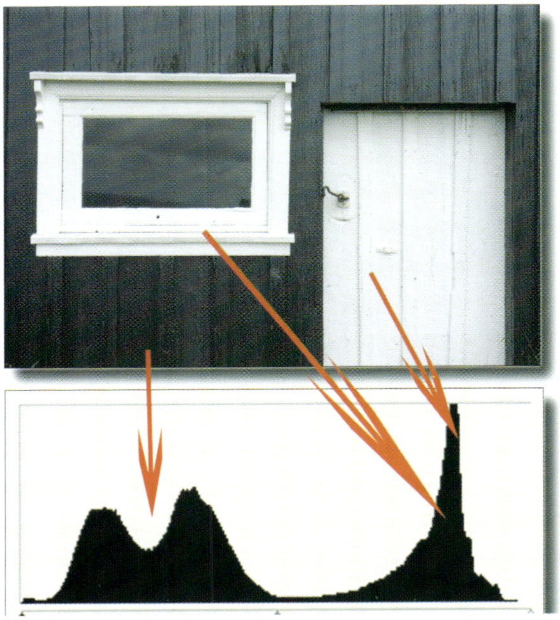

Brightness Levels and Amounts

A Window in Frame

In the histogram of this image, the dark wooden frame is displayed on the left side of the graph and the white window on the right. The vertical line displays the amount of each light level in a "bar".

The large amount of dark wooden frame is represented by a number of higher and wider peaks on the left side of the graph. The smaller amount of white window in the frame is shown by the smaller peak on the right side of the histogram.

A Window and a Door in Frame

Here, a white door was added to the image. The additional amount of white areas increases the height of the peak on the right side of the histogram.

Since the amount of dark area in the image has been diminished by the frame, the height of the peak on the left side of the histogram has decreased in size.

In both pictures, the brightness of the window, door and frame are the same. Their positions along the horizontal line axis are identical. The only thing that has changed is the heights of the vertical lines. This change represents the change in the amount of white and dark areas that is present in the image.

Panda Bear

The pictures of the panda bear below contain dark, medium and light tones. As the amount of these tones changes, the height of each tone will change in the histogram.

Three Basic Tones

These panda images contain three basic levels of brightness, or tones:

A) The black part of the bear,

B) The mid-tone grass and

C) The white part of the bear.

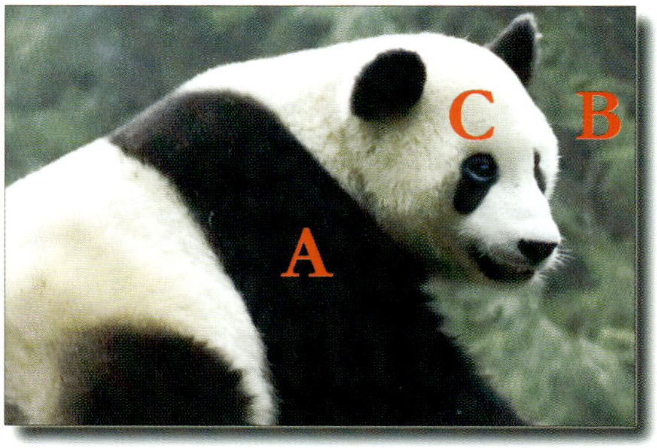

The three peaks in this histogram show the three basic levels of brightness in this image. The highest peak on the left shows the black parts of the bear. The middle peak represents the foliage and the right peak shows the white parts of the bear.

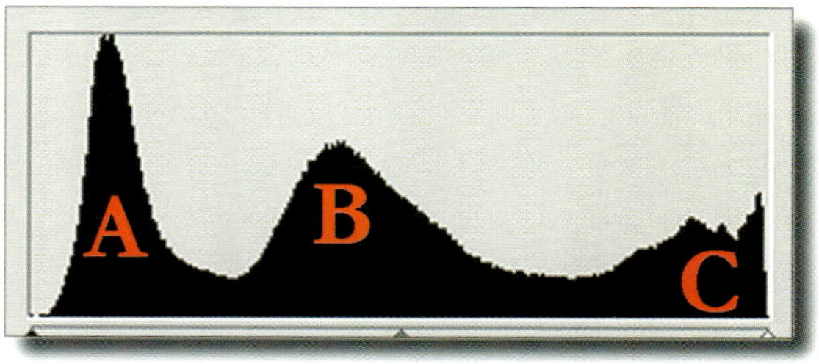

Large Amount of Midtones

The bamboo occupies a large part of this picture. Since the bamboo appears medium in brightness, it is displayed in the large middle peak on the graph. The smaller dark parts of the panda bear are shown on the left side of the graph and the smallest white parts are seen on the right side of the histogram.

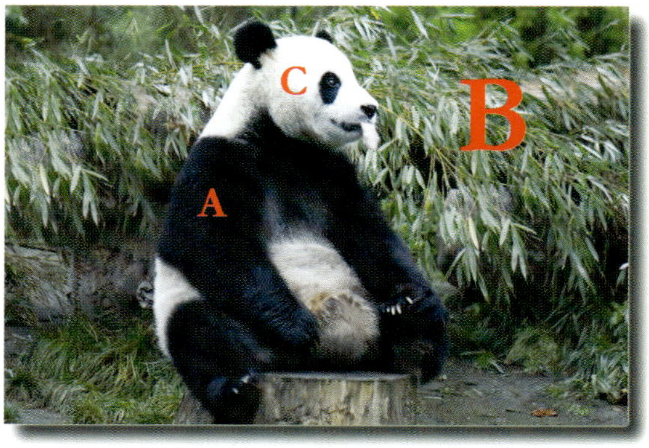

To illustrate the different levels of brightness, the large area of bamboo is marked "B" in the picture as well as on the graph. The smaller dark parts are marked "A" and the white parts are marked "C" on both the picture and the histogram.

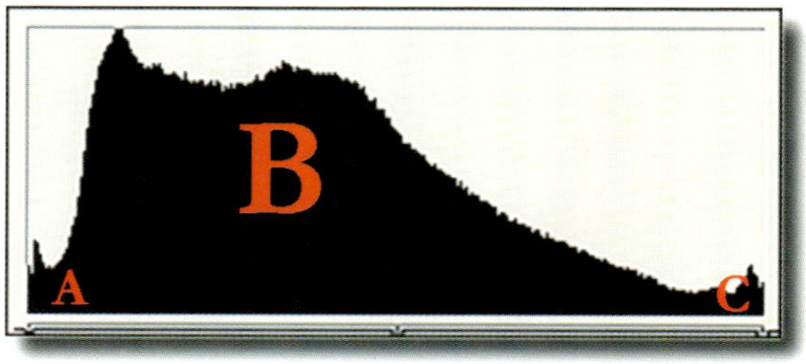

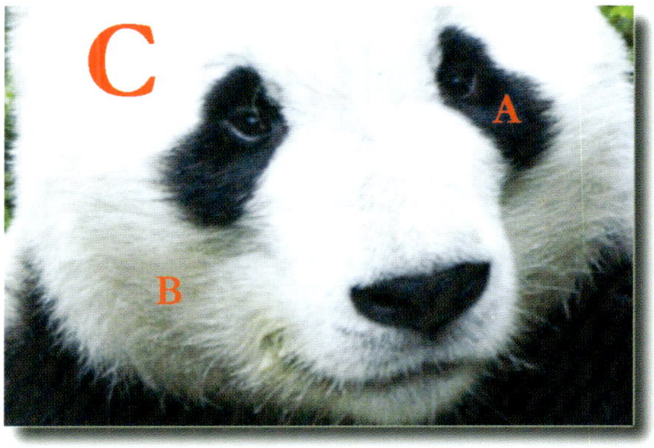

Large Amount of White Tones

The face of the panda in this picture is very light in tone and occupies a large portion of this image. As you would expect, the graph of the panda's face is bunched up higher at the right, or white, end of the histogram.

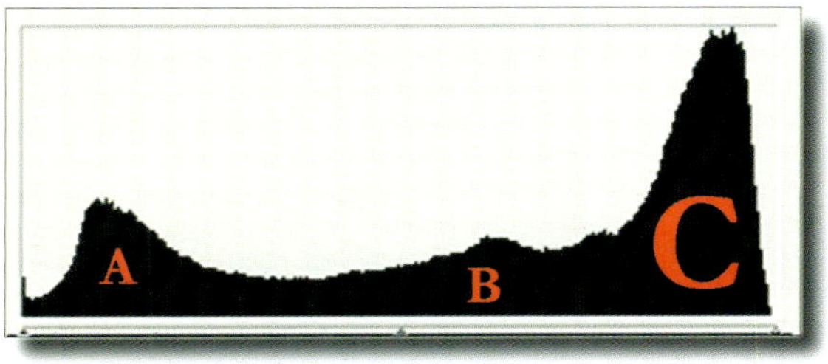

The panda's face is marked "C" in the picture as well as the histogram.

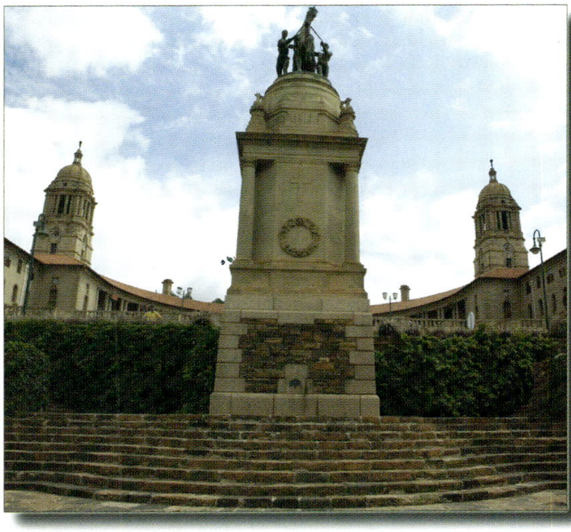

Statue and Sky

This image has two basic tones: the light sky and the dark building. The sky is shown on the right side of the histogram. The building and the hedges are shown by the shorter, but longer, peak on the left side of the graph.

A histogram can only show you the distribution of the level of brightness in an image. It does not tell you anything about your subjects or the quality of your image.

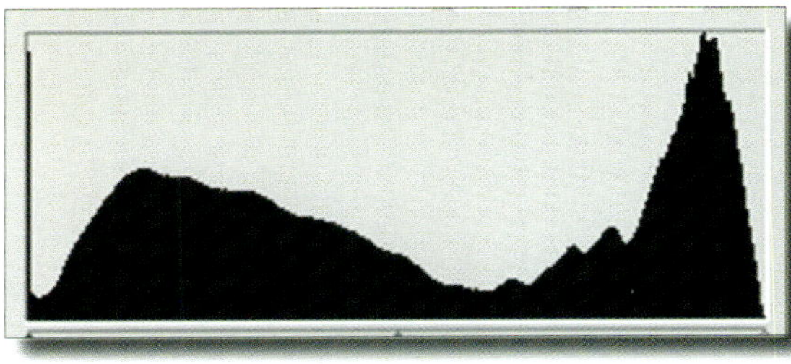

As you can see on this page, the histogram of the picture and the histogram of the image of the panda bear have a very similar appearance. However, when we look at the images themselves, they are radically different.

Histograms display the amount of light at different levels of brightness in a graph. When you look at an image with its histogram, it becomes easy to understand the distribution of light in a photograph.

Conclusion

"Reading" Histogram

You will understand more about lighting and exposure if you spend more time "reading" histograms while comparing them to the images they represent.

Dark Tones

Histograms of mostly dark images will have the tones bundled to the left side of the graph.

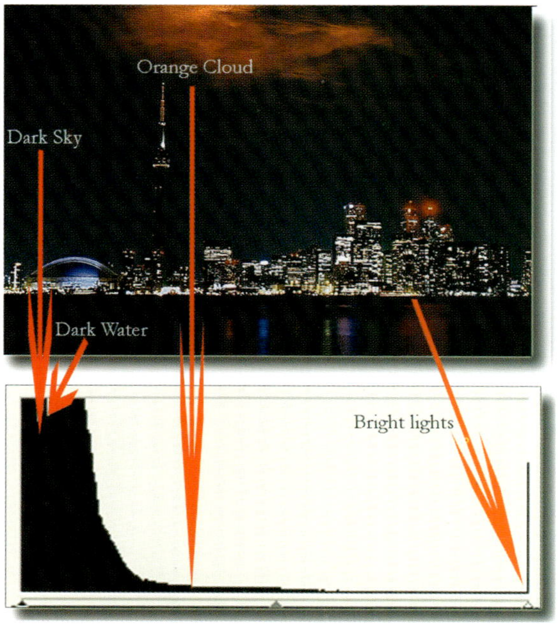

CN Tower (Toronto, Canada)

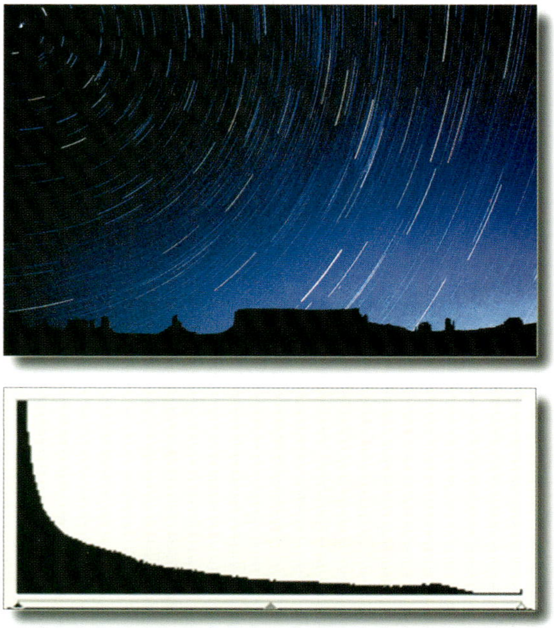

Stars at Night (Alaska, US)

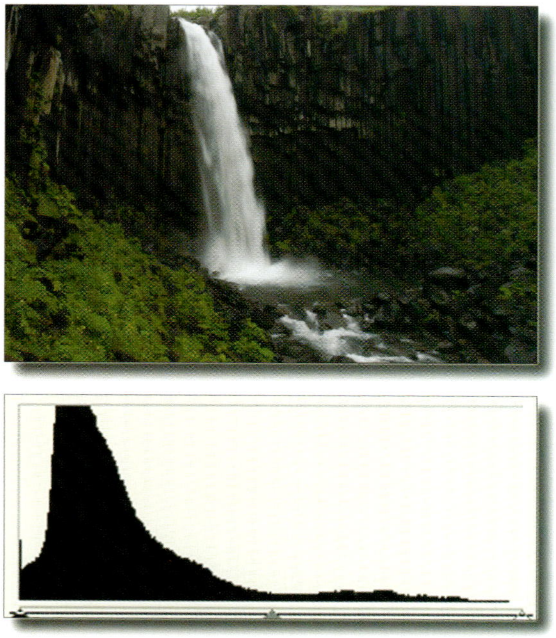

Svartifoss (Iceland)

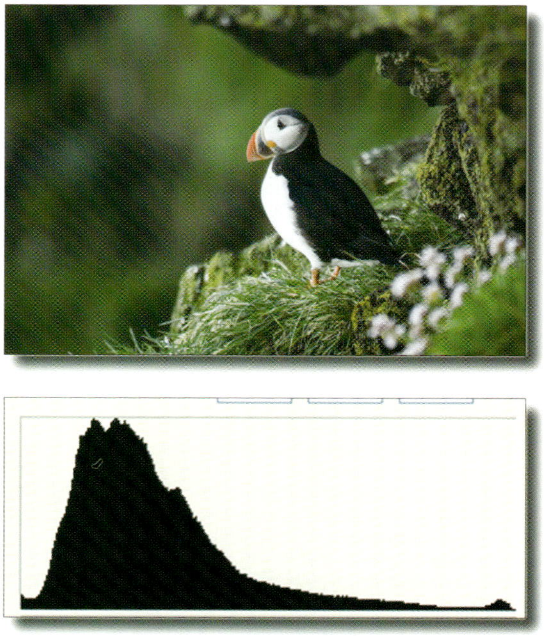

Puffin (Iceland)

An Image that contains mainly mid-tones will have the tones in the histogram concentrated in the middle of the graph.

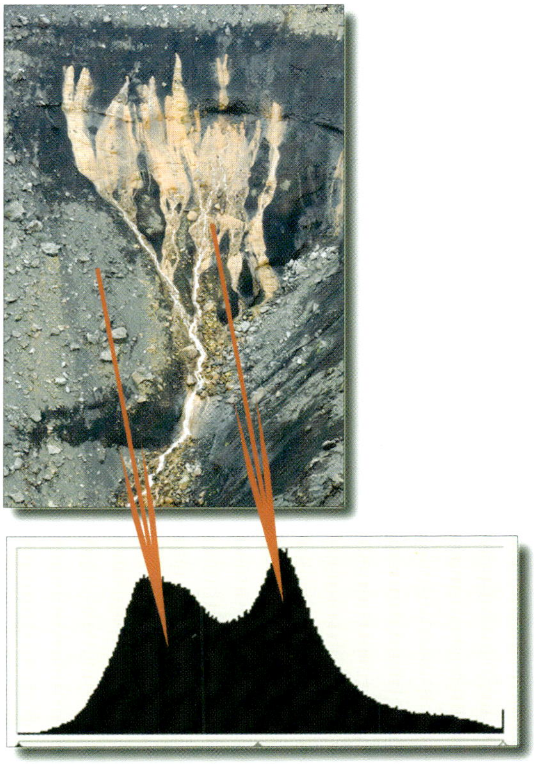

Canyon (Iceland)

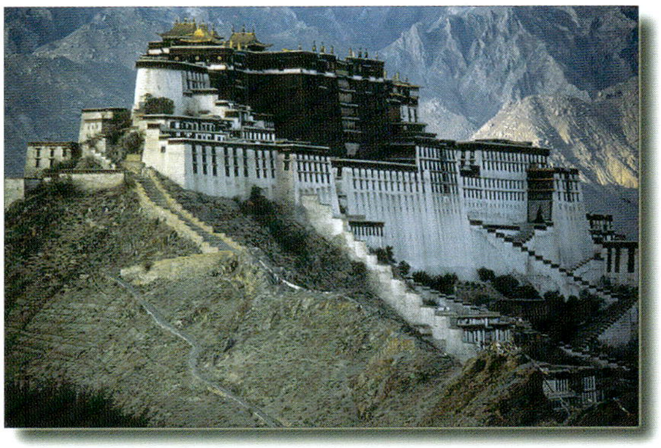

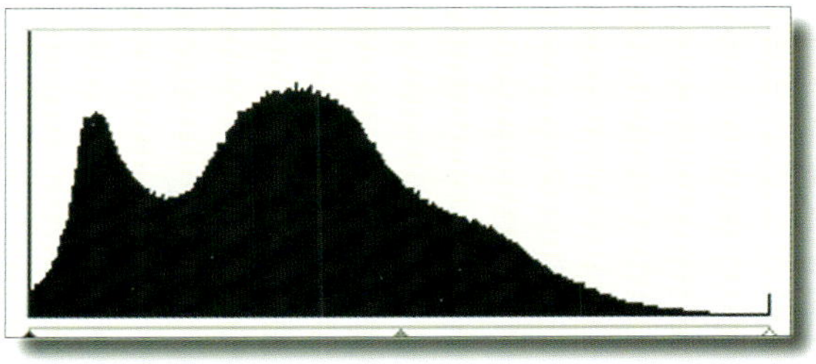

Palace (Tibet)

Mid-tones

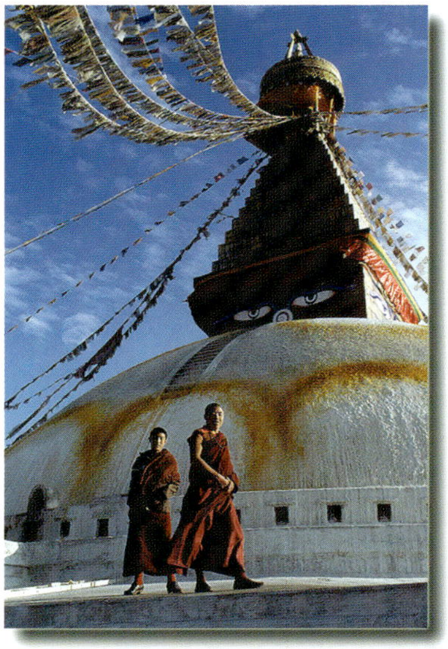

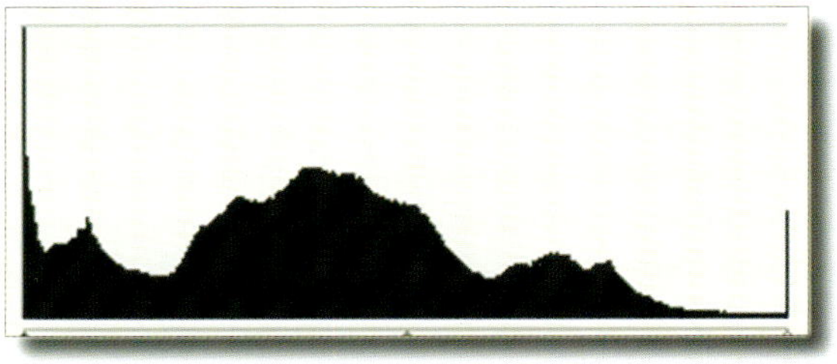

Monks (Tibet)

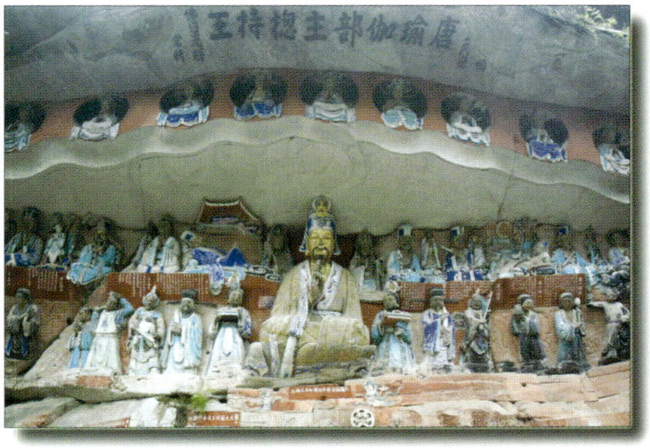

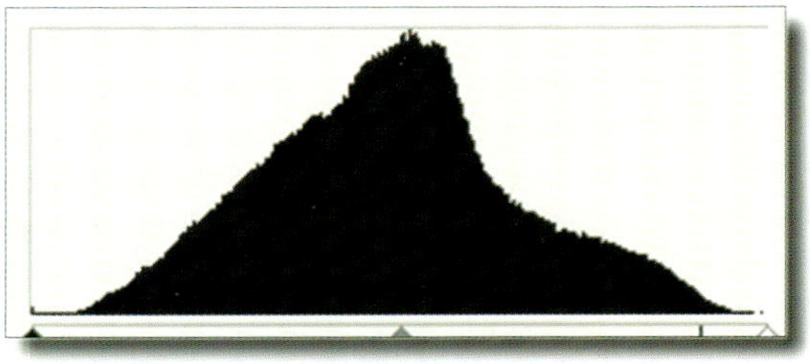

Dazu Rock Carving (China)

White Tones

Histograms of mostly light images will have the tones concentrated on the right side of the graph.

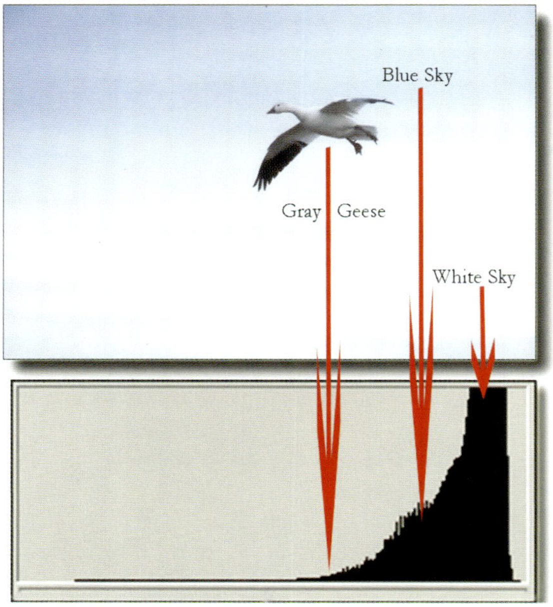

Snow Geese (New Mexico, US)

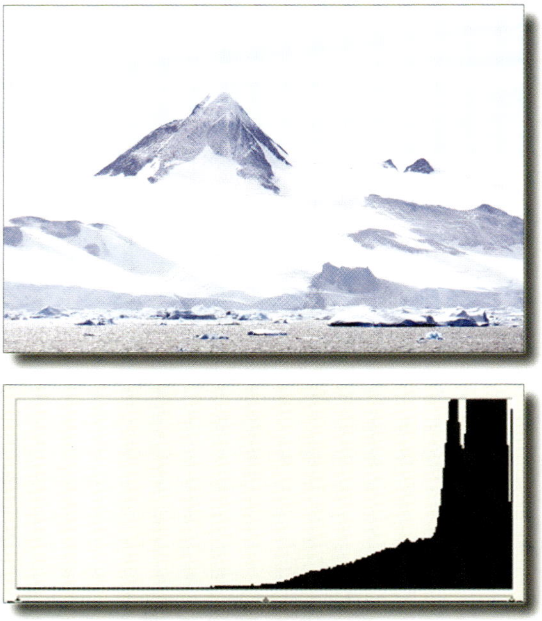

Iceberg (Antarctica)

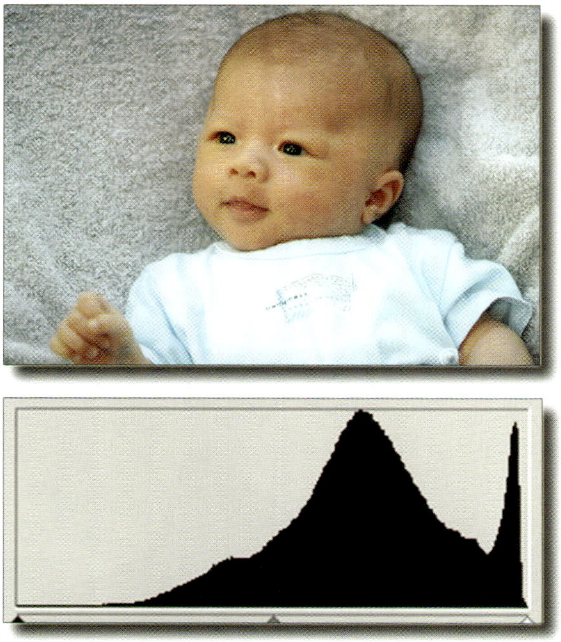

Baby Nick (Toronto, Canada)

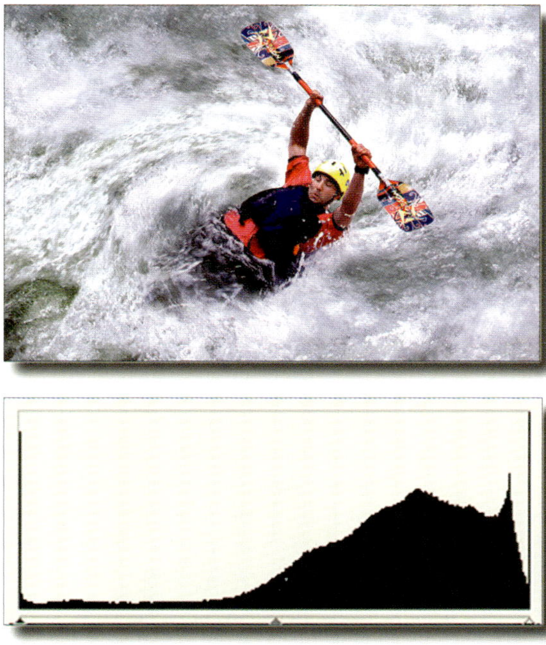

Kayak (Minden, Canada)

A Variety of Tones

Histograms of images with a number of distinctive tones will show numerous peaks and valleys along the graph.

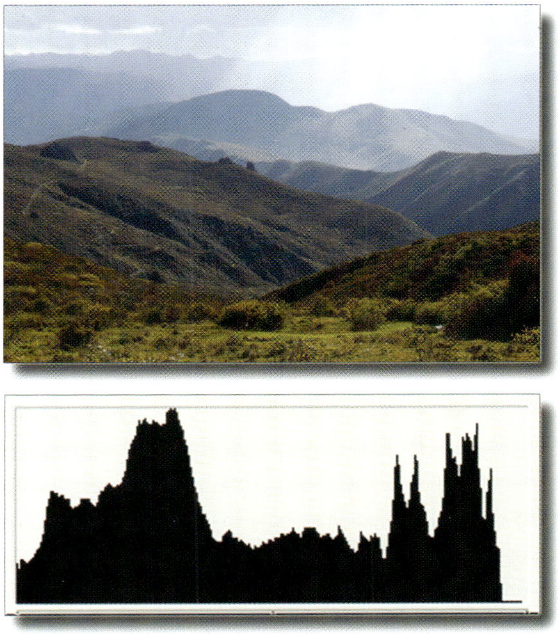

Lights on Mountain (China)

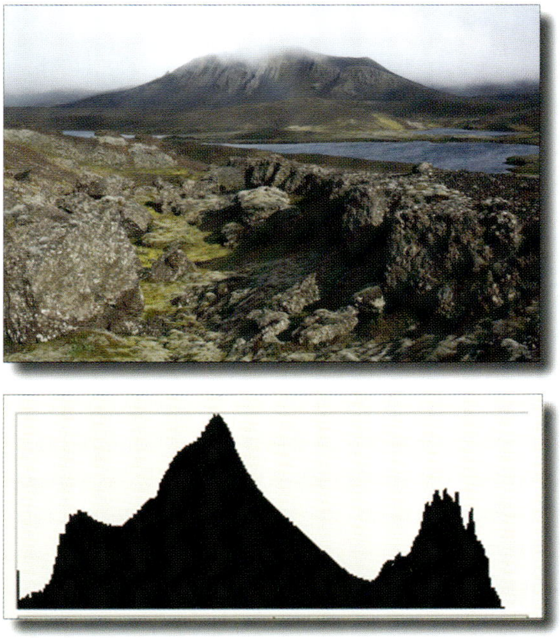

Rauofossafoll Mountain (Iceland)

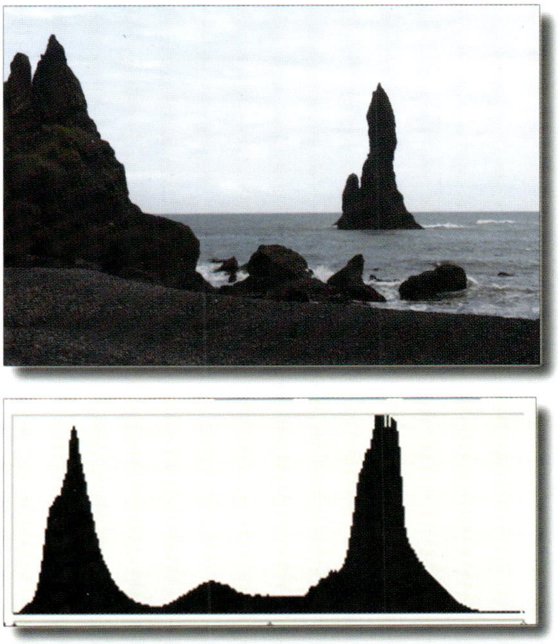

Reynisdrangar (Iceland)

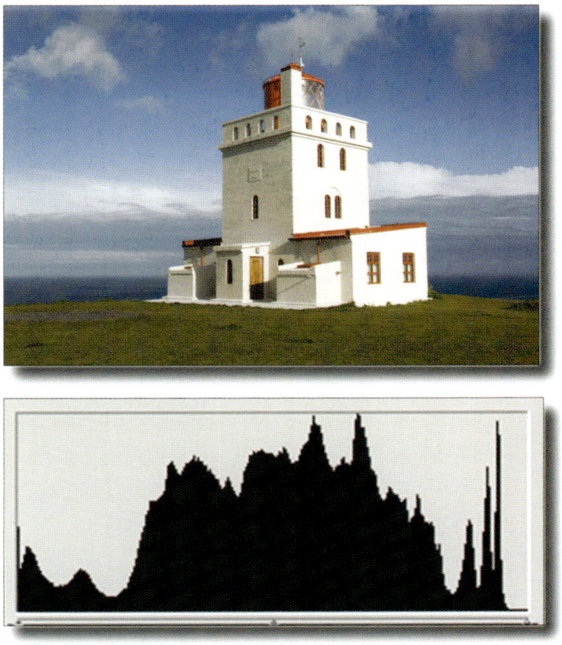

Lighthouse (Iceland)

Conclusion

The appearance of your histograms can vary dramatically from picture to picture due to the unique level of brightness in each image.

Correcting Exposure with Histogram

Once you know how to "read" a histogram, it's simple to correct pictures that are underexposed or overexposed.

Introduction

Your histogram gives you the level light of your images in a graph. You should evaluate the histogram while you are taking your pictures and adjust it if necessary in order to a get an better exposed image.

Underexposure

You will know your image is underexposed when there is a large gap at the right edge of the histogram. Underexposure means your sensor didn't capture enough light and the picture will be too dark. In this image, there is no light area and the areas of shadow have very little detail.

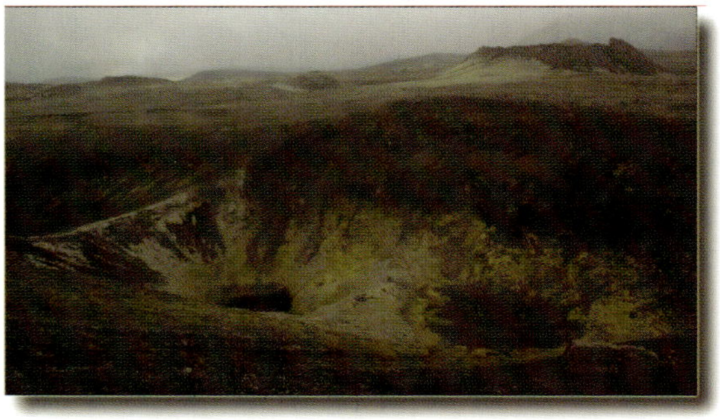

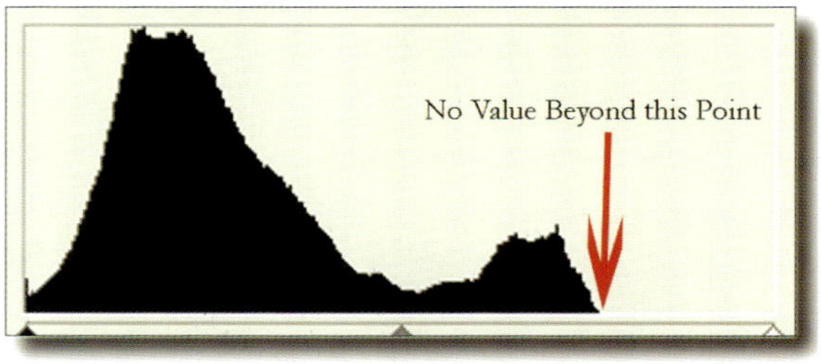

Dormant Volcano (Iceland)

Correcting Underexposure

To correct underexposure in auto exposure mode, dial a plus value in exposure compensation until there is no gap on the right side of the histogram. When you dial in a plus value in exposure compensation, you add more light to the image, and the overall picture will be lighter. You might need to try different plus values until the values in your histogram graph move all the way to the right side.

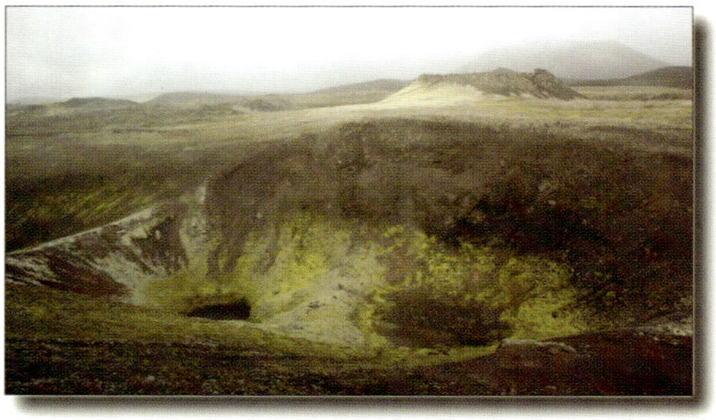

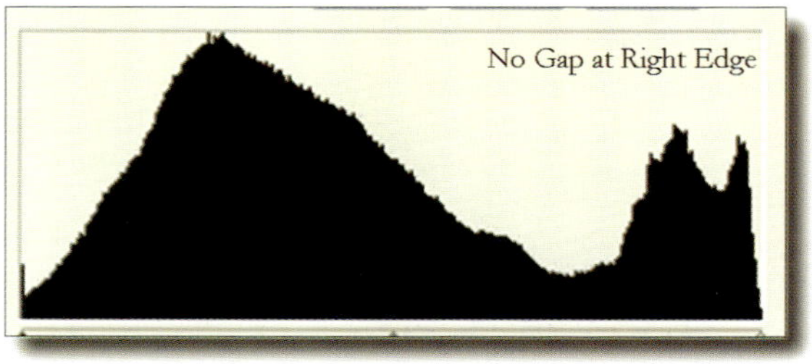

Dormant Volcano (Iceland)

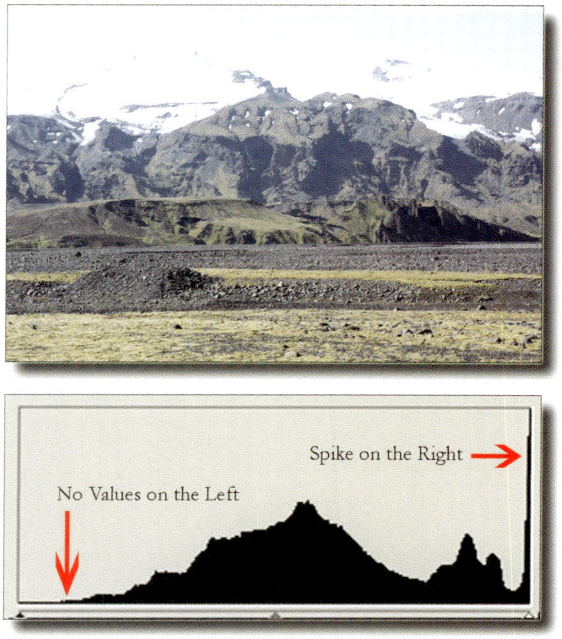

Icecap Mountain (Iceland)

Overexposure

When you see values running up to the right side of the histogram and no values on the left side, your image is overexposed. Overexposure means the brightest areas of your image have no detail. This condition is called "blowing out the highlights". Some digital cameras show this information to you by "blinking" at the areas with blown out highlight. If your camera has this feature, you should turn it on and pay attention to it.

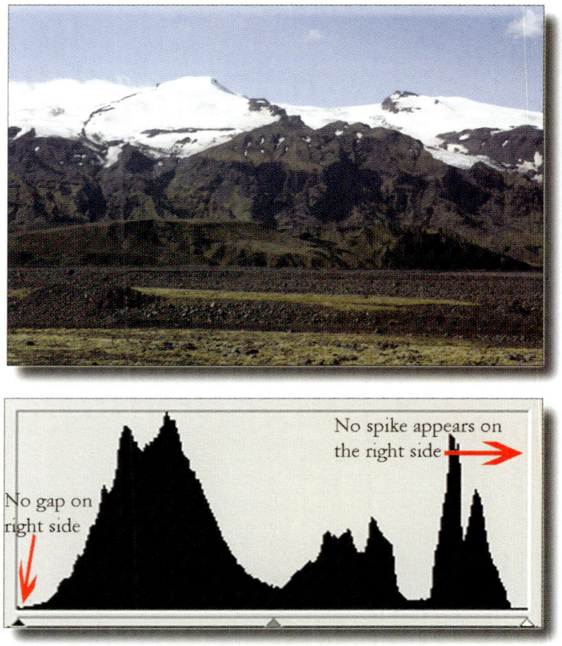

Icecap Mountain (Iceland)

Correcting Overexposure

To correct overexposure in auto exposure mode, dial a minus value in exposure compensation until no spike appears on the right side of your graph. The gap on the left side will also decrease. When you dial in a minus value you subtract light from the image, and the overall picture will be darker. You will also see more detail in the light areas in your image.

When light is decreased, the "blinking" on the light areas will stop. This indicates that there is no over-exposed area in the image.

White Spike and Black Spike

The human eye can see a much greater range of tones than the digital camera can record. If the level of brightness is too dim for the camera to record, it will show up as a black spike on the left side of the histogram. A spike on the right side indicates that the level of brightness is too bright to record.

White Spike

In this landscape picture, the white sky is recorded as a spike on the right side of the histogram. Some cameras have an overexposure warning whereby the overexposed areas blink. We ignored this warning to capture this image.

In this image, the white sky is acceptable because it is not the dominant subject. We can capture more detail in the sky by using a minus value in exposure compensation mode. This will reduce the right spike and push the histogram to the left. If we choose to use this camera setting, the overall picture will be very dark and the main subject will be underexposed. Thus, our picture will be less desirable.

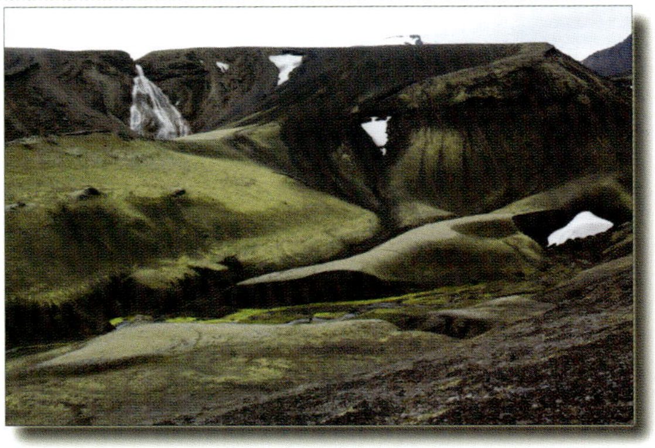

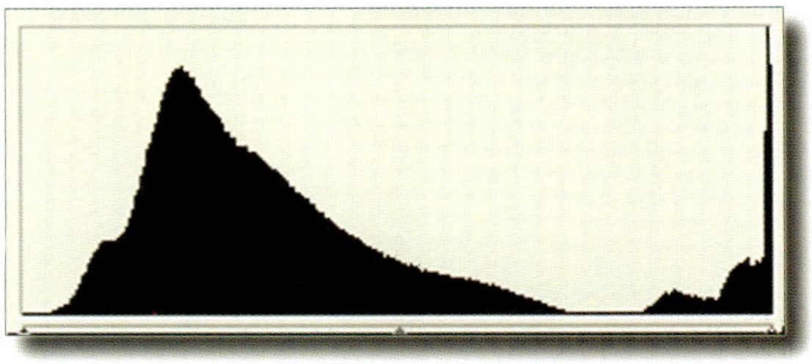

Waterfall (Iceland)

White Spike and Black Spike

In this picture, the dark face of the weaver, the mid-tones of the nest and weaver, and the bright white background have too great a range of contrast for the camera to capture.

We want to get the most pleasing exposure of the bird and thus record no detail in the very dark and white parts of the image. As a result, there is a spike on the right side as well on the left side of the histogram.

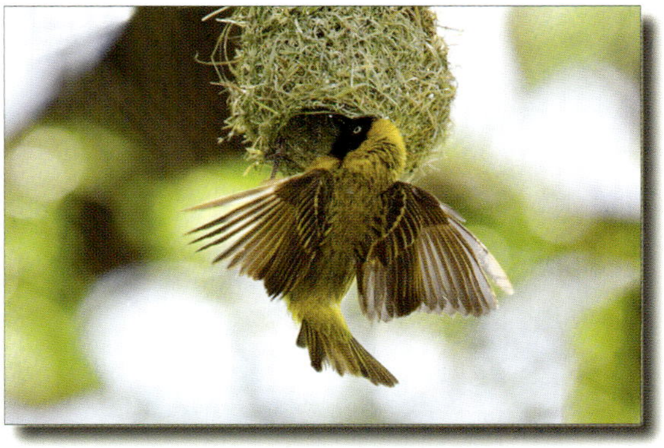

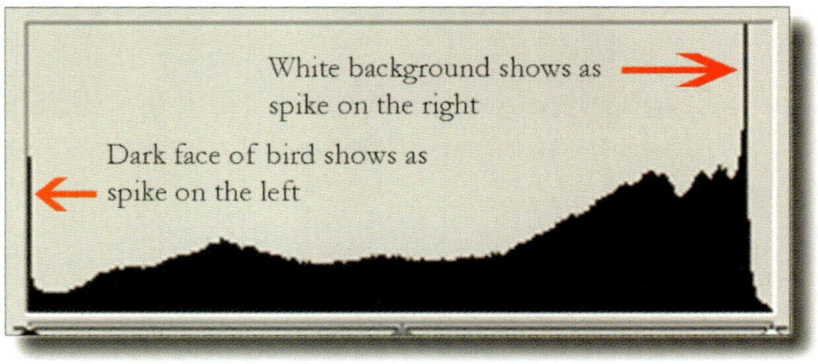

Weaver (South Africa)

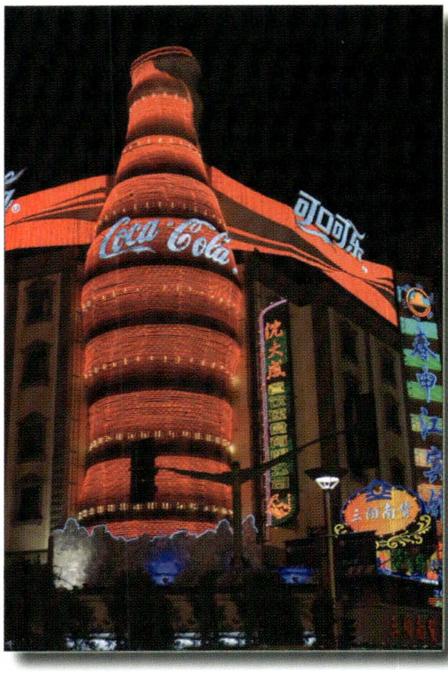

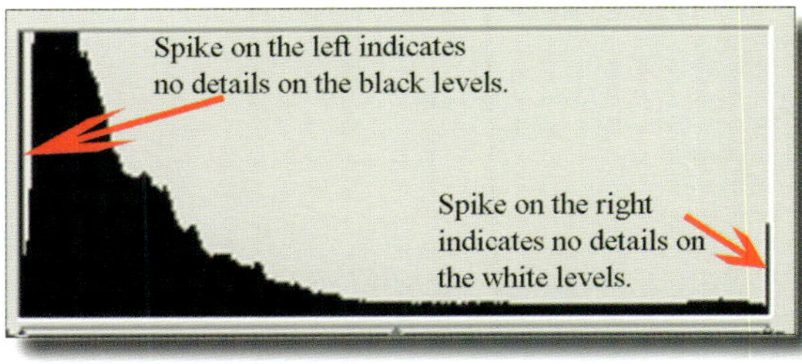

Shanghai at Night (China)

White Spike and Black Spike

The histogram of this image has spikes on the left as well as on the right. This indicates that the range of the levels of brightness in this image exceeds the range that this camera is capable of capturing.

This image has a black sky and bright neon lights. Our eye can see the details in both the dark and bright areas, but our camera is unable to capture all the levels of brightness that are available.

In this situation, you should ignore the deep shadow and the bright highlights of the histogram. Concentrate only on the mid-tones of the image. Use plus or minus exposure compensation in auto exposure mode to obtain the most pleasing mid-tones for the image.

Conclusion

Histograms give us useful information about the exposure of an image. We need to understand histograms, be able to "read" a histogram and use this information in order to take better exposed pictures.

Shutter Speed - Fast or Slow

Shutter speed can be used to freeze or blur water.

Introduction

Shutter speed is a time value expressing how long the camera's shutter is allowed to remain open. Along with aperture (the size of the opening that lets light into the camera), it is one of two settings that control the amount of light that reaches a camera's sensor. To show how fast and slow shutter speeds affect an image, we will use various shots of water rushing over Niagara Falls.

Camera Settings – Shutter Speed Priority

Note: Shutter Speed Priority is available in certain camera model only.

In most instances when your subject matter is in motion, like the water moving over the falls in this example, you should choose to use your camera's Shutter Speed Priority Mode. In Shutter Speed Priority Mode, you select the shutter speed you desire and your camera automatically chooses a matching aperture that will result in a proper exposure.

The table to the right shows the standard combinations of aperture and shutter speed:

Faster Time - Less Light				Slower Time - More Light			
1/500	1/250	1/125	1/60	1/30	1/15	1/8	1/4
F/2.8	F/4	F/5.6	F/8	F/11	F/16	F/22	F/32
Larger Aperture-More Light				Smaller Aperture-Less Light			

In some newer cameras you will find intermediate combinations:

1/125	1/100	1/80	1/60
F/16	F/15	F/13	F/11

Fast Shutter Speeds

In this picture, with a fast shutter speed of 1/500th of a second the water appears clear and sharp.

We selected the shutter speed (1/500th of a second), and the camera set a matching aperture of f/2.8. This combination gave us a proper exposure.

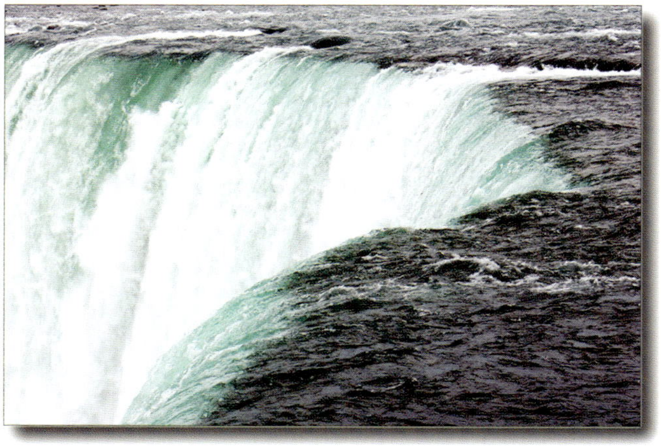

Niagara Falls at 1/500 sec., f/2.8 (Ontario, Canada).

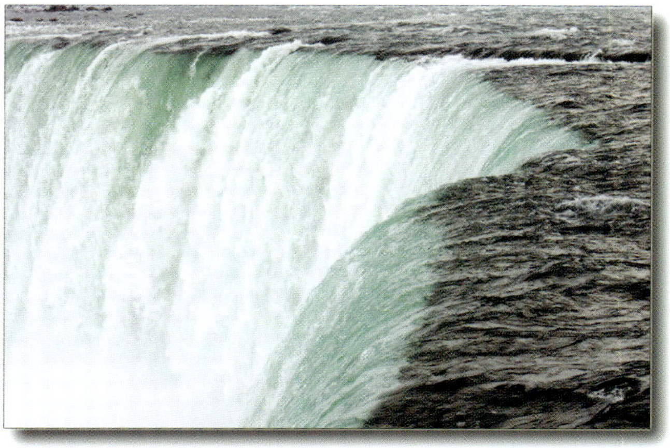

Niagara Falls at 1/125 sec., f/5.6 (Ontario, Canada).

Normal Shutter Speeds

When the shutter speed is set to a slightly slower 1/125th of a second, the water appears less crisp – closer to the way a human eye would see it.

We selected a medium shutter speed (1/125th of a second), and the camera set a matching aperture of f/5.6. Again, this combination gave us a proper exposure.

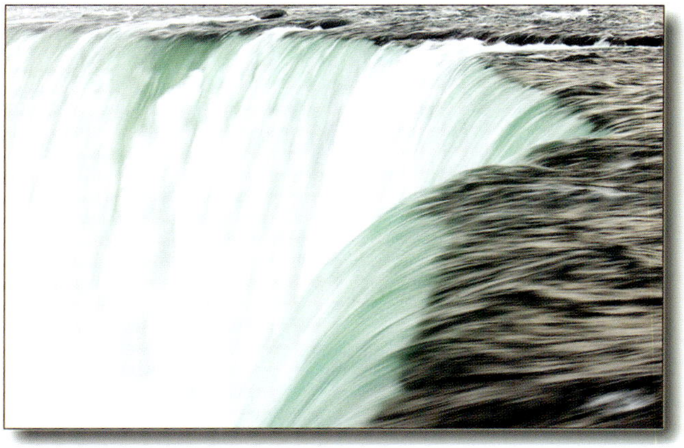

Niagara Falls at 1/8 sec., f/22 (Ontario, Canada).

Slow Shutter Speeds

With a very slow shutter speed of 1/8th of a second, a cotton wool effect is achieved. Here, the camera chose an aperture of f/22.

To avoid any unwanted camera movement that would blur the picture when one is using a slow shutter speed, be sure to mount the camera on a tripod and use a cable release to reduce camera vibration. Generally, to obtain acceptable sharpness when hand holding a camera, you need a shutter speed at least equal to the 35 mm equivalent focal length of the lens that you're using. For example, if your lens has a focal length of 100 mm, you should use a shutter speed of at least 1/100th of a second to prevent camera shake.

Slower Speeds

The moving effect of the water is enhanced even further with a shutter speed of ¼ of a second (aperture f/32).

Blurring the motion of the water suggests movement and presents an image to the viewer that differs from what the photographer actually saw. We like the effect of this image the best. The soft cotton wool effect adds an element of serenity to the fast running water of Niagara Falls.

In other situations, slower speeds can last up to several seconds (see the Antelope Canyon picture on page 35).

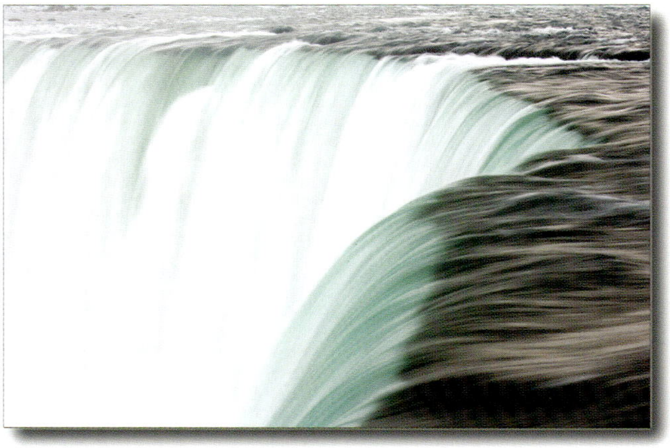

Niagara Falls at 1/4 sec., f/32 (Ontario, Canada)

Comparison

These images illustrate how different shutter speeds capture the feeling of moving water in different ways. Freezing the water with a shutter speed 1/500th of a second can be dramatic, while blurring the water at ¼ of a second adds an element of serenity. Both produce images that can't be seen by the human eye.

In all these examples, you select the shutter speed that gives the effect you desire. Your camera will select a matching aperture to give you a proper exposure. However, you may need to add plus exposure compensation for light subjects as discussed on page 17.

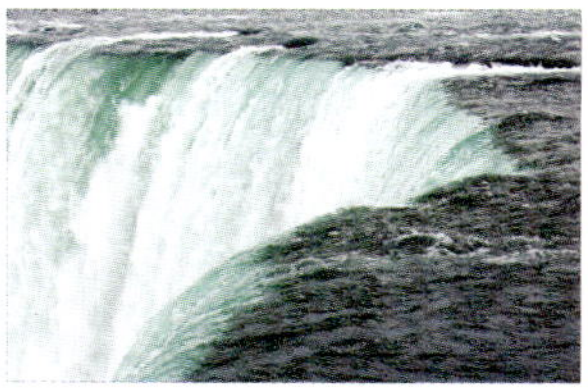

1/500 sec.

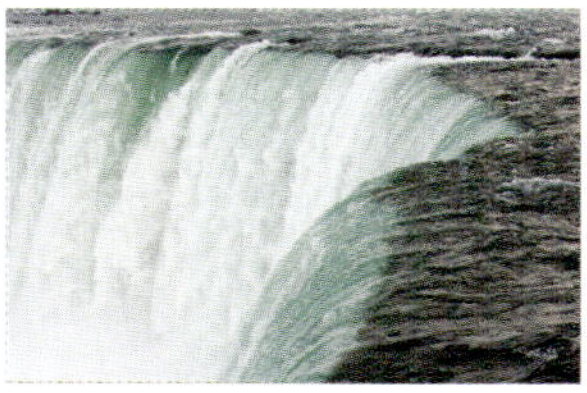

1/125 sec.

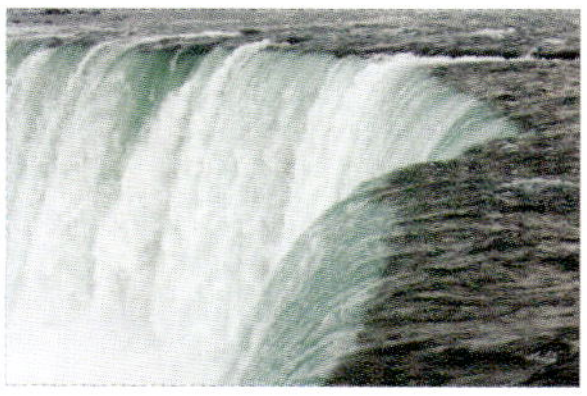

1/8 sec.

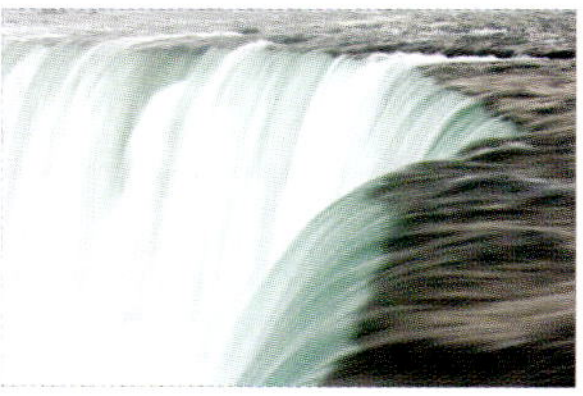

1/4 sec.

Faster Time - Less Light				Slower Time - More Light			
1/500	1/250	1/125	1/60	1/30	1/15	1/8	1/4
F/2.8	F/4	F/5.6	F/8	F/11	F/16	F/22	F/32
Larger Aperture-More Light				Smaller Aperture-Less Light			

Conclusion

Fast shutter speeds allow you to freeze action while slow shutter speeds let you blur motion. Experimentation will be required to find a shutter speed that produces the effect you most desire. A slow shutter speed makes the movement of the water more apparent and dramatic while stationary elements still appear sharp.

Shutter Priority-Slow

A slow shutter speed can be used to let more light reach the camera's sensor, as well as to create implied motion in pictures.

Introduction

Shutter speed is a time value expressed in seconds or fractions of seconds. It is one of two factors (the other being aperture size) that determine how much light reaches the camera's sensor. The slower the shutter speed, the longer the shutter is open. The longer the shutter is open, the more light that is allowed into the camera and the brighter the resulting picture. Shutter speeds generally range from 1/500th of a second (fast) up to 30 seconds (slow). A shutter speed longer than 1/30th of a second is usually considered slow.

Low Light

In extreme low light situations, such as this image of Antelope Canyon, the only option for a properly exposed picture is to use a very slow shutter speed. In this picture the shutter speed was 8 seconds with an aperture of f/11.

When using a slow shutter speed, it is necessary to use a tripod and cable release to keep the camera absolutely still. Any vibration of the camera will result in a blurred photo.

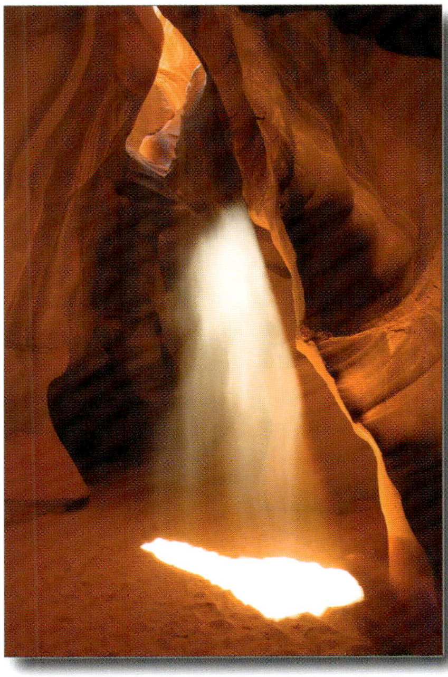

Antelope Light Ray (Arizona, US)

Macro Photography

In close-up photography, the shallow depth of field (the area in focus in an image) provides an added challenge for the photographer. Because of the optical properties of the camera lens, the depth of the area in focus decreases as we move closer to our subject. One can compensate for this by using a smaller aperture. In this picture of a spider, an aperture of f/22 was required to maintain a sufficient depth of field or focus and keep the entire body of the spider in focus. In order to compensate for the smaller aperture, a slower shutter speed - 1/4 of a second - was needed to allow enough light into the camera for a proper exposure. We used a tripod and a cable release to prevent blurring.

In this case, a slow shutter speed was used to allow a smaller aperture to give the image a larger depth of field.

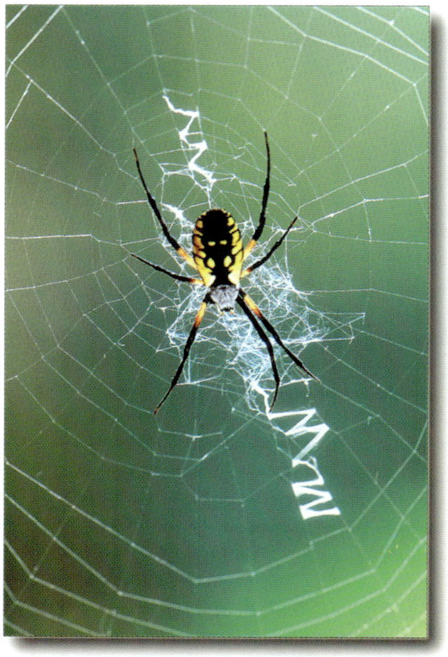

Black and Yellow Argiope (Toronto, Canada)

Blurred Motion

In this picture, when a slow shutter speed - ½ of a second - was used to capture the ferris wheel, the moving cars became a blur. In contrast, the stationary objects in the picture – the supporting structure and the Giant Wheel sign – remained in focus. Once again, a tripod and cable release were used.

When blurred and focused objects are combined in the same image, a sense of motion is implied. In this photo there is no doubt that the "Giant Wheel" is in motion.

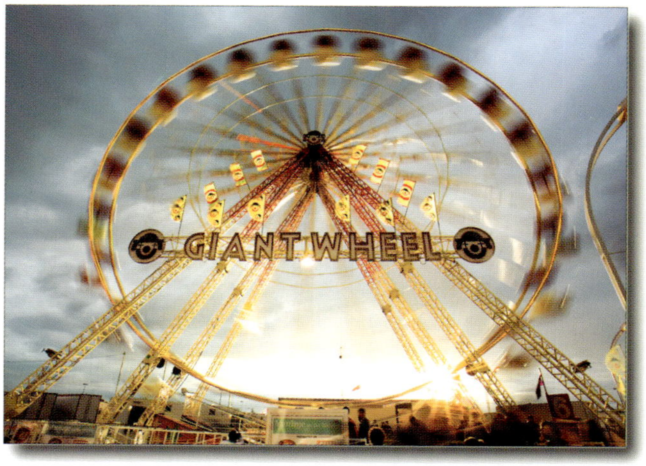

Giant Wheel (Toronto, Canada)

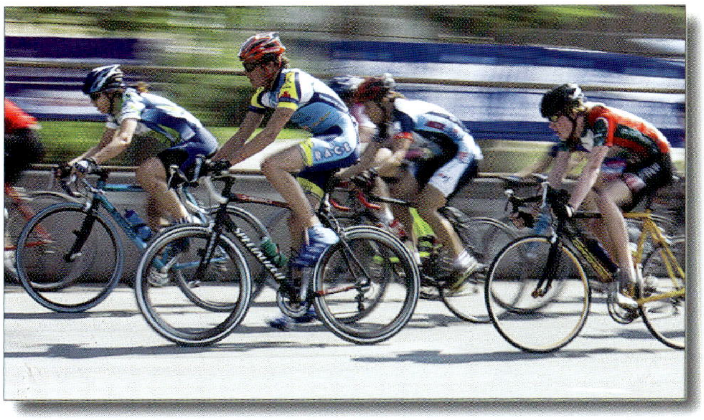

Cycling (Toronto, Canada)

Panning

Panning, a technique commonly used in film and video, can also be used with a still camera. In this picture, the photographer moved the camera to keep pace with the leading cyclist. The result was a sharp image against a blurred background. Here, a Shutter Priority Mode of 1/30th of a second was used. In other situations, you may need to experiment with different shutter speeds.

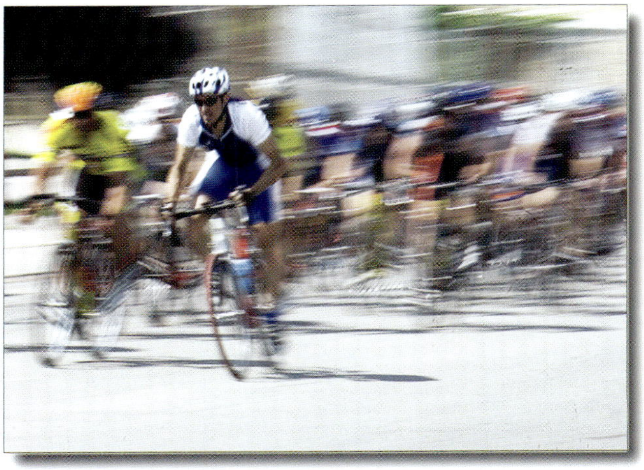

In the Midst (Toronto, Canada)

Panning with Selective Focus

In this example of panning, the photographer focused on a single cyclist in the middle of a large group of racers all moving at slightly different speeds. The result was one sharp cyclist in the midst of a pack of blurred and out of focus bicycles and racers. In this instance a shutter speed of 1/15th of a second was chosen. As in the previous picture, it may be necessary to take pictures with different shutter speeds and move the camera along with your subject in order to get the desired result. The secret is to pan while maintaining a focus on your subject - here, the cyclist in the middle of the pack.

Conclusion

Slow shutter speeds are a useful photographic technique. They can be used in low light situations, when dramatic action pictures are the photographer's goal, for panning and for panning with selective focus and also in macro photography. Experimenting with shutter speed may give you just the effect you are looking for, so don't be afraid to experiment with various shutter speeds.

Shutter Priority-Fast

Fast shutter speeds can be used to freeze action.

Introduction

Fast shutter speeds are often used to freeze action sequences. This photographic technique allows you to take sharp pictures of moving subjects. In this section, we have included a number of illustrations that show the effects this can produce.

Sports - Volleyball

In this image, a Shutter Priority Mode with a shutter speed of 1/200th of a second was used to capture the striker in action. At this shutter speed, the volleyball appears sharp and the striker's hand is a slightly blurred.

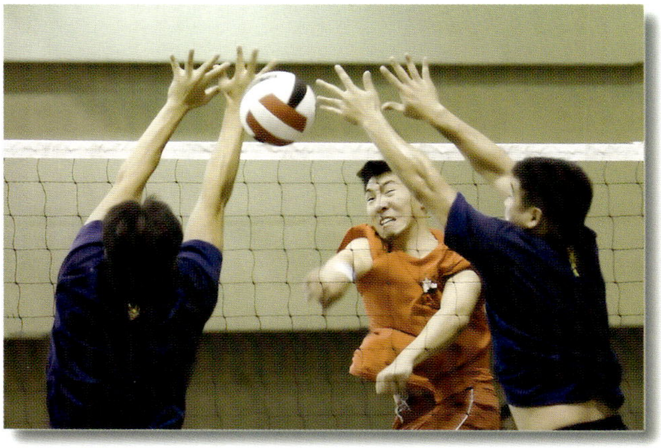

Spike (Toronto, Canada)

Sports – Wheel Chair Race

Here, we used the Shutter Priority Mode and set the shutter speed to 1/500th of a second. As the racer moves towards the viewer, this shutter speed is sufficient to render the wheel sharp and the racer in focus.

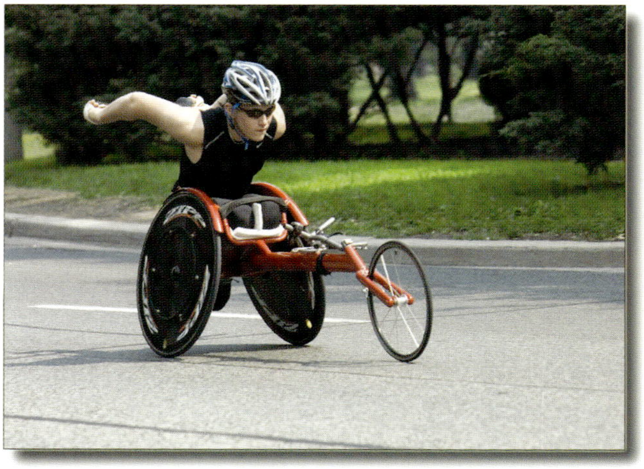

Wheel Chair Race (Toronto, Canada)

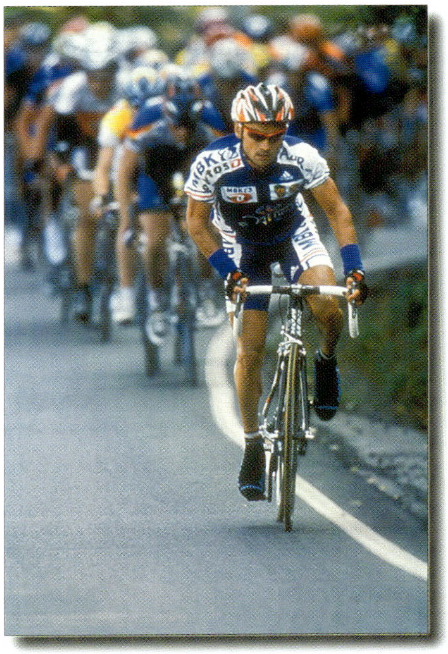

World Cycling (Hamilton, Canada)

Sports - Cycling

In this photograph, a Shutter Priority Mode with a shutter speed of $1/250^{th}$ of a second was used to freeze the leading cyclist. Note that a picture taken with the movement coming toward the camera implies less speed to the viewer than when the subject is traveling across our field of vision.

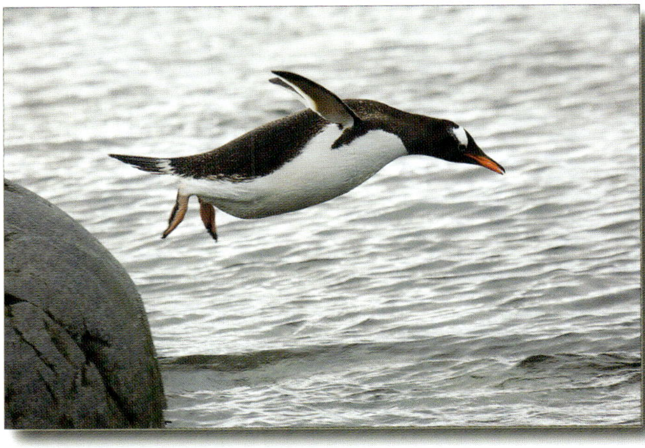

Penguin Jumps (South Georgia, Antarctica)

Freezing Action

In this picture, a Shutter Priority Mode with a slightly faster shutter speed of $1/320^{th}$ of a second was used to freeze the penguin in mid-air.

Here the penguin jumped sideways, across the camera's lens. This implies faster action than if the penguin were moving toward the camera. As a result, a slightly faster shutter speed was needed to ensure the penguin's motion was captured in sharp focus.

Water Droplets

Here, a shutter speed of 1/320th of a second was used to freeze the drops of water thrown up by the horse into crisp detail. The cowboy and the horse were kept in focus by using the Auto Focus Mode while they were further away and by shooting as many images as possible as they moved closer to the photographer.

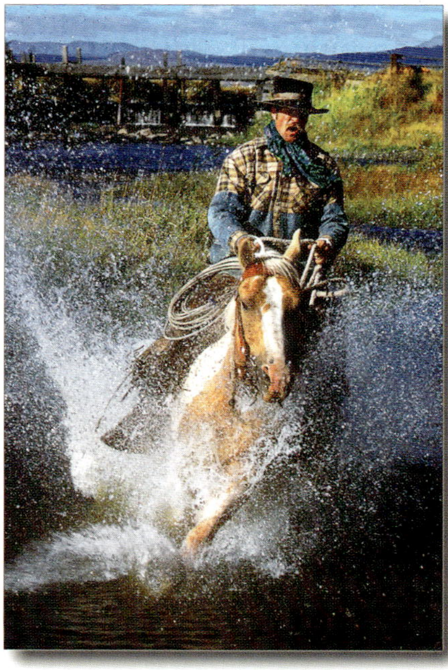

Dashing (Idaho, US)

Stopping Action

Capturing a special moment is one of the joys and challenges in action photography. In this image, a shutter speed of 1/500th of a second allowed the photographer to stop the action as the cheetah was jumping down the tree.

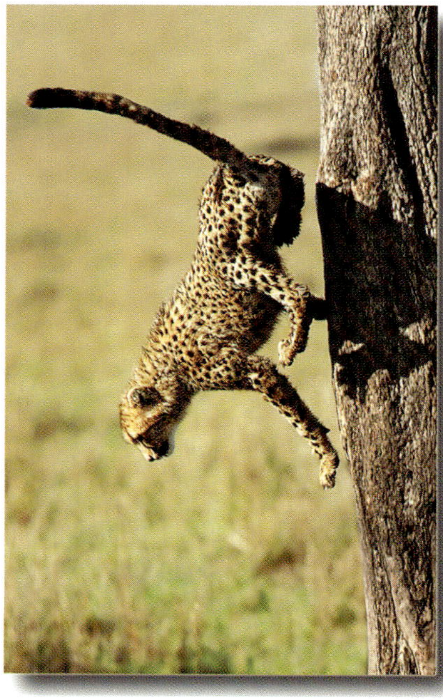

Cheetah Jumps (Kenya)

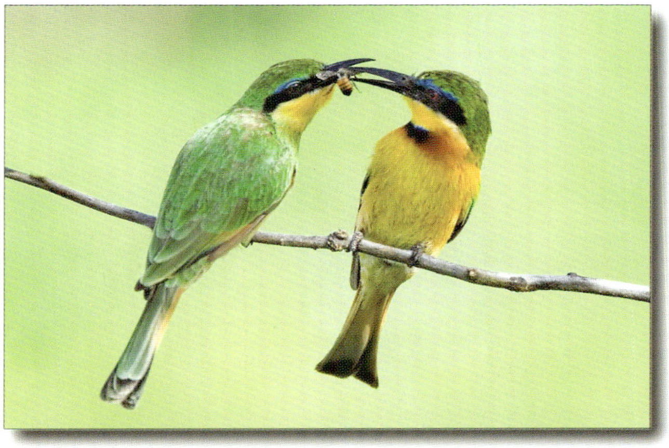

Little Bee-Eater Sharing (Kenya)

Capturing the Moment

Photography is about capturing a given moment. This is made more challenging when fast camera action is required to take pictures of moving subjects. In this image, a shutter speed of 1/500th of a second enabled the photographer to capture the precise moment when the Little Bee-Eater was sharing a meal with his companion.

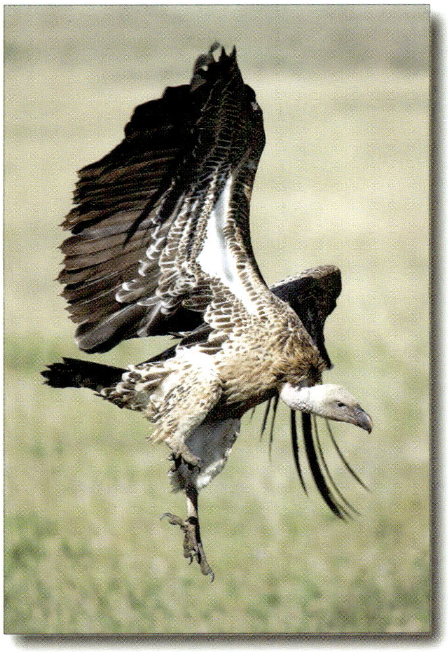

Vulture Landing (Kenya)

Freezing Motion

Here, an even faster shutter speed was used to capture the details of the vulture about to land. The Continuous Focus Mode (in which the camera keeps the subject in focus until the shutter is pressed) was employed when the vulture was approaching, and a shutter speed of 1/1000th of a second was used. This let the photographer take multiple images of the subject in a quest for the perfect perspective.

Conclusion

Fast shutter speeds allow the photographer to capture moving subjects effectively. They also increase the number of frames that can be taken during a short, but often critical, time span.

Aperture Priority

Using the camera's Aperture Priority Mode will allow you to control your camera's aperture and depth of field.

Introduction

The aperture - the opening that permits light to pass into the camera - is controlled by an adjustable diaphragm. Obviously, a larger opening will allow more light into the camera than a smaller one. Aperture sizes are expressed as f-numbers, as illustrated in the diagram below:

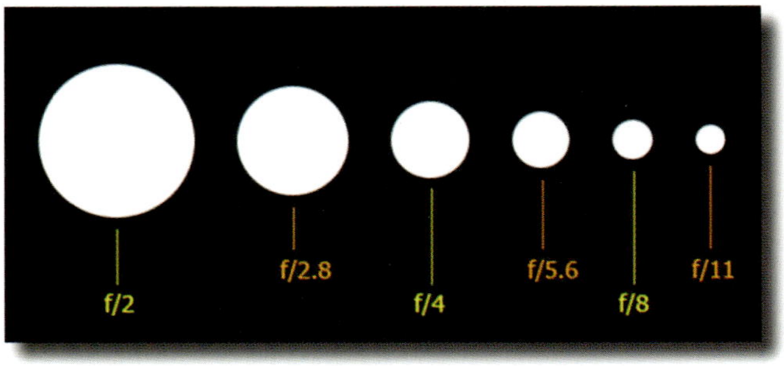

F-numbers are expressed as fractions rather than whole numbers.

F-numbers	Fraction	Opening & Amount of Light
F/2.8	1/ 2.8ths	Large – More Light
F/5.6	1/ 5.6ths	Medium – Average Light
F/16	1/ 16ths	Small – Less Light

This causes some confusion for many people because a smaller f-number (like f/2.8) represents a larger aperture opening than larger f-number (such as f/16). In summary:

Bigger F-number =	**Smaller Aperture Opening**
Smaller F-number =	**Larger Aperture Opening**

The standard f-numbers are:

F/2.8	F/4	F/5.6	F/8	F/11	F/16
More Light		Average Light		Less Light	

You can control the amount of light that enters the camera's sensor by adjusting the size of the aperture.

Note: Aperture Priority Mode is available in certain camera model only.

When you use your camera's Aperture Priority Mode, you fix the size of the opening. Your camera then selects the appropriate shutter speed that will, in combination with the aperture, yield a proper exposure.

You can use large apertures or small apertures to create a variety of photographic effects.

Aperture Priority for Creative Effect

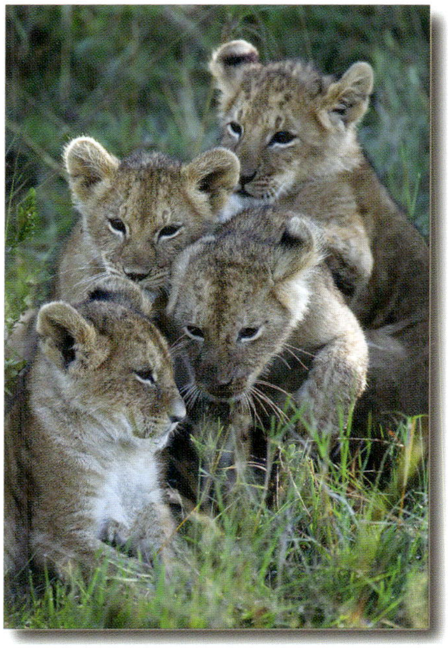

Lion Cubs (Kenya)

Large Apertures Outdoors for Low Light

In early morning, the available light is soft and low. Using a large aperture allows the maximum amount of light to enter the camera. In this case, setting the aperture at f/2.8 necessitated a shutter speed of $1/60^{th}$ of a second.

Had the Auto Exposure Mode been chosen, the camera might have selected a small aperture and a slower shutter speed. That would likely have resulted in unwanted blurring because of the motion of the cubs.

Smaller F-number =	**Larger Aperture Opening**

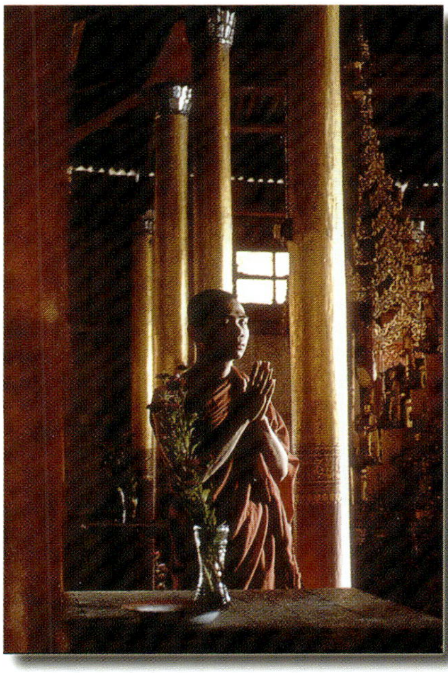

Monk Praying (Burma)

Large Apertures Indoors for Low Light

There are occasions when indoor lighting is very dim. In this temple the main source of natural light was the window. The selected aperture of f/5.6 gave a reasonable depth of field. The resulting shutter speed of $1/15^{th}$ of a second was the minimum speed needed to render the monk sharply. We used tripod and cable release to eliminate any camera vibration.

Smaller F-number =	**Larger Aperture Opening**

Small Apertures at Night

Small apertures such as f/11 and f/16 allow less light to reach the camera's sensor. As a result, the camera automatically slows down the shutter speed in order to obtain the correct exposure.

Setting the Aperture Priority Mode at f/16 for this picture meant the camera chose a shutter speed of 1/30th of a second. The slower shutter speed resulted in a slight blurring of the carousel lights and captured the sense of movement the photographer sought.

Bigger F-number =	Smaller Aperture Opening

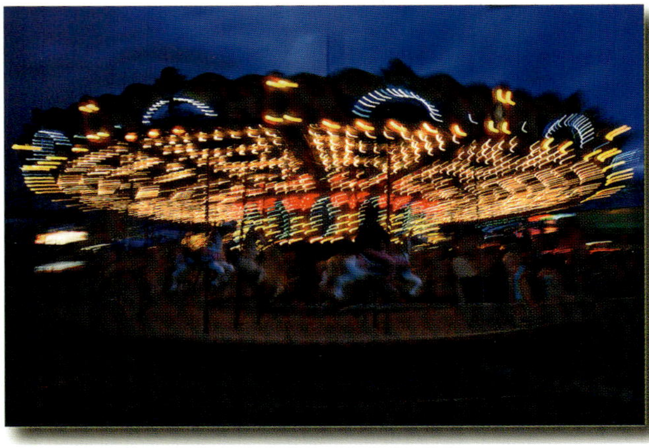

Carousel (Toronto, Canada)

Small Apertures during the Day

In this photograph of a waterfall, we set the camera's Aperture Priority Mode to its smallest aperture f/16. In this case, the shutter speed automatically defaulted to 1/15th of a second.

The slower shutter speed gave the water in the picture a soft cotton wool effect. A tripod and cable release were used to avoid camera movement.

Bigger F-number =	Smaller Aperture Opening

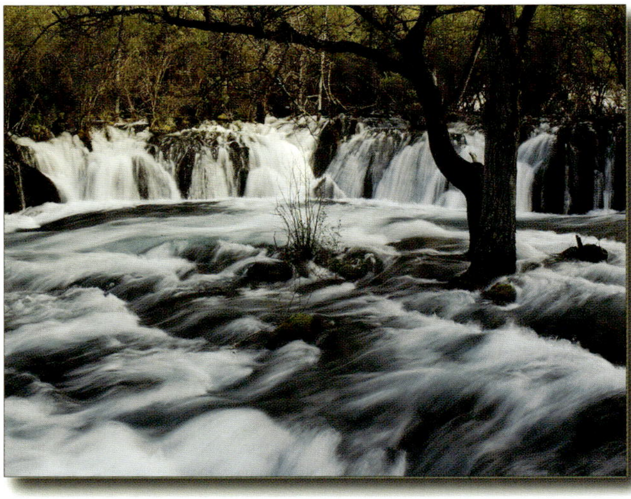

Waterfall (Sichuan, China)

Conclusion

Once you become accustomed to the principle that a larger aperture will result in a faster shutter speed and that a smaller aperture will force the camera to select a slower shutter speed, you can create a variety of interesting photographic effects using the Aperture Priority Mode.

Aperture Priority for Depth of Field

You can use your camera's Aperture Priority Mode to control the depth of field (the area of sharpness) within your photograph.

Introduction

The term "depth of field" refers to the area of an image in which the subject matter will appear acceptably sharp. It is measured from front to back. The smaller the aperture (such as F/16), the larger the area of sharpness; the larger the aperture (such as F/2.8), the smaller the depth of field, and the smaller the area of sharpness.

Smaller Area of Sharpness		Average Area of Sharpness		Larger Area of Sharpness	
F/2.8	F/4	F/5.6	F/8	F/11	F/16
Large Aperture		Med. Aperture		Small Aperture	

Depth of field is best illustrated through examples. The following pictures will show how depth of field affects the overall appearance of your pictures.

Small Apertures

Smaller apertures, such as f/11 and f/16, will result in a larger amount of the photograph (from the foreground to the background) being in clear focus. In this example, with an aperture of f/16, the two penguins in the foreground, the groups of penguins in the middle of the image, and the distant iceberg and mountain, are all in focus.

Larger Area of Sharpness	
F/11	F/16
Small Aperture	

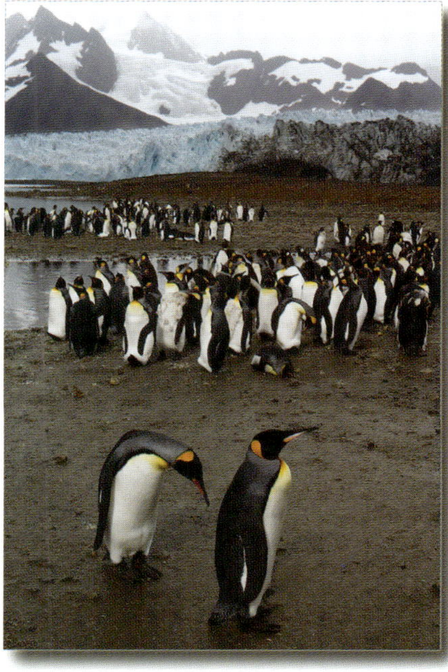

Penguins (South Georgia, Antarctica)

Small Apertures

This is another example of a photograph shot with a small aperture, f/16. The tea vendors in the foreground, the trees in the middle and the Blue Mosque in the background are all in focus. To get the maximum depth of field in your image, you must use the camera's optics to your advantage. Optics tell us that the depth of field extends from 1/3rd of the way in front of the point of focus to 2/3rd's of the way behind it. Therefore, to keep the most amount of space in your picture in focus, you should focus 1/3rd of the way in front of your image. In this picture, the result came from focusing on the faces of the tea vendors.

Larger Area of Sharpness	
F/11	F/16
Small Aperture	

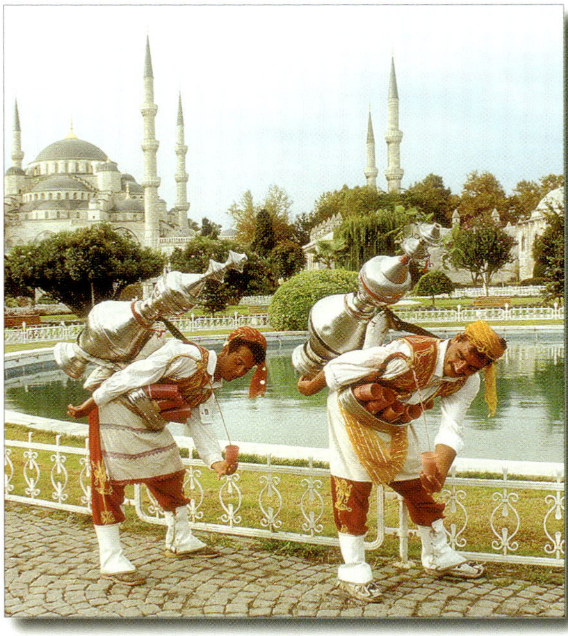

Tea Vendors (Turkey)

Medium Apertures

Medium apertures, with f-numbers such as f/5.6 and f/8, are used when depth of field is not an important element in the composition. A medium aperture will give you the best quality picture that your camera's optics are capable of. In this image, the monk is the only subject that needs to be sharp and depth of field – the area in focus – is not important.

Average Area of Sharpness	
F/5.6	F/8
Med. Aperture	

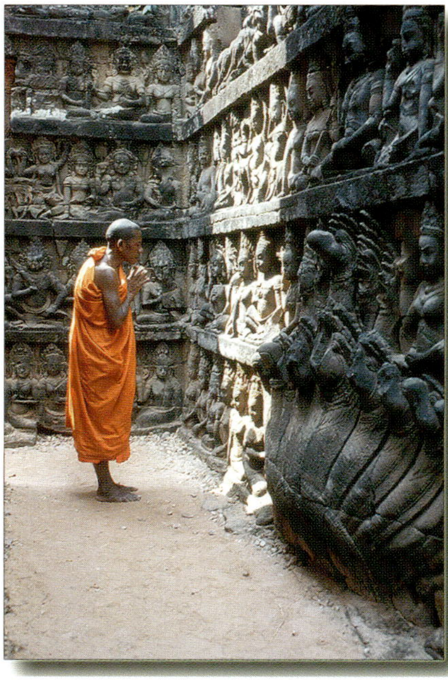

Monk in Corridor (Cambodia)

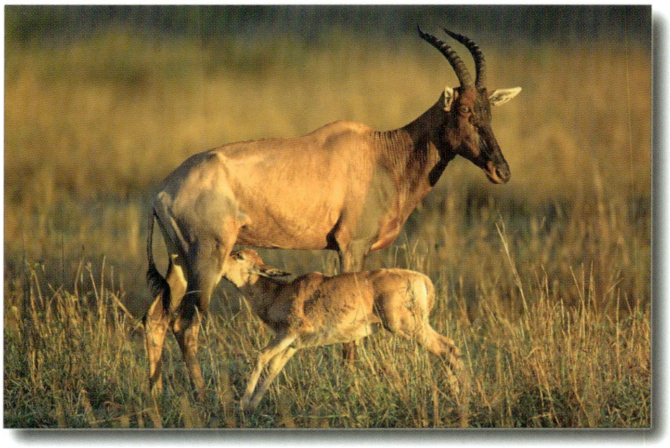

Fawn Nursing (Kenya)

Large Apertures

Large apertures such as f/2.8 and f/4 reduce the depth of the area in your photograph that will appear in focus. In this image, the area of sharpness is limited to the mother and calf. The grass in the foreground and the sky in the background are both out of focus in terms of tone and shape. This prevents the foreground and background from competing for the viewer's attention.

Smaller Area of Sharpness	
F/2.8	F/4
Large Aperture	

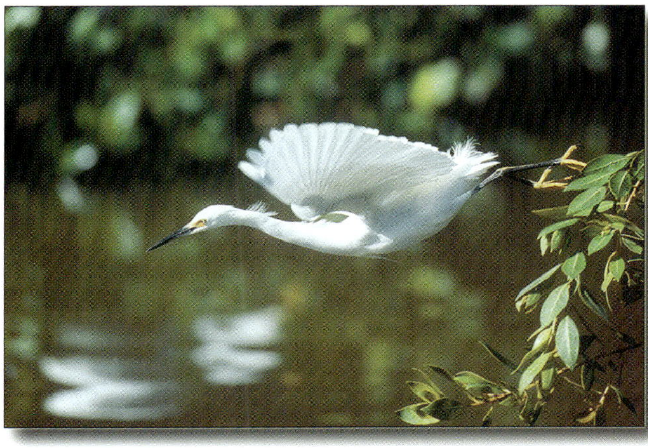

Great Egret Taking Off (Florida, US)

Large Apertures

Again here, a shallow depth of field left the egret and branches in focus with the trees and water in the background out of focus. The large aperture also resulted in the faster shutter speed required to freeze the action of the egret.

Smaller Area of Sharpness	
F/2.8	F/4
Large Aperture	

Conclusion

A mastery of depth of field can produce dramatic and varied results. A small aperture enables the photographer to keep virtually everything in the picture in focus while a large aperture makes it possible to isolate the specific portion of the picture you wish the viewer to focus upon.

Smaller Area of Sharpness		Average Area of Sharpness		Larger Area of Sharpness	
F/2.8	F/4	F/5.6	F/8	F/11	F/16
Large Aperture		Med. Aperture		Small Aperture	

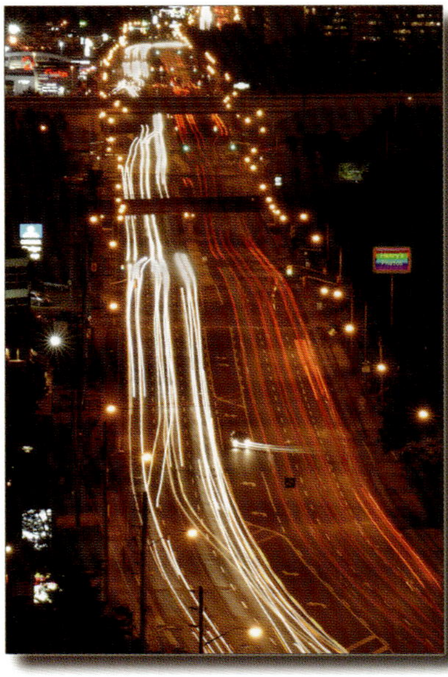
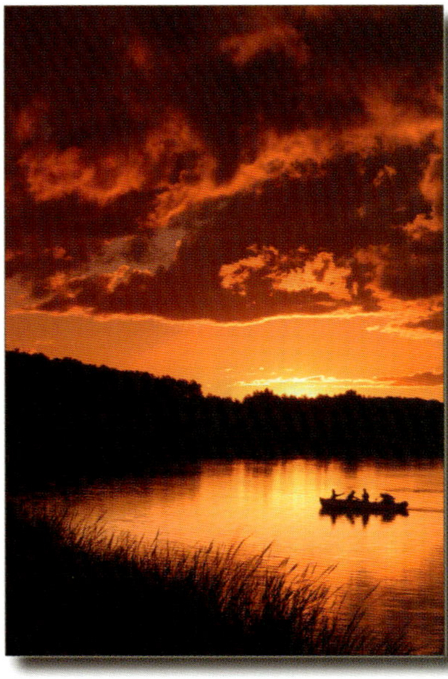
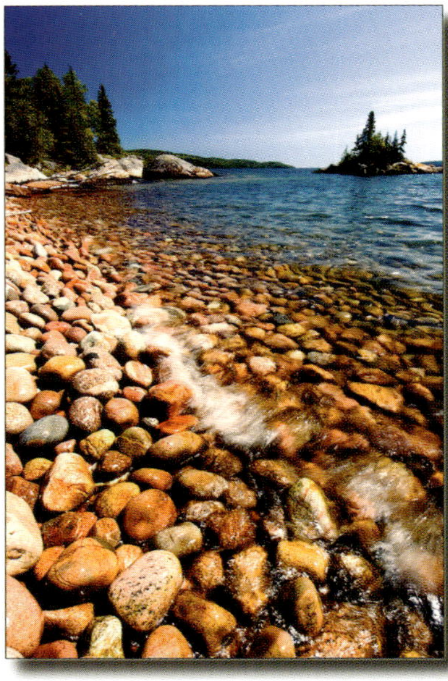
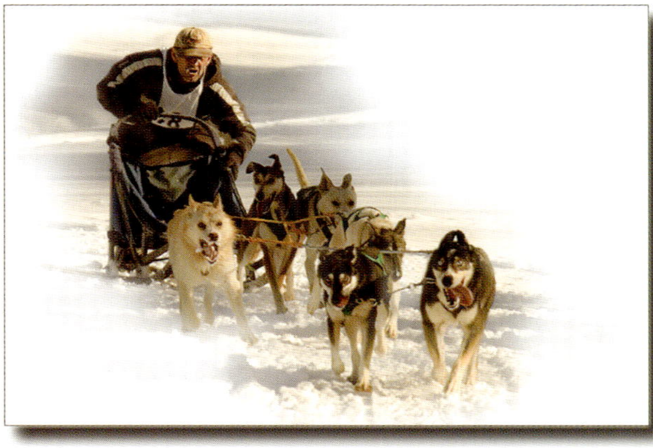
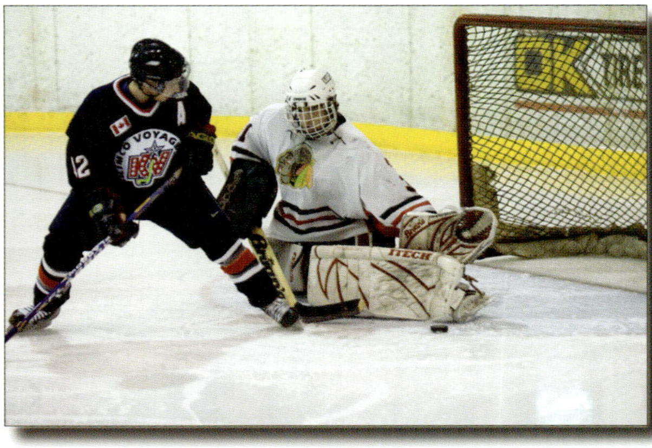
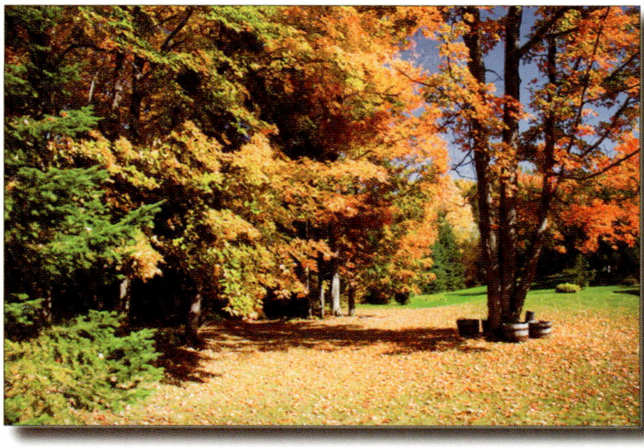
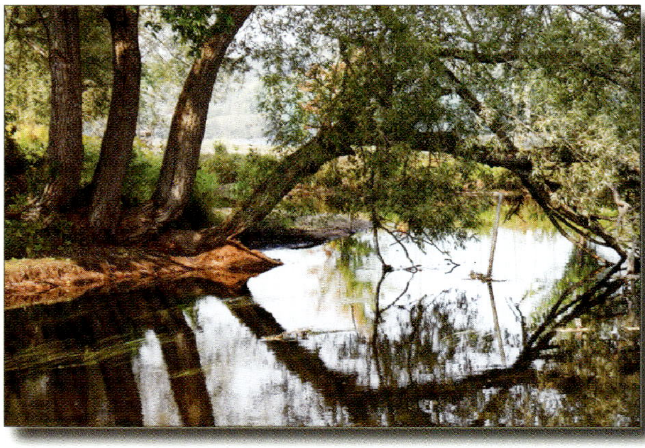

Photos by Henry Christiansen

Chapter 3 COMPOSITION

Composition

Becoming familiar with basic principles of composition such as quality of light, straight lines, straight and curved lines, the Rule of Thirds, the Points of Power, the Golden Rule, and framing can help you create better pictures. In this chapter we will explain how these principles work and give you a wide variety of examples to illustrate how they can be used in many different photographic situations.

Quality of Light

Various directional properties of light are top lighting, front lighting, side lighting, back lighting and overcast light.

Introduction

The two aspects of light that you must consider in photography are quantity and quality. Your camera's built-in light meter will measure the quantity, and you can follow up by utilizing the correct aperture and shutter speed to get a perfectly exposed photograph. However, there is no meter that will measure the quality of light. When taking photographs, you must learn to look for, recognize and exploit the different lighting opportunities that are available.

Top Lighting

Top lighting occurs at midday when the sun is directly on top of the subject. This is considered the worst kind of natural light because it casts harsh shadows on the subject. Try to avoid top lighting as much as possible.

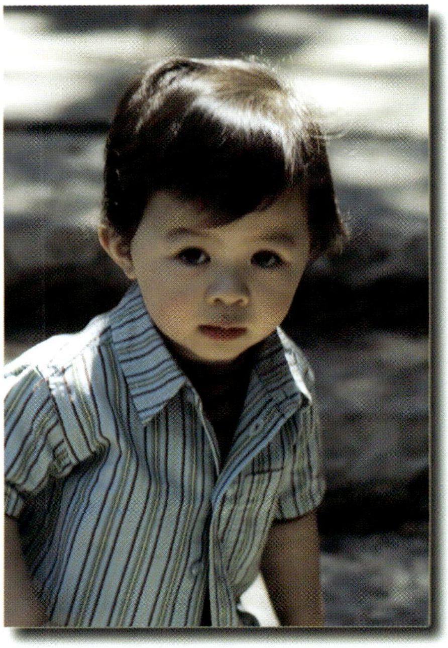

Nick (Toronto, Canada)

Front Lighting

Front lighting occurs when the light source is coming from over your shoulder, and you can see your own shadow at least five feet long in front of you. A disadvantage of front lighting is that your subject will cast very little shadow. Shadow often brings a sense of perspective to a photograph. To bring out the main subject in these cases it's a good idea to choose a background that is lighter or darker than the subject.

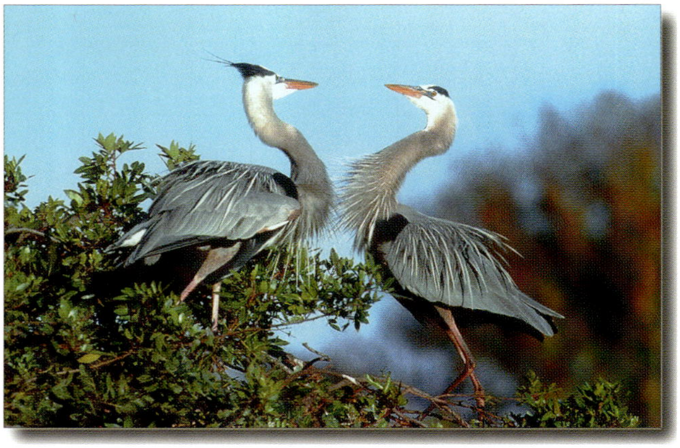

Great Blue Herons (Florida, US)

Front Lighting with Reflection

Usually front lighting means that the subject casts very little shadow. However, this can change under certain conditions, and with direct reflection. In this case, the white penguins are in shallow water, and front lighting gives the subjects an interesting reflection in the water. Recognizing and utilizing the properties of front lighting will help you capture more dynamic pictures.

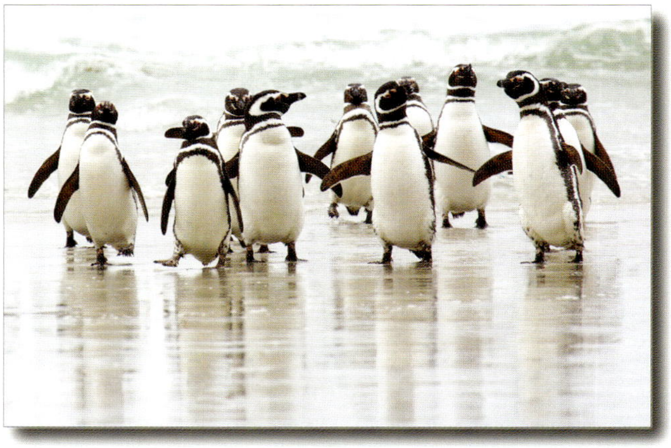

Penguin's Reflection (South Georgia, Antarctica)

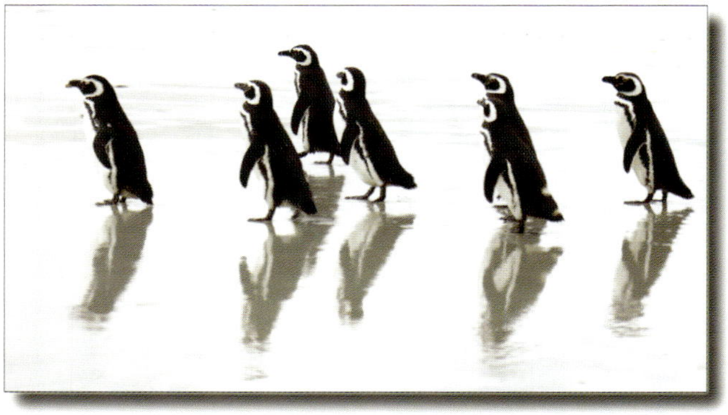

Penguin's Reflection (South Georgia, Antarctica)

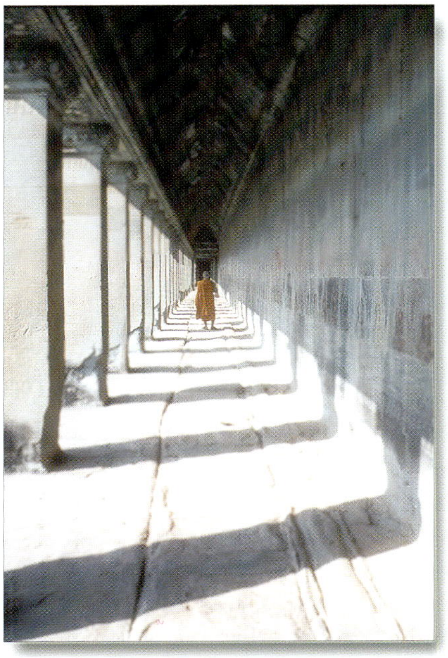

Monk in First Gallery (Cambodia)

Side Lighting

Shadows are most prominent when the light is coming from the side of the photograph. Side lighting can give a picture a sense of perspective and dimension. In this image, the dominant shadows of the columns add depth and perspective to the photograph. The angled shadows also lead the viewer's eye toward the figure of the monk.

Side lighting shows texture and can be used to express emotion in an image.

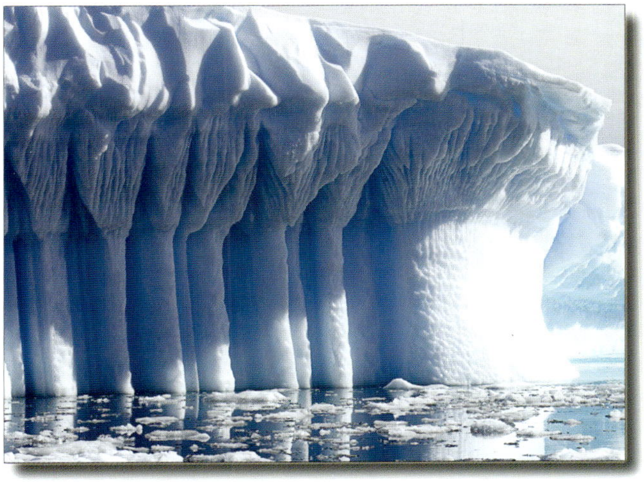

Iceberg (Antarctica)

Side Lighting - Landscapes

In this landscape photograph, the dominant shadows produced by side lighting add depth and texture to this iceberg image.

Back Lighting

Back lighting occurs when the subject is positioned between the sun and the photographer. In this example of back lighting, the egret's feathers are caught by the sun's rays and seem to hold the light. With a proper amount of contrast between the subject and the background, this can be the most striking type of lighting.

When the camera points directly at the sun, lens flare may occur. Be careful to shift your camera angle to eliminate undesirable bursts of light and use a lens hood if possible.

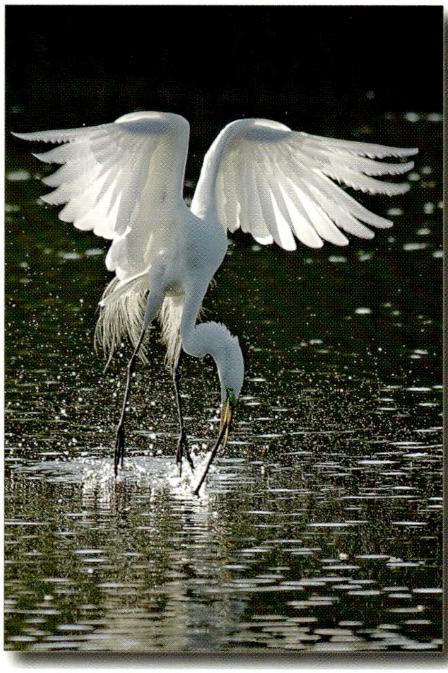

Great Egret Picking up Stick (Florida, US)

Overcast Lighting

On an overcast day, the entire sky is one giant and gentle light source. This type of diffused light creates little contrast. In this example, the light produces few shadows and brings out the subtle yellow and green hues in the flowers and leaves of the Yellow Lady Slippers.

Many people put their camera away on cloudy days. Often, this overcast light provides the richest color that is available in nature.

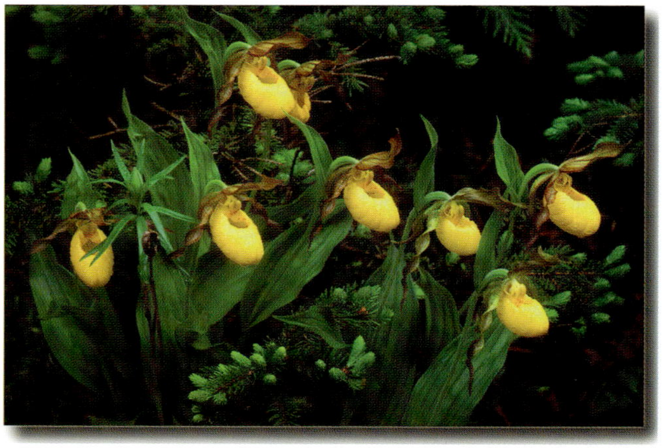

Yellow Lady Slippers (Ontario, Canada)

Conclusion

Since camera meters don't measure the quality of light, you must learn to recognize the directional aspects of the light source and work with them. Exposure compensation, camera angles and composition guidelines, in combination with your own creativity, can make for remarkable results.

Straight Lines

One simple, yet remarkably effective compositional secret is to use straight lines in your photographs.

Introduction

Straight lines occur in nature as well as in human creations. For photographers, they often become compositional elements. The following pictures will illustrate the effectiveness of using straight lines in composing photographs.

Straight Lines

In photography, lines lead the viewer's eye across the picture. Longer lines hold the viewer's eye for a longer amount of time, resulting in greater impact.

Vertical or horizontal lines can give your picture a sense of stability and purpose. Conversely, lines that are not absolutely straight can evoke feelings of unease or restlessness.

In this example, you would want to choose a shooting angle which would ensure that all the vertical lines (columns), and all the horizontal lines (steps), were straight and, where possible, framing other "straight line" elements in the picture.

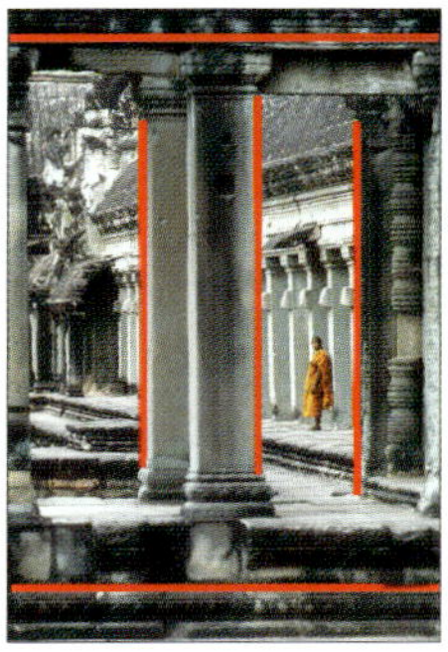

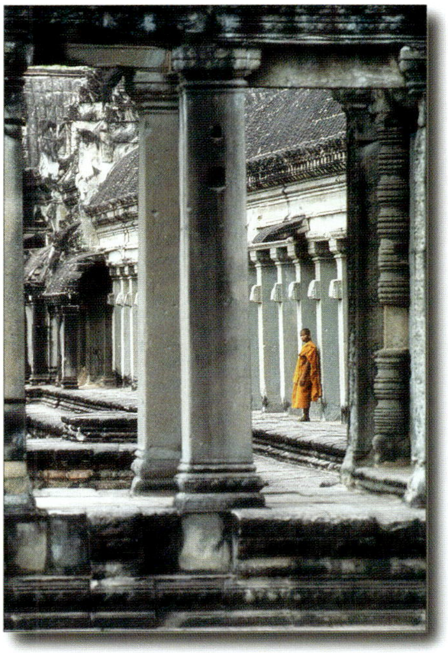

Courtyard (Cambodia)

Horizontal Lines

The main building blocks of this picture are a series of horizontal lines formed by the birds, trees, mist and fence. Straight and parallel lines produce an image of stability.

It is important to ensure that horizontal lines are as straight and parallel as possible.

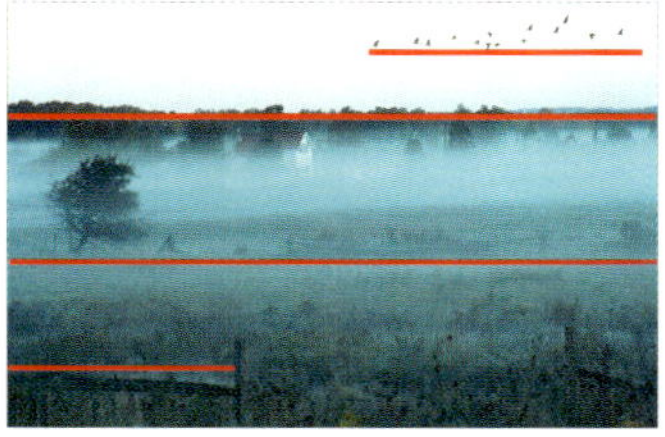

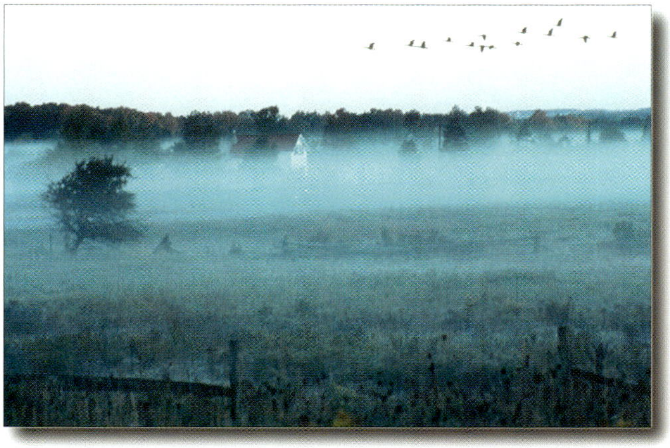

Misty Morning (Ontario, Canada)

Vertical Lines

This picture is composed of a series of vertical lines (columns). The repetition of vertical lines suggests strength, power and precision.

In this case, the photographer chose a shooting location that presented the columns with an adequate amount of space between them, and avoided overlapping or merging them. The angle of the shot kept the horizon low, capturing more of the sky and enhancing the height of the columns.

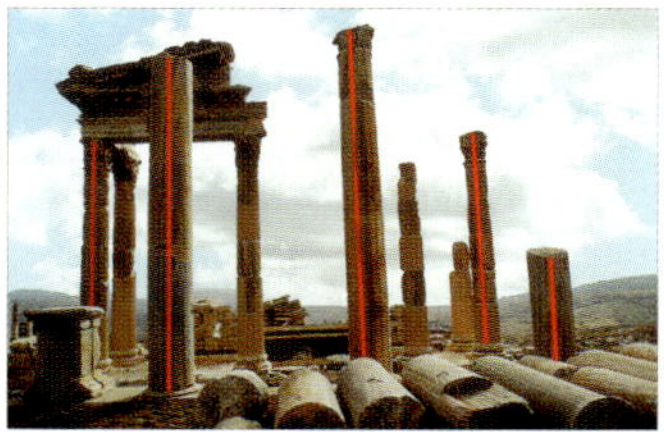

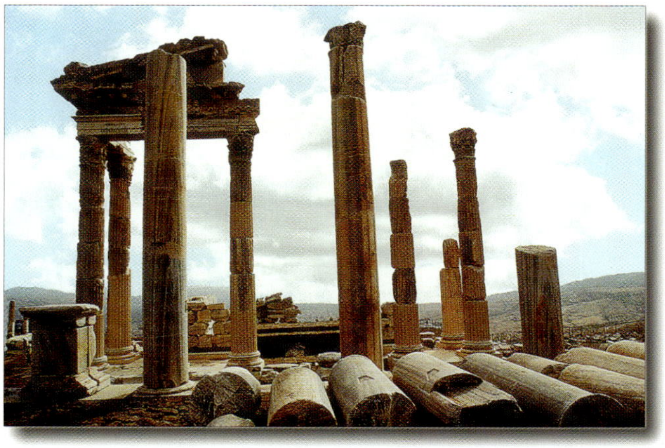

Temple of Trojan (Turkey)

Oblique Lines - Nature

Oblique lines can be more dynamic than vertical and horizontal lines, suggesting movement and change.

This picture presents the diagonal lines of the rocks in the foreground against the straight line of the horizon.

Using oblique lines in addition to straight vertical and horizontal lines can add an extra dimension to your pictures.

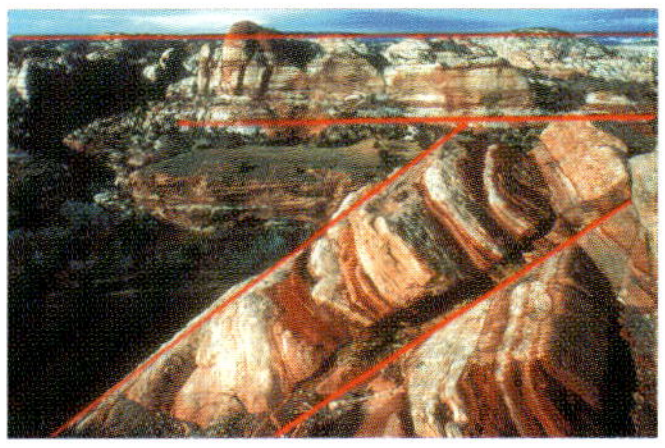

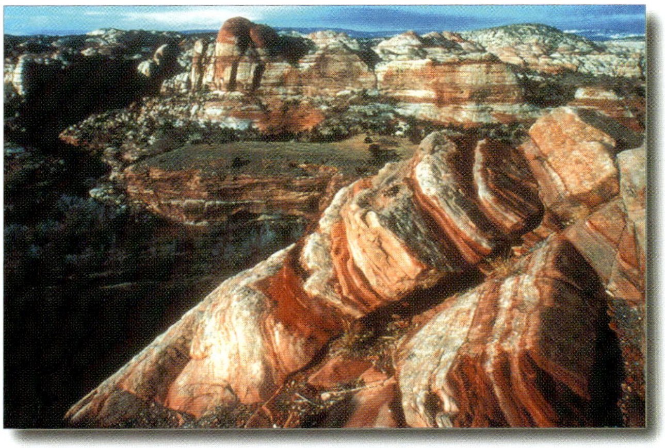

Bryce Canyon (Utah, US)

Oblique Lines - Action

As the huskies and their driver turn a corner during a race, oblique lines are formed. The resulting diagonal lines against the straight line of the horizon add motion and dynamic tension to this image.

The oblique lines in this picture are only available for a brief moment. In action photography, it's important to select a good vantage point in order to capture the precise moments lines are formed. Using oblique lines can make pictures more dynamic.

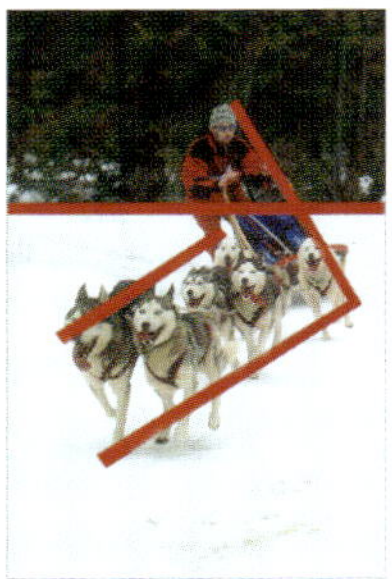

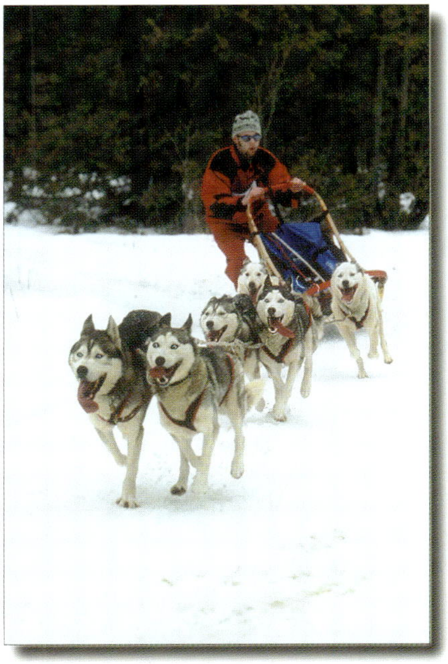

Husky Sled Race (Haliburton, Canada)

Conclusion

Lines are building blocks in many photographic compositions. Using straight lines effectively will certainly help you take better pictures.

Straight and Curved Lines

Combining straight and curved lines is a powerful method of composition which can produce interesting and dynamic images.

Introduction

Many notable photographs result from capturing arrangements of lines. The following pictures illustrate the characteristics of straight and curved lines and show how to combine them for better pictures.

Minimizing the Number of Lines

We often use both straight and curved lines in photography.

This image has two main lines: a curved line formed by a river and a straight line formed by the horizon. The curved 'S' line of the river leads the eye from the rock in the foreground, up through the path of the river. It ends at the horizon.

When combining straight and curved lines, you should attempt to use as few lines as possible. This will prevent the viewer's attention from being drawn in conflicting directions.

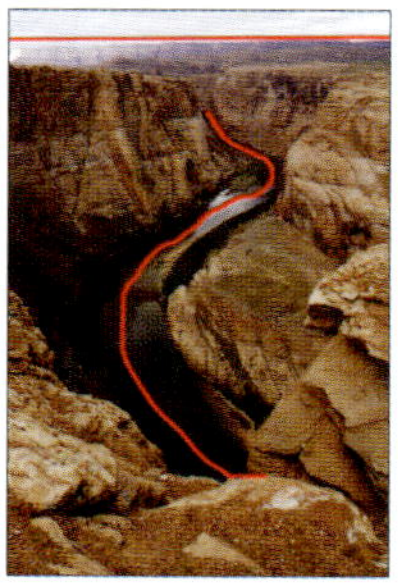

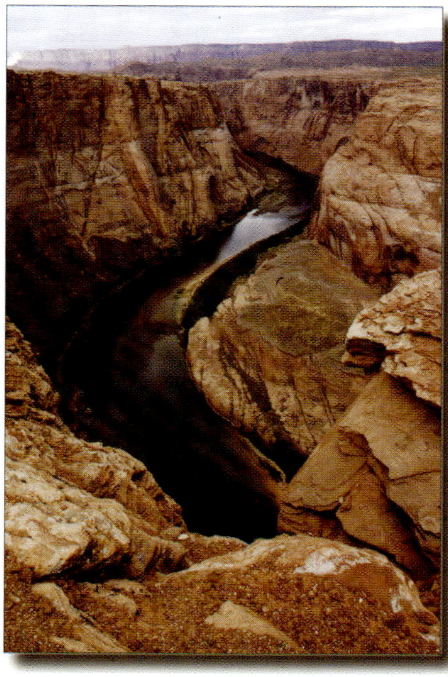

Colorado River (Arizona, US)

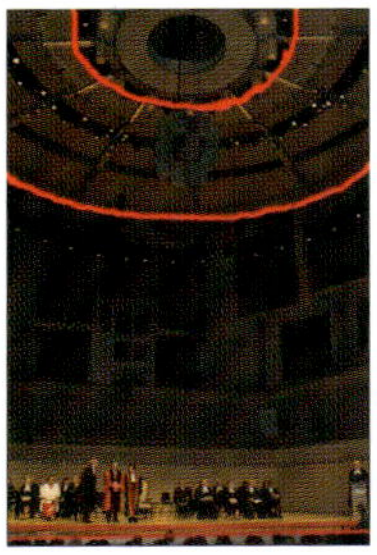

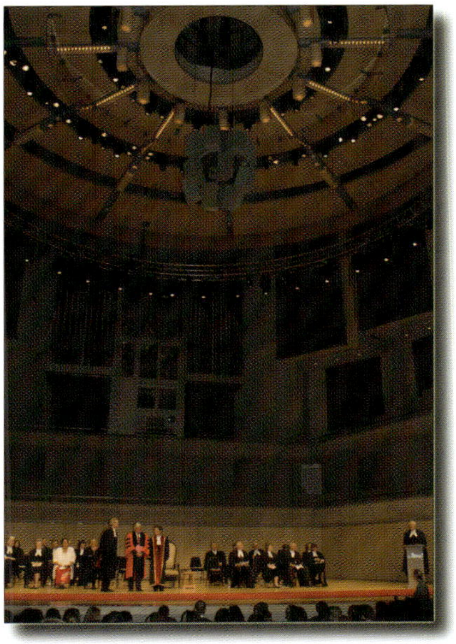

Roy Thomson Hall (Toronto, Canada)

Semi-circles and a Straight Line

The semi-circles at the top of this image bring an interesting element to the photograph. The repetition of the semi-circles also add symmetry to the image.

In contrast to the curves at the top of this photograph, the straight line at the stage anchors the image from the bottom.

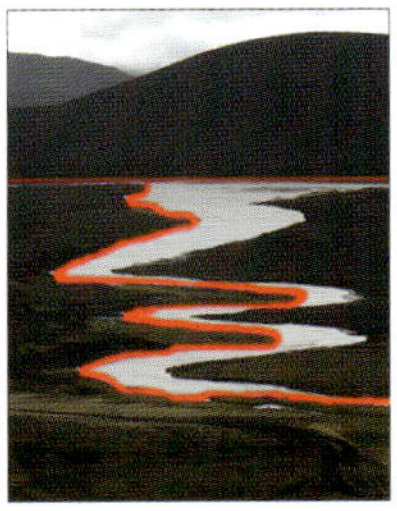

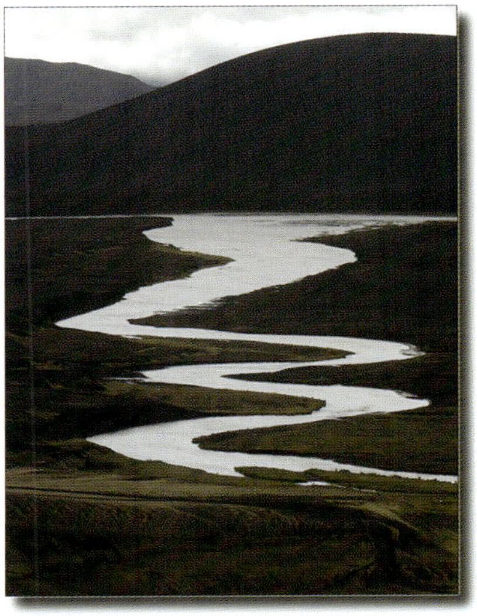

River (Iceland)

Curving River

The rock in the foreground and the mountain in the background anchor the river which winds through the middle of this image.

The bends in the river lead the viewer's vision slowly through the picture.

By using fewer colors, the photographer has made this image almost black and white. The simplicity of the color scheme keeps the viewer from being distracted. It also compliments the curved lines in this image, which are graphic and simple.

The slow moving water which flows down through the curves of the river, across the relatively flat land, bring a sense of peacefulness to this image.

U-Shaped Line

The dominant curve of the u-shaped shoreline in this image is anchored by the straight lines of the hills in the background.

Color, light and shadow play an important role in the curves of this photograph. The dark curve of the shoreline in the foreground stands out sharply from the light blue water, which in turn stands out from the lighter shoreline in the background.

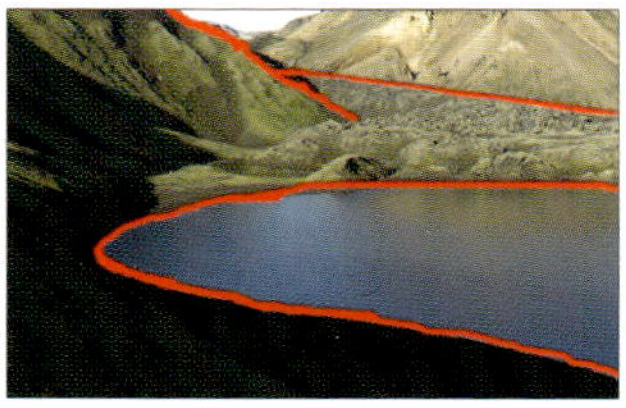

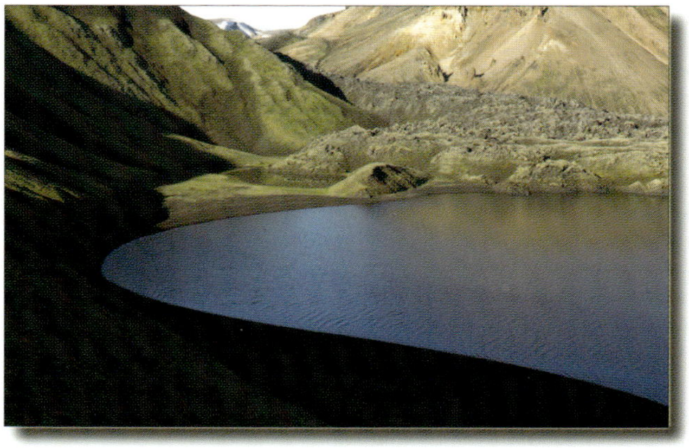

Shore Line (Iceland)

Elliptical Line

In this image, the rock protruding in the foreground breaks up the elliptical shape of the lake.

The rock brings an element of interest to the photograph. It also anchors the curve, and thus, the picture as a whole.

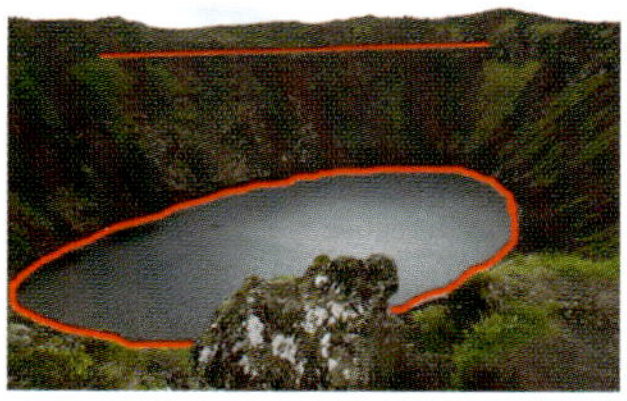

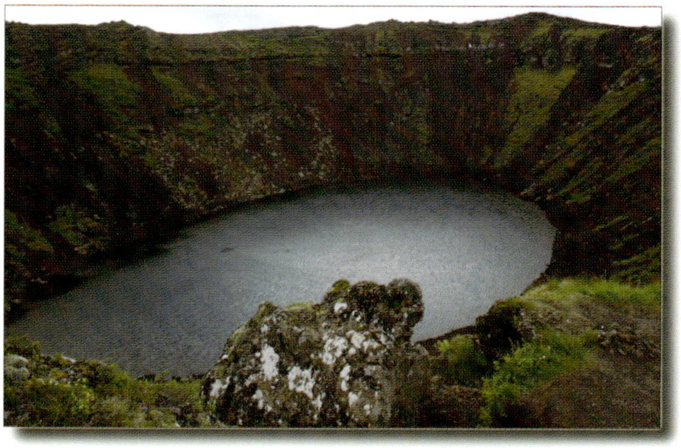

Hnausapollur (Iceland)

Anchoring Curved Lines

In this picture, a curved line of shadow leads the viewer slowly through the lupines until the eye stops at the straight horizontal line at the base of the trees. The straight line anchors the curved line of shadow. The result is a suggestion of stability and unhurried travel.

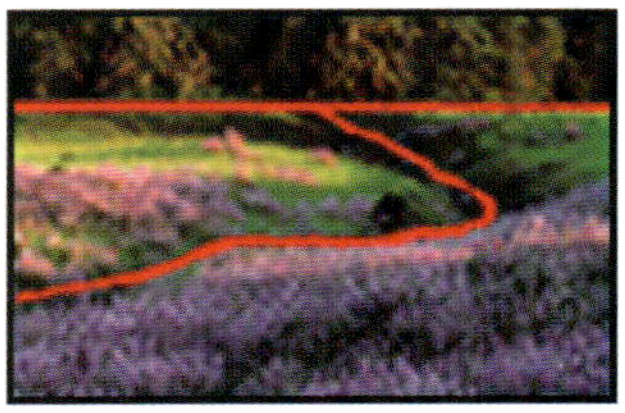

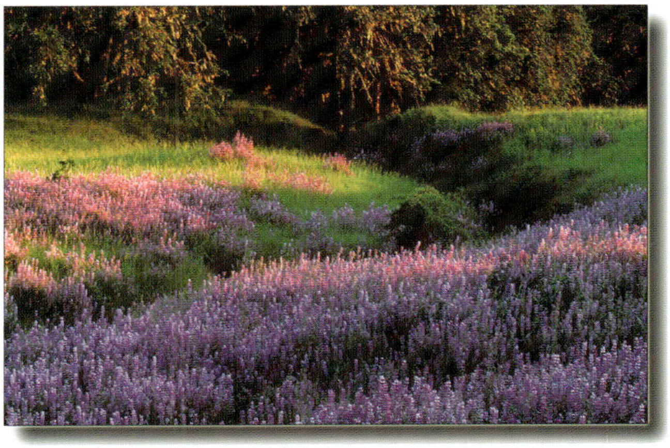

Lupines (Oregon, US)

Finding Lines

Lines are not always as obvious. In fact, the curved line in this photograph is not an object, but is created by the shadow of the canyon. It starts at the right edge of the picture, moves across the frame and then up to the horizon. In this case, the shape and intensity of the line will change with the movement of the sun, and the time of day the photograph is taken will affect its overall composition.

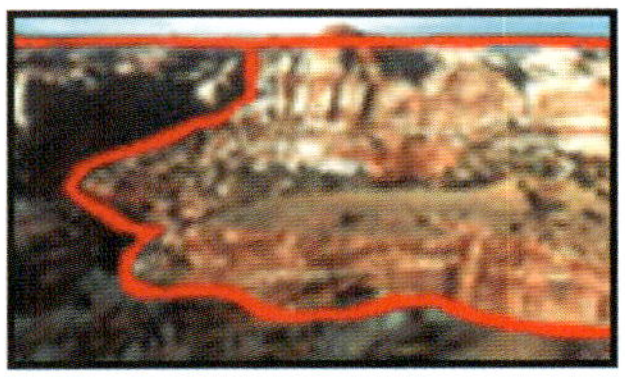

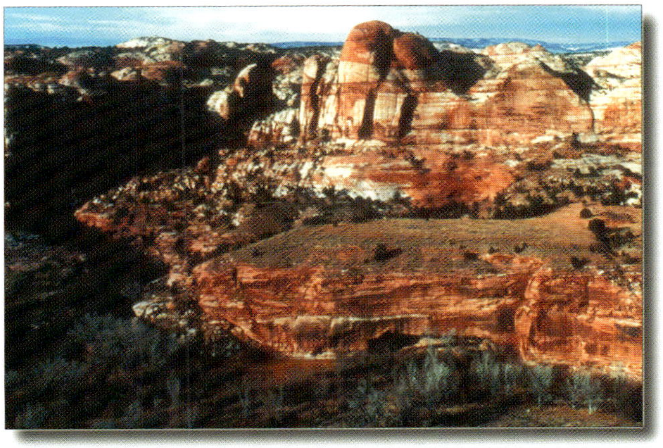

Bryce Canyon (Utah, US)

Conclusion

Great pictures can come from identifying and using curved and straight lines, including those created by light and shadow. When mixing straight and curved lines it is better to use fewer lines and to have your curved lines anchored by a straight line.

The Rule of Thirds

Using the Rule of Thirds when composing your photographs is an easy way to get better results.

Introduction

The Rule of Thirds has emerged as an important component of basic photographic composition. Awareness and use of the Rule of Thirds can help you create more dynamic pictures.

A Line through the Middle

When a viewer first looks at a picture, the eye usually moves immediately to the center of the photograph, following a natural instinct to find the main subject. Once the subject is identified, the viewer often loses interest. This is the principle reason that experienced photographers seldom place the main subject in the middle of a picture.

By centering the sun and positioning the horizon in the middle of the photograph, this picture becomes less interesting than it has the potential to be.

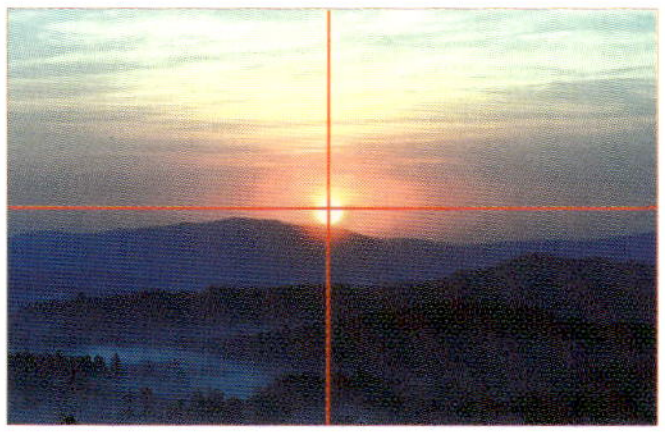

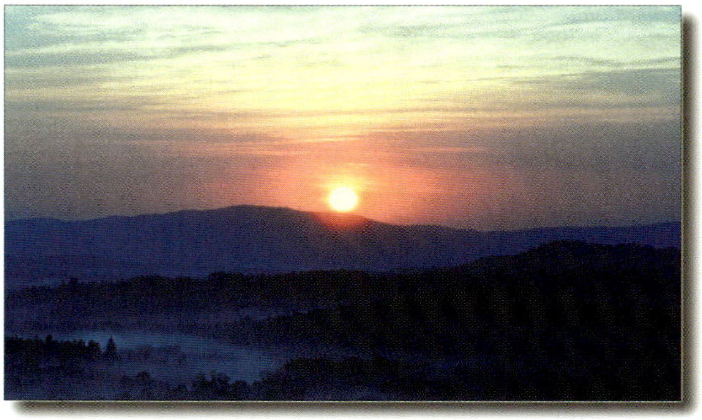

Dawn (Boulter, Canada)

Rule of Thirds - Landscapes

The Rule of Thirds divides a rectangular picture into three equal horizontal sections.

In this picture, the center of the picture is empty and the focus of the picture – the sun – is in the upper third of the photograph, offset to the right. When the eye doesn't find what it seeks in the middle of the frame it is forced to explore the picture further, and interest is maintained for a longer amount of time.

This is but one illustration of why it's best not to place the main subject in the middle of your picture.

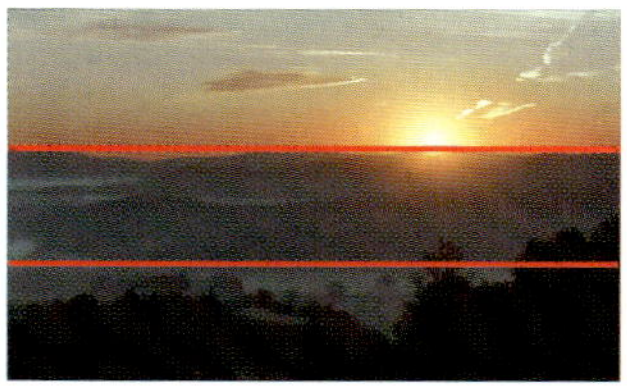

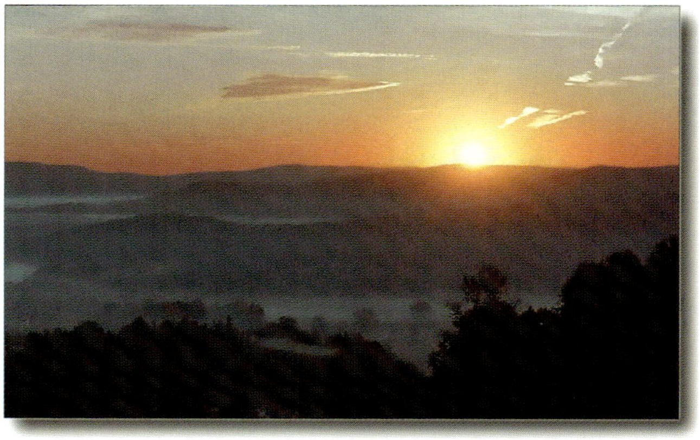

Dawn (Boulter, Canada)

Rule of Thirds - Nature

Using the Rule of Thirds you can also divide a rectangular picture into three vertical sections.

The trees in the background divide this image into three equal vertical sections with the flowers in the foreground occupying two of the three sections. Again, this photograph shows how the Rule of Thirds is an effective way of uniting different elements in a picture and creating a more attractive arrangement.

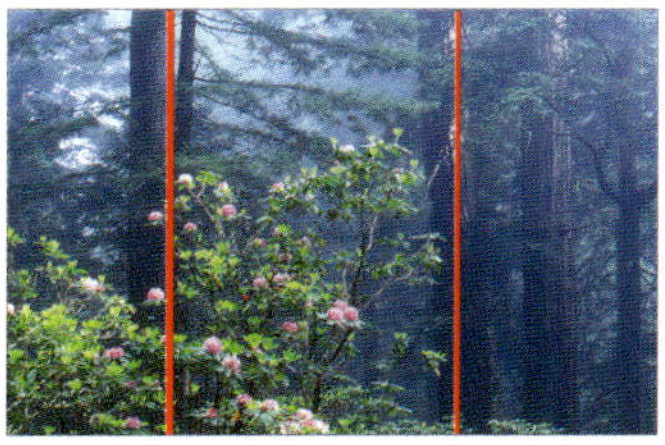

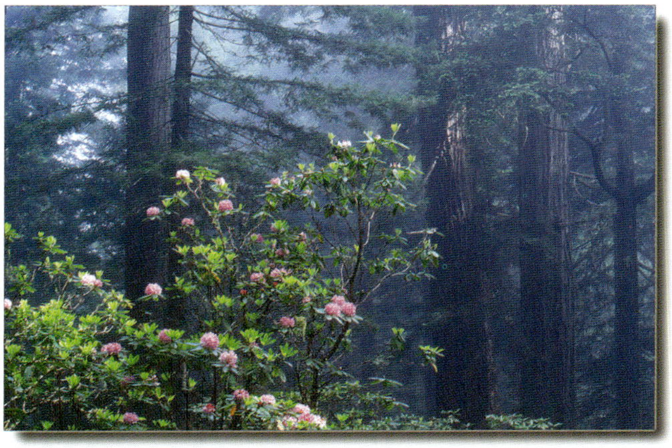

Rhododendrons (Oregon, US)

Rule of Thirds - Landscapes

In this photograph of an iceberg, the two distinctive textures and colors of the iceberg divide the picture into three horizontal sections.

When taking photographs of landscapes, you should observe the scene carefully in order to find interesting designs, lines, colors or patterns, even when they do not appear to be obvious at first glance. Such natural wonders often provide the photographer with a remarkable composition.

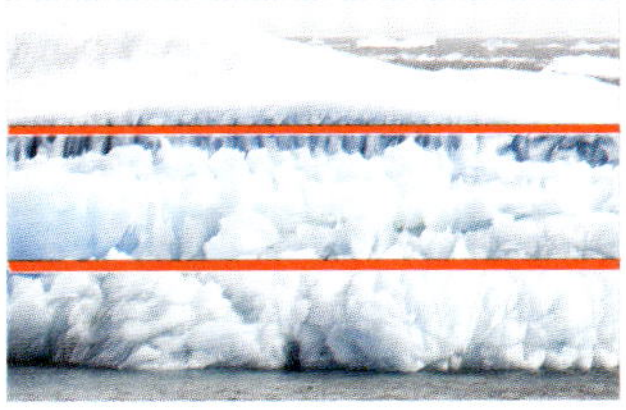

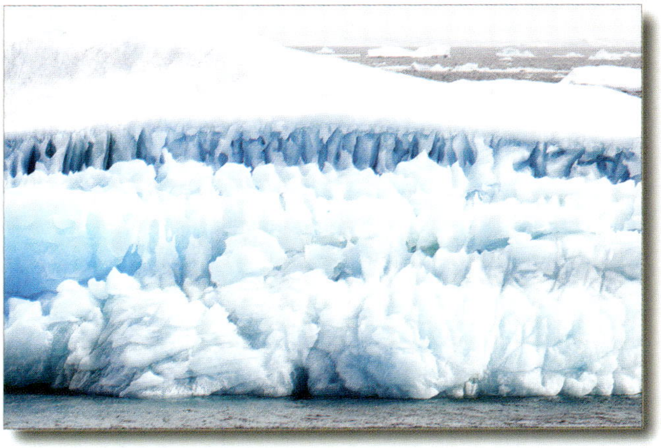

Iceberg (Antarctica)

Conclusion

Recognizing the Rule of Thirds as a basic compositional element is an important step. If you don't always place your subject in the middle of your image, you will find yourself taking more interesting pictures.

The Points of Power

Expanding on the Rule of Thirds brings us to the Points of Power – yet another element of composition that can help improve the structure of your photographs.

Introduction

Recognizing the Rule of Thirds as a basic compositional element in photography is an important step in taking better photographs. By not always placing your subject in the centre of the picture, you will take more interesting pictures. By placing your subject on one or more Points of Power, your subject can be even further accentuated.

Rule of Thirds - Points of Power

The Rule of Thirds divides a picture into three equal horizontal and vertical sections. This creates a grid with nine spaces and four intersecting points. These intersecting points are known as the Points of Power.

In this picture, the caterpillar is positioned along a grid line and at two points of intersection, creating a sense of dynamic tension. This demonstrates the positive effect of placing a key subject on one or more Points of Power.

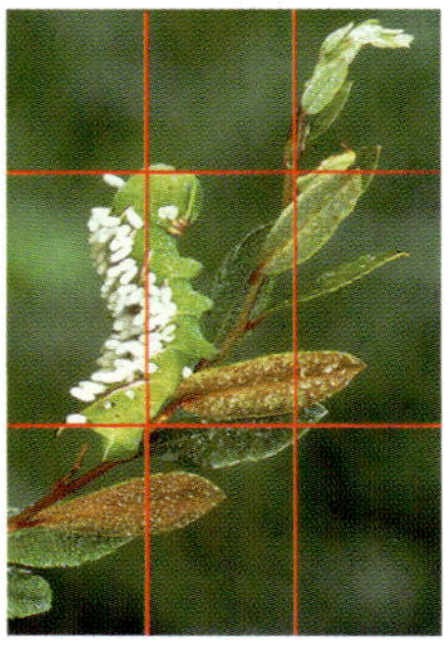

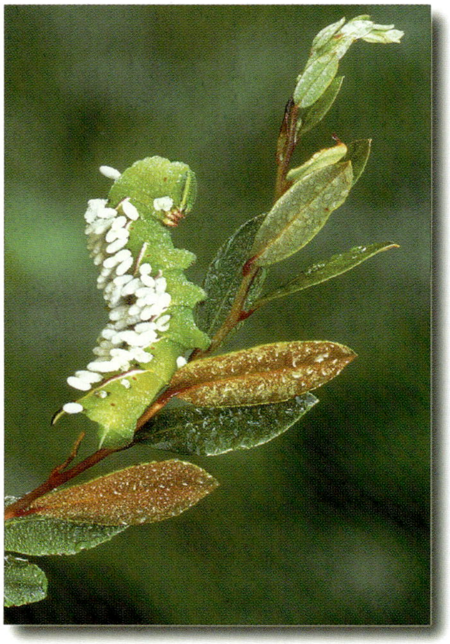

Caterpillar (Michigan, US)

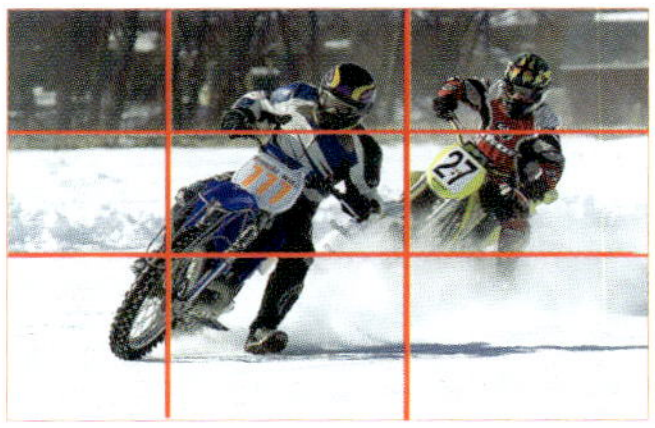

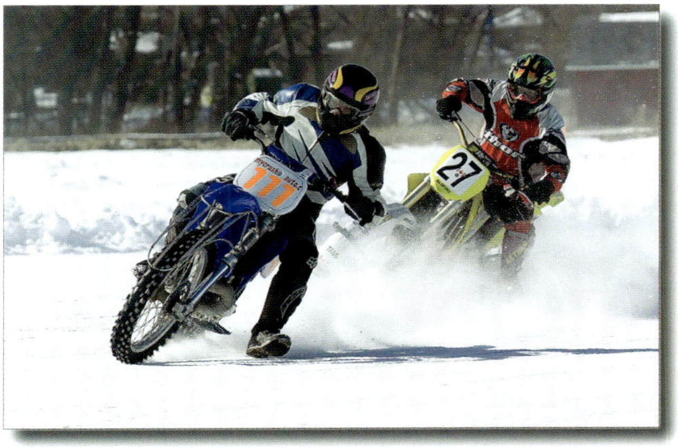

Motorcycle (Ontario, Canada)

Points of Power - Action

You can also utilize the Rule of Thirds when you take action pictures. In this example, the top third of the background consists of trees and the bottom two-thirds, of snow. The hub of the front wheel of the leading bike is at a Point of Power.

By not centering and dividing scenes in half, you move the subject away from the middle of your picture creating a more active and visually pleasing composition.

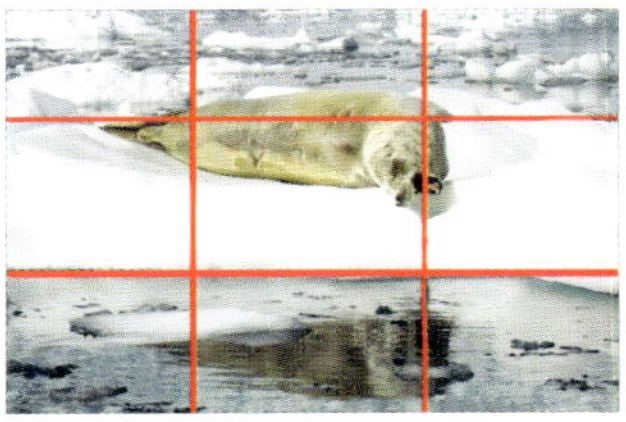

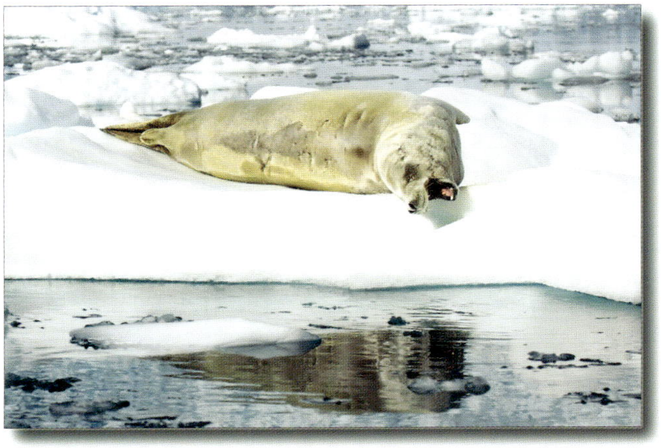

Harp Seal on Ice (Antarctica)

Points of Power - Nature

In this nature picture, the ice divides the scene into three equal parts with the seal positioned at two points of power.

The head of the seal and its reflection are placed vertically in line, following the Rule of Thirds.

The Rule of Thirds and the Points of Power are basic principles of composition that can improve your pictures.

Points of Power - Wildlife

This picture tells the story of two snow geese looking for food. The background obeys the Rule of Thirds with the mountains in the upper third of the frame and the cornfield in the lower third. The eye of the upper goose is on a Point of Power. There is enough open space in this picture for the eye to travel, and the combination of compositional principles enhances interest.

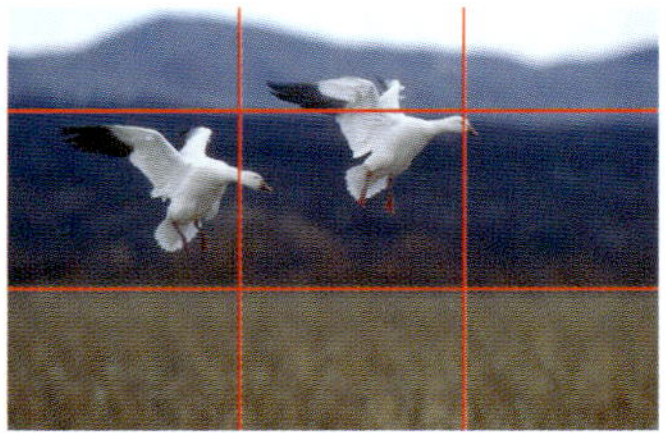

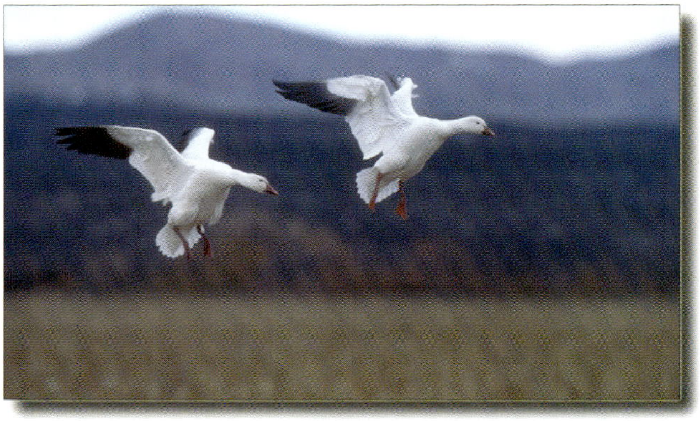

Snow Geese Searching (New Mexico, US)

Points of Power - Rodeo

In this rodeo photograph, the top third of the image consists of fence and the lower two-thirds of ground. This division obeys the Rule of Thirds.

The cowboy's face and the horse's head are located at two Points of Power. The positioning of the two main subjects strengthens the compositional aspects of this image.

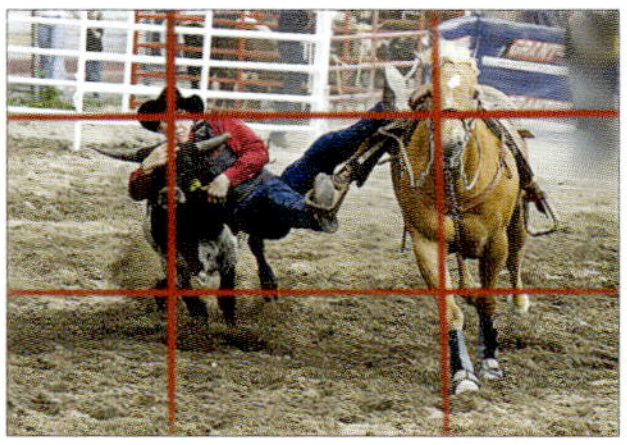

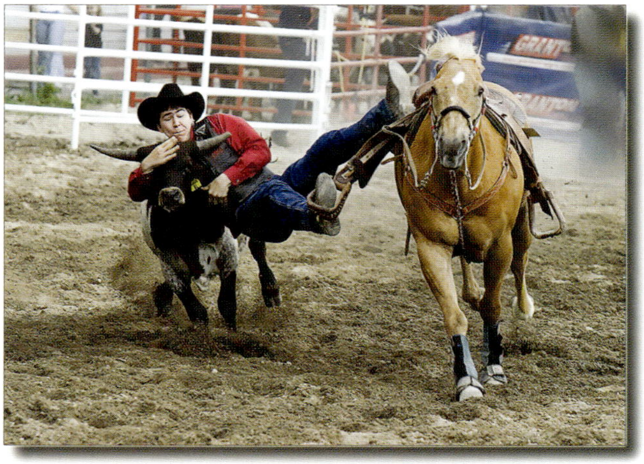

Steer Wrestling (Barrie, Canada)

Conclusion

Awareness of the Rule of Thirds and the Points of Power will enable you to position the main components of your photographs more effectively, resulting in vibrant attention-grabbing pictures.

The Golden Rule

Consider using the Golden Rule to position your most important subject.

Introduction

The Golden Rule originated in ancient Greece many centuries before the invention of the camera and was later rediscovered during the Renaissance. It states that the most important area in a picture is located at the bottom right hand corner, about one quarter up from the bottom and one quarter in from the right.

The Theory of the Golden Rule

The Theory of the Golden Rule is based on our reading patterns. We read from left to right and top to bottom. The eye's natural stopping point is at the bottom right of the page, before turning to the next one.

If we "read" a picture in the same way we read a book, then the right corner should hold our attention for the longest amount of time. "Meditation" is composed in a way that reflects this, with the main subject – the woman in prayer – positioned at the bottom right.

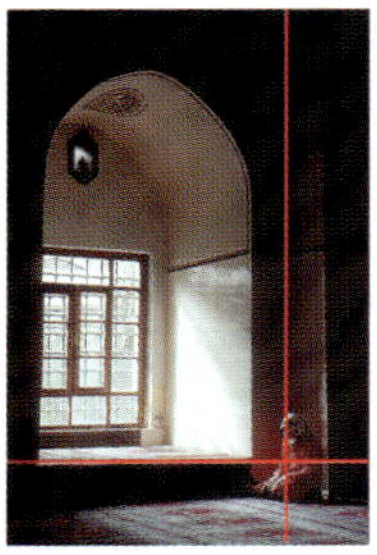

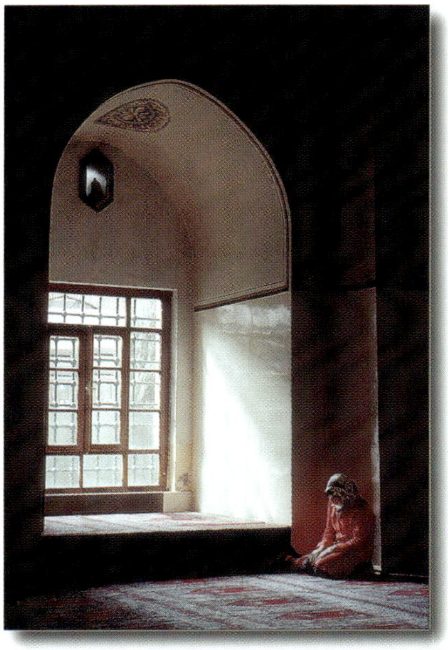

Meditation (Turkey)

In this landscape picture, a small bush is positioned in the bottom right hand corner following the theory of the "Golden Rule". The bush acts as an anchor and thus stops the eye from wandering off the image.

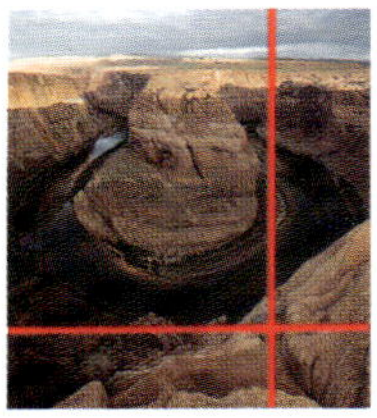

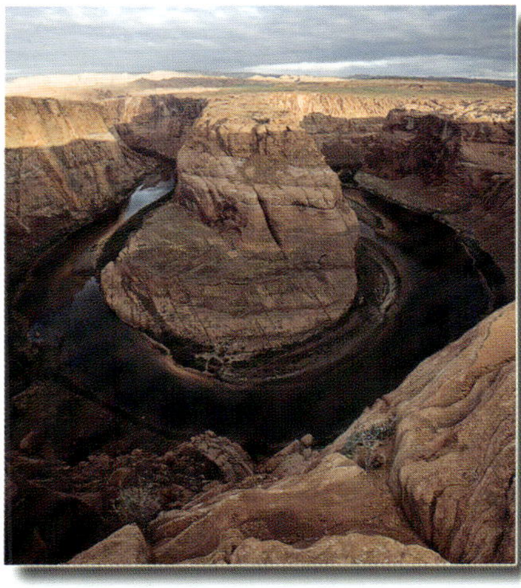

Horseshoe Bend with Bush (Arizona, US)

Positioning with the Golden Rule

This picture, "Elephant Playing" portrays a mother elephant and her baby playing in the water. To get the viewer to focus on the baby, we have used the Golden Rule and positioned the baby elephant roughly a quarter of the way up from the bottom and in from the right side.

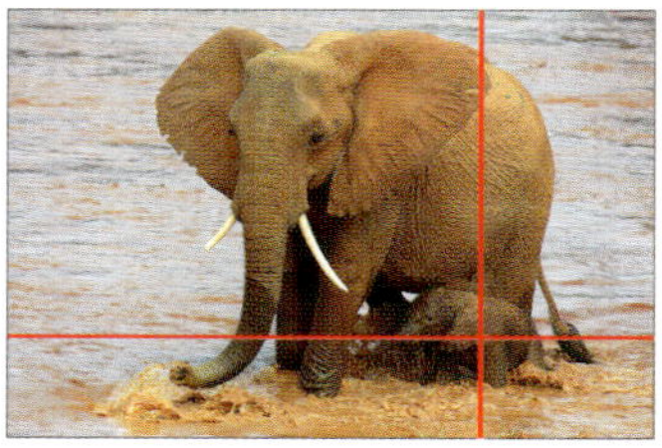

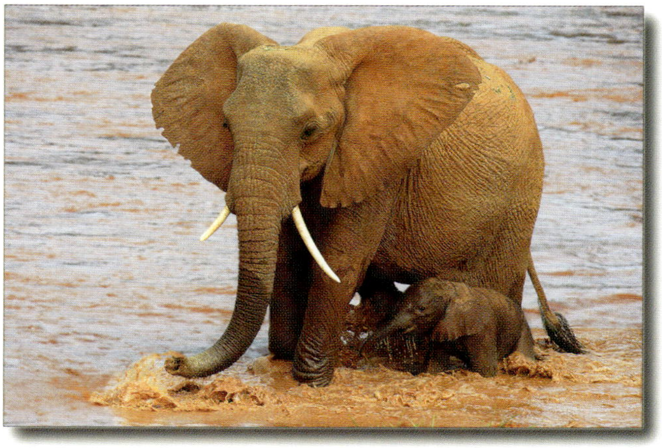

Elephant Playing (Kenya)

Cultural Differences

While the Roman alphabet is read from left to right and from top to bottom, the Japanese and Chinese read from right to left and from top to bottom. The Golden Rule works differently in those cultures. In "Charging Bull" we have positioned the cowboy's face to the bottom left of the picture instead of the bottom right to achieve maximum emphasis for those cultures.

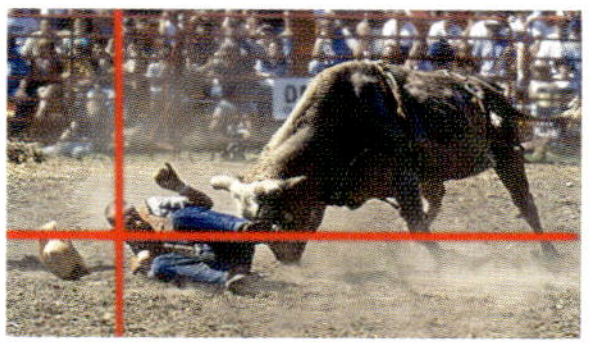

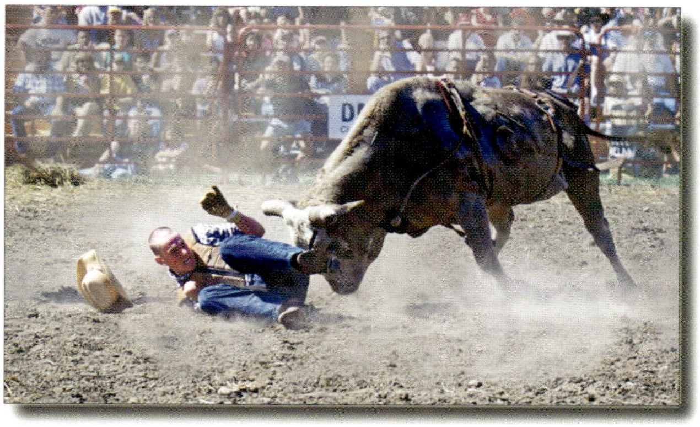

Charging Bull (Peterborough, Canada)

Conclusion

When positioning your main subject to attract the maximum amount of attention, try emulating the ancients by using the "Golden Rule".

Simple Framing

Use simple natural objects to frame your picture.

Introduction

Another element in photographic composition is framing. A careful selection of your photographic vantage point with an eye to natural framing can make a big difference in the final product.

Landscape

In landscape photography, the sky is often uninteresting. Its emptiness can draw attention away from the primary focus of the photograph. This picture of the Toronto skyline is flat, lacking three-dimensional qualities.

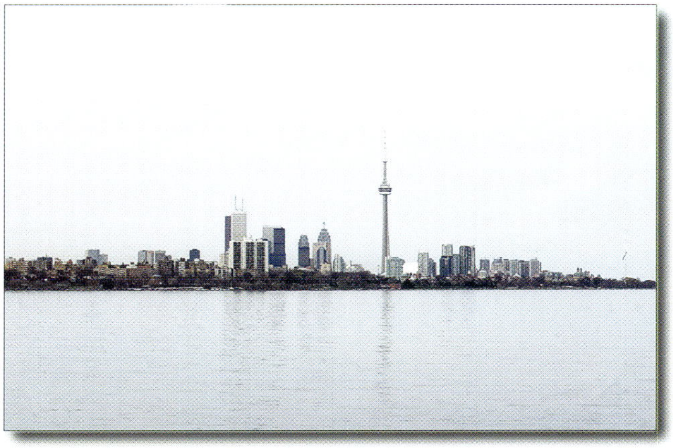

Skyline (Toronto, Canada)

Framing Around the Subject

In this version of the picture, we have used overhanging branches to frame the skyline. They take up some of the empty space in the sky and water, and bring a sense of distance and depth to the picture.

Framing Note:

It is important to choose framing objects carefully. If they are too intrusive, colorful or noteworthy, they can draw the viewer's attention away from the center of interest. However they must also be dominant enough to act as framing elements. Using too few branches would serve as a distraction instead of pulling the viewer into the photograph.

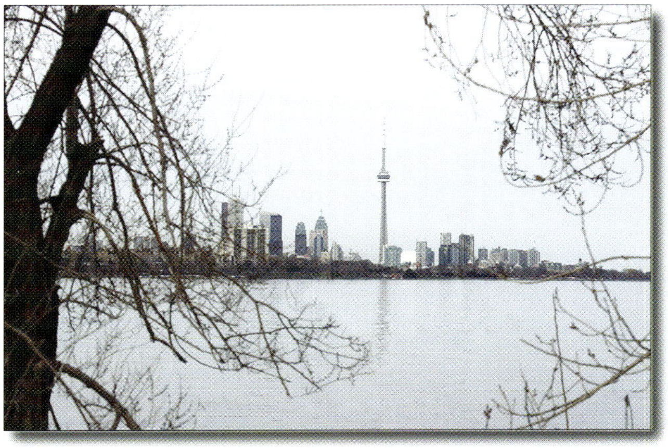

Skyline with Branches (Toronto, Canada)

Framing from the Sides

Here, we used branches on both sides of the picture to frame the waterfall. By serving as elements of interest and depth, they help put the viewer into the photographer's shoes.

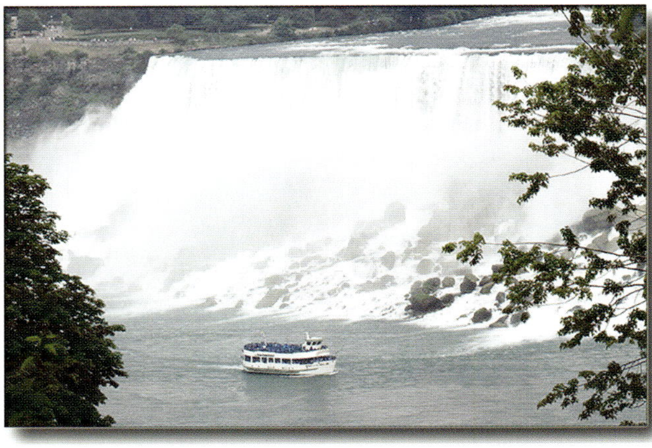

Niagara Falls (Ontario, Canada)

Framing from the Sides and Bottom

In the upper picture, we used the rock, shadow and sky to frame the "Watika" structure. In the lower picture, it is almost completely framed by the natural rock formation. This technique draws the viewer's attention from inside the framing rock to the brighter structure in the middle of the photograph.

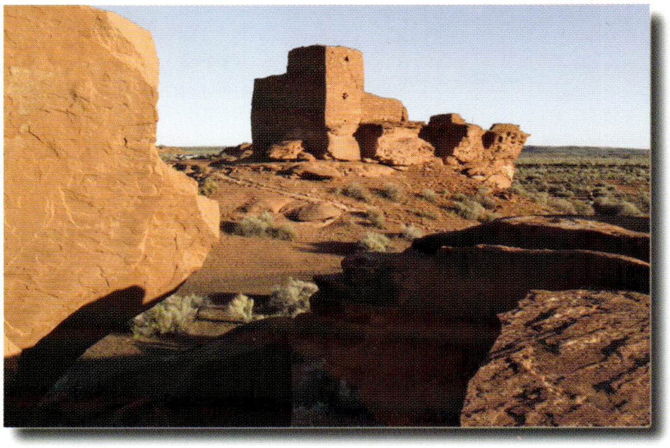

Watika (Arizona, US)

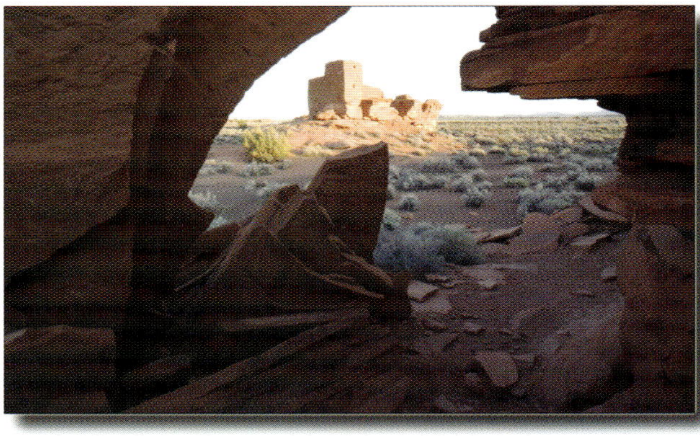

Watika (Arizona, US)

Conclusion

Effectively using peripheral objects as framing elements can help keep your viewer focused on the primary subject of your photograph.

General Framing

Subjects in the background can be framed by a simple element in the foreground.

Introduction

In photography, framing is more than just a method of display. It can also serve as an element in the photograph itself.

Basic Framing

This picture of a monk in an open stone window is an example of simple framing. By not including any other building features or background, the stone acts as a simple frame to keep the viewer's attention from wandering away from the main subject - the monk.

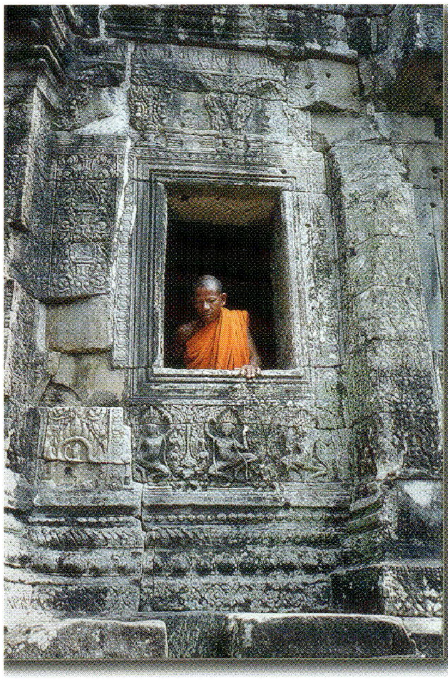

Monk at Bayon (Cambodia)

Aesthetic Value

Whenever possible, the framing object should have some aesthetic value of its own. In this picture, an inner portion of the Great Wall of China was used to frame another section of the wall in the distance. In this instance, it was necessary to crouch down in order to silhouette the tower in the distance against the sky.

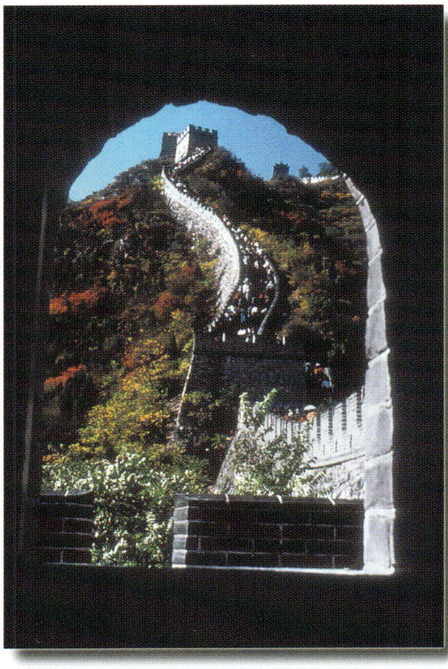

Great Wall (China)

Framing with Details

In this example of framing, we entered one chimney in order to use its opening to frame another chimney in the distance. The detail and sharpness of the rocks and sand in the foreground enhanced the three-dimensional aspects of this image.

An aperture setting of f/16 was used for this picture. The small aperture permitted both the near and distant images to appear in focus. (see "Depth of Field", page 45.)

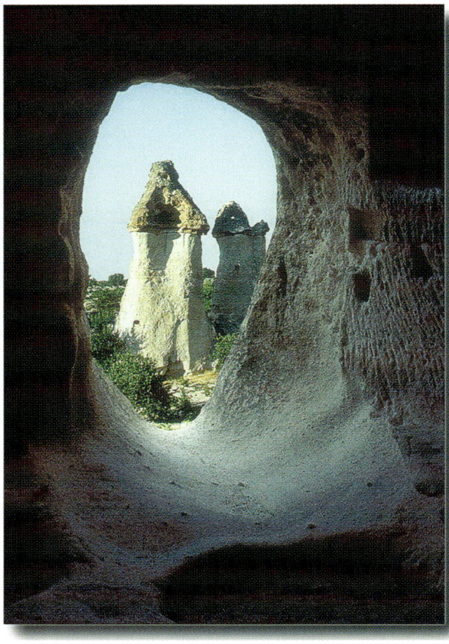

Fairy Chimney (Turkey)

Framing with Natural Formations

We framed this image of Victoria Falls, or "The Smoke that Thunders" with the surrounding rock formation. We walked around the scene and finally selected a vantage point which included rocks on the sides and the river at the bottom of the falls. The rocks act as a frame to keep the viewer's focus on the falls. The river acts as a leading line, allowing the water to flow down to the very bottom of this image.

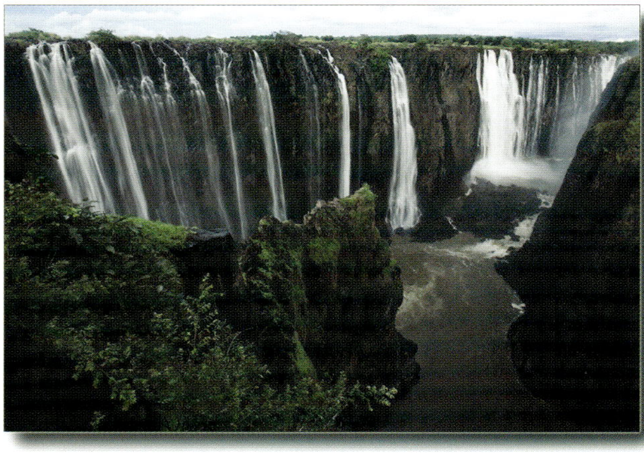

Victoria Falls (Zimbabwe)

Conclusion

Framing is an important part of photographic composition. A careful selection of framing elements will result in better pictures.

Foreground and Background Framing

Subjects in the background and foreground of a photograph can act as framing elements for each other.

Introduction

In some situations, a photographer will exercise a great deal of ingenuity to create engaging pictures by using more than one key element in framing the photograph.

Foreground Framing - Table

In this picture, the door and the table in the foreground act as a frame to the monk and the people praying inside the temple.

Foreground framing can be used to focus the viewer's attention on the main subject of a picture.

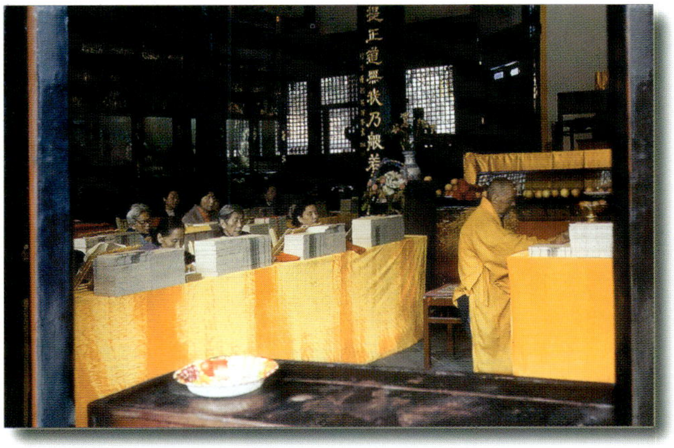

Praying (China)

Foreground Framing - Window

In this picture, the cowboy hat and lasso framed by the window in the foreground are the main subjects of the photograph.

Adding the additional framed silhouette of a cowboy in the background brought even more depth to the picture.

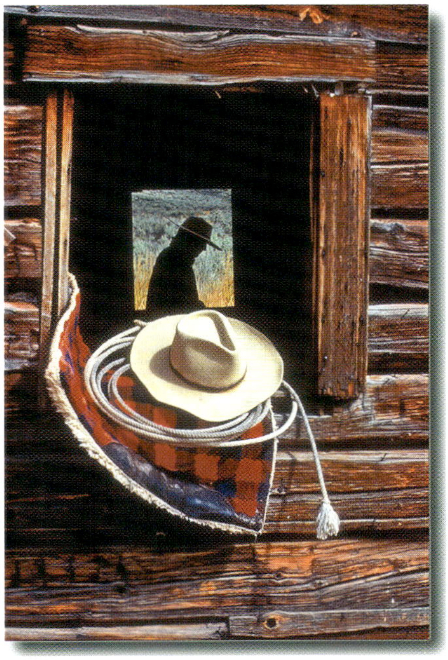

Cowboy and his Hat (Idaho, US)

Foreground and Background Framing Out of Focus

The out of focus grass in the foreground, and the out of focus trees in the background framed the jackal in the center of this picture.

Using a wide-open aperture of f/4, and a 500mm lens, allowed the photographer to achieve this effect.

The out of focus foreground and background add more drama to the sharply focused jackal and its prey.

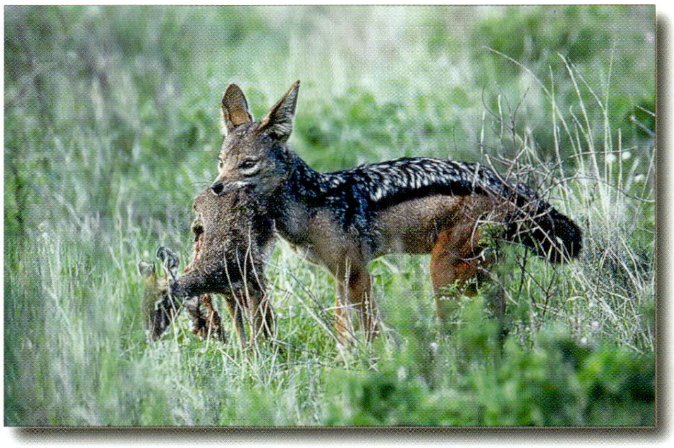

Jackal with Kill (Kenya)

Foreground and Background Framing In Focus

The two main elements in this picture are the door in the foreground and the cowboy in the background.

We kept the details and texture of the old doorframe in the foreground in focus, and then maintained a correct exposure to allow the second door in the background to be framed by shadow. The result is that the viewer is drawn from the very front of the old building to the cowboy in the background.

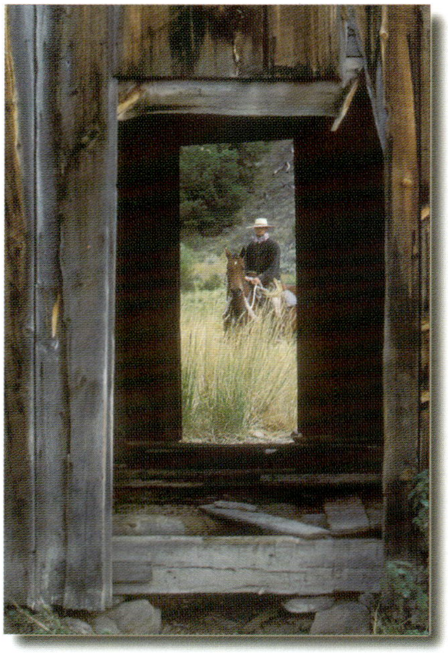

Cowboy through the Doorways (Idaho, US)

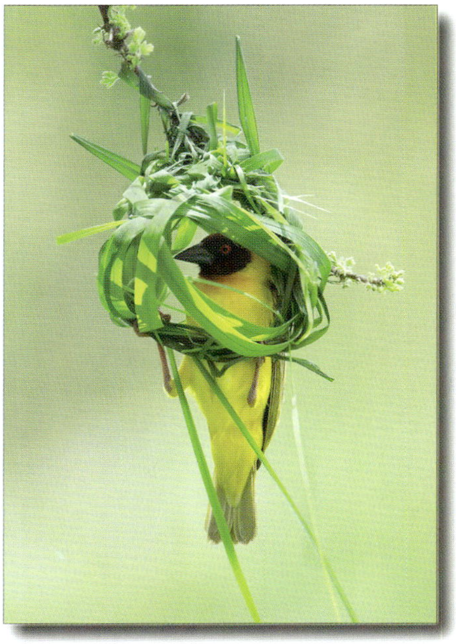

Masked Weaver (Kenya)

Foreground and Background Framing In Focus

Sometimes framing occurs naturally. This image was taken while the masked weaver was building its nest. We waited for the moment that the weaver took a rest, when his head appeared in the middle of the nest. The nest acted as natural foreground framing for the weaver in this image.

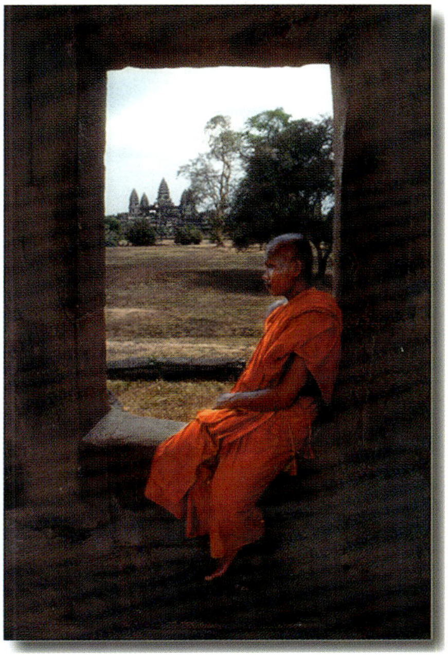

Monk at Angkor Wat (Cambodia)

Foreground and Background Framing with Fill-Flash

In this picture, the monk in the foreground is equally as important as the distant spires of Angkor Wat in the background. As there was less natural light where the monk was sitting, a fill-flash was used to add light to the monk in the foreground and to meet the ultimate goal of getting a good exposure for both subjects.

A fill flash can add some light to the dark areas in your image. In this image, we dialed minus 1 on our flash unit. You can find an explanation of setting the fill-flash in your camera manual.

Conclusion

Employing creativity when choosing shooting locations can result in appealing pictures that contain multiple elements. Be careful to use lighting to reflect the relative importance of your subjects.

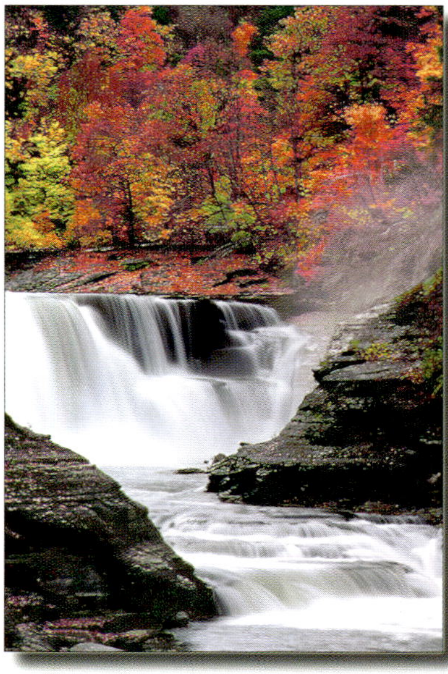

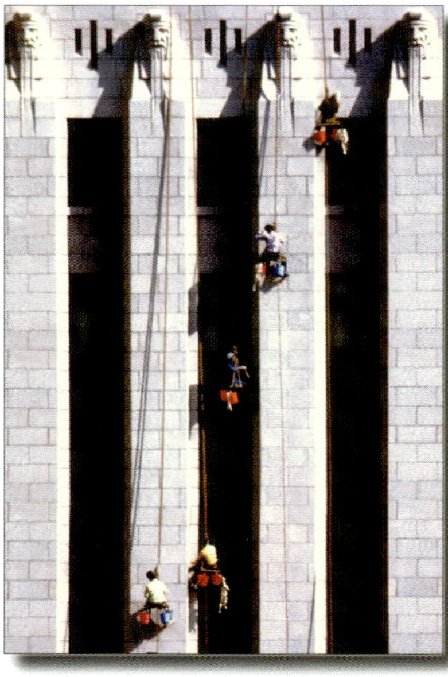

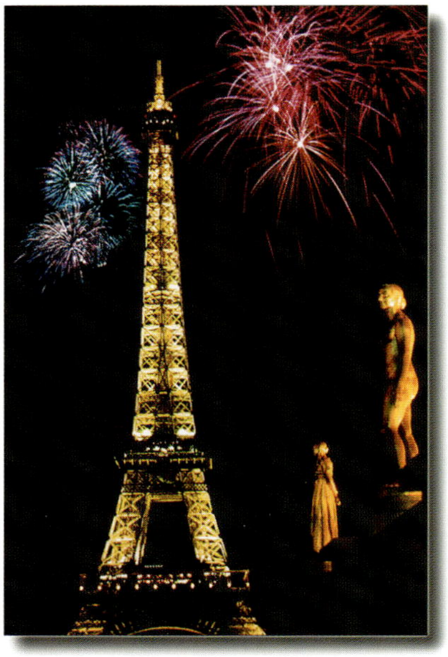

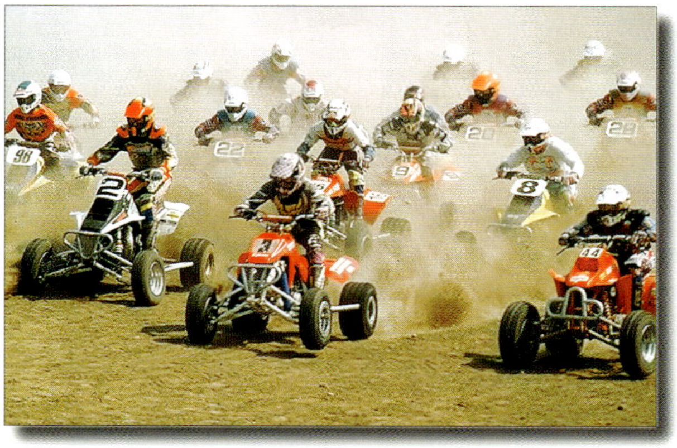

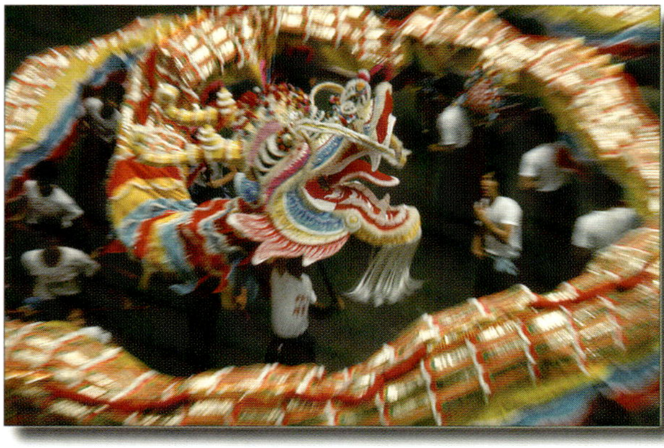

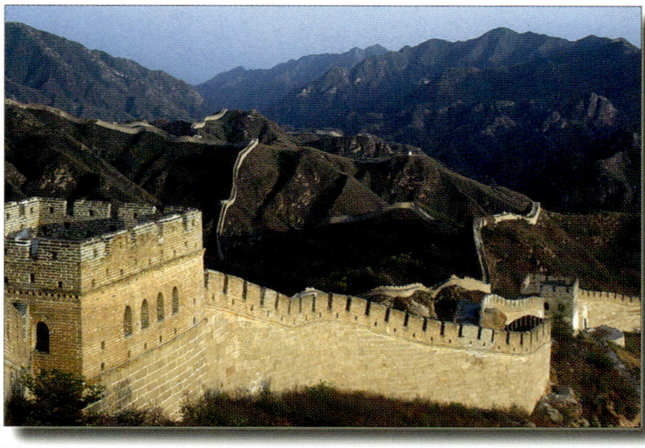

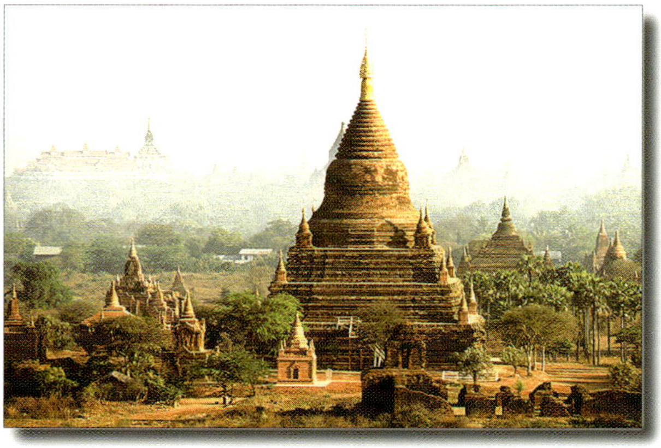

Photos by Antony Chow

Chapter 4 ON-LOCATION

On-Location

Different types of photographs have different needs: landscapes are best captured by shooting at morning and evening, at time intervals and at the precise moment. Children are often photographed well when the photographer lets them be at home in their natural environment. In this chapter, we will show you how to take advantage of a number of different photographic situations in order to take better pictures.

Landscapes - Morning and Evening

Taking pictures in the morning and evening can yield interesting results.

Introduction

Being in the right place at the right time is an important aspect of photography. Pictures taken in the middle of the day are quite different from those taken in the early morning or late evening. Below are some examples that illustrate how images taken at different times of the day can vary dramatically.

Midday

As a general rule, most photographers consider the middle of the day the worst time to capture landscapes. At midday the sun casts very little shadow, reducing the three-dimensional elements in the picture.

Also, when the sun is high the light is stronger. This tends to diminish the colors in landscapes, leaving one with a flat effect. This is called "top lighting".

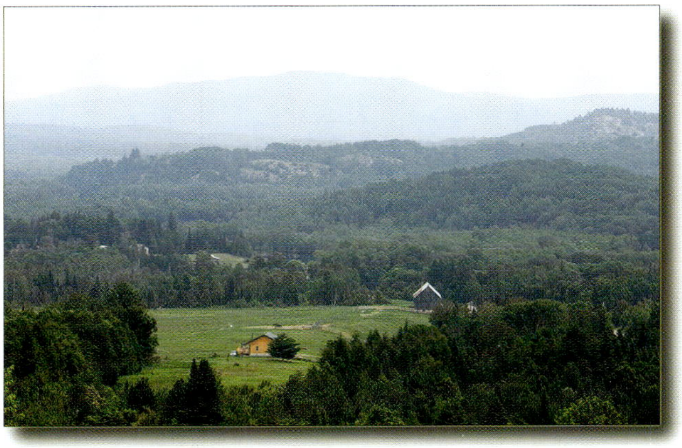

Midday (Boulter, Canada)

Sunrise

Sunrise is considered the prime time of day to photograph landscapes. As the sun rises, multiple layers of the landscape appear through the mist. These layers can bring a strong three-dimensional quality to your photographs. In addition, when the sun is close to the horizon its light passes through a larger amount of the earth's atmosphere before it reaches the ground. As you can see in this picture, the resulting light is soft and warm.

Sunrise (Boulter, Canada)

Early Morning

Early morning is also a good time to take landscape pictures. As the sun's ray shine through the mist, layers of the mountain break through and come into focus.

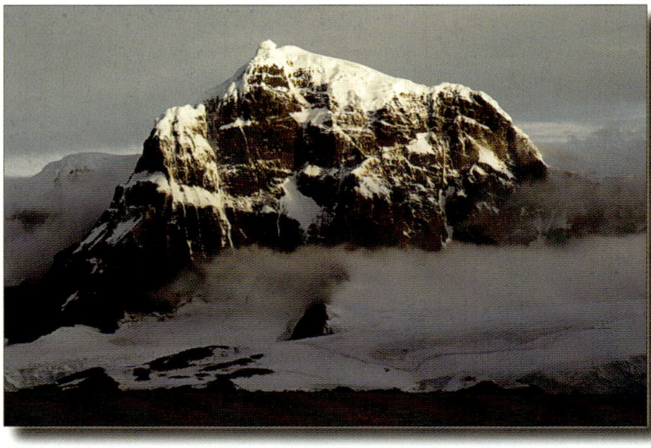

Misty Mountain (Antarctica)

Late Evening

As the sun sets with the icebergs along the horizon, it casts a number of golden orange lines across this picture.

Using a very long horizontal format enhanced the long lines cast by the sun's rays.

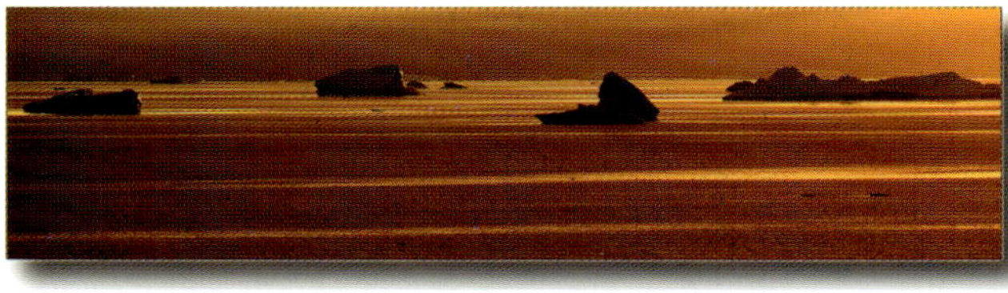

Iceberg (Antarctica)

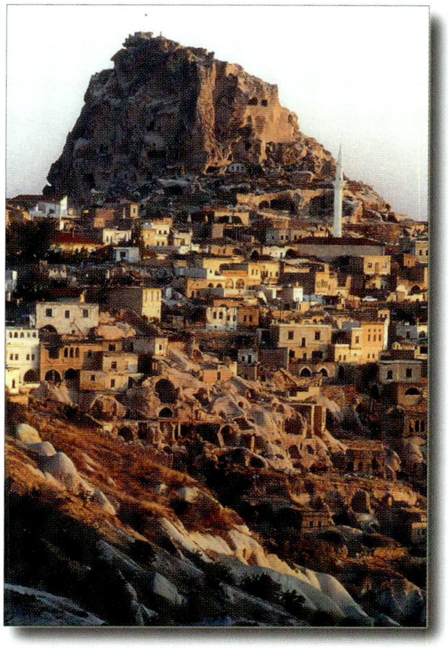

Cappadocia (Turkey)

Late Evening

Late evening is another good time of day to take pictures of landscapes. The evening sun casts different shadows than the morning sun. These distinctive shadows lend an intriguing quality to photographs such as the urban landscape shown here.

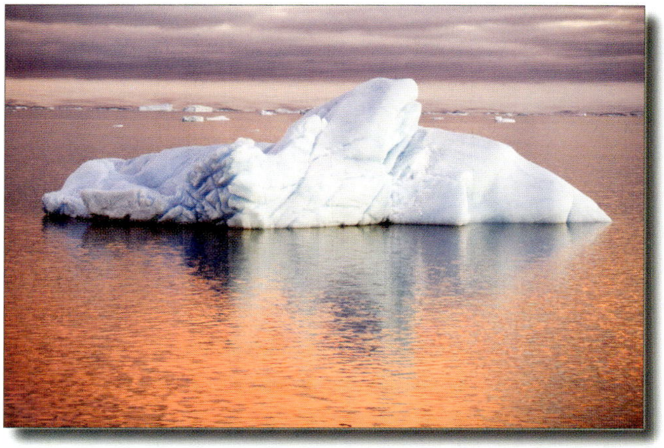

Sunset (Antarctica)

Sunset

The light at sunset is warm, adding an orange and red tint to the landscape.

Try taking advantage of the qualities of light that occur at a specific time of day in the composition of your photographs.

Conclusion

While it isn't always possible to take advantage of the natural lighting at sunrise and sunset, the benefits inherent in morning and evening photo shoots are something you should take into consideration when engaging in landscape photography.

Landscapes - Time Intervals

Taking pictures at time intervals can be a good learning tool for photographers.

Introduction

Opportunities for great pictures are often best at the beginning and the end of the day. During the hour after sunrise and the hour before sunset, the light changes very quickly. The following pictures illustrate just how dramatic those changes can be.

Twenty Minutes after Sunrise

In this picture, taken just after first light, the sun's rays reflect from one canyon wall to the other, creating a warm red glow.

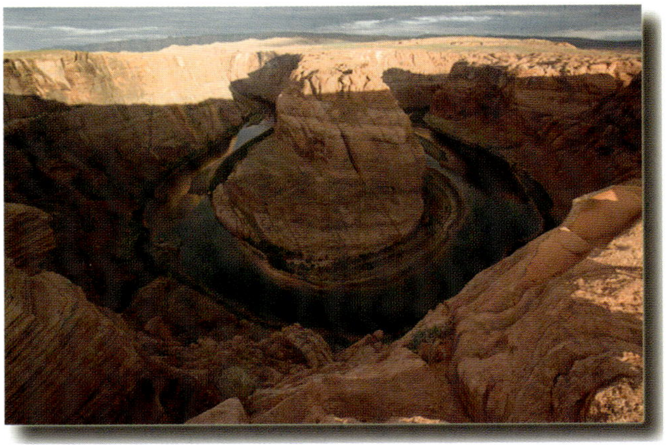

Horseshoe Bend (Arizona, US)

One Hour after Sunrise

As the sun rises higher in the sky, the intensity of the light increases, creating a sharper contrast between shadow and light and diminishing the earlier glow.

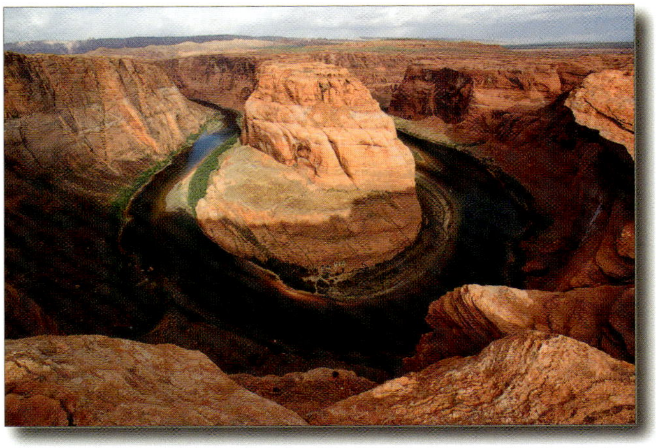

Horseshoe Bend (Arizona, US)

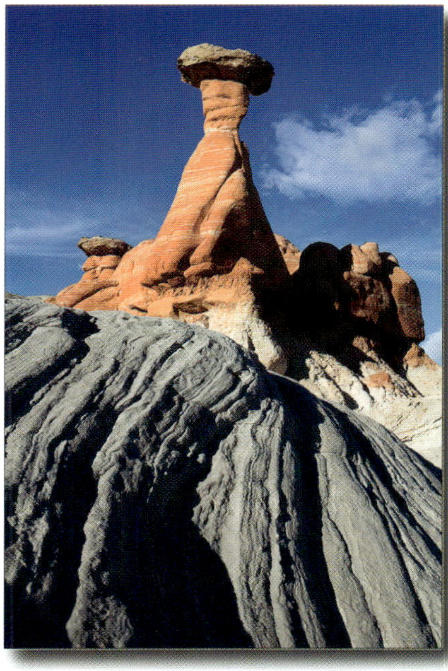

Whimsical Rock (Arizona, US)

One Hour before Sunset

As the sun moves lower in the sky, the light coming from the side of the picture creates stronger shadows in the foreground, emphasizing the texture and contours of the rock.

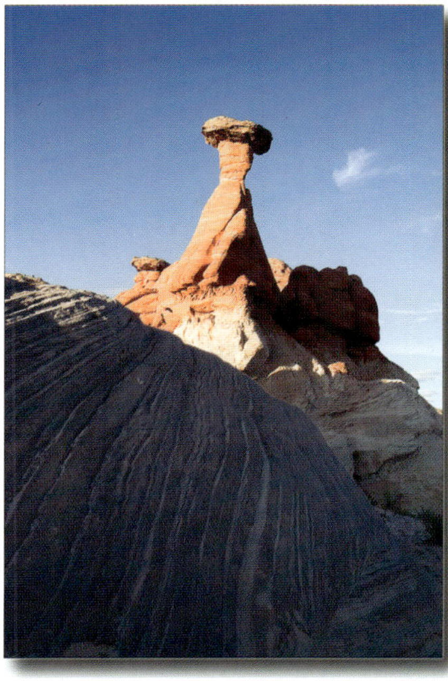

Whimsical Rock (Arizona, US)

Twenty Minutes before Sunset

Just before sunset, the angle of the sun has changed and the detail in the rock in the foreground of the photograph is no longer as arresting. This forces the viewer to focus on the "Whimsical Rock" in the background.

Forty Minutes before Sunset

An hour before sunset is usually a prime time to photograph landscapes. As the sun moves down, the light coming from its lower angle creates shadows and highlight in the foreground as well as background, emphasizing the texture and contours of the rock formation in the foreground.

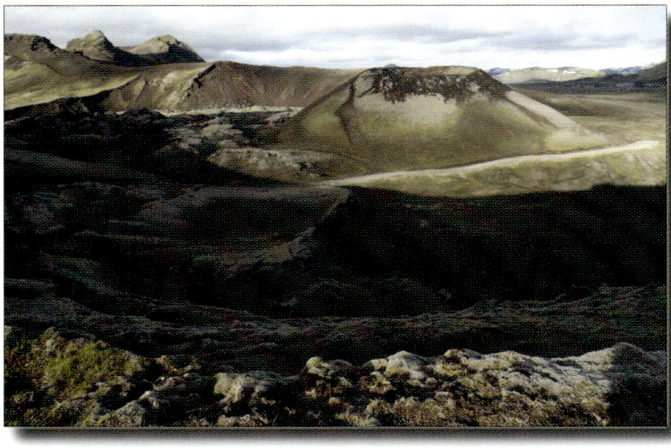

Dormant Volcano (Iceland)

Thirty Minutes before Sunset

A few minutes after the previous picture was captured, the sun is down even further. The shadowed area in the foreground has increased, creating a slightly different image.

In landscape photography, the mid-ground and background change very little. It is generally the foreground that distinguishes each individual picture.

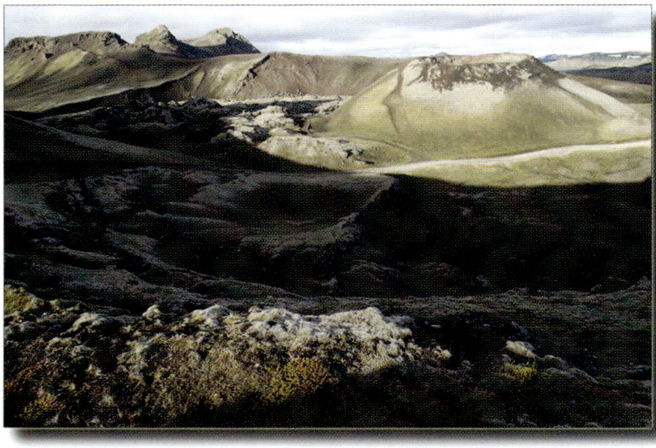

Dormant Volcano (Iceland)

Twenty Minutes before Sunset

As the sun gets even lower, the light in the foreground has decreased a great deal.

In landscape photography, foreground elements such as rocks, flowers, or grass lead the viewer into the picture. It is important to observe and select them carefully.

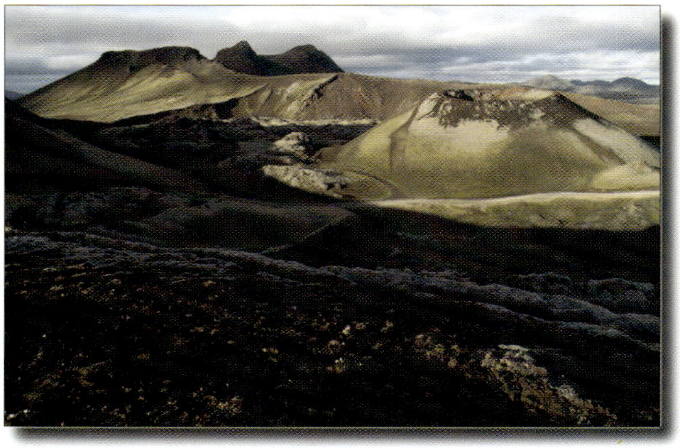

Dormant Volcano (Iceland)

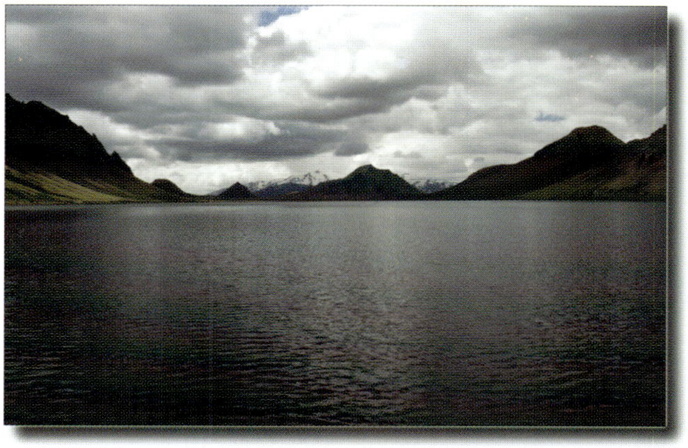

Lake (Iceland)

Windy Conditions

Here, a slight breeze is blowing over the lake, creating small ripples. Because of the ripples, the lake is unable to hold a reflection.

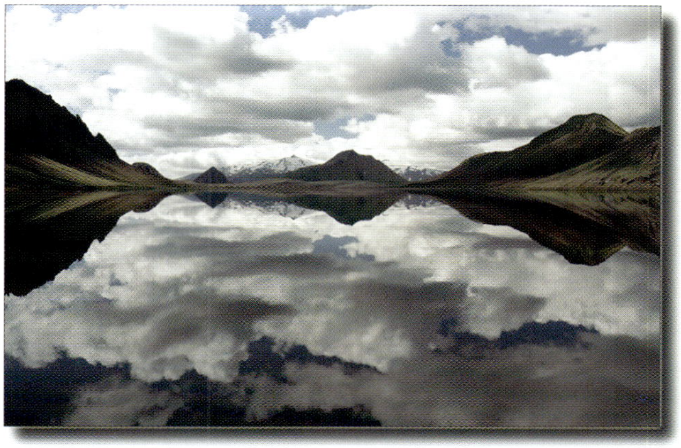

Lake Reflection (Iceland)

Reflection

A few minutes later, the wind has died down. Suddenly, the lake acts as a mirror, creating a perfect reflection of the clouds in the sky.

Conclusion

Attempting to select the very best time to take good photographs is challenging. As the light changes, the picture changes. Waiting carefully and observing the condition of light and wind and taking pictures at intervals of ten to fifteen minutes can provide you with an interesting variety of photographs of the same subject.

Landscapes - Capturing the Moment

Try to take landscape pictures at the perfect moment.

Introduction

One element of the photographer's art is to make each picture unique. In landscape photography that often means shooting at the precise moment when the natural light is at its best for each individual subject. The following pictures illustrate some examples of "capturing the moment".

Sunburst

Photography is all about light. In fact, the word "photography" means drawing with light. In this picture, the sun bursting through the trees demonstrates how natural light can be used to dramatic effect.

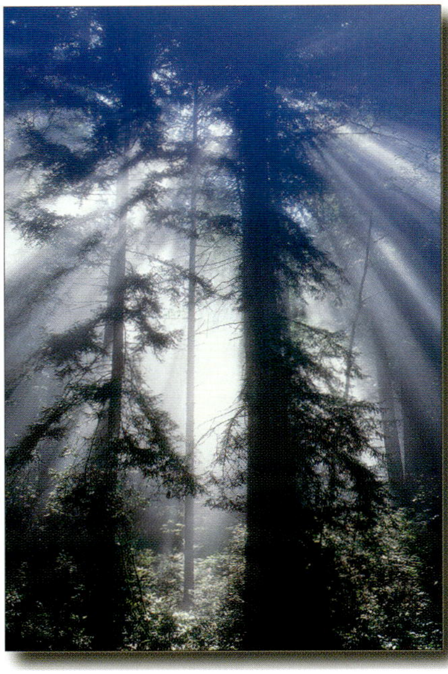

Sun's Rays (Oregon, US)

Cloud Formation

This continuously changing cloud formation provided the photographer with a unique picture taking opportunity. Cloud patterns are often the most interesting after bad weather, and this cloud picture was taken the day after a storm.

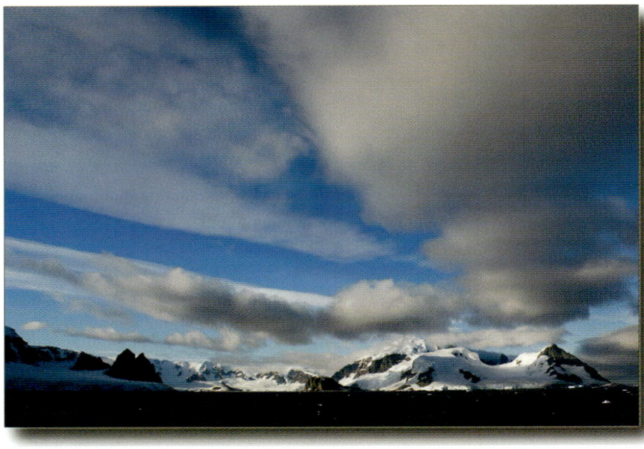

Cloud (Antarctica)

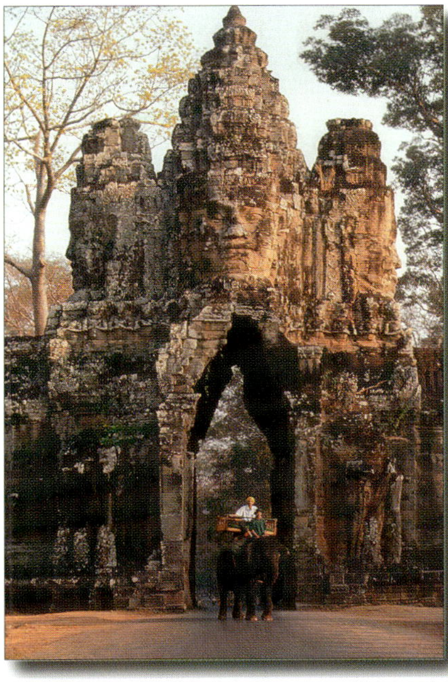

South Gate of Angkor Wat (Cambodia)

Morning Light

The gentle morning sun casts a softer shadow. The resulting low contrast allows the subtle tones and rich hues of the stone to come through beautifully in this picture. Catching the elephant walking through the gate added an element of depth and interest to the photograph.

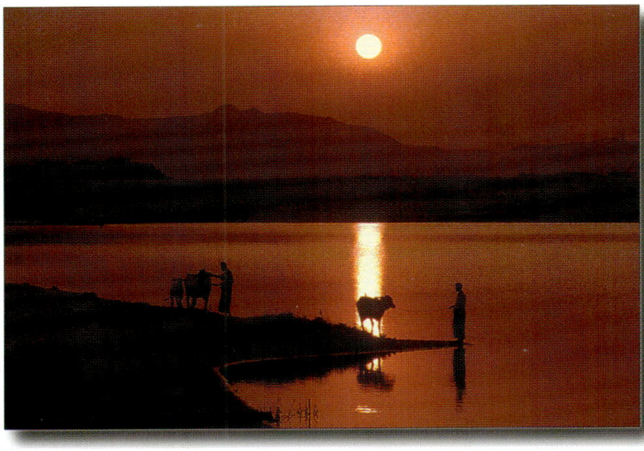

Sunset (Burma)

Sunset

Shooting toward the setting sun will put your subjects in silhouette. When photographing silhouettes, make sure each figure is separated as the men and cows are in this picture, taken at the exact moment the cow was in line with the sun. Try to position yourself to line up your subjects for the best effect.

Conclusion

Learning how to "capture the moment" can turn your pictorial subjects into great photographs.

People - Families

When photographing people, you should look for moments to occur naturally instead of using studied poses.

Introduction

Families are a favorite and frequently photographed subject. Ultimately, these are the pictures we cherish the most. When photographing families, one should look for natural expressions and use different photographic techniques to capture memorable moments.

Getting Closer

A term often used in photography is "less is more". Getting closer to your subject means less background. In fact, your whole picture can be your subject.

You have two options to get closer. The first is to move physically closer to the subject. The second is to zoom in on your subject using a lens with a longer focal length. Zooming in is often preferable because there is less distortion. The natural properties of a camera lens mean that getting in close to your subject with a focal length of less than 50 mm can distort a face, making the nose look big and the ears small. However, in this picture taken with a 135 mm focal length, there was no lens distortion.

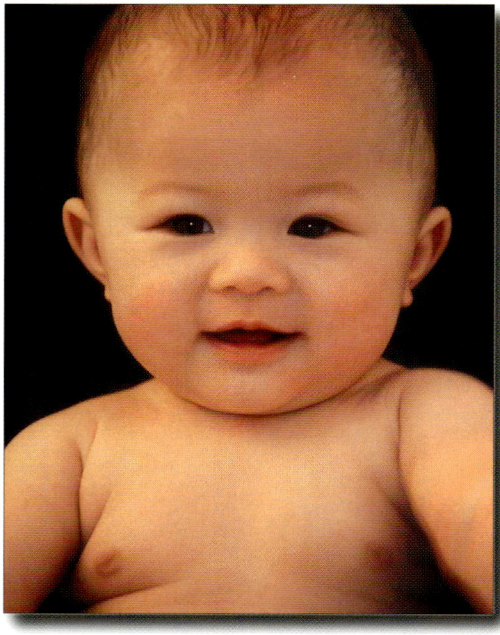

Baby Nick

Side Lighting

Side lighting can be an interesting element in the composition of a picture because of the shadows created by the subject. Here, both the lit and shadowed areas of the child are emphasized, plus the shadow itself serves as an additional three-dimensional element in the photograph. The lone shadow also emphasizes how the child is being allowed to walk freely.

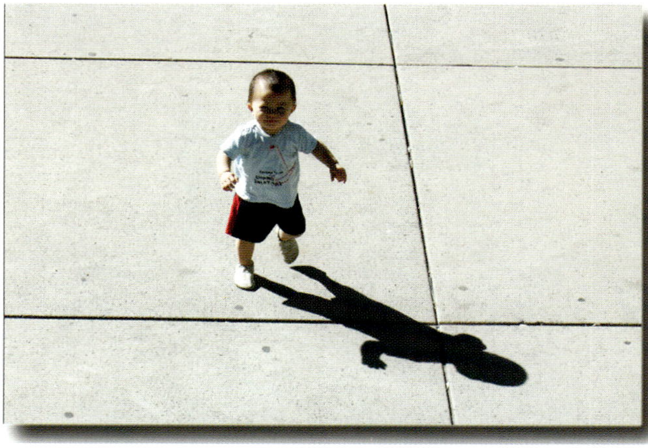

Walking in the Square

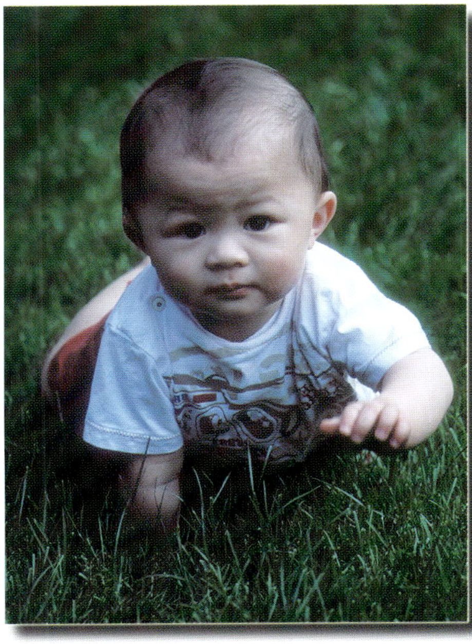

Playing in the Grass

Natural Poses

When taking pictures of children, it is often best to let your subject be at home in his or her natural environment. In this picture, the child is moving freely through the grass while the photographer is lying down to keep the camera at the child's eye level. Taking pictures this way requires more time and effort, but often yields better results.

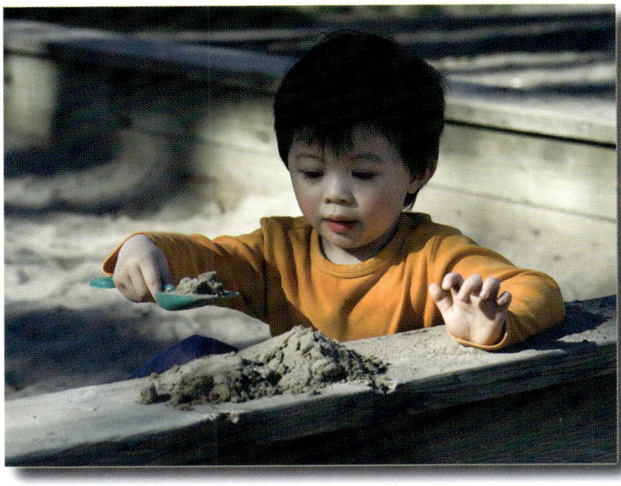

Playing in the Sandbox

Various Photo Techniques

In this image, we used a number of photographic techniques such as: getting closer to the subject, side lighting, natural poses and framing to capture the child playing freely in the sandbox.

Technique	Result
Getting Close	Less Background
Natural Poses	Not Static
Side Lighting	Creates Shadows
Framing (Sandbox)	Adds Focus

Action

Capturing a child in action is an excellent way to take a good picture. As the child is going down the slide, he is in motion, at ease and moving freely. This is preferable to a static posed image.

Again photographic techniques such as side lighting and framing were used in this picture.

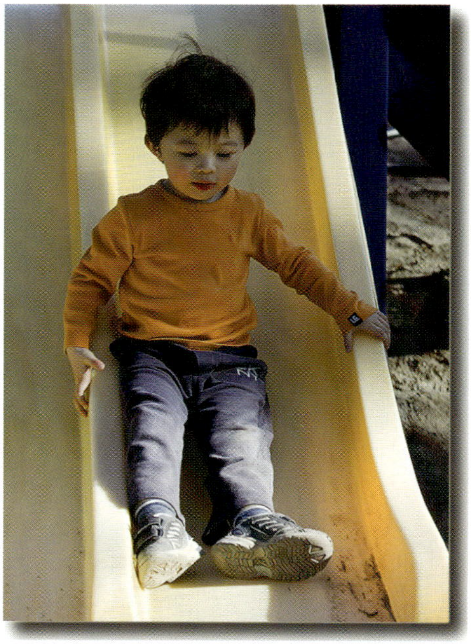

Down the Slide

Emotion

Family pictures are usually taken to capture and preserve the intimacy and emotion of a given moment. In many cases, emotions can be transformed into subtle works of art. By moving in closer and keeping the background to a bare minimum, the photographer lets the expressions of the mother and child dominate this picture, capturing an everyday moment in an artistic way.

Technique	Result
Getting Closer	Very Little Background
Natural Poses	Capture the Emotion

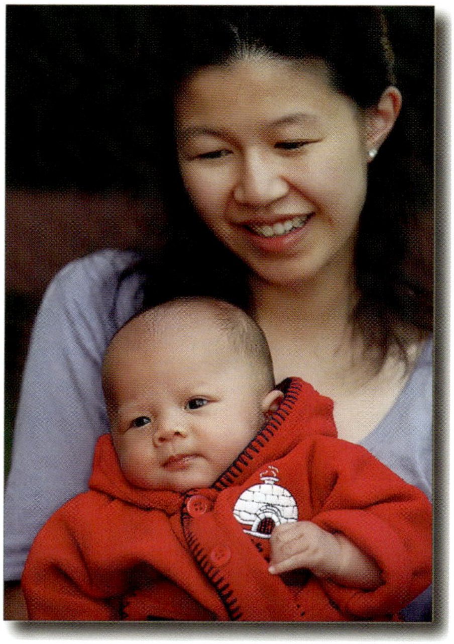

Mother and Baby

Conclusion

Outstanding family pictures can often be best achieved through the use of close-ups, capturing the subjects as naturally as possible, and remembering that techniques such as side lighting and framing can add artistic elements to the photograph.

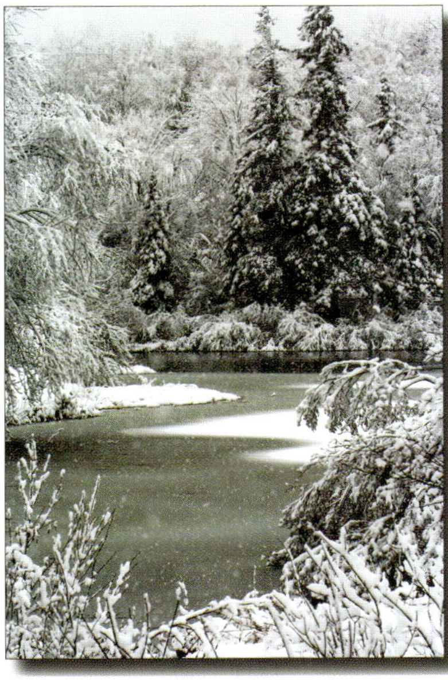

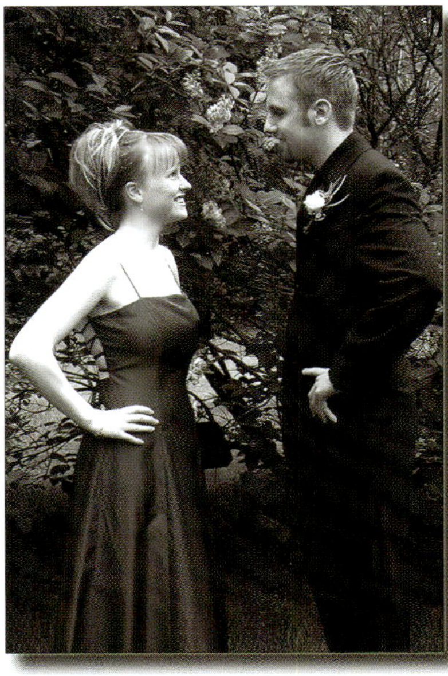

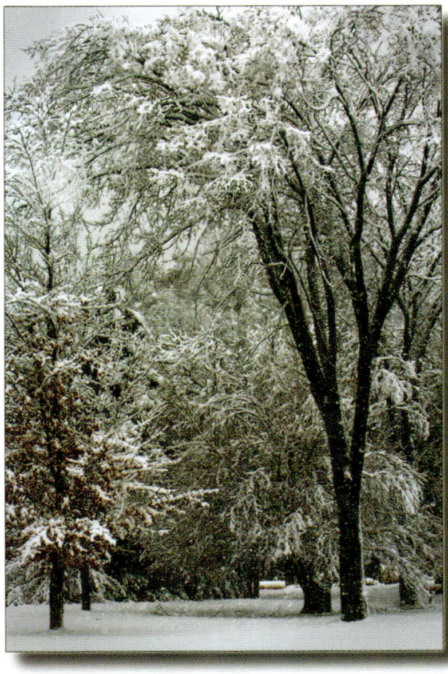

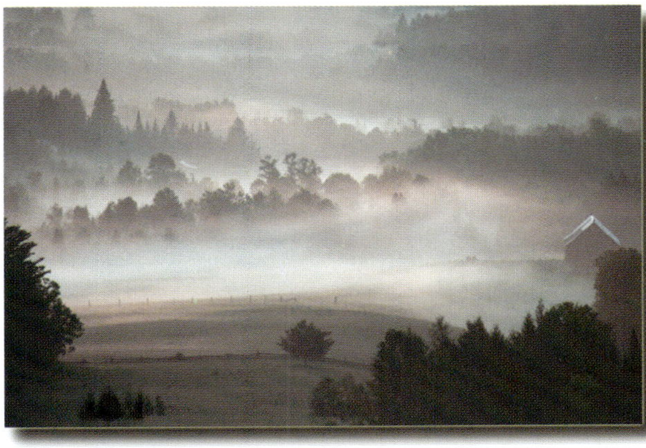

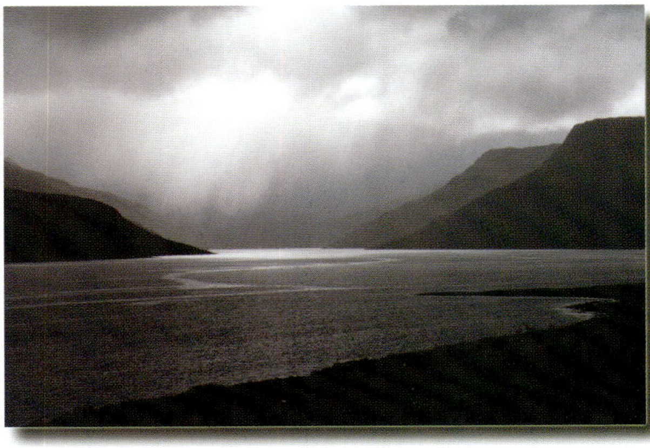

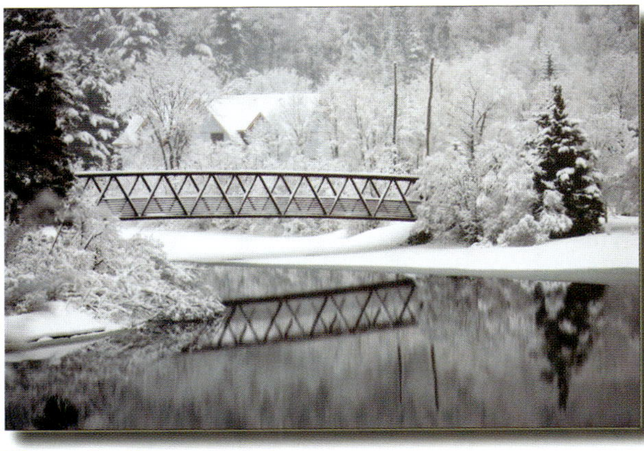

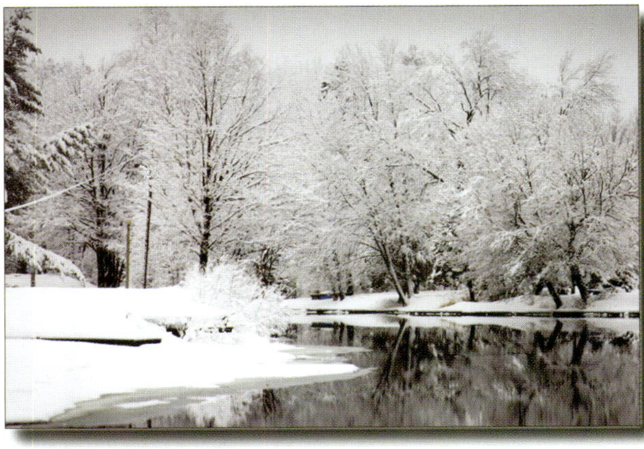

Photos by Henry Christiansen

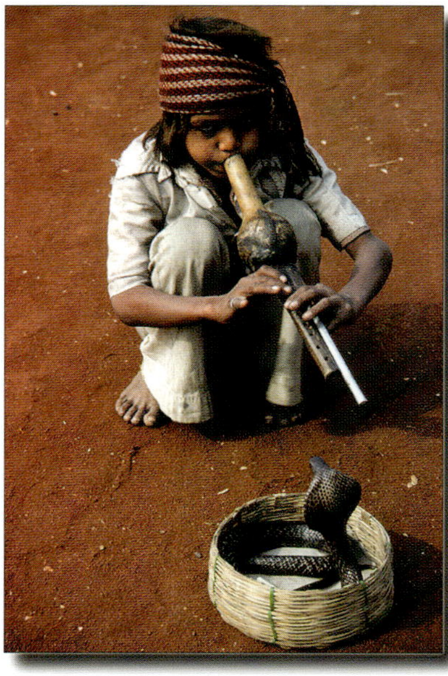

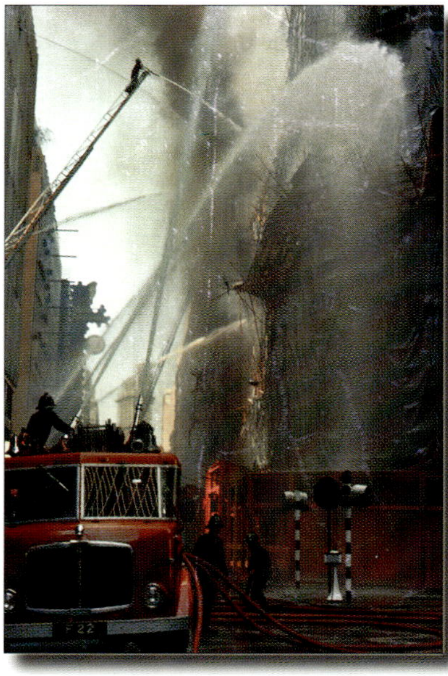

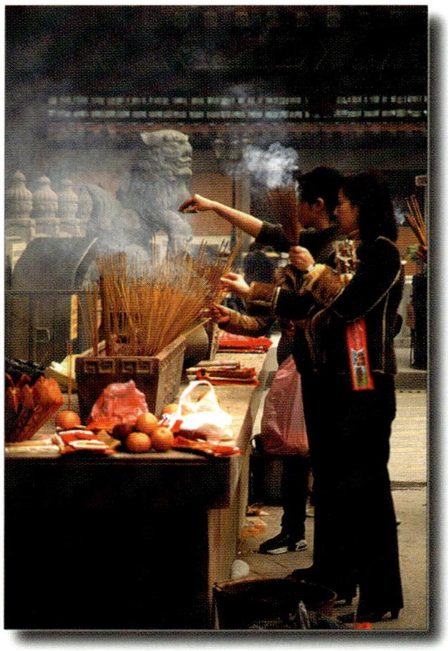

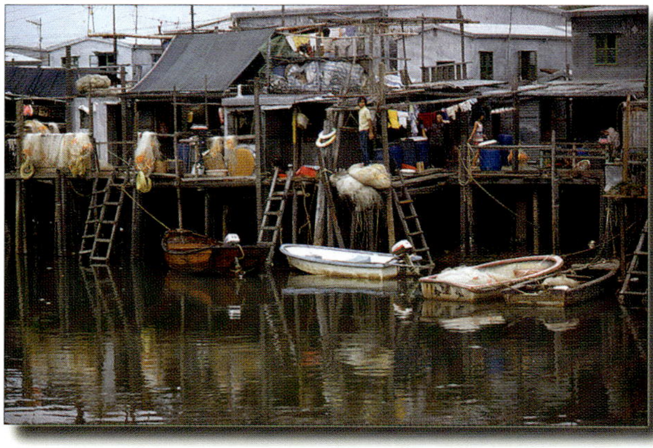

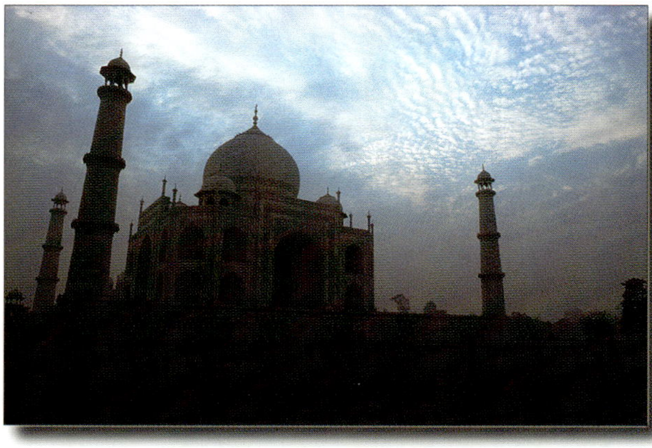

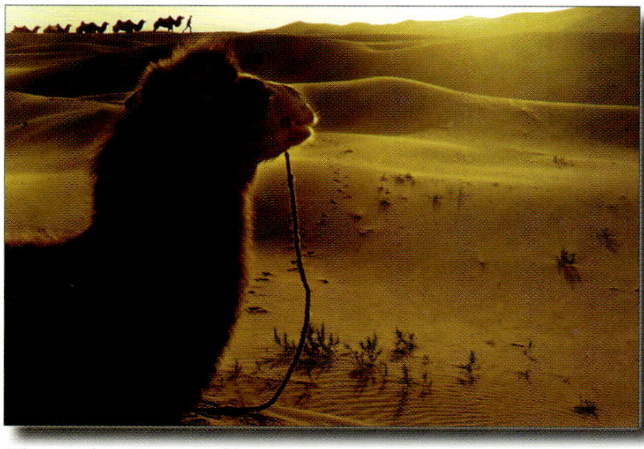

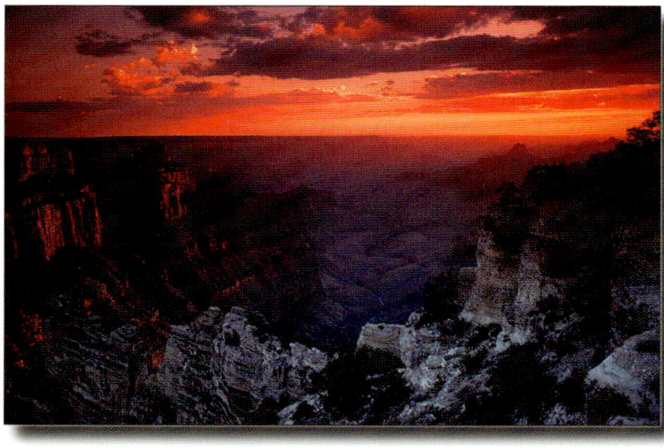

Photos by Antony Chow

Chapter 5 PHOTO EDITING SOFTWARE

Photo Editing Software

Once you have taken some digital pictures, you will need editing software. Your images are stored on the memory card in your camera. Once your memory card is full, you need to get these images copied onto your computer's hard drive so you can re-use your memory card.

Editing software will do this and much more. After images are copied onto your computer, you will be able to save, view, improve, print and email them. Editing software does not have to be complex or difficult. However, it is important that you pick appropriate software for your needs and level of experience.

We would like to make this process easy for you. Often, software is included in the purchase of a new digital camera. We suggest that you do not use this and instead follow the recommendations below.

Adobe Editing Programs

We recommend the Adobe line of editing software because Adobe is the industry standard. They have a product suitable for every user from the complete beginner to the most advanced. As well, the knowledge you will gain from mastering the most basic product is upward compatible, allowing you to grow and learn at your own pace. Here is an overview of the Adobe Editing Programs:

Album Starter	It is appropriate for the novice with automatic corrections.
Album Full	This upgrade from the Starter version is perfect for the novice who wants some manual capability over the automatic corrections.
Elements Basic	Elements Basic program allows for automatic corrections with more manual override than the Album Full program.
Elements Advanced	Elements advanced program allows for complete and extensive manual image corrections.
Photoshop CS2	This is the software used by professionals in the editing industry.

Note: Album Starter does not have back up feature.

Note: We strongly recommend Album Full over Album starter because Album Full has back up feature.

Note: This book does not cover **Photoshop CS2**. We feel it does not suit our target audience.

Adobe Photo Editing Programs

Adobe Album Starter **Chapter 6**	Adobe Album Starter is the most basic editing program offered by Adobe. It allows the complete beginner to copy pictures into a computer, organize, view, print and email them with little difficulty. The program will also perform basic automatic corrections and image improvements. The best part of Album Starter is that the program is completely free from Adobe and can be easily upgraded. This version does not allow CD and DVD back up.
Adobe Album Full **Chapter 7**	Adobe Album Full is one step up from the most basic editing program offered by Adobe. Like the Starter version, it allows you to copy pictures into a computer, organize, view, print and email them with little difficulty. The program will also perform basic, automatic corrections and image improvements. What distinguishes Album Full from the Starter version is the ability it gives you to manually override the automatic corrections. This version allows CD and DVD back up.
Adobe Elements - Basic **Chapter 8** **Note:** Elements Basic and Elements Advanced come together in one program called Elements. You get both modes when you purchase the program.	Adobe Elements is the next step up from Adobe Album. This program can be used in two modes: Basic or Advanced. In Basic, you can copy pictures into a computer, organize, view, print and email them. In this mode, the program will also perform basic, automatic corrections and image improvements. However, Elements Basic allows more control over the manual override of automatic corrections than Album Full. This version allows CD and DVD back up.
Adobe Elements - Advanced **Chapter 9**	Adobe Elements is the next step up from Adobe Album programs. This program can be used in two modes: Basic or Advanced. Like the other programs we have discussed, Elements Advanced allows you to copy pictures into a computer, organize, view, print and email them. In its Advanced mode, Elements will also perform the powerful edits and corrections associated with full featured editing software. This version allows CD and DVD back up.
Conclusion	Once you have decided on the appropriate Adobe product for your needs, refer to the appropriate chapter that follows. In each chapter, we provide step-by-step instructions for that program. If you upgrade in the future, you can refer back to this book to help you with instructions on your new software.

Chapter 6 ADOBE ALBUM STARTER

Adobe Album Starter

Adobe Album Starter is the most basic editing program offered by Adobe. It gives the complete beginner the ability to copy pictures into a computer, organize, view, print and email them with little difficulty. The program will also perform basic automatic corrections and image improvements.

The best part of Adobe Starter is that the program is completely free from Adobe and can be easily upgraded.

This version does not allow CD or DVD backup.

Introduction

In this chapter, we will cover using Adobe Album Starter to download your images with a Card Reader. We will illustrate how you can view your images and select one or more images for automatic corrections, printing and emailing.

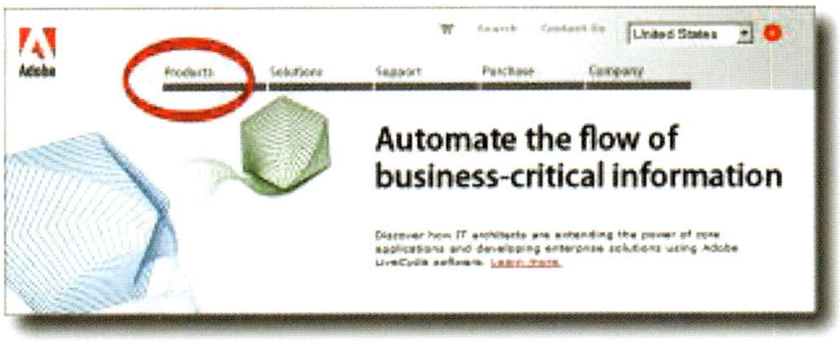

Getting The Program

To acquire this free program, you must go on the internet to: www.adobe.com. Choose **Products**, and follow the links to Album Starter. Save the program to your desktop. You will then have an **Installer** icon on your desktop.

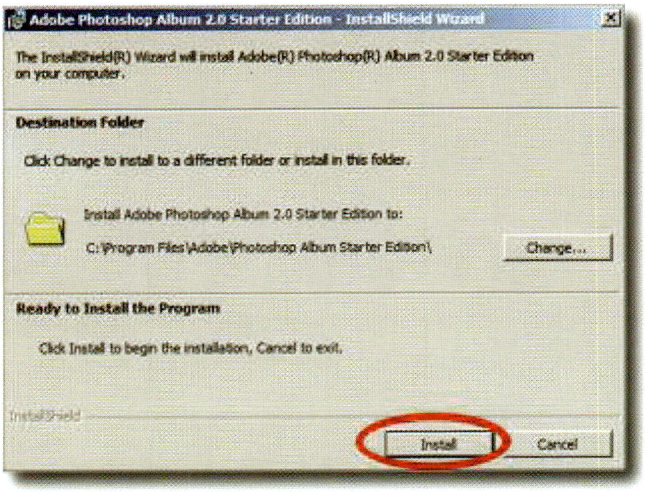

Installing The Program

Click on the **Installer** icon on your desktop. This will open a dialog box. Click on the program named: **Setup**. Follow the screen instructions to finish the installation of the actual program itself. You will have to accept their legal agreement. The **Quick Guide** will then appear on the screen. Turn it off by clicking on the lower left hand corner. Go to the Main menu and choose **Help**. Click on **Registration** and then enter the **Unlock Code** that you receive from Adobe by email.

Card Readers

Memory Card Readers are an inexpensive accessory that will streamline your digital workflow. They allow you to continue to use your camera while downloading images. The card reader you buy must match the type of memory card used by your camera.

Installing the Card Reader

After purchasing a card reader for your type of memory card, plug it into one of the unused USB ports on your computer. Windows should recognize it and state:

New hardware found

Then Windows should announce:

New hardware is installed and ready to use

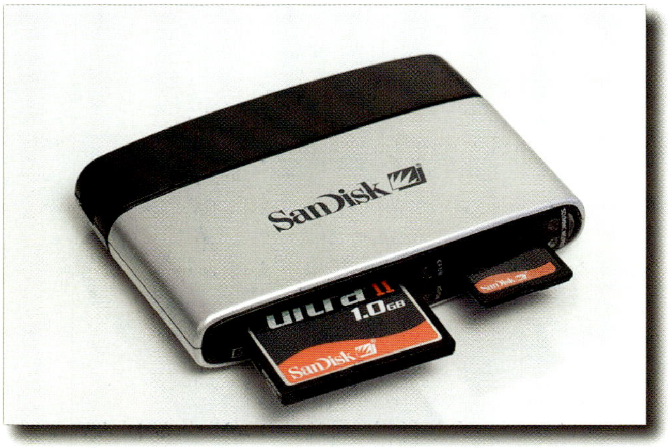

Using the Card Reader

Insert your full memory card into the card reader.

There are two ways to download photos:

1. The Adobe Downloader will pop up and offer to download your images. **<u>Or</u>**

2. From the Main menu, choose:

Get Photos

From Camera or Card Reader…

Click **OK** to load the images.

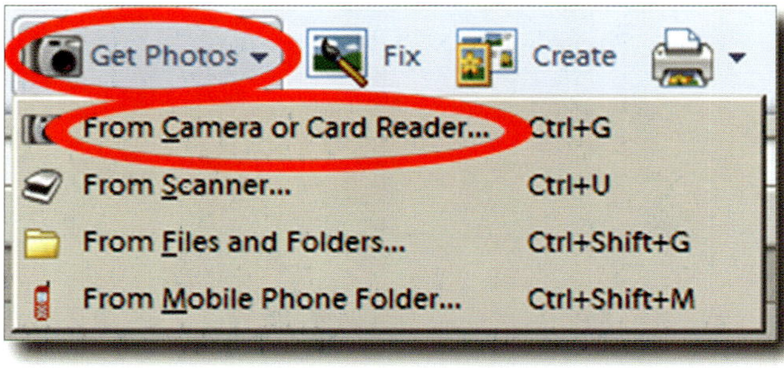

Unplugging the Card Reader

You may then remove your memory card. We recommend that you don't unplug your card reader. However, if you wish to unplug it to free up USB ports, you should click the **green arrow** on the right lower part of the Windows screen to do so.

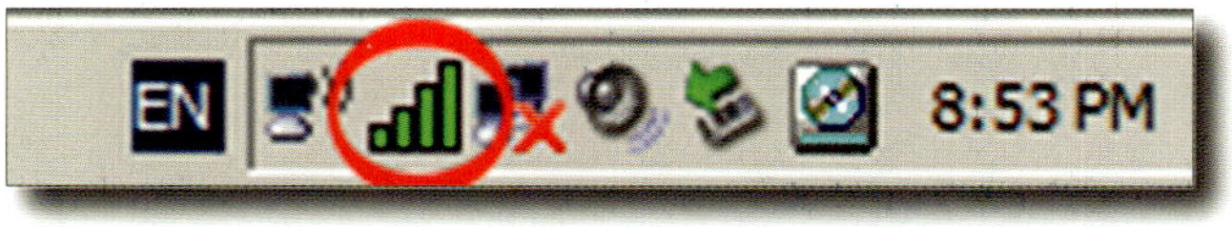

Selecting a Photo

Once your images have been downloaded from your memory card reader, the Photo Well will display them for you.

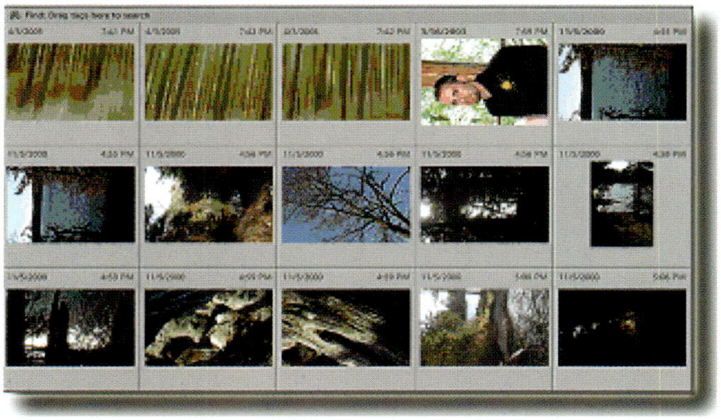

The Photo Well

All your downloaded images will be added to the **Photo Well**.

The **Photo Well** is the thumbnail representation of all your images. It appears in the center part of the screen.

If you do not see any of your images displayed, click on the **Show All** button.

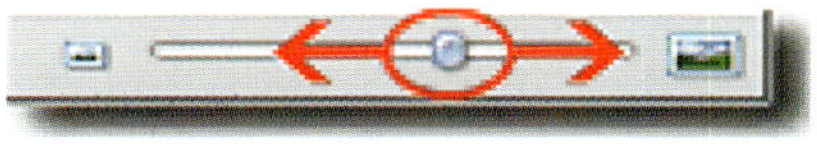

Thumbnail View Size

Use the **Thumbnail Views** slider at the bottom right corner of the screen to resize the images in the **Photo Well** as desired.

As the slider is moved to the right, the images get bigger and fewer images fit on the screen.

As the slider is moved to the left, the images get smaller and more images fit on the screen.

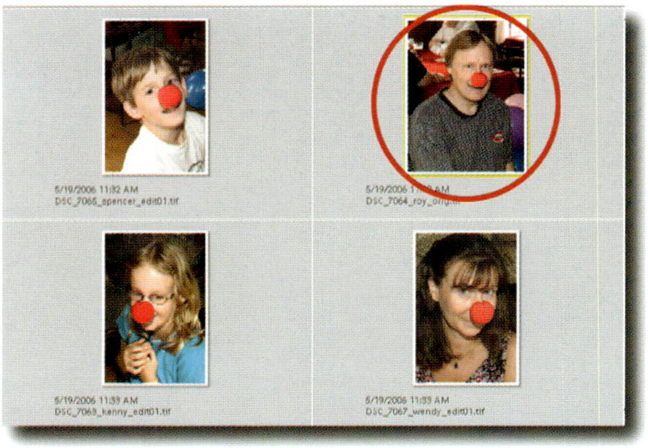

The Selected Photo

When you find the photo that you want in the **Photo Well**, click on it.

A colored box will appear around this image to indicate that you have selected it to work on.

Fixing a Photo - Getting Started

You may wish to improve some of your images. In this chapter we will deal with the initial set-up for the repair process.

The Fix Screen

Once you have selected the image you wish to work on, you should select the **Fix** button from the Main menu.

This action will bring up the Main Fix Screen interface where you will make all of your repairs.

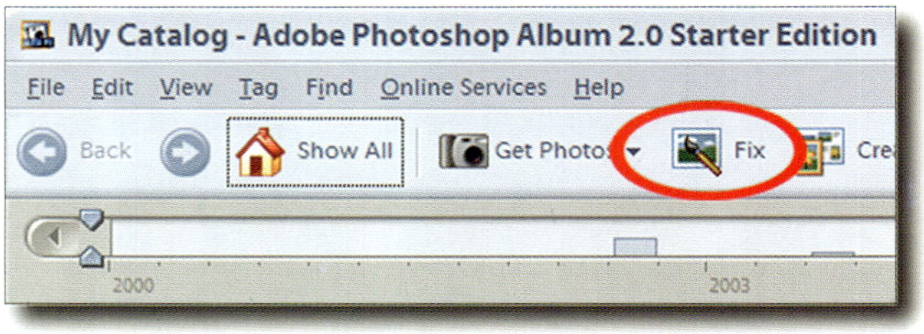

Before & After

When making changes to images, it is helpful to see the before and after images.

Click the **Before & After** button.

The left pane will show the photo without any changes.

The right pane will show the cumulative effect of your changes.

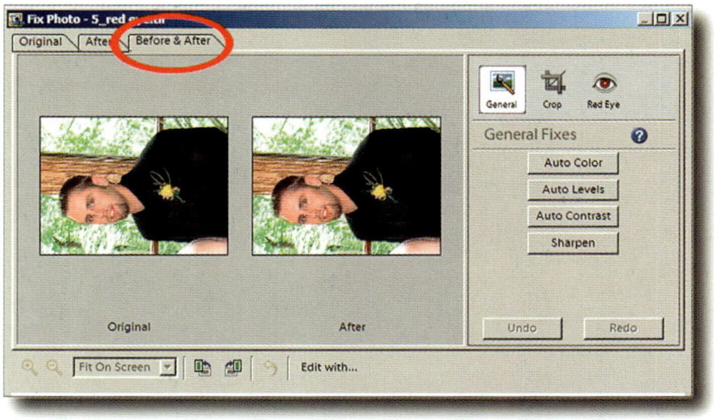

Rotate Image

We recommend that you rotate the image if it is necessary.

This is done by clicking on one of the icons circled in red.

The **left icon** will rotate the image to the left, or counter-clockwise.

The **right icon** will rotate the image to the right, or clockwise.

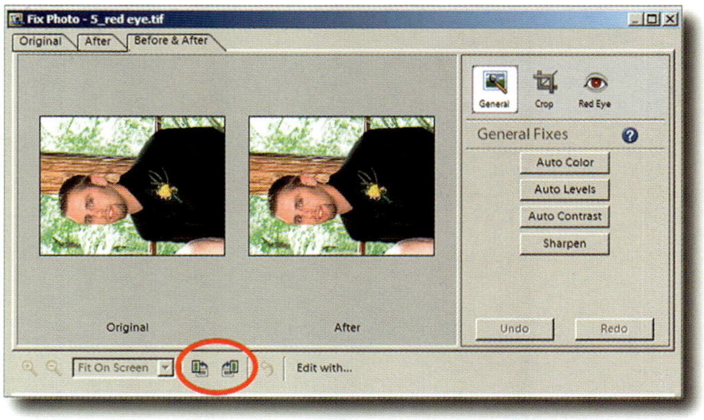

Fixing a Photo - General Fixes

In this section we will use Adobe Album Starter to make automated image repairs. We will cover general repairs.

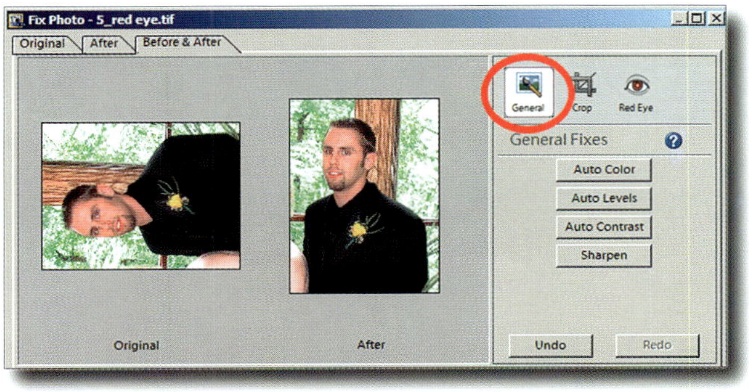

The General button

Once you have selected the image you wish to work on and clicked the **Fix** button, you will be taken to the **Fix** section of the program.

To make general corrections, you must click the **General** button.

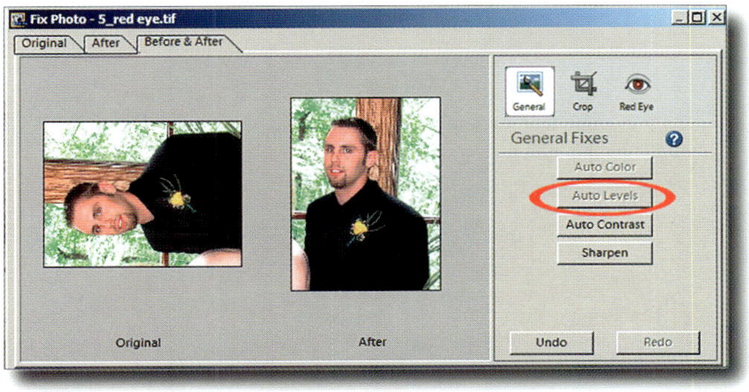

Fixing Things

This will fix the following:

Color

Tone (Auto Levels)

Contrast

Sharpness

When you click any of these correction buttons, you will notice:

1. The selected button will gray out, indicating the step has been performed.

2. The **After** view will change to reflect the effect of the repair.

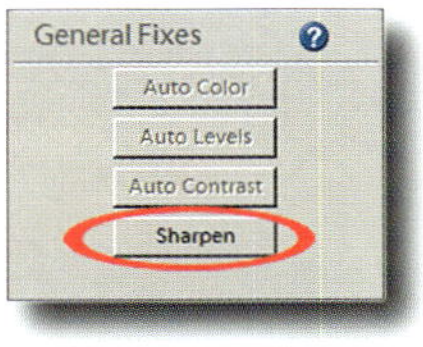

Sharpening

Sharpening is different. There is no grey out to indicate the action has been performed. You should only sharpen once.

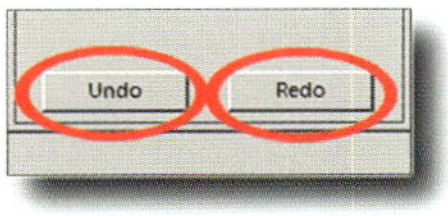

Undo/Redo

The **Undo** and **Redo** buttons move you back and forward one step at a time to allow you to cancel any repairs.

Fixing a Photo – Cropping

In this chapter we will deal with cropping your image without restriction or to a specific size and/or shape.

The Crop Button

Once you have selected the image you wish to work on and clicked the **Fix** button, you will be taken to the **Fix** section of the program.

To crop, you must click the **Crop** button.

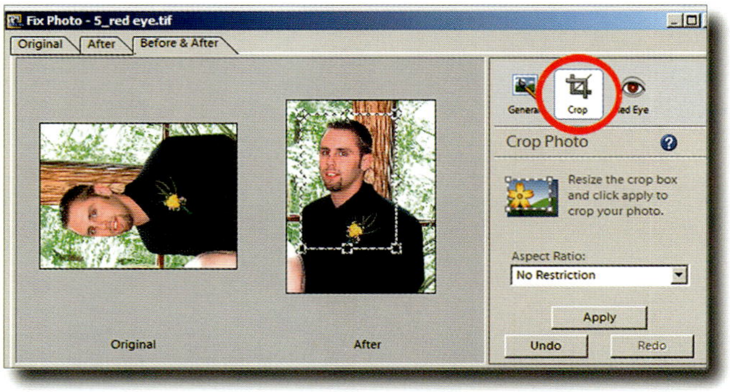

Unrestricted Crop

Sometimes you will want to crop an image to any shape – whatever you deem makes the best photograph.

Any Size = No Restriction

You will notice a white square appear on top of your image. You can drag this box around the image to resize it as desired.

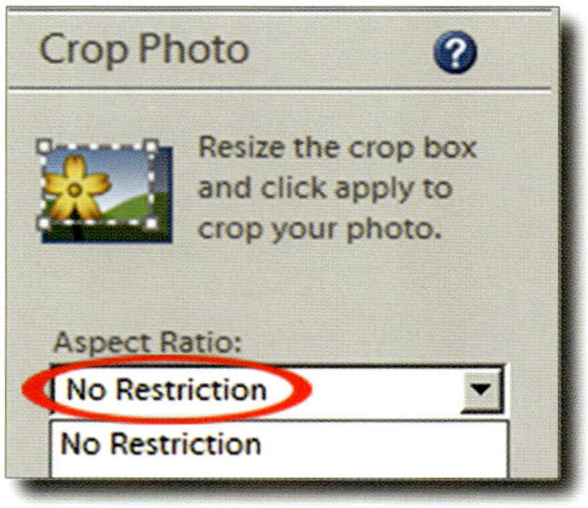

Restricted Crop

Sometimes you will want to crop the image to a specific shape, or aspect ratio.

Standard Size = Restriction

This is selected using the drop down box below **Aspect Ratio**.

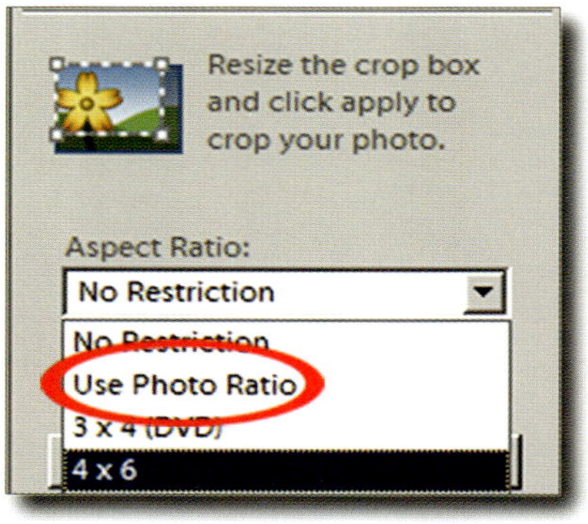

Applying the Crop

Click the **Apply** button to complete cropping. The **After** image will appear cropped.

This step can be **Undone** and **Redone**.

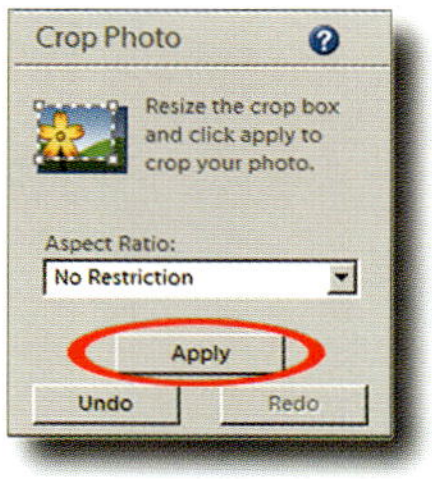

Fixing a Photo - Red Eye

Often after images are captured by digital flash photography, you will want to get rid of **Red Eye** - red pupils. **Red Eye** is a tool that allows you to do this.

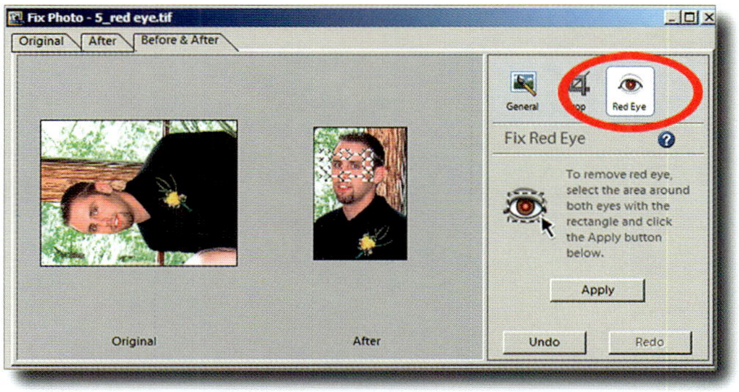

The Red Eye Button

Once you have selected the image you wish to work on and clicked the **Fix** button, you will be taken to the **Fix** section of the program.

To fix red eye, you must click the **Red Eye** button.

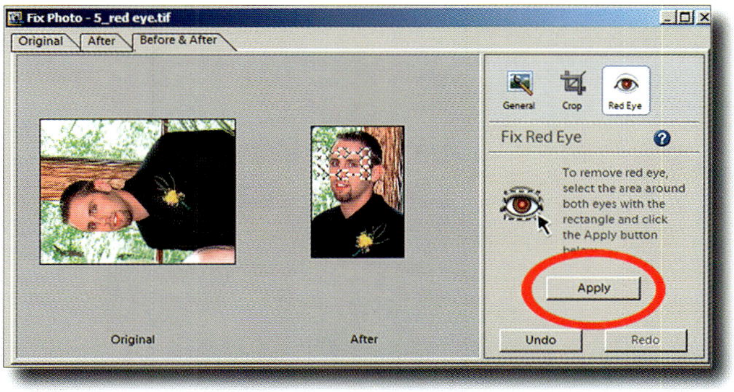

Applying Red Eye Correction

You will notice a white square show up on top of your image.

You can move this white box around the image by dragging it with the left mouse button held down.

You can resize the box by grabbing any corner of it with the left mouse button held down and dragging it to the desired size.

Once you have placed the white box around your subject's eyes, click the **Apply** button.

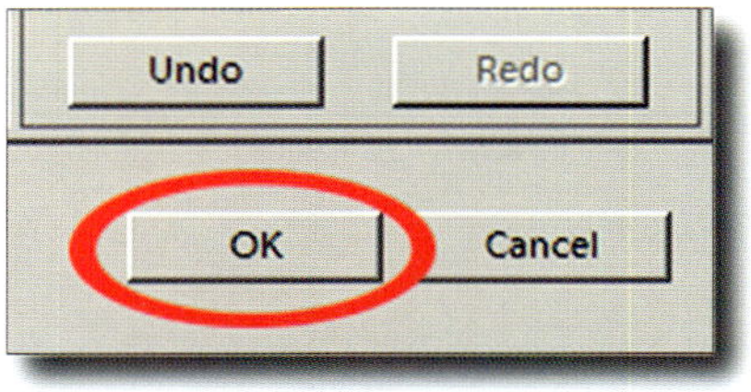

Finishing Red Eye Correction

At this point you can still use the **Undo** and **Redo** buttons to go back and forth through your fixes.

When you are happy with everything, click the **OK** button.

Printing Photos

In this section, we will use Adobe Album Starter to select an image, or several images, from the **Photo Well** to print.

Selecting Photo(s) to Print

If you want to print one photo, click on a photo in the **Photo Well**.

If you want to select several photos to print as a group hold down the **Ctrl** key and click on all the photos you want to print in the **Photo Well**.

A border will appear around each picture you have selected.

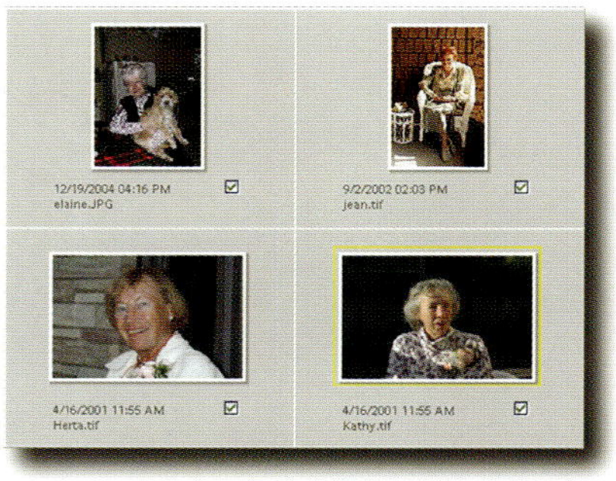

Select Print Function

From the Main menu, select the **Print…** function.

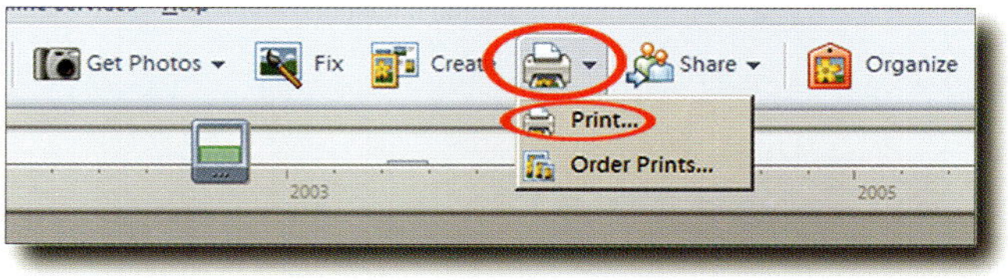

Selecting Printer and Layout

You must select the printer you wish to use as well as the number of copies.

1. Select a layout:**Individual Print:** use this to print __one__ photo.
2. **Contact Sheet:** use this to print small prints of __several different__ images on the same page in columns and rows.
3. **Picture Package:** use this to print __several copies__ of the __same__ image on one page.

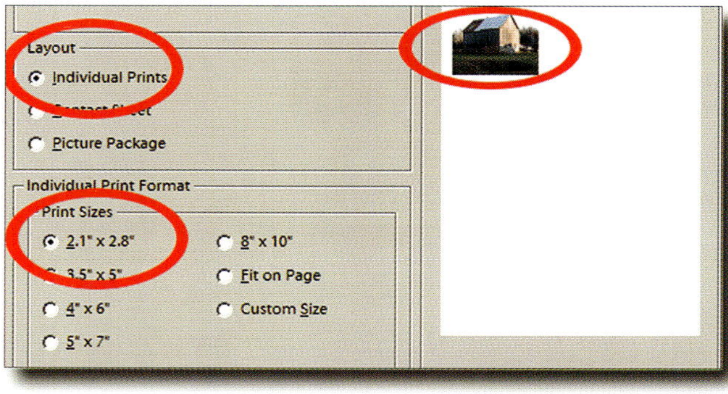

Print It

When you are ready to print, click the **Print** button.

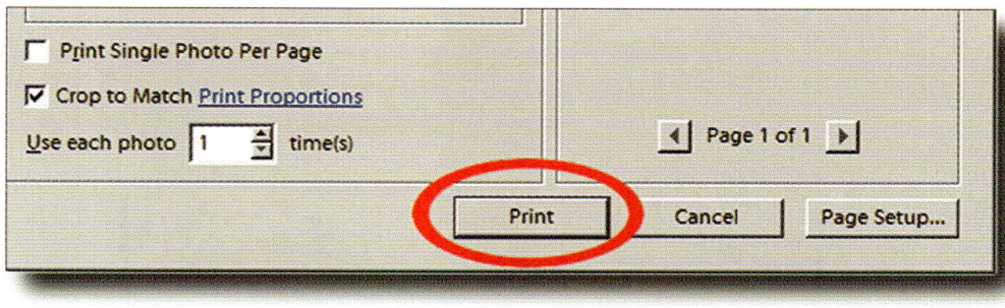

Emailing Photos

In this section, we will select a photo to email. The photo will then become an attachment in our usual email program.

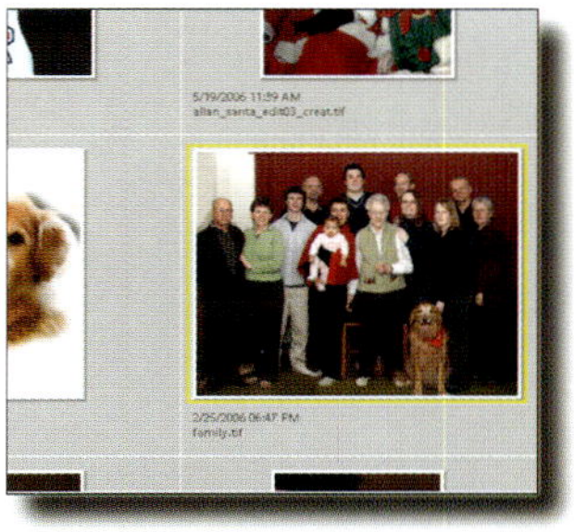

Selecting Photo(s) to Email

Click on the photo that you wish to email.

A border will appear around the selected photo.

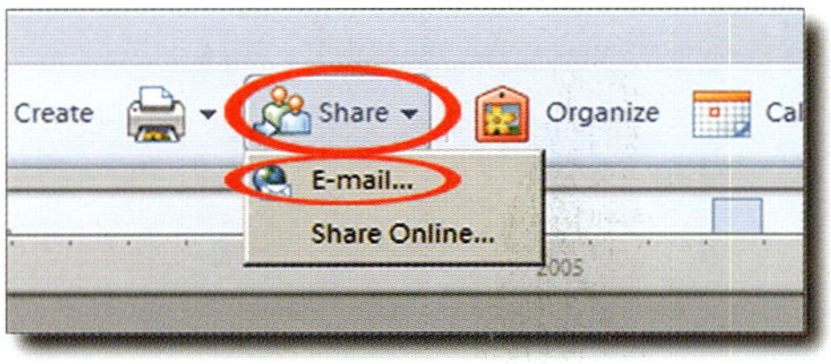

Select Email Function

In the Icon menu, click the **Share** button.

In the drop down menu, click the **Email…** button.

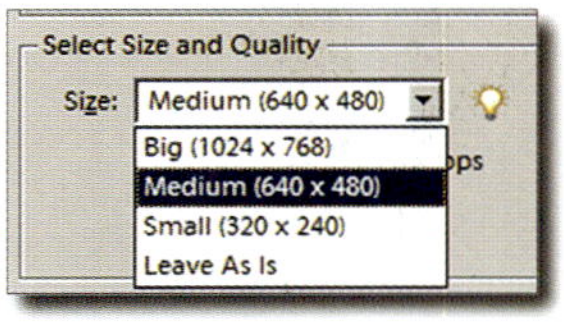

Setting Size and Quality

Select a size and quality. A larger size will give a higher image quality, but it will also take more time to send.

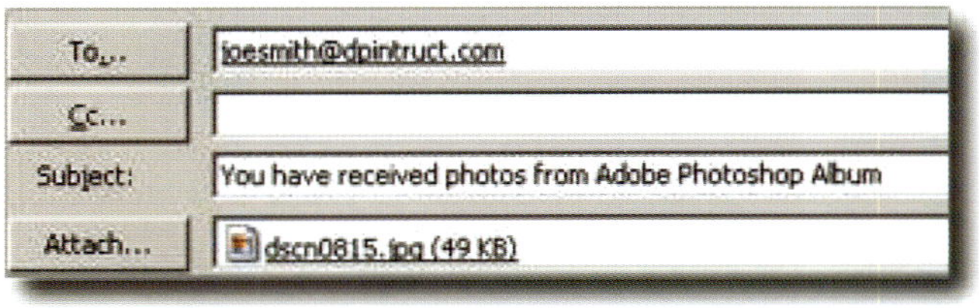

Send Email

After this, you will be dropped into your email program. The photo will automatically be attached to your email. Select recipient, insert subject and message, then click the **Send** button.

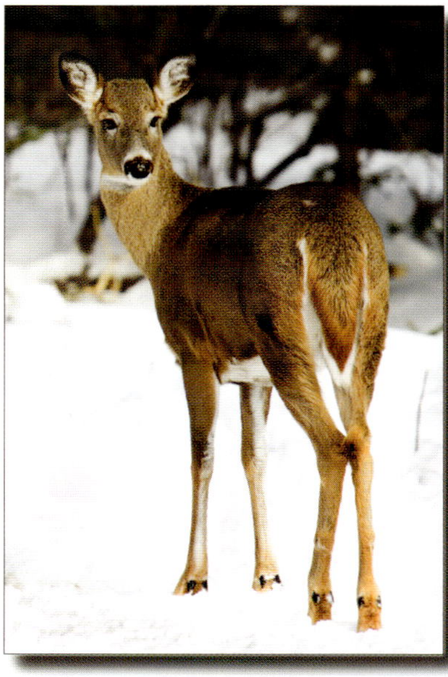

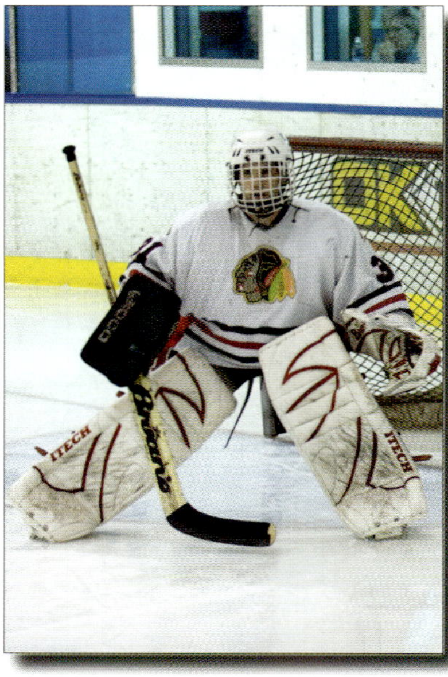

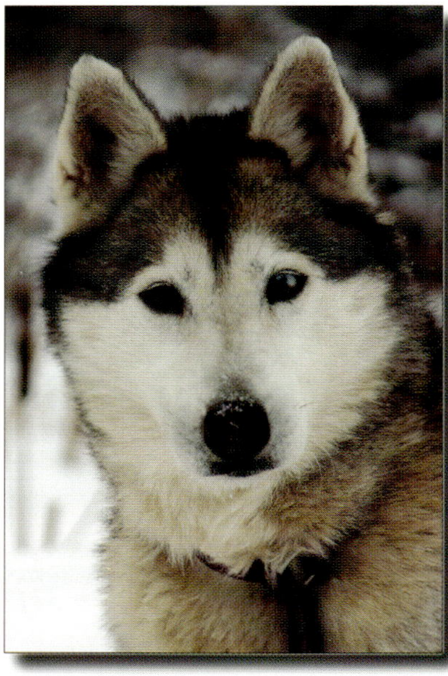

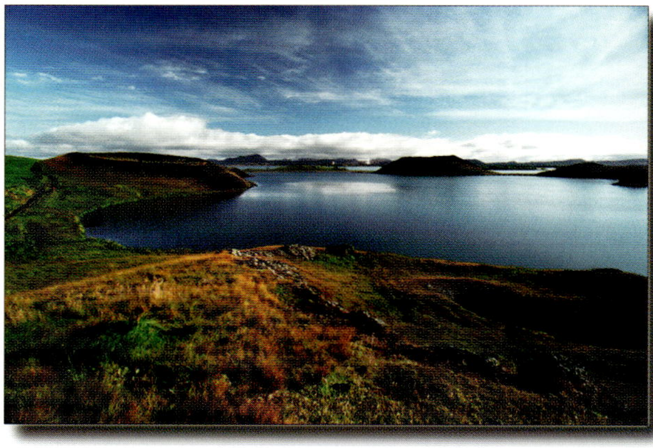

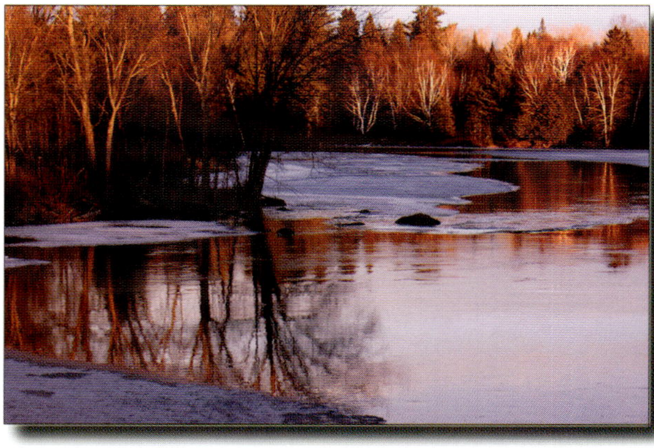

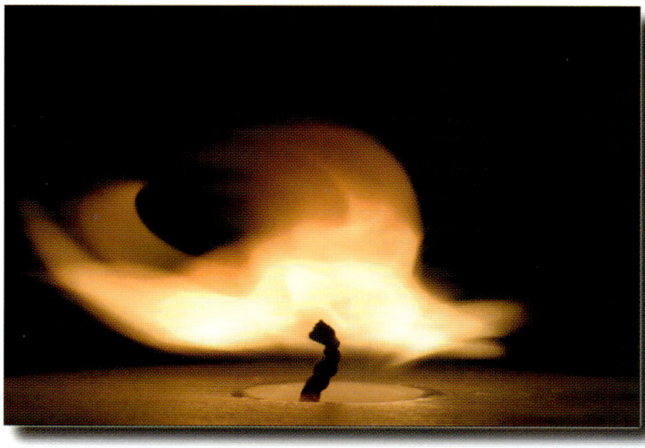

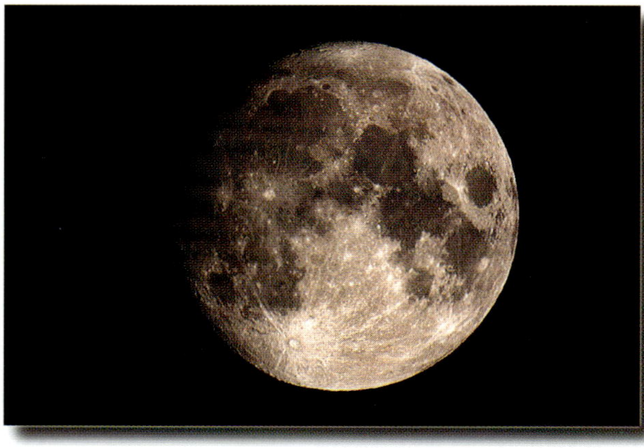

Photos by Henry Christiansen

Chapter 7 ADOBE ALBUM FULL

Adobe Album Full

Adobe Album Full is one step up from the most basic editing program offered by Adobe. Like the Starter version, it allows you to copy pictures into a computer, organize, view, print and email them with little difficulty. The program will also perform basic automatic corrections and image improvements. What distinguishes Album Full from the Starter version is the ability it gives you to manually override the automatic corrections.

This version allows CD and DVD back up.

Introduction

In this chapter, we will cover using Adobe Album Full to download your images using a Card Reader. We will illustrate how you can view your images and select one or more images for automatic and manual corrections, printing and emailing.

Getting the Program

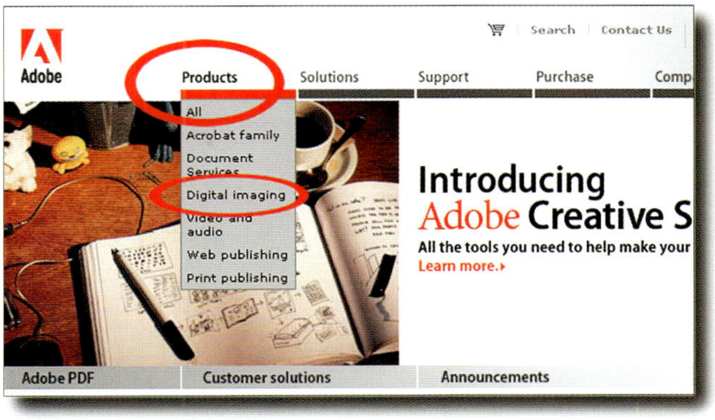

To acquire this program, you must purchase it for about $50 US (in 2006).

You can purchase it online at www.adobe.com. Select **Products**, and follow the links to Album Full.

You can also purchase the program through various commercial outlets.

Installing the Program

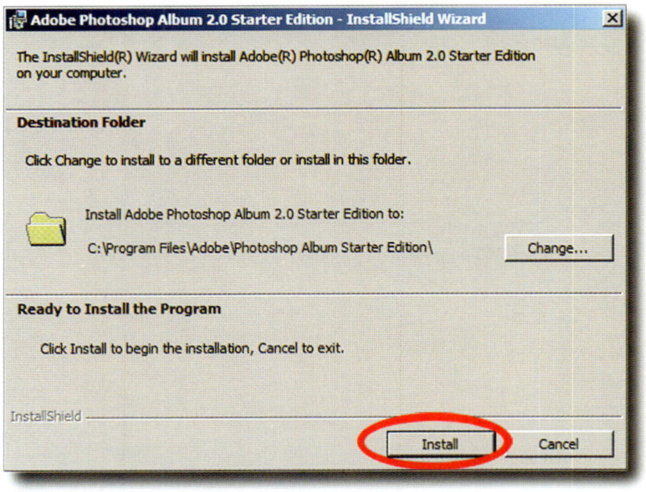

Click on the **Installer** program you have downloaded from Adobe, or place the CD you have purchased, in your computer. Follow the screen instructions to finish the installation of the actual program. You will have to accept their legal agreement. The **Quick Guide** will then appear on the screen. Turn it off by clicking on the lower left hand corner. Go to the Main menu and choose **Help**. Click on **Registration** and then enter the **Unlock Code** that you received from Adobe by email, or with your CD.

Card Readers

Memory Card Readers are an inexpensive accessory that will streamline your digital workflow. They allow you to continue to use your camera while downloading images. The card reader you buy must match the type of memory card used by your camera.

Installing The Card Reader

After purchasing a card reader for your type of memory card, plug it into one of the unused USB ports on your computer. Windows should recognize it and state:

New hardware found

Then Windows should announce:

New hardware is installed and ready to use

Using the Card Reader

Insert your full memory card into the card reader.

There are two ways to download photos:

1. The Adobe Downloader will pop up and offer to download your images. **Or**

2. From the Main menu, choose:

Get Photos

From Camera or Card Reader…

Click the **OK** button to load the images.

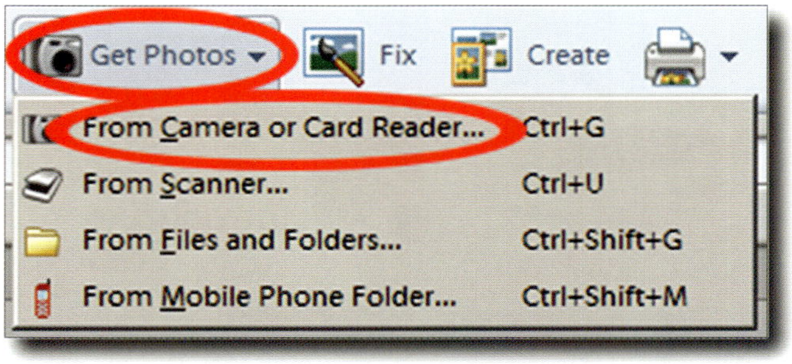

Unplugging the Card Reader

You may then remove your memory card. We recommend that you don't unplug your card reader. However, if you wish to unplug it to free up USB ports, you should click the **green arrow** on the lower right part of the Windows screen to do so.

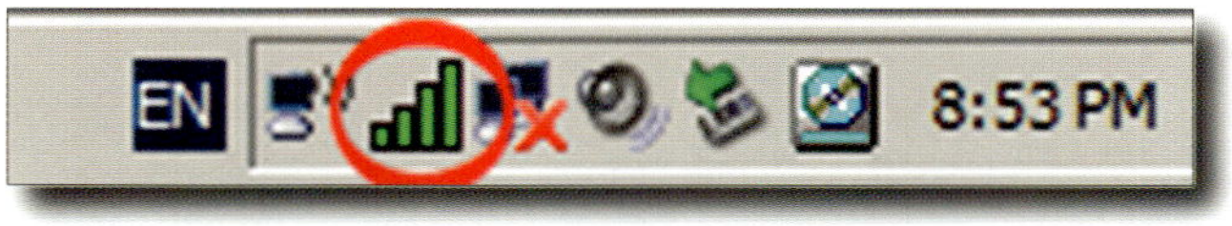

Selecting a Photo

Once your images have been downloaded from your memory card reader, the Photo Well will display them for you.

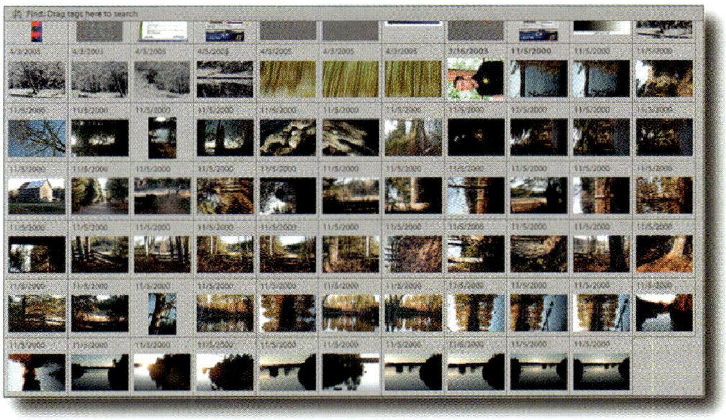

The Photo Well

All your downloaded images will be added to the **Photo Well**.

The **Photo Well** is the thumbnail representation of all your images. It appears in the center part of the screen.

If you do not see any of your images displayed, click the **Show All** button.

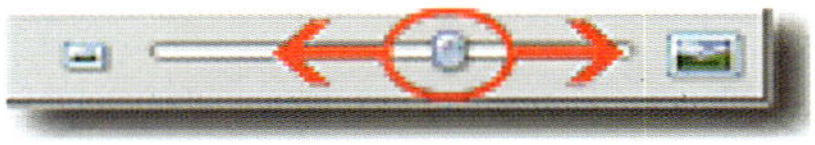

Thumbnail Size & Scroll Bars

Use the **Thumbnail Views** slider at the bottom right corner of the screen to resize the images.

As the slider is moved to the right, the images get bigger and fewer images fit on the screen.

As the slider is moved to the left, the images get smaller and more images fit on the screen.

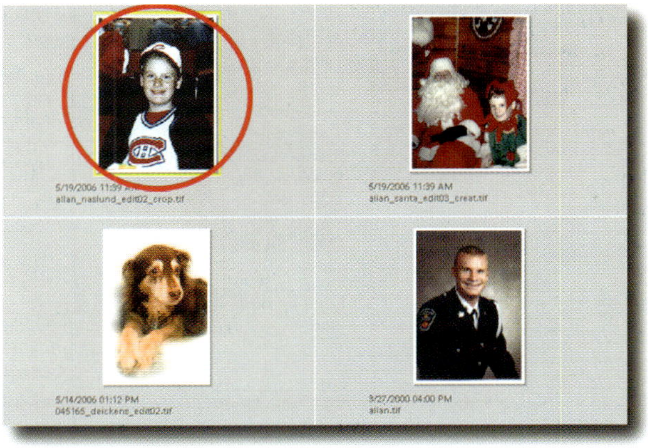

The Selected Photo

When you find the photo that you want in the **Photo Well**, click on it.

A colored box will appear around this image to indicate that you have selected it to work on.

Fixing a Photo - Getting Started

You may wish to improve some of your images. In this chapter we will deal with the initial set-up for the repair process.

The Fix Screen

Once you have selected the image that you wish to work on, you should select **Fix** from the Main menu.

This action will bring up the Main Fix Screen interface where you will make all of your repairs.

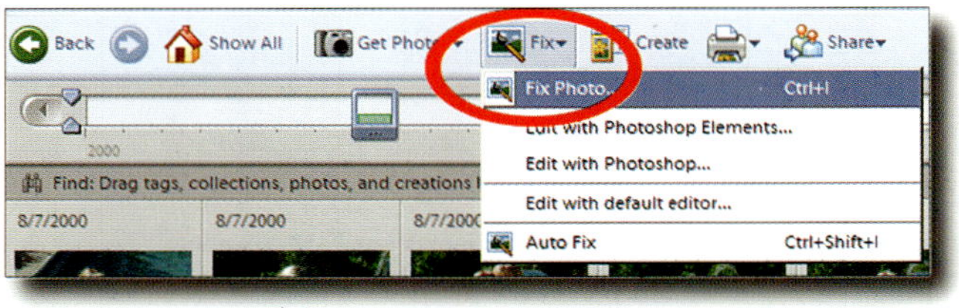

Before & After

When making changes to your images, it is helpful to see the before and after images.

Click the **Before & After** button.

The left pane will show the photo without any changes.

The right pane will show the cumulative effect of your changes.

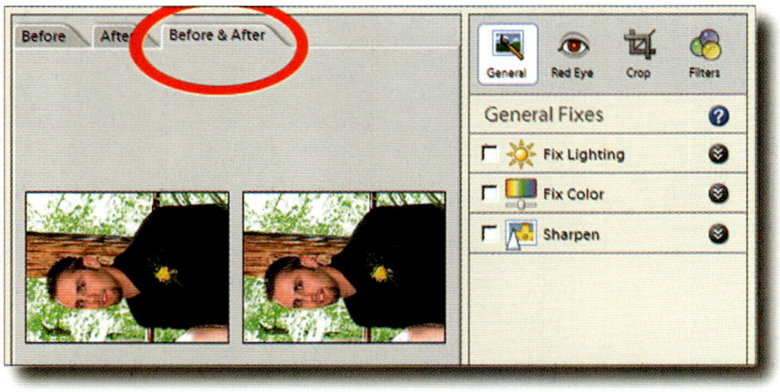

Rotate Image

We recommend that you rotate the image if it is necessary.

This is done by clicking on one of the icons circled in red.

The **left icon** will rotate the image to the left, or counter-clockwise.

The **right icon** will rotate the image to the right, or clockwise.

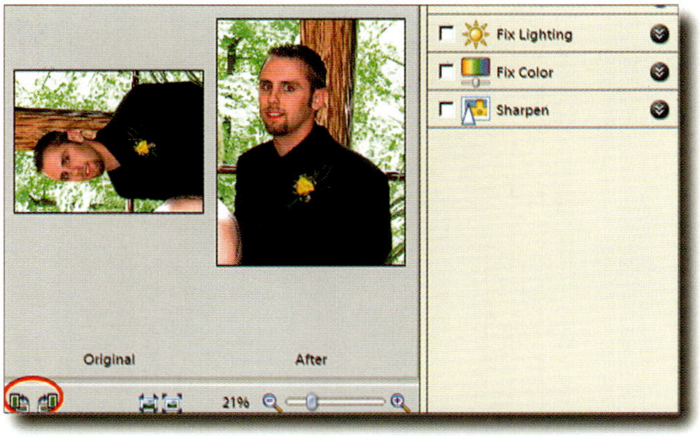

Fixing a Photo - General Fixes

In this section we will use Adobe Album Full to make automated image repairs. The Full version of the program allows manual override of the automatic fixes. We will now cover general repairs.

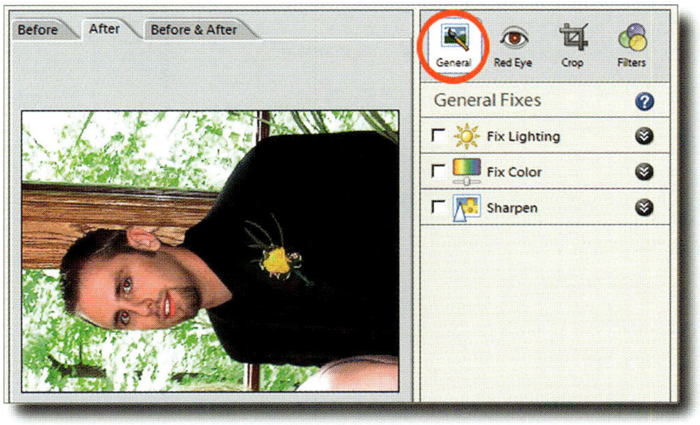

The General Button

Once you have selected the image you wish to work on and clicked the **Fix** button, you will be taken to the **Fix** section of the program.

To make general corrections, you must click the **General** button.

Fixing Things

This will fix the following:

Fix Lighting

Fix Color

Sharpen

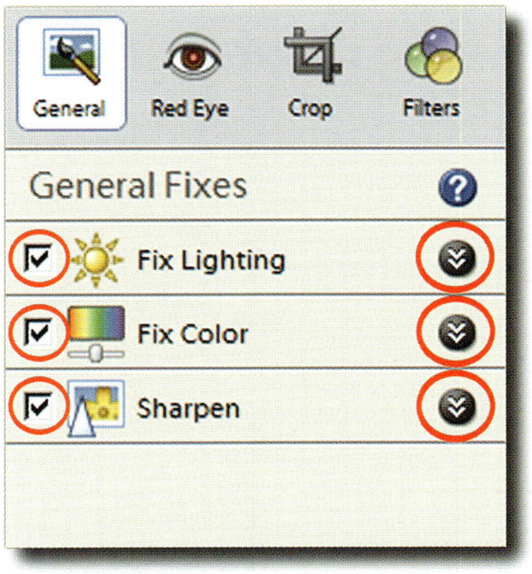

Automatic Fixes

If you only wish to make automatic fixes without any manual override, proceed as follows:

Click the small check box in front of the corrections desired. Here we have shown all corrections checked.

Leave the manual override toggle switches (on the right side) in the arrow-down mode to prevent the manual override sliders from appearing.

The pane on the right is in total automatic mode, with no provision for manual override.

Manual Fixes

If you wish to make automatic fixes with the option for manual override, proceed as follows:

Click the small check box in front of the corrections desired. Here we have shown all corrections checked.

Click the manual override toggle switches (on the right side) to the arrow-up mode in order to make the manual override sliders visible.

The pane on the right is in automatic mode, with complete provision for manual override.

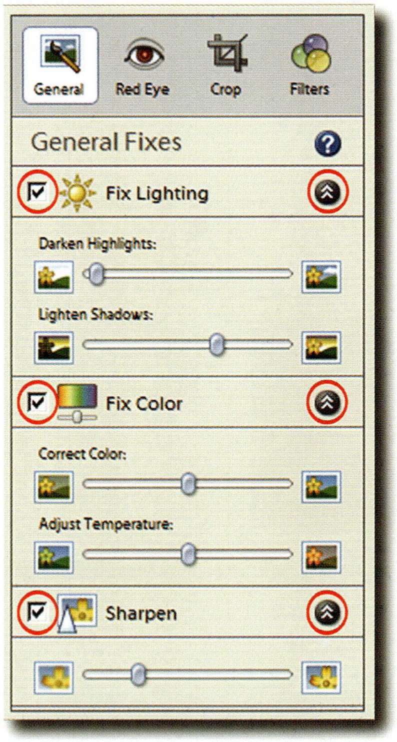

Slider Effects:

Darken Highlight Slider: Moving this slider to the right darkens any light areas. Moving slider all the way to the left adds no effect.

Lighten Shadows Slider: Moving this slider to the right lightens any dark areas. Moving slider all the way to the left adds no effect.

Correct Color Slider: Moving this slider to the right increases the colors. Moving slider all the way to the left adds no effect.

Adjust Temperature Slider: Moving this slider to the right makes colors appear warmer, enhancing the red & yellow tones.

Moving this slider to the left makes colors appear cooler, enhancing the blue tones.

Sharpening Slider: Moving the slider to the right increases the sharpness of the image. Moving the slider all the way to the left adds no sharpening effect

Undo/Redo

In this instance, there are no **Undo** and **Redo** buttons. You can just uncheck and recheck corrections as needed.

Fixing a Photo - Red Eye

Often after images are captured by digital flash photography, you will want to get rid of **Red Eye**, or red pupils. **Red Eye** is a tool that allows you to do this.

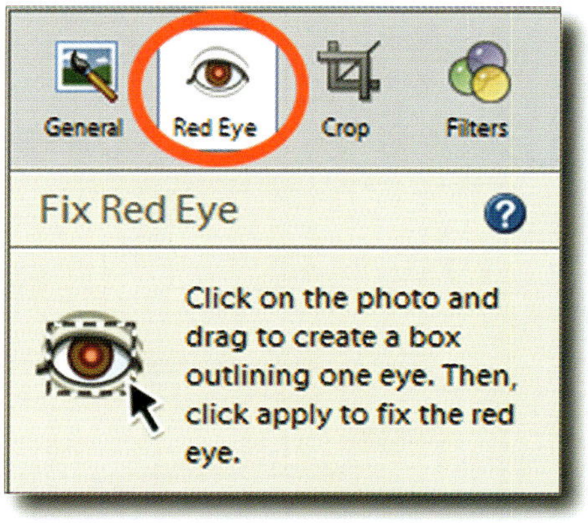

The Red Eye Button

Once you have selected the image you wish to work on and clicked the **Fix** button, you will be taken to the **Fix** section of the program.

To fix red eye, you must click the **Red Eye** button.

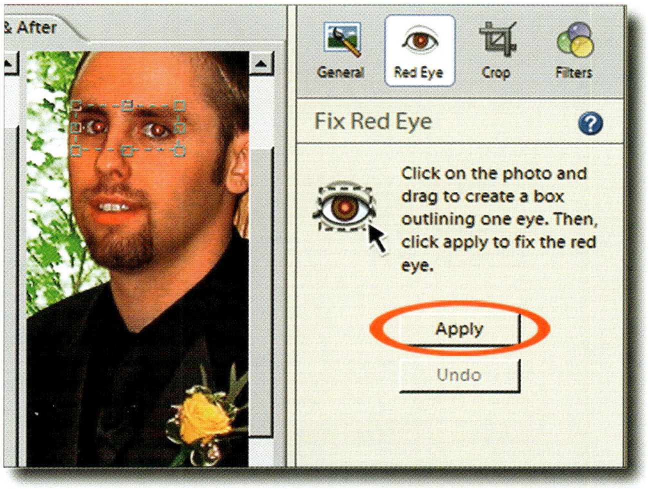

Applying Red Eye Correction

You will notice a white square show up on top of your image.

You can move this white box around the image by dragging it with the left mouse button held down.

You can resize the box by grabbing any corner of it with the left mouse button held down and dragging it to the desired size.

Once you have placed the white box around your subject's eyes, click the **Apply** button.

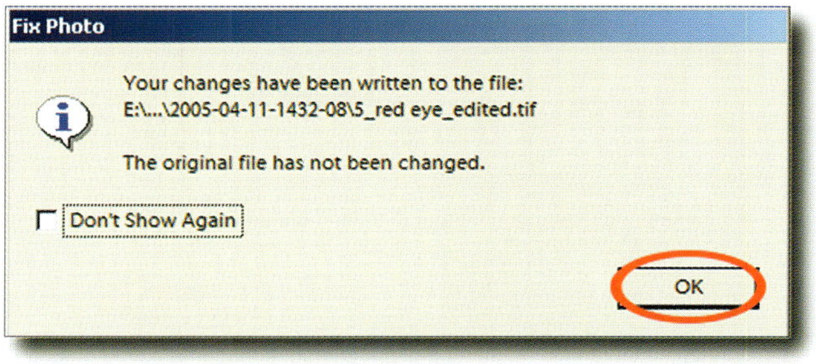

Finishing Red Eye Correction

At this point you can still use the **Undo** button to go back.

When you are happy with everything click the **OK** button.

Fixing a Photo - Cropping

In this section we will deal with cropping your image either without restriction or to a specific size and/or shape

The Crop Button

Once you have selected the image that you wish to work on and clicked the **Fix** button, you must click the **Crop** button.

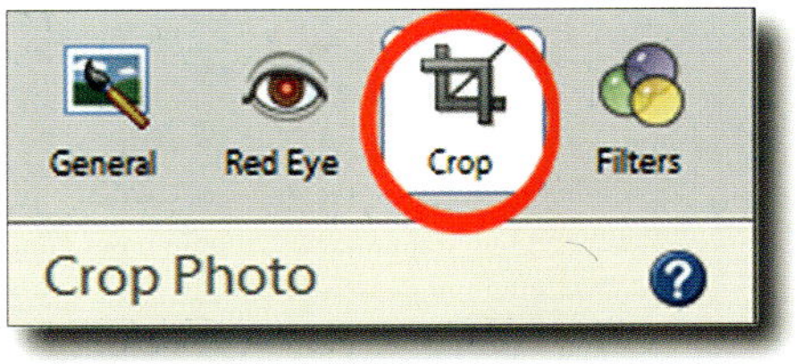

Unrestricted Crop

Sometimes you will want to crop an image to any shape – whatever you deem makes the best photograph.

Any Size = No Restriction

You will notice a white square at the top of your image. You can drag this box around the image and resize it as desired.

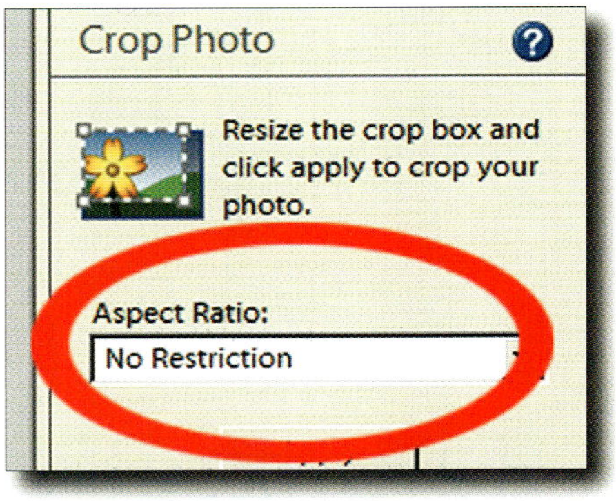

Restricted Crop

Other times you will want to crop an image to a specific shape or aspect ratio.

Standard Size = Restriction

This is selected using the drop down box below **Aspect Ratio**.

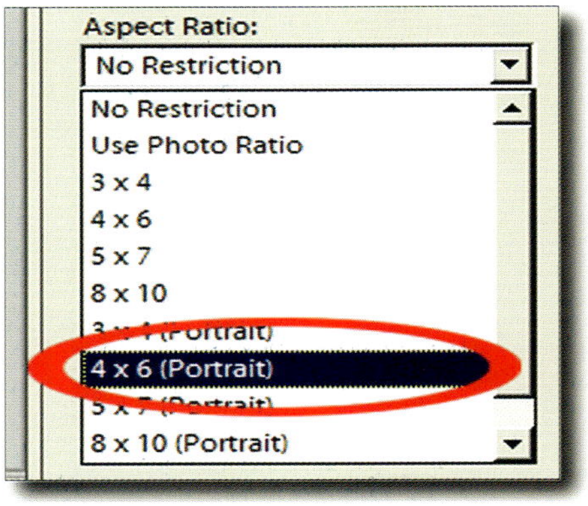

Applying the Crop

Click the **Apply** button to complete cropping. The **After** image will appear cropped.

This step can be **Undone** and **Redone**.

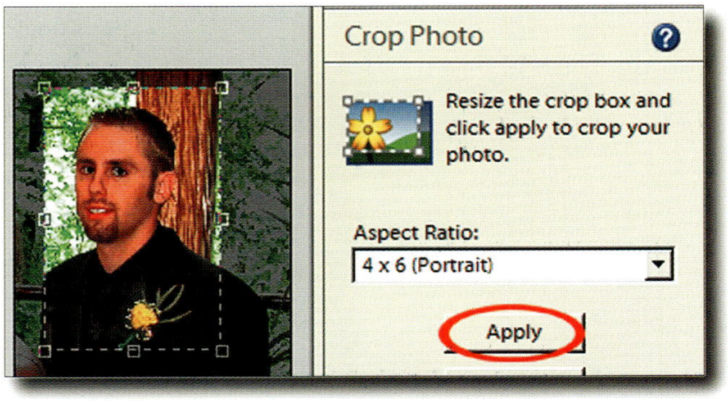

Fixing Photo - Filters

In this section, you will learn to apply special filters to your images.

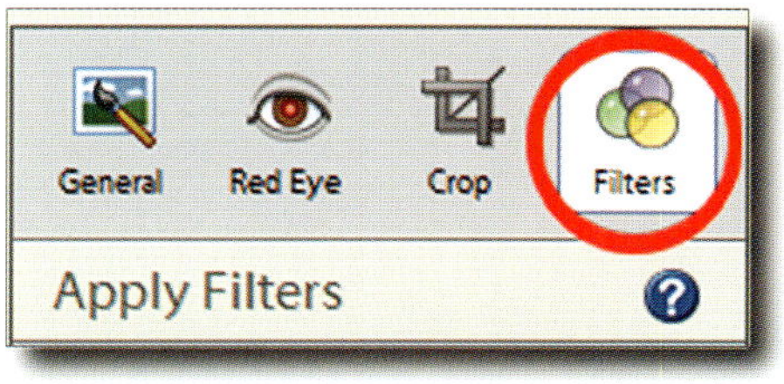

The Filter Button

Once you have selected the image that you wish to work on and clicked the **Fix** button, you must click the **Filters** button.

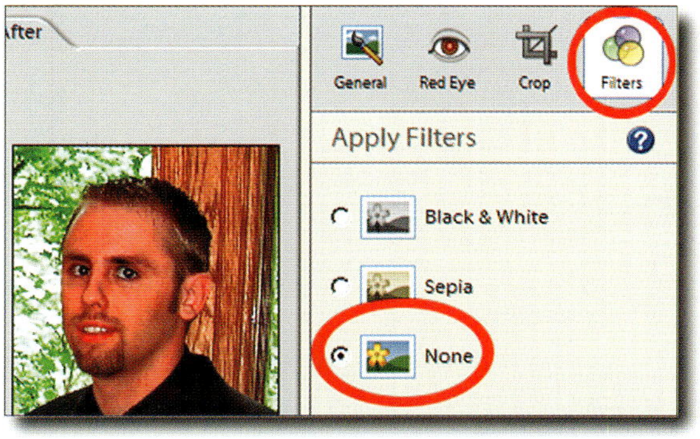

No Filter

When the pane opens up, it shows **None** checked as the default – this means that the program will leave the color as is.

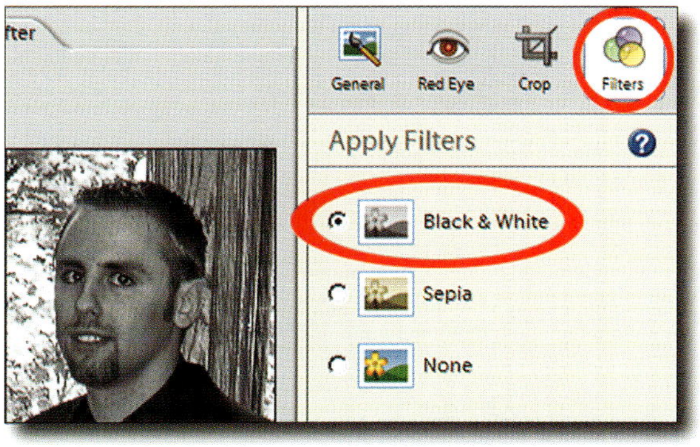

Black & White Filter

If you click on the button beside **Black & White**, the color image will be transformed into a black and white one.
Remember, this only happens to the copy of your original.

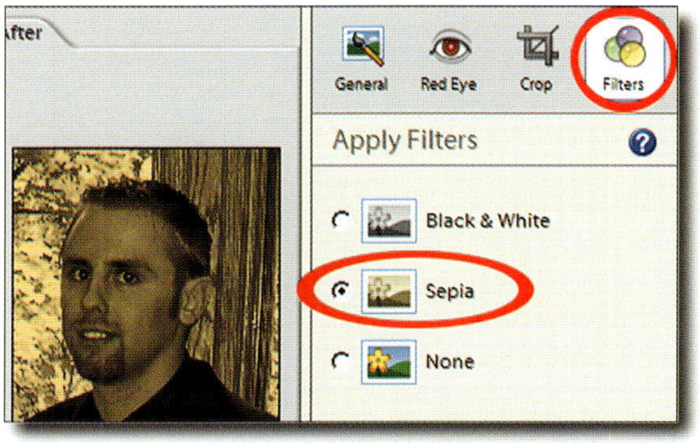

Sepia Filter

If you click on the button beside **Sepia**, the image will be transformed into a Sepia one.
Remember, this only happens to the copy of your original.

Printing Photos

In this section, we will use Adobe Album Full to select an image, or several images, from the **Photo Well** to print.

Selecting Photo(s) to Print

If you want to print one photo, just click on a photo in the **Photo Well**.

If you want to select several photos to print as a group, hold down the **Ctrl** key and click on all the photos you want to print in the **Photo Well**.

A colored border will appear around each picture you have selected.

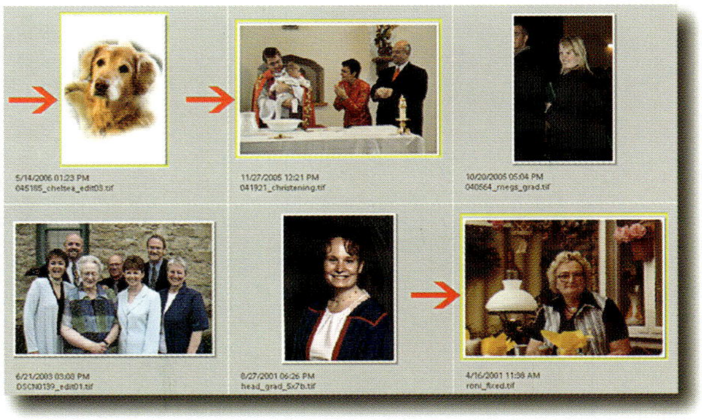

Selecting Print Function

From the Main menu, select the **Print...** function.

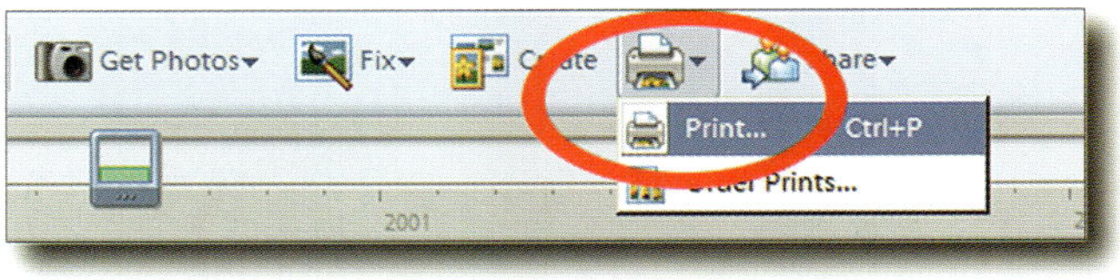

Selecting Printer and Layout

You must select the printer you wish to use as well as the number of copies.

Select a layout:

1. **Individual Prints:** use this to print **one** photo.
2. **Contact Sheet:** use this to print small prints of **several different** images on the same page in columns and rows.
3. **Picture Package:** use this to print **several copies** of the **same** image on one page.

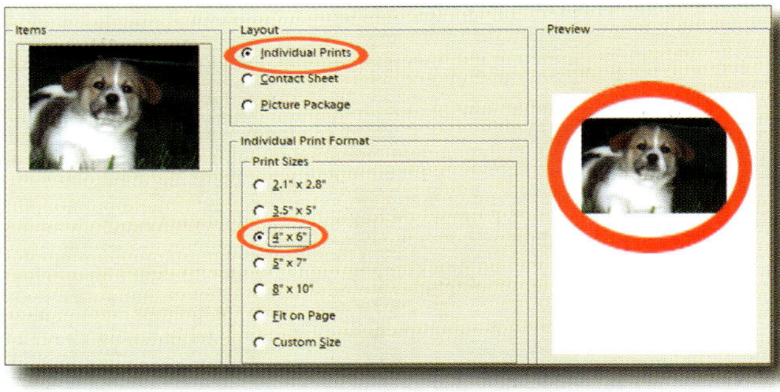

Print It

When you are ready to print, click the **Print** button.

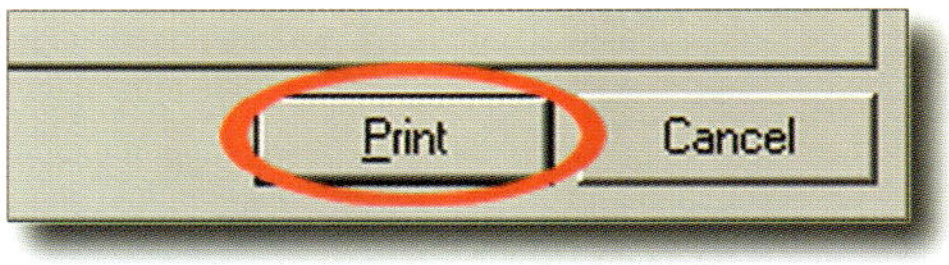

Emailing Photos

In this section, we will select a photo to email. The photo will then become an attachment in your email program.

Selecting Photo(s) to Email

Click on the photo that you wish to email.

A border will appear around the selected photo.

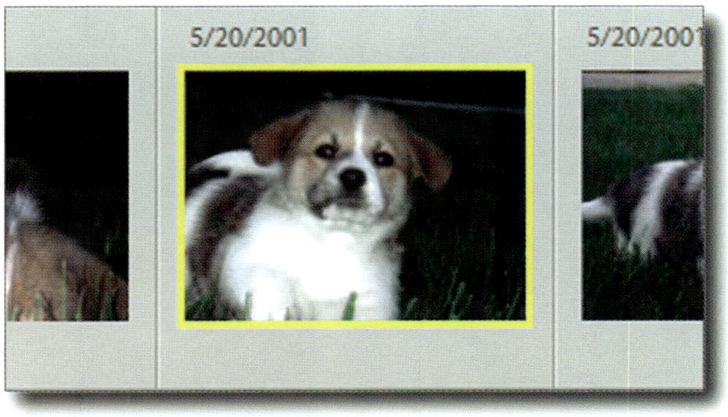

Select Email Function

In the Icon menu, click the

Share and **E-mail…** buttons.

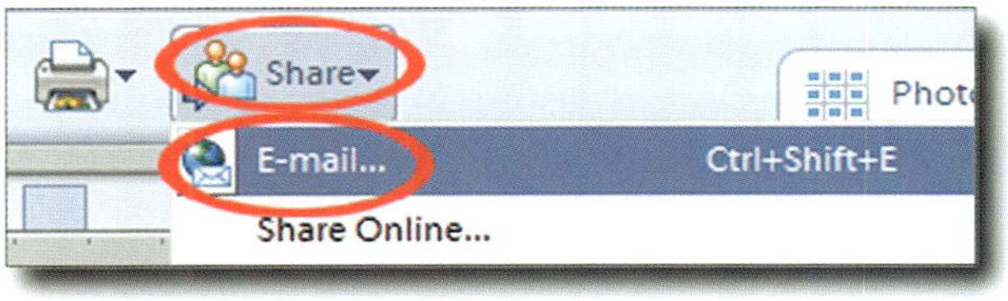

Select Size and Quality

This program will give you an estimated transmission time for the image (i.e. 16 sec @ a transmission speed of 56Kbps).

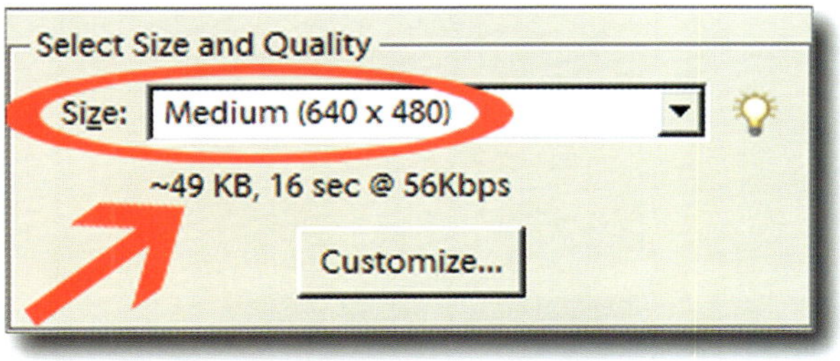

Send Email

After this, you will be dropped into your email program. The photo will automatically become an attachment.

Click the **Send** button.

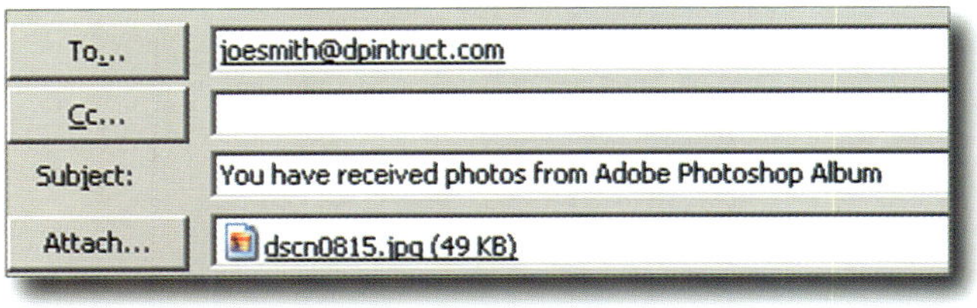

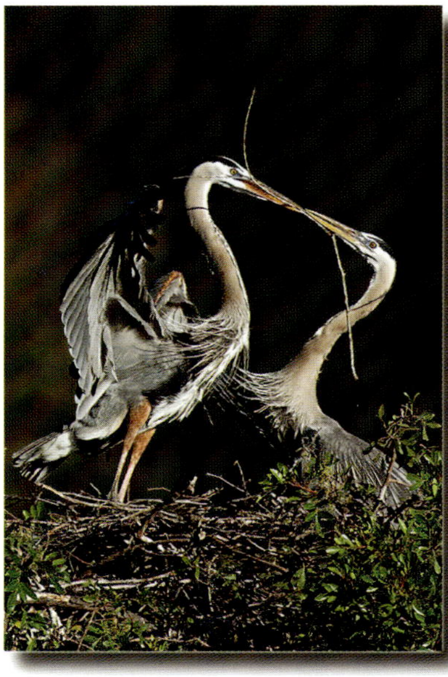
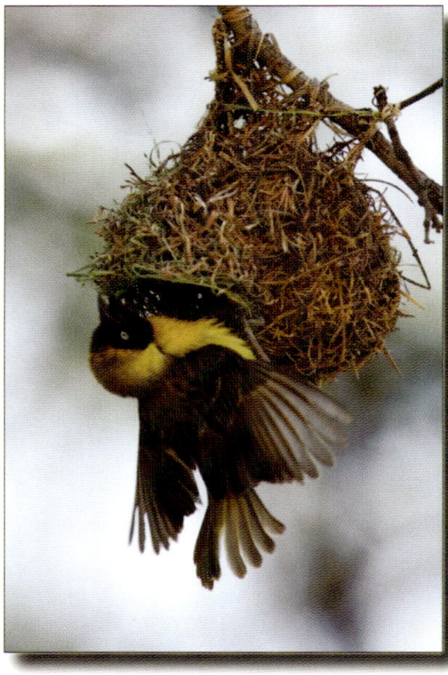
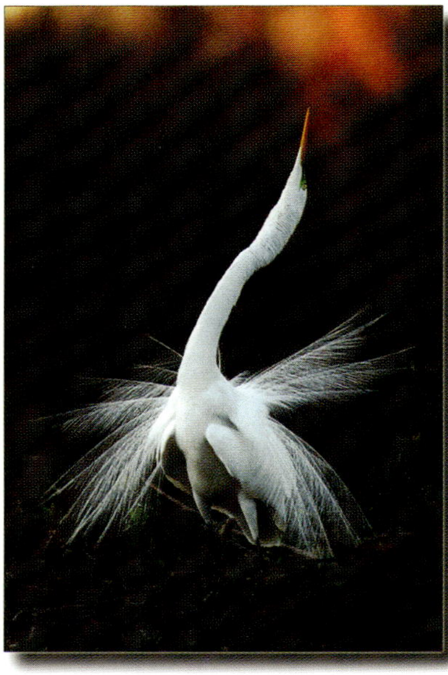
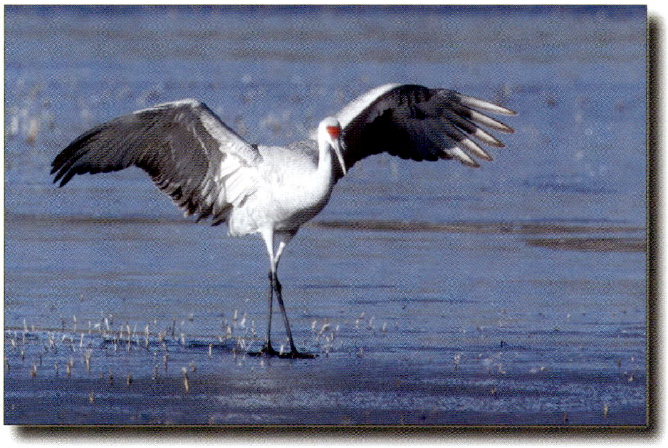
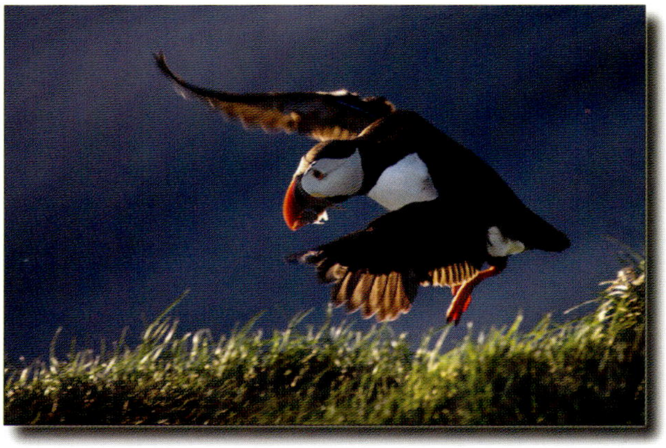
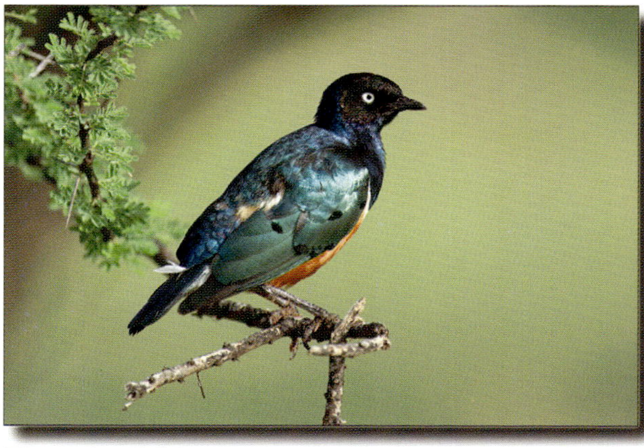
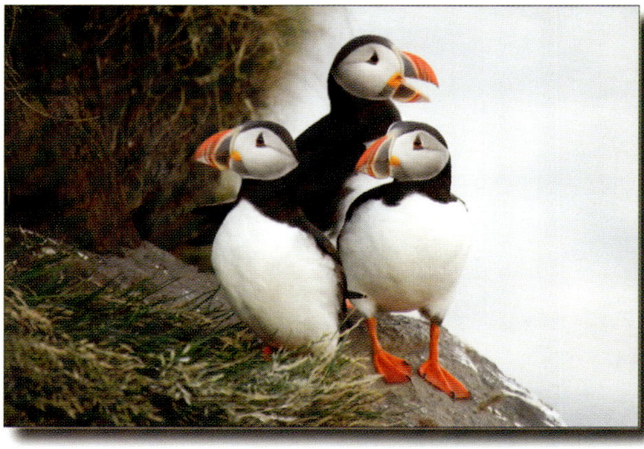

Photos by Phil Kwan

Emailing Photos

In this section, we will select a photo to email. The photo will then become an attachment in your email program.

Selecting Photo(s) to Email

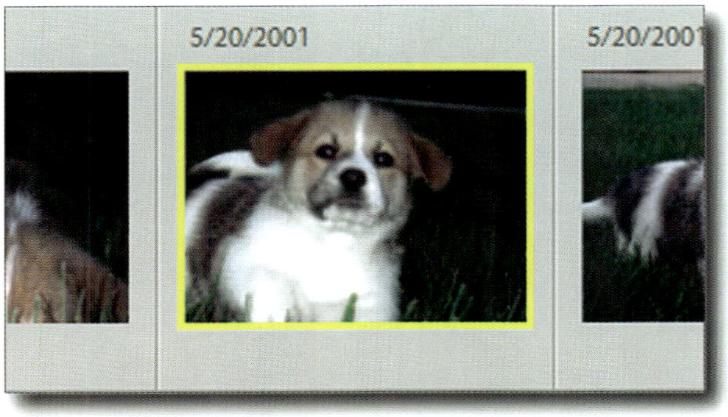

Click on the photo that you wish to email.

A border will appear around the selected photo.

Select Email Function

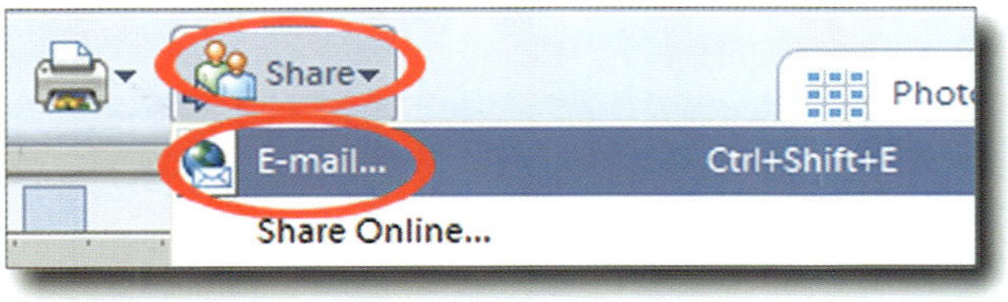

In the Icon menu, click the

Share and **E-mail…** buttons.

Select Size and Quality

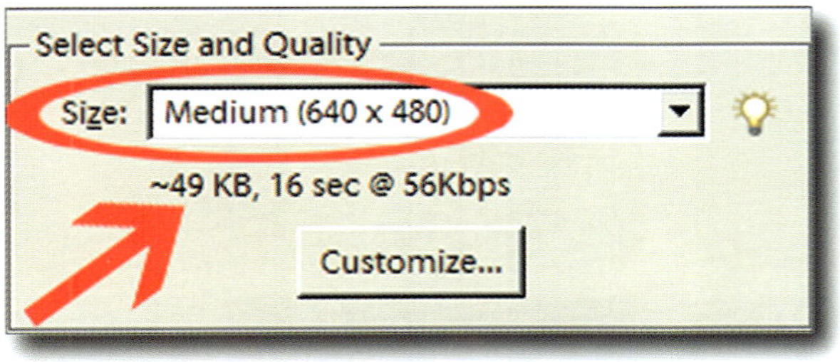

This program will give you an estimated transmission time for the image (i.e. 16 sec @ a transmission speed of 56Kbps).

Send Email

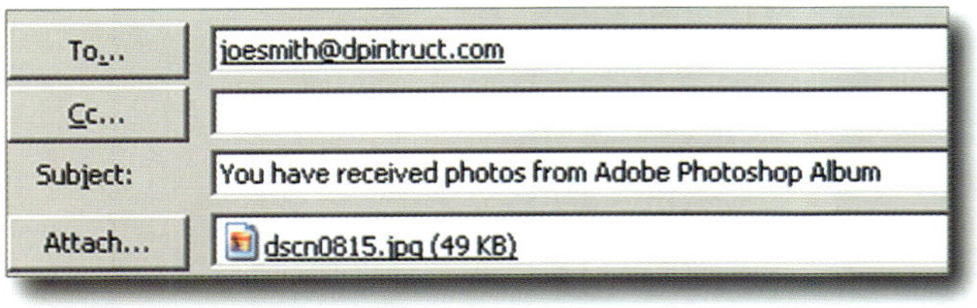

After this, you will be dropped into your email program. The photo will automatically become an attachment.

Click the **Send** button.

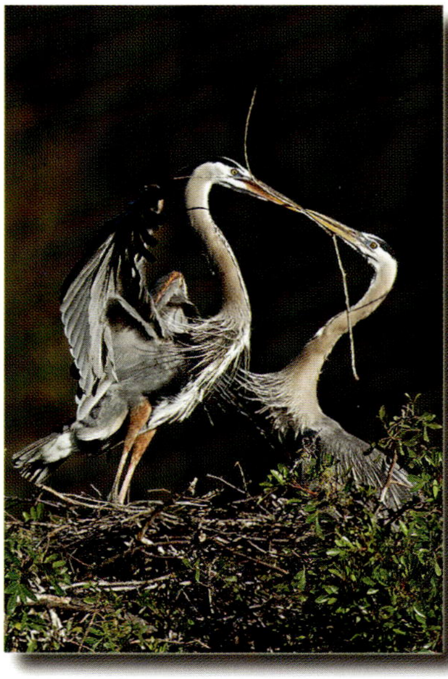

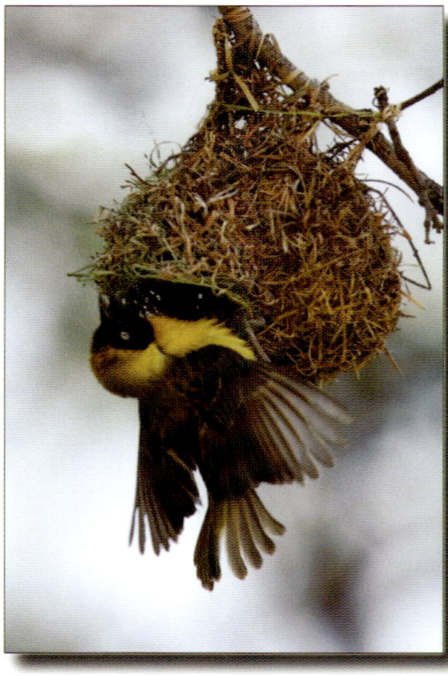

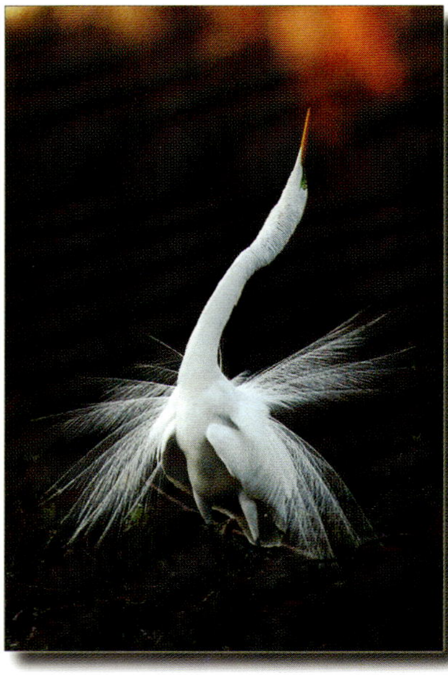

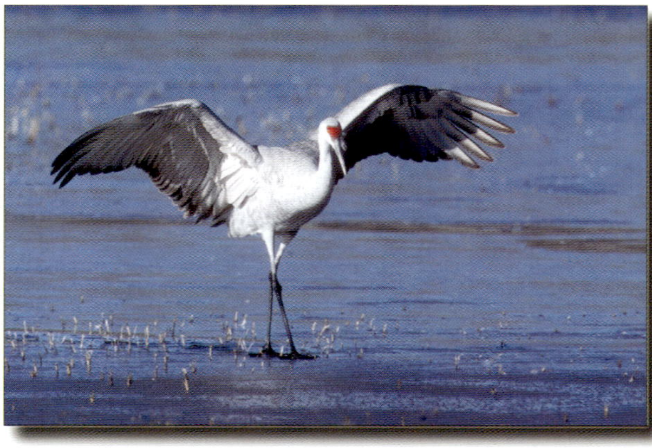

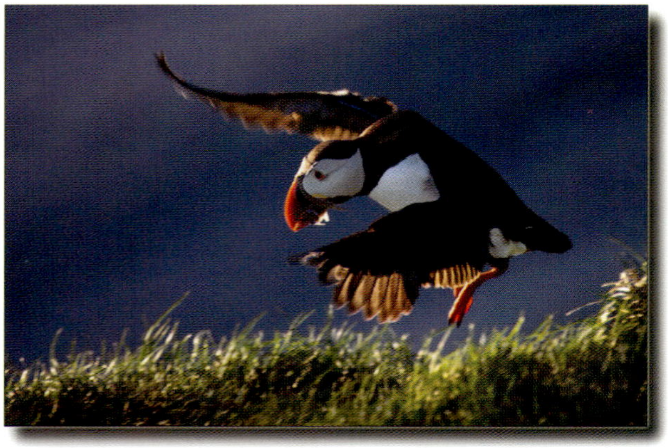

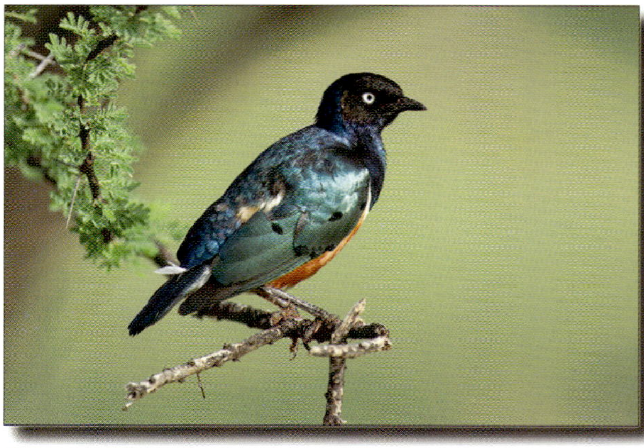

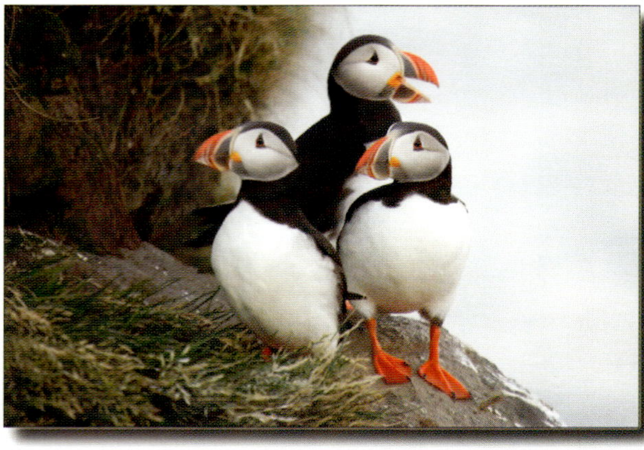

Photos by Phil Kwan

Chapter 8 ADOBE ELEMENTS BASIC

Adobe Elements Basic

Adobe Elements is the next step up from Adobe Album Full. This program can be used in two modes: Basic or Advanced.

In Basic, you can copy pictures into a computer, organize, view, print and email them. In this mode, the program will also perform basic automatic corrections and image improvements. However, Elements Basic gives more control over the manual override of the automatic corrections than Album Full.

This version allows CD and DVD back up.

Introduction

In this chapter, we will cover using Adobe Elements in its Basic Mode to download your images using a Card Reader. We will illustrate how you can view your images and select one or more images for automatic and manual corrections, printing and emailing.

Getting the Program

To acquire this program, you must purchase it for about $90 US (in 2006).

You can purchase it online at www.adobe.com. Select **Products**, and follow the links to **Elements**.

You can also purchase the program through various commercial outlets.

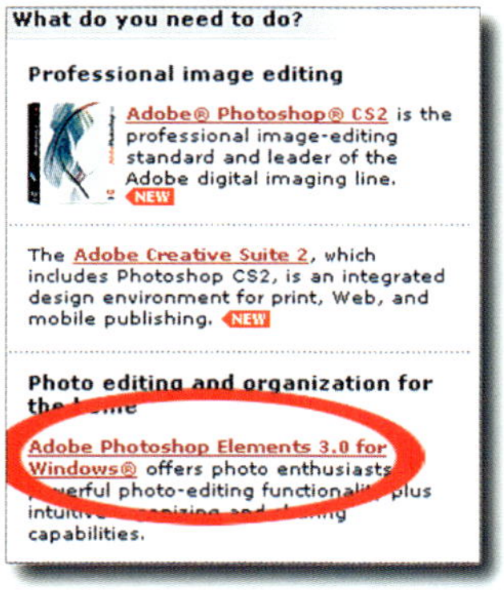

Installing the Program

Click on the **Installer** program you have downloaded from Adobe, or place the CD you have purchased in the computer. Follow the screen instructions to finish the installation of the program itself. You will have to accept their legal agreement. The **Quick Guide** will then appear on the screen. Turn it off by clicking on the lower left hand corner. Go to the Main menu and select **Help**. Click on **Registration** and then enter the **Unlock Code** that you received from Adobe by email, or with your CD.

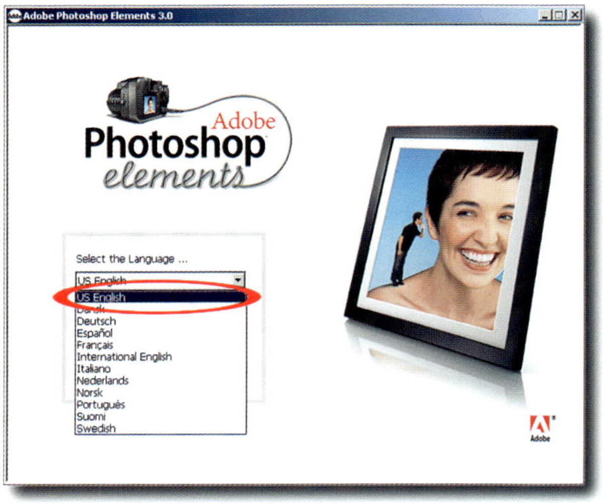

Card Readers

Memory Card Readers are an inexpensive accessory that will streamline your digital workflow. They allow you to continue to use your camera while downloading images. The card reader you buy must match the type of memory card used by your camera.

Installing the Card Reader

After purchasing a card reader for your type of memory card, plug it into one of the unused USB ports on your computer. Windows should recognize it and state:

New hardware found

Then Windows should announce:

New hardware is installed and ready to use

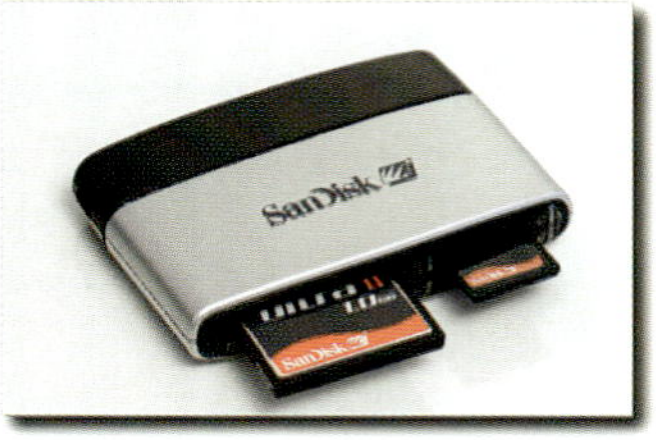

Using the Card Reader

Insert your full memory card into the card reader.

There are two ways to download photos:

1. The Adobe Downloader will pop up and offer to download your images. **<u>Or</u>**

2. From the Main menu, choose:

Get Photos

From Camera or Card Reader

Click **OK** to load the images.

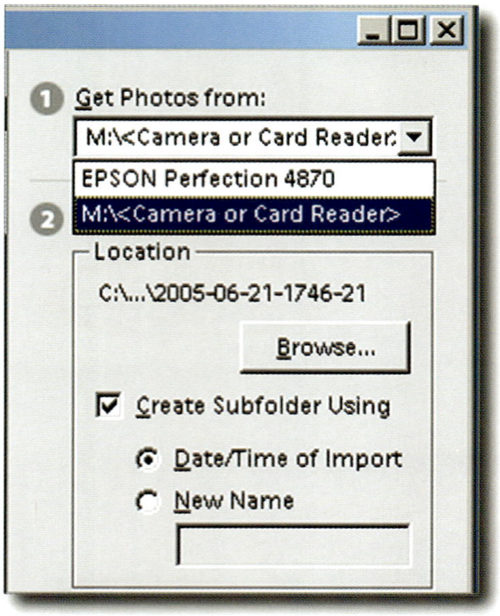

Unplugging the Card Reader

You may then remove your memory card. We recommend that you don't unplug your card reader. However, if you wish to unplug it to free up USB ports, you should click on the **green arrow** on the lower right part of the Window screen to do so.

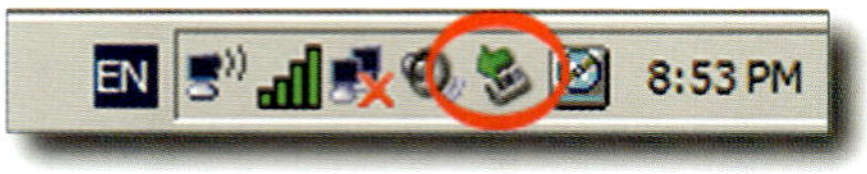

Elements Basic - Setup

Adobe Elements is a very versatile program. It is essentially two programs in one.

It can be used in its basic form to make quick fixes to photos, or in its advanced form to make high-powered photo edits.

In this chapter we will deal with the ***basic form*** and ***quick fixes.***

The Welcome Screen

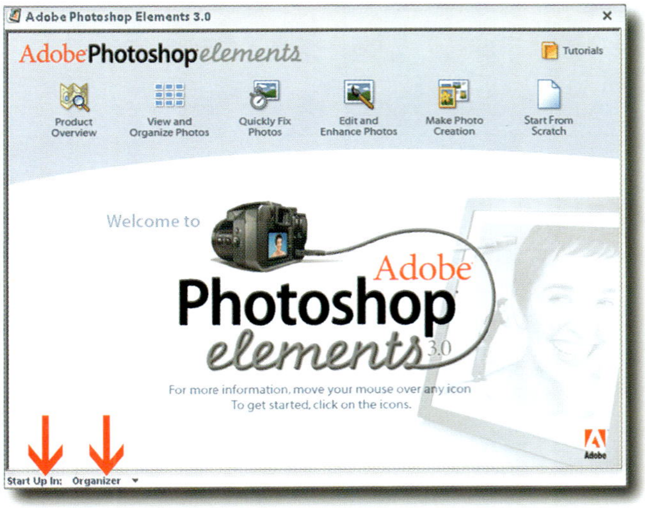

When you open Elements, the Welcome Screen appears as shown on the left. This is fine for our first time in the program, but we don't want it to appear every time we start the program. We have to get rid of it. If you look at the bottom left of the Welcome Screen, it should read: **Start Up In.**

Click the drop down menu.

No More Welcome

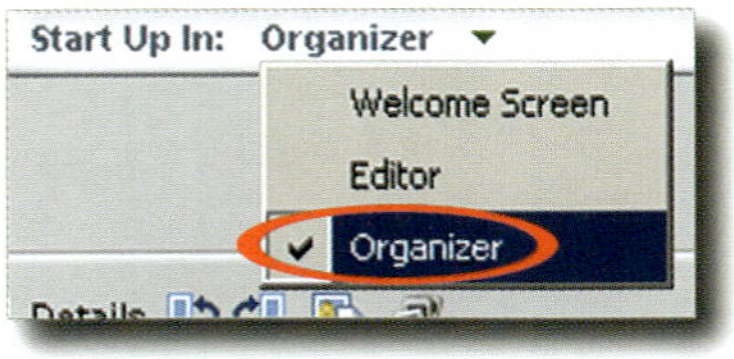

Now we want to get rid of the check mark beside "Welcome Screen". You can do this by checking something else. In this case, check the **Organizer**.

The Organizer

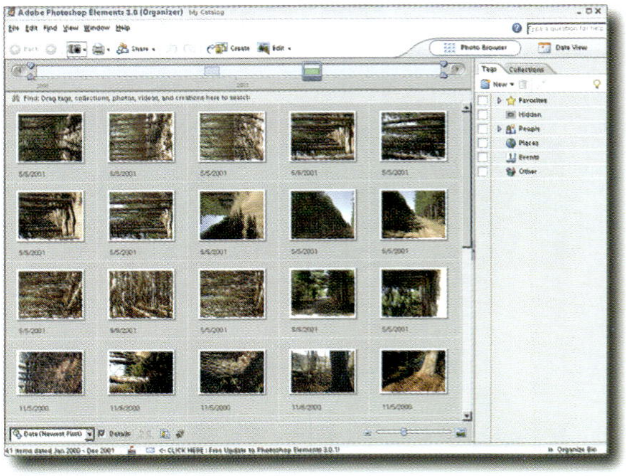

The Organizer is new for Elements 3.0. It was not present in Elements 2.

It is a major step forward and the way of the future for Elements.

Elements previously used the **File Browser**. You can still use this in Elements 3.0, but we do not advise it.

Selecting a Photo

Once your images have been downloaded from your memory card reader, the Organizer will display them for you in the Photo Well.

The Photo Well

All your downloaded images will be added to the **Photo Well**.

The **Photo Well** is the thumbnail representation of all your images. It appears in the center part of the screen.

If you do not see any of your images displayed, click the **Show All** button.

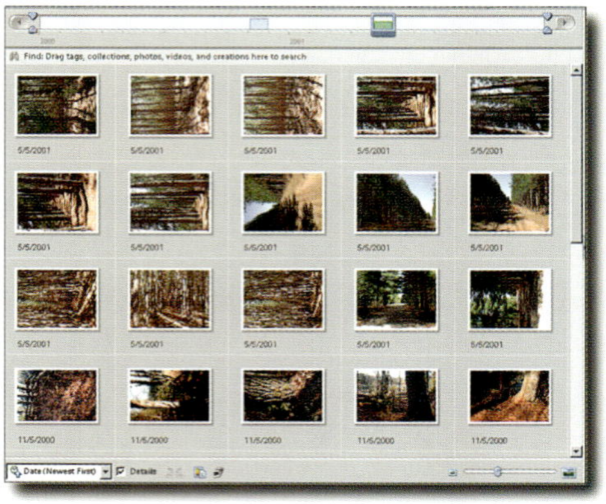

Thumbnail View Size

Use the **Thumbnail Views** slider at the bottom right corner of the screen to resize the images in the **Photo Well** as desired.

As the slider is moved to the right, the images get bigger and fewer images fit on the screen.

As the slider is moved to the left, the images get smaller and more images fit on the screen.

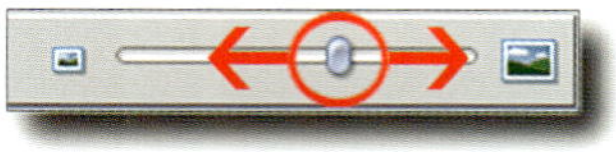

The Selected Photo

When you find the photo that you want in the **Photo Well,** click on it.

A colored box will appear around this image to indicate that you have selected it to work on.

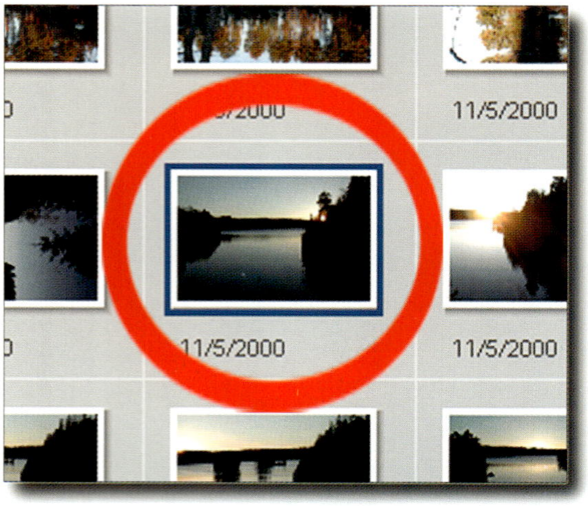

Quick Fix - Getting Started

You may wish to improve some of your images. In this section we will deal with the initial set up for the repair process.

The Fix Screen

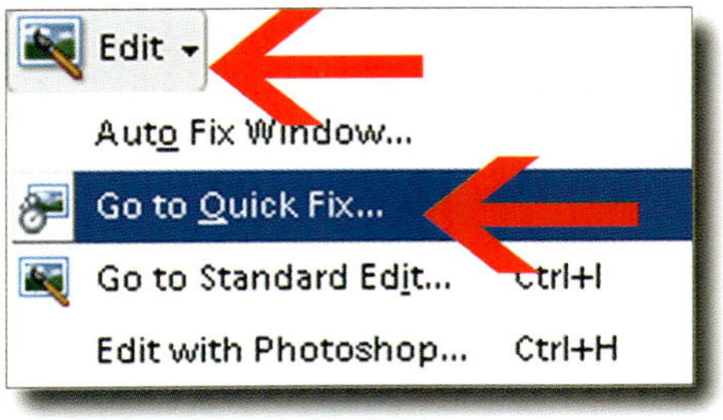

Once you have selected the image you wish to work on, you should select the following from the Main menu:

Edit > Go to Quick Fix…

This action will bring up the Main Fix Screen interface where you will make all of your repairs.

Before & After

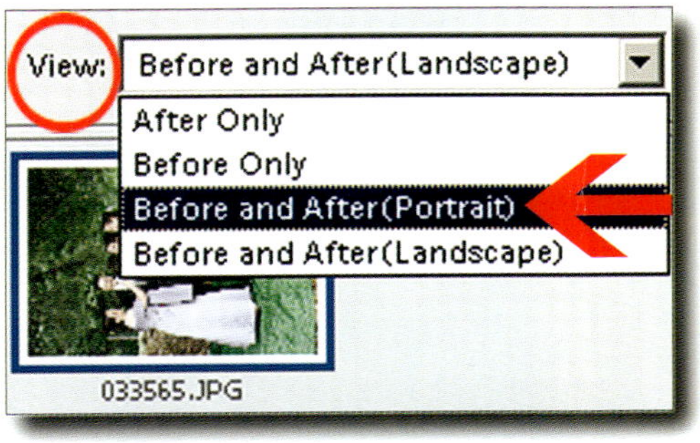

When making changes to your images, it is helpful to see the before and after images.

Select the following:

View > Before and After (Portrait)

The left pane will show the photo without any changes. The right pane will show the cumulative effect of your changes.

You may need to click on **Fit On Screen** to see your images properly.

Rotate Image

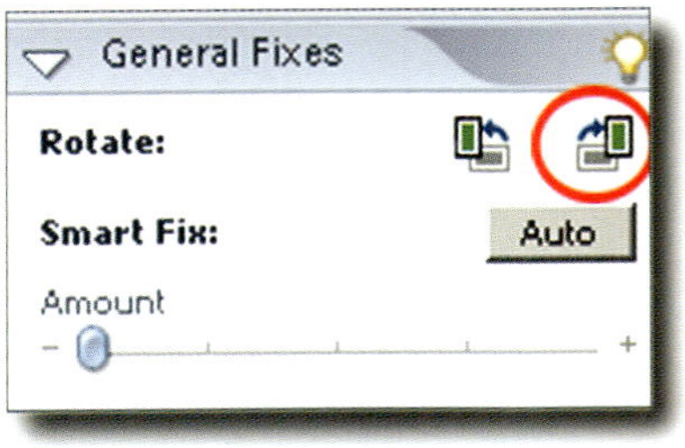

We recommend that you rotate the image if it is necessary.

To rotate, click on one of the icons circled in red.

The **left icon** will rotate the image to the left, or counter-clockwise.

The **right icon** will rotate the image to the right, or clockwise.

Quick Fix - Smart General Corrections

In this section we will use Adobe Elements Basic to make automated image repairs with a possible manual override of the automatic fixes.

The General button

Once you have selected an image and clicked **Edit > Go to Quick Fix**, you'll be taken to the **Fix** section of the program.

To make general corrections, click the **General Fixes** button.

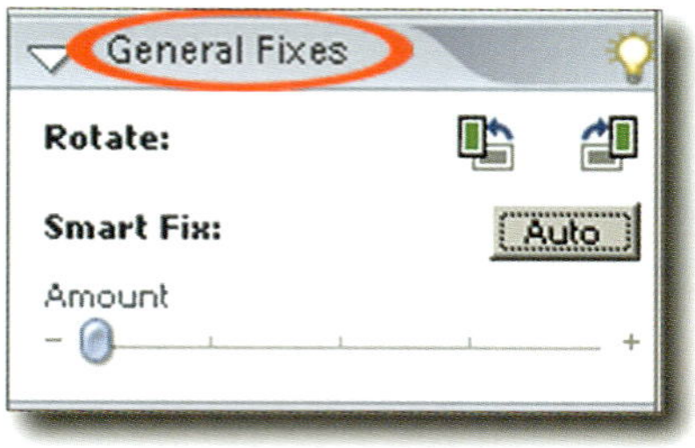

Automatic Smart Fix

Elements can attempt to complete an Automatic fix for the entire image.

We do ***not recommend*** this. We feel the program can rarely make the image the way you want it. But you should try it out first.

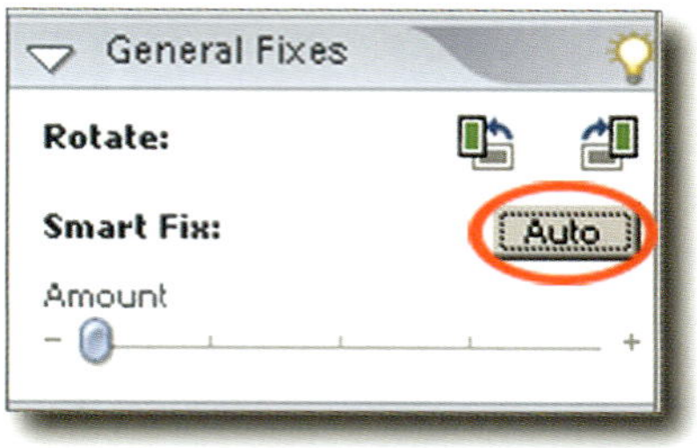

If you are unhappy with the **Auto** Fix, you can click the **Reset** button.

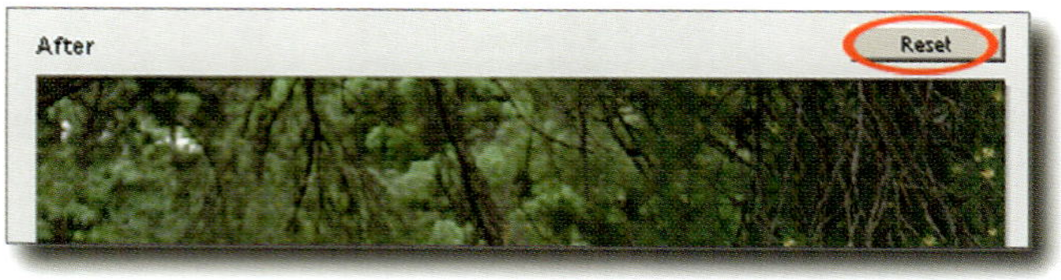

Manual Fixes

After the **Auto** Fix, you can apply a **Manual Override**.

This is accomplished by using the **Amount** slider.

We do ***not recommend*** this approach for most images. You can only adjust what the program thinks you want your image to look like. But you can give it a try.

If you want to <u>undo</u> your Manual Override, click the **Cancel** button marked by a circle with a line through it.

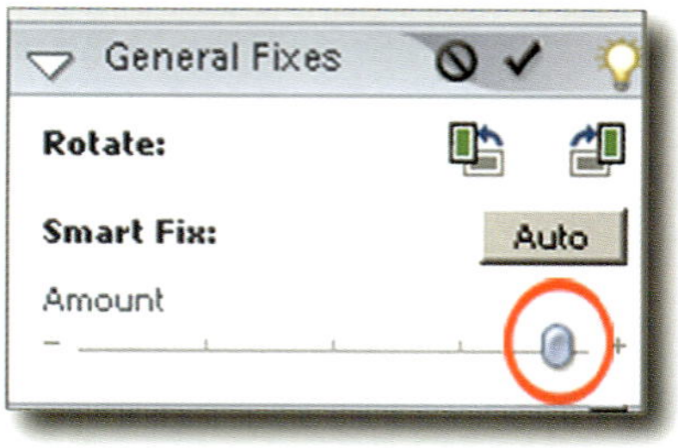

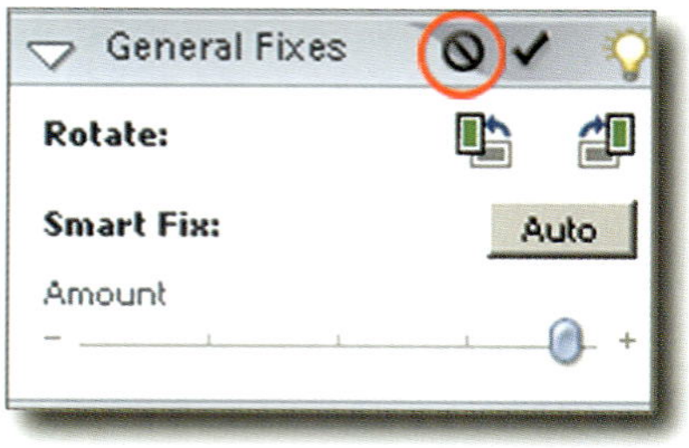

Quick Fix - Smart Specific Corrections

We can use Adobe Elements Basic to make automated image corrections with manual overrides.

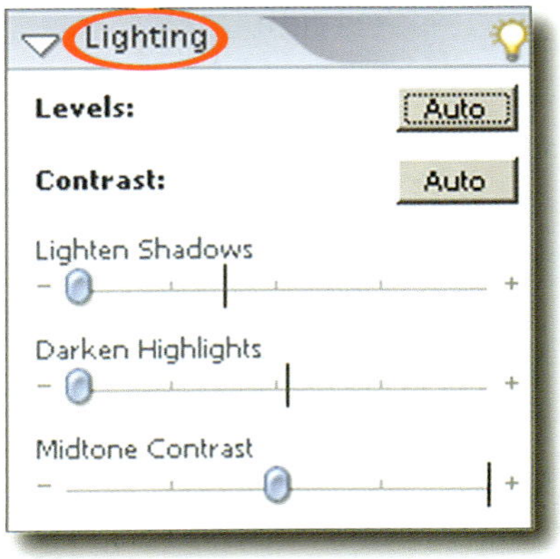

The Lighting button

Once you have selected the image you wish to work on and clicked the **Edit** button > **Go to Quick Fix**. You will be taken to the **Fix** section of the program.

To make tone corrections, click the **Lighting** button.

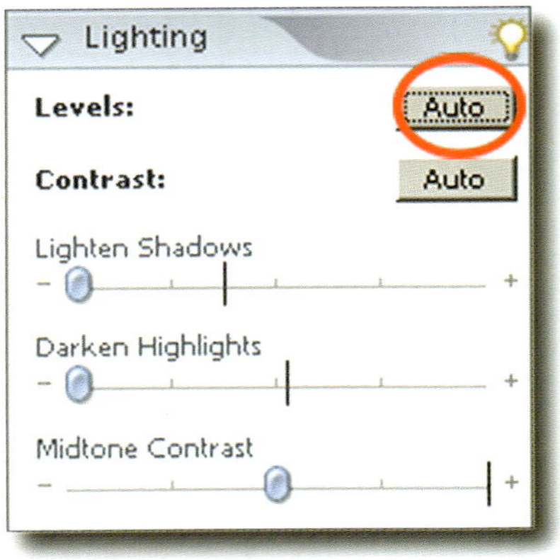

Auto Levels

Levels is a tool used by Elements to correct the tones in your image.

Elements can attempt to complete an Automatic Levels Fix for the entire image.

We ***recommend*** you let the program do so initially. It's best to correct the tones automatically, and you will have some manual override.

Beside **Levels**, click the **Auto** button.

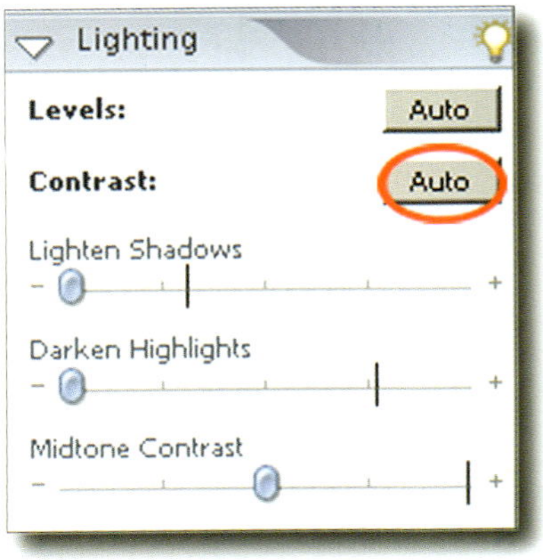

Auto Contrast

Contrast is a tool used by Elements to give images more punch. It does this by darkening the dark parts and lightening the light parts of the image.

Elements can attempt to complete an Automatic Contrast Fix for the entire image.

We do ***not recommend*** you let the program attempt to correct the contrast.

Recommended: Auto Level + Manual

We recommend that you use **Auto Levels** and then ***manually*** make the fine-tuning adjustments listed below.

Auto Levels

No **Auto Contrast**

Use **Lighten Shadows** Slider to taste

Use **Darken Highlights** Slider to taste

Use **Midtone Contrast** Slider to taste

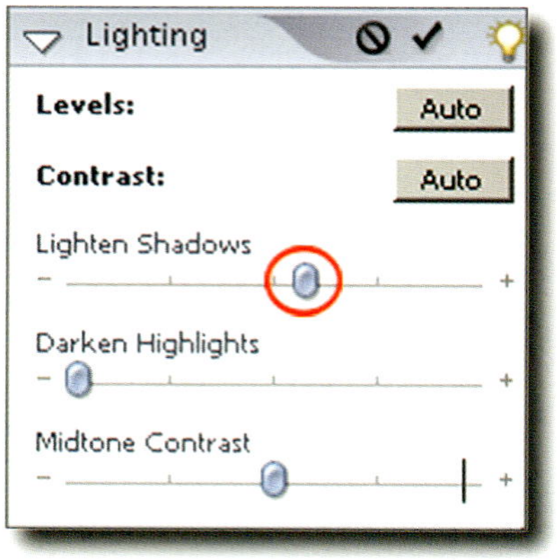

Recommended: Auto Color + Manual

We recommend that you let Elements attempt to set the colors automatically.

It usually does a good job of color correction.

If you wish to fine-tune any of the color settings, you can move the sliders to taste.

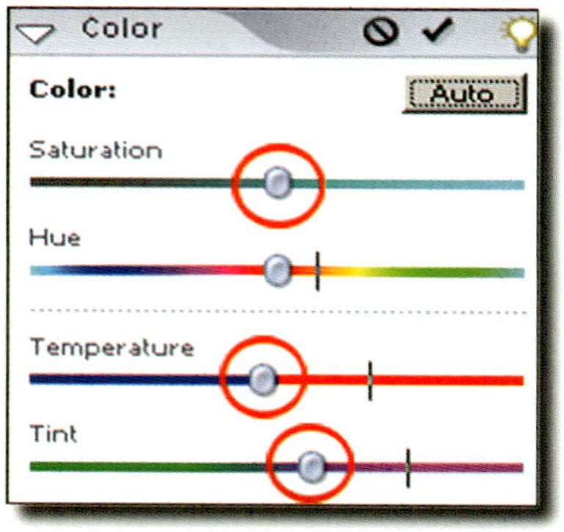

Recommended: Auto Sharpening + Manual

Almost all digital images need to be sharpened. Sharpening is difficult to assess on the screen and may look entirely different in print.

We recommend that you use **Auto Sharpen** and then possibly use a little extra gentle manual sharpening in a few images for extra sharpness.

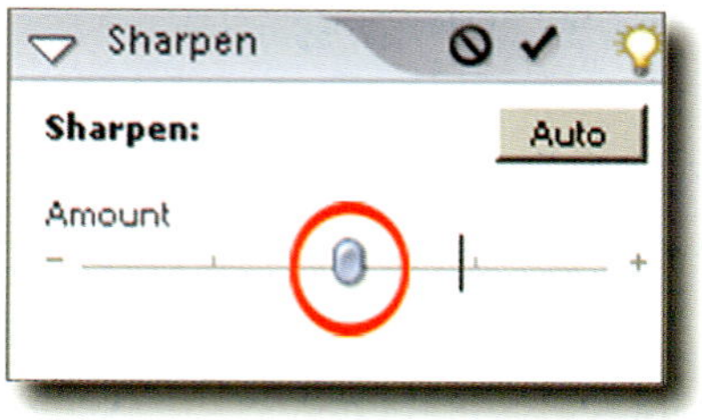

Undoing Adjustments

If you are unhappy with your adjustments at any time, you can click the **Undo** button. It is a circle marked with the line through it.

This will take you back to the beginning of your changes. You may have to rotate the image again.

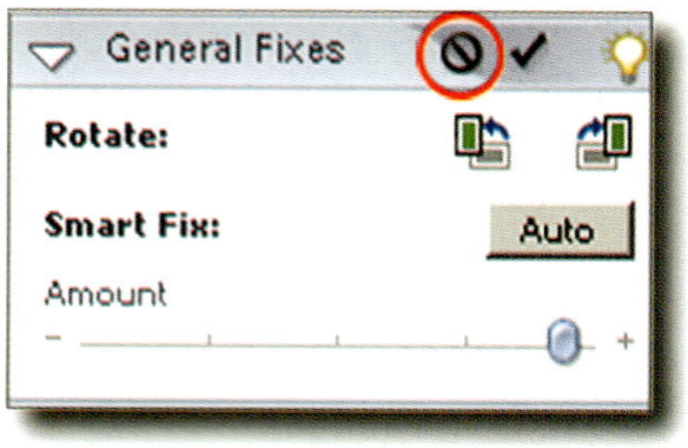

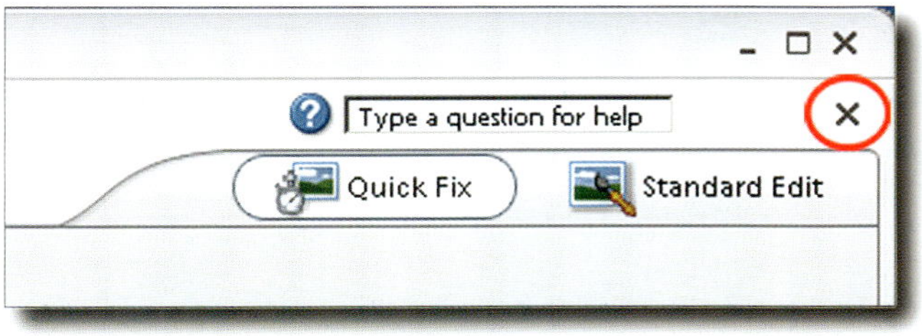

Exit Quick Fix

To leave the **Quick Fix** screen, click the **X** button.

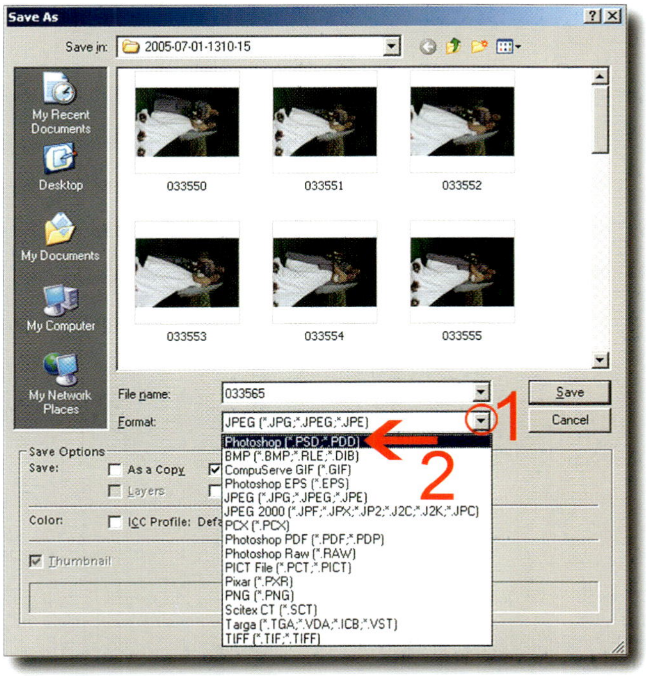

Save Format

The image from your camera was probably saved in a file format called **JPEG**. This format will recompress your image every time it saves it. This will result in a loss of quality.

We recommend that you convert your corrected image to Adobe's file format: **PSD**. This is a lossless format that will not damage the quality of your image.

To accomplish this, click the down arrow beside **Format.**

Then choose

Photoshop PSD

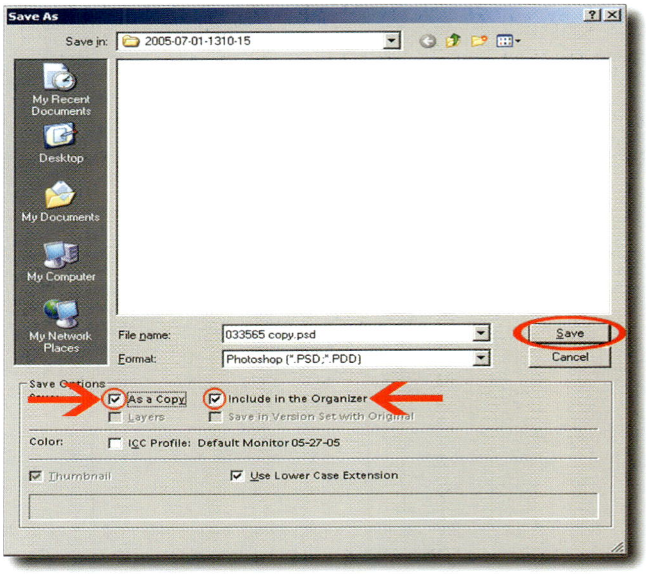

Where to Save your Photos

Click the indicated check boxes to save the image:

As a Copy

Include in the Organizer

The corrected image will now appear to the right of the original image in the **Photo Well**.

Note: The original image still exists untouched.

There is now a ***second image*** with your ***changes in effect***.

Fixing a Photo - Red Eye

Often after images are captured by digital flash photography, you will want to get rid of **Red Eye** - red pupils. **Red Eye** is a tool that allows you to do this.

The Red Eye Button

Once you have selected the image you wish to work on and clicked the **Fix** button and **Go to Quick Fix**, you will be taken to the **Fix** section of the program.

To fix red eye, you must click the **Red Eye Correction** tool button.

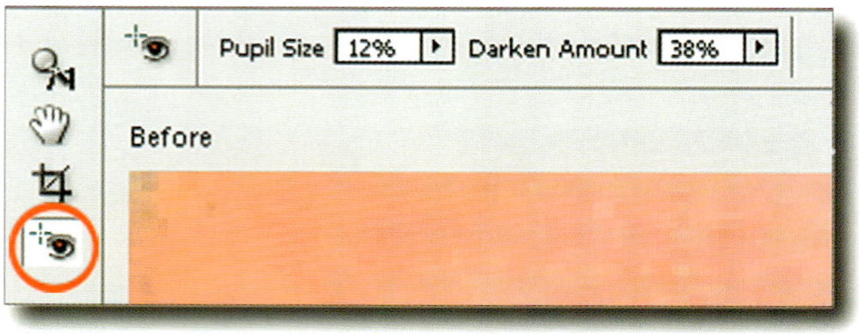

Applying Red Eye Correction

With the **Red Eye Removal** tool selected, drag it over one red eye area so there is a square selection around the entire eye.

The red will be replaced with a neutral color.

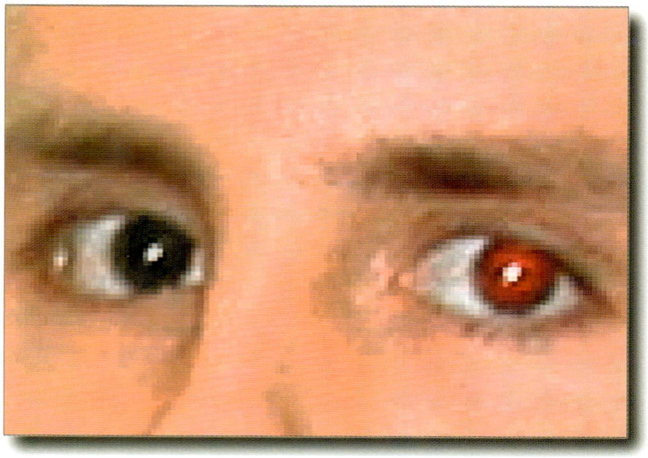

Fine-Tuning Corrections

You can now fine-tune the size and darkness of the pupil.

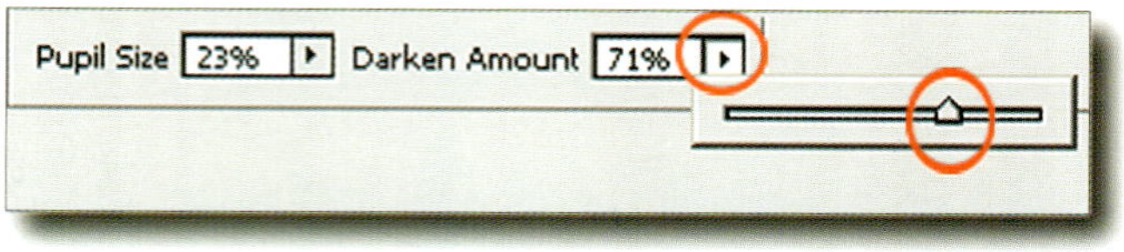

Finishing Red Eye Correction

Now you should exit the **Quick Fix** screen and save the changes to your image.

Methods for exiting and saving were outlined in chapter 7, page 107.

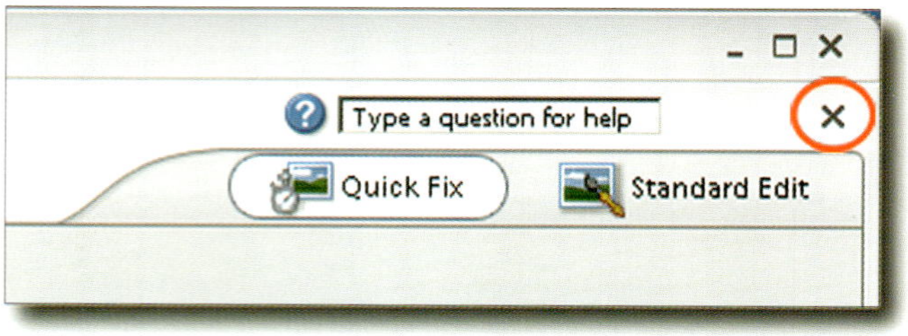

Fixing a Photo – Cropping

In this chapter we will deal with cropping your image either without restriction or to a specific size and/or shape.

The Crop Button

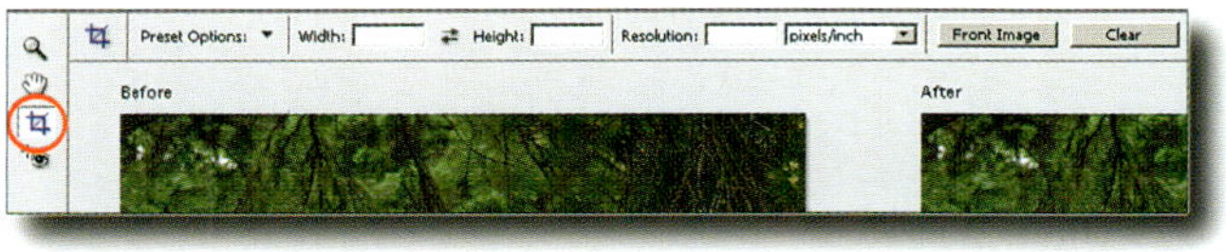

Once you have selected the image you wish to work on and clicked the **Fix** button and **Go to Quick Fix**, you will be taken to the **Fix** section of the program.

To crop, you must click the **Crop** button.

Unrestricted Crop

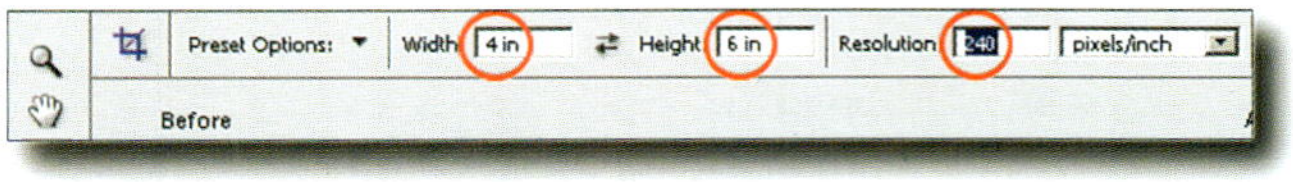

Sometimes you will want to crop an image to any shape – whatever you deem makes the best photograph.

Using this method, you can set your preferred dimensions for your image:

1. **Width**
2. **Height**
3. **Resolution**
   240 for prints
   72 or 96 for emailing

You will notice a white square show up at the top of your image. You can drag this box around your image to resize it as desired.

Cropping to Preset Dimension

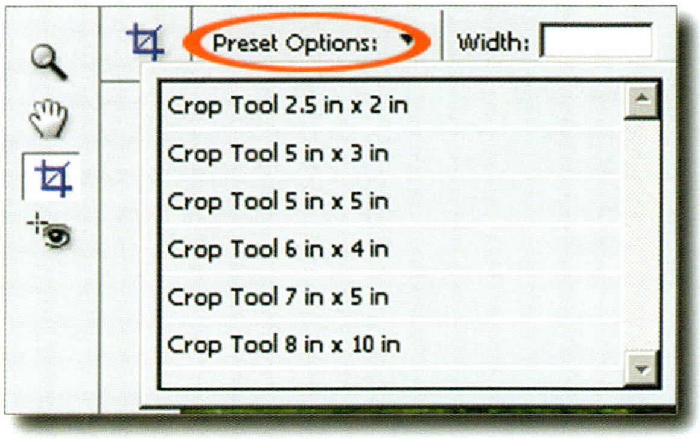

Other times you will want to crop the image to a specific shape, or aspect ratio.

There are a number of **Preset Options** that contain the most common aspect ratios.

You can select one of these to use.

Printing Photos

In this lesson, we will use Adobe Elements Basic to select an image, or several images, to print.

Selecting Photo(s) to Print

If you want to print one photo, click on a photo in the **Photo Well**.

If you want to select several photos to print as a group, just hold down **Ctrl** and click on all the photos you want to print in the **Photo Well**.

A border will appear around each picture you have selected.

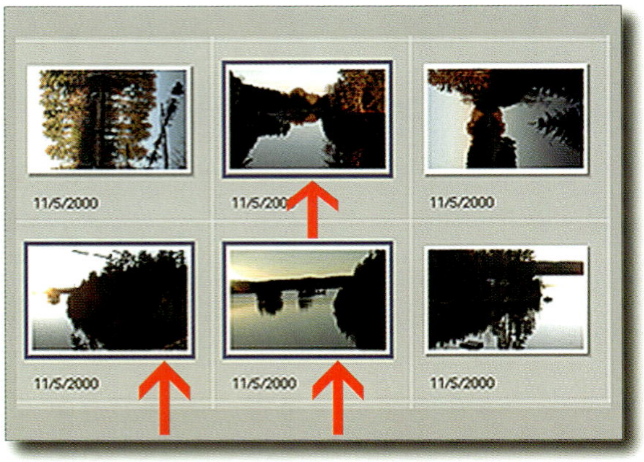

Selecting Print Function

From the Main menu, select the **Print…** function.

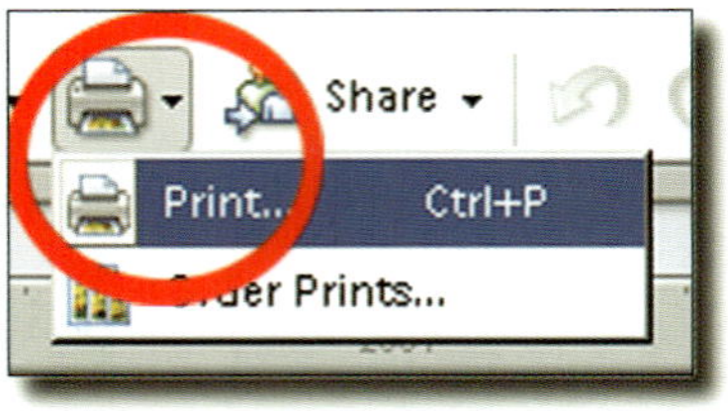

Select Printer and Layout

You must select the printer you wish to use as well as the number of copies.

Select a layout:

1. Individual Prints: use this to print <u>one</u> photo.

2. Contact Sheet: use this to print small prints of <u>**several different**</u> images on the same page in columns and rows.

3. Picture Package: use this to print <u>**several copies**</u> of the <u>**same**</u> image on one page.

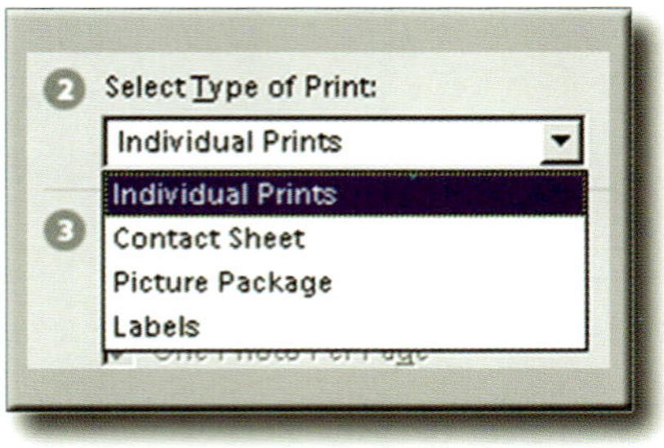

Print It

When you are ready to print, click the **Print** button.

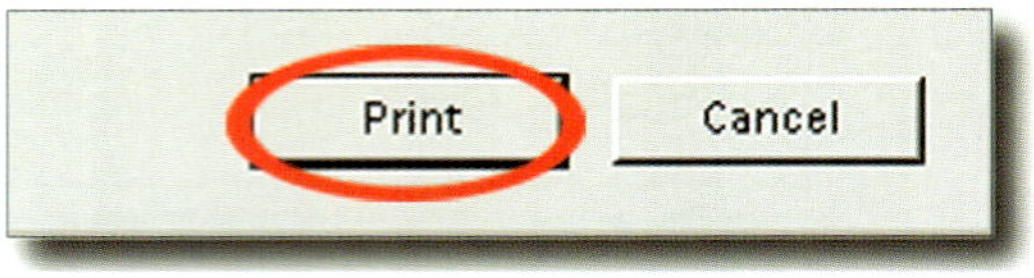

Emailing Photos

In this lesson, we will select a photo to email. The photo will then become an attachment in our usual email program.

Selecting Photo(s) to Email

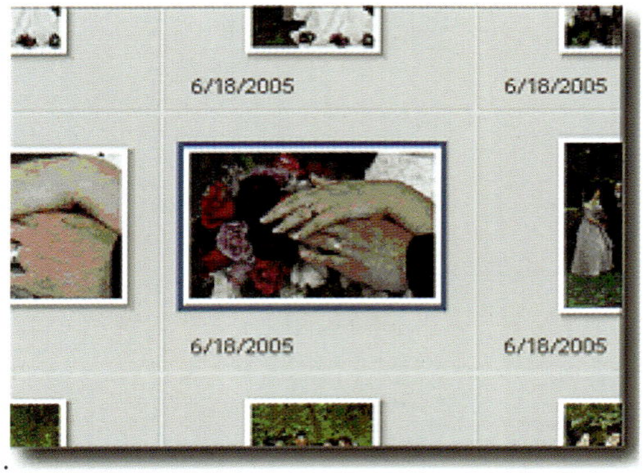

Click on the photo you wish to email.

A border will appear around the selected photo.

Select Email Function

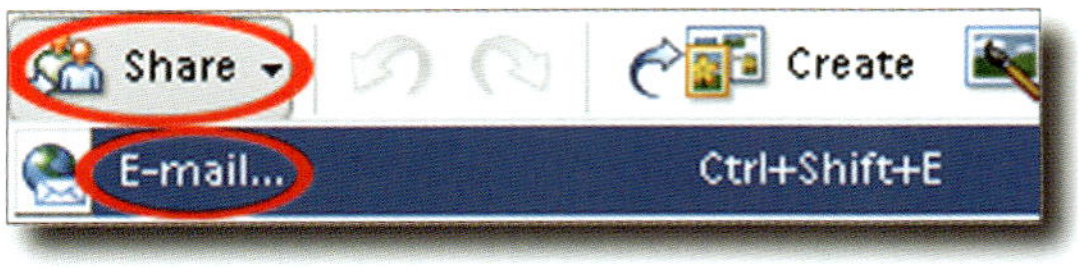

In the Icon menu, click the **Share** button.

In the drop down menu, click the **E-mail...** button.

Select Size and Quality

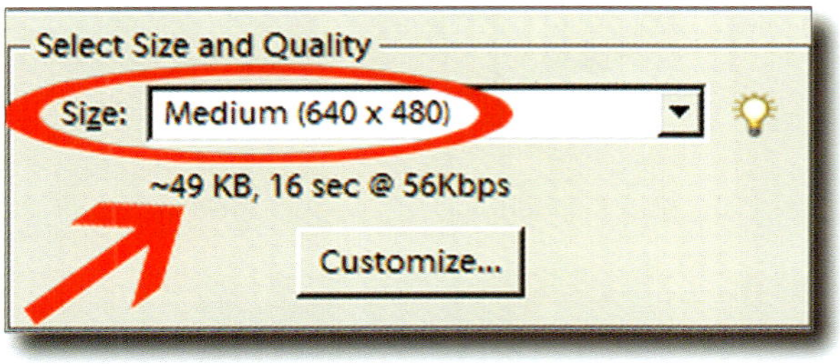

An estimated time of 16 sec is required to transmit this image. (16 sec @ transmission speed of 56Kbps).

Send Email

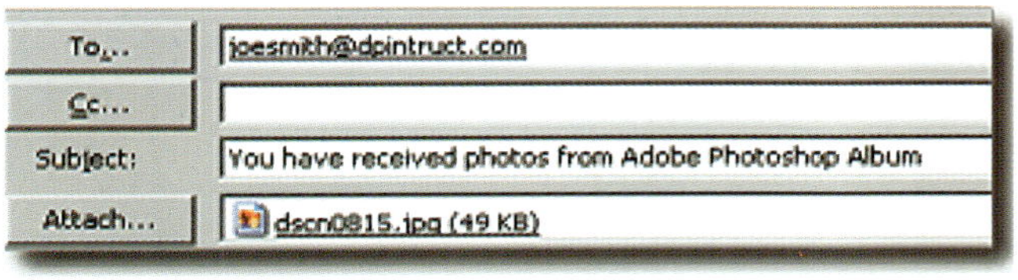

After this, you will be dropped into your email program. The photo will automatically become an attachment.

Click the **Send** button.

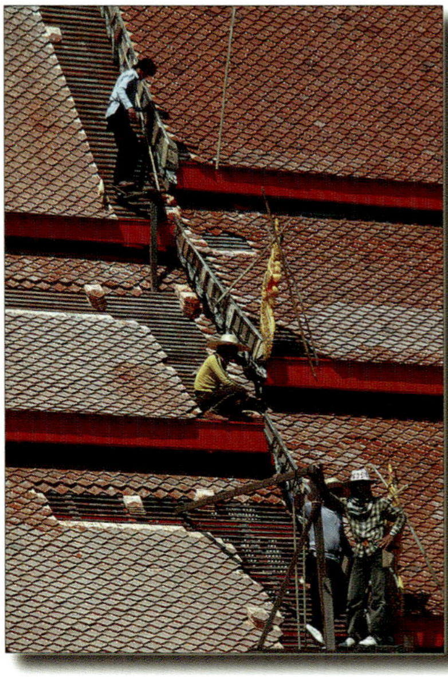
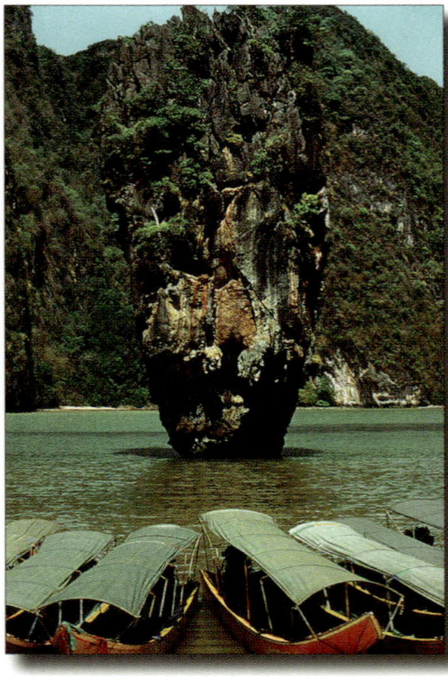
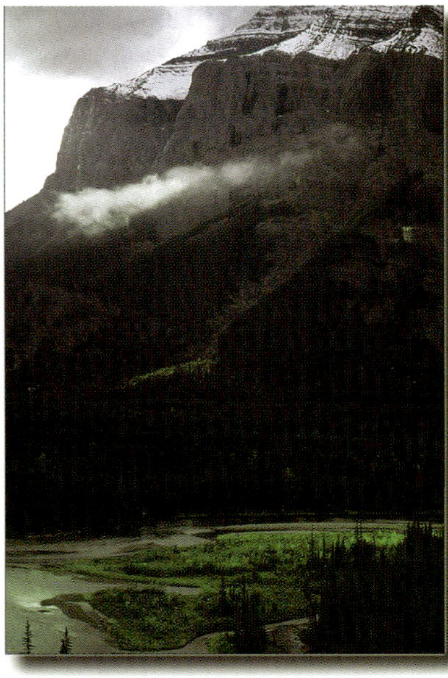
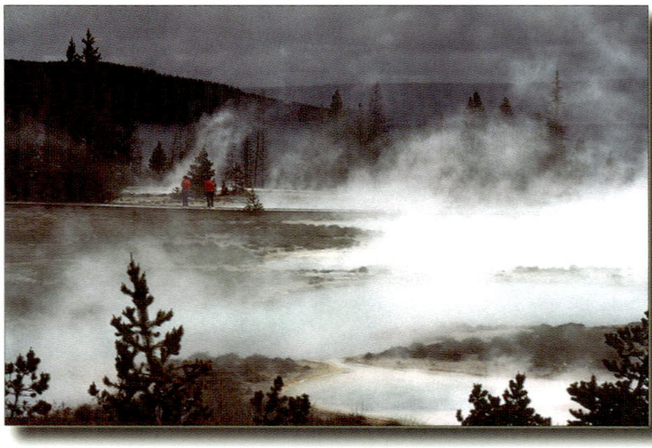
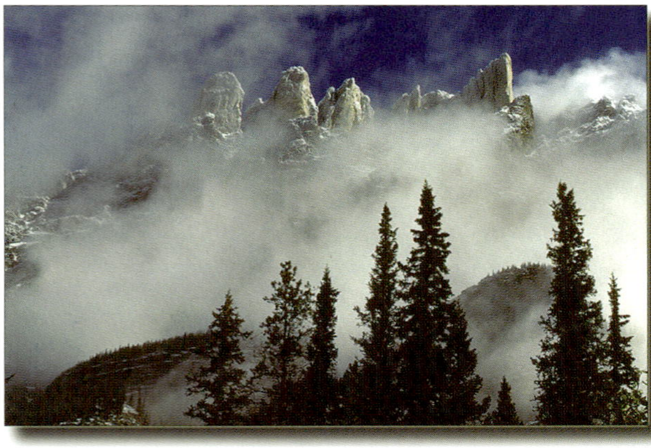
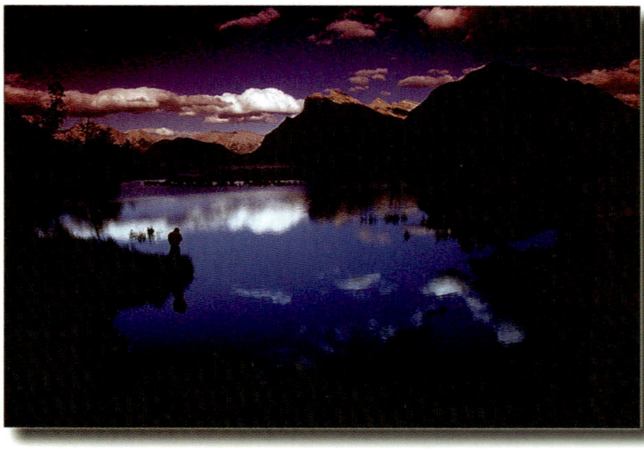
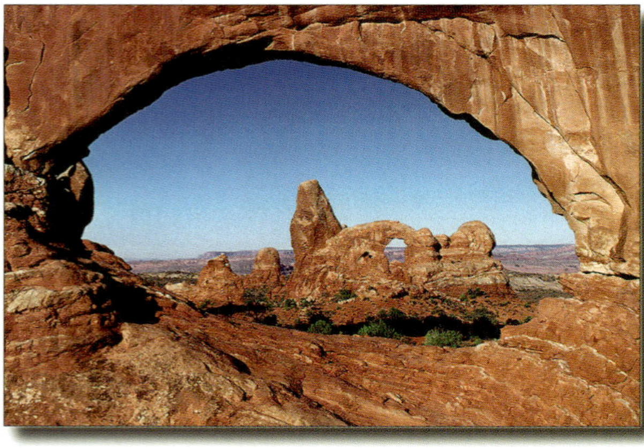

Photos by Antony Chow

Chapter 9 ADOBE ELEMENTS ADVANCED

Adobe Elements Advanced

Adobe Elements is the next step up from Adobe Album Full. This program can be used in two modes: Basic or Advanced.

In Basic you can copy pictures into a computer, view, print or email them. However, Elements Advanced allows you to perform many of the sophisticated advanced editing techniques used by professional photographers.

This version allow CD and DVD back up.

Introduction

Elements 3.0 Advanced will give you the ability to download your pictures directly into the program. It will organize your pictures and show you thumbnails of them. In addition, it will allow you to make advanced manual corrections to your pictures. You will then be able to print or email your pictures.

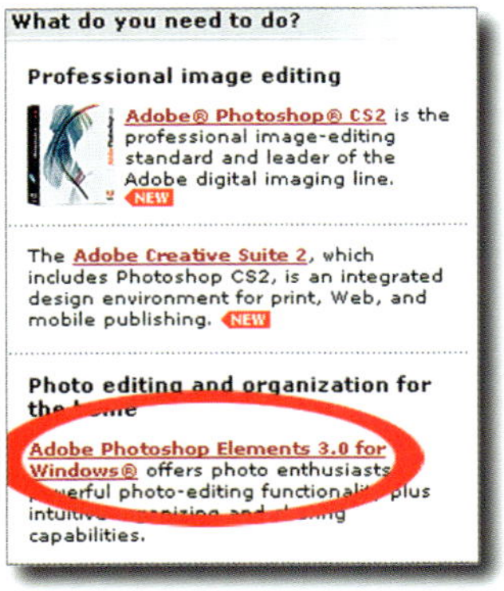

Getting the Program

To acquire this program, you must purchase it for about $90 US (in 2006).

You can purchase it online at www.adobe.com. Select **Products**, and follow the links to **Elements**.

You can also purchase the program through various commercial outlets.

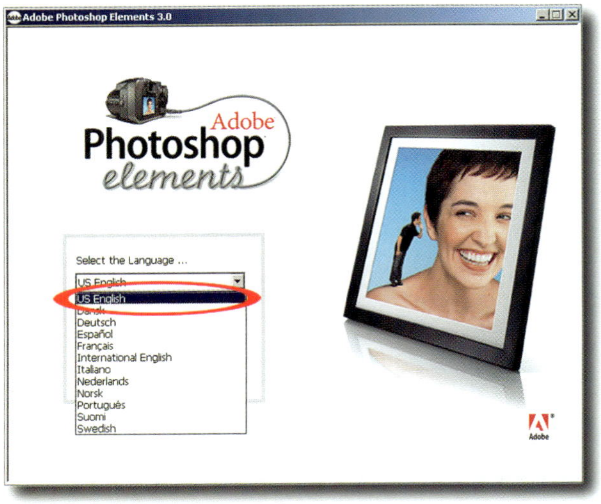

Installing The Program

Click the **Installer** program you have downloaded from Adobe or place the CD you have purchased in the computer. Follow the screen instructions to finish the installation of the actual program itself. You will have to accept their legal agreement. The **Quick Guide** will then appear on the screen. Turn it off by clicking in the lower left hand corner. Go to the Main menu and select **Help**. Click on **Registration** and then enter the **Unlock Code** that you received from Adobe by email, or with your CD.

Card Readers

Memory Card Readers are an inexpensive accessory that will streamline your digital workflow. They allow you to continue to use your camera while downloading images. The card reader you buy must match the type of memory card used by your camera.

Installing The Card Reader

Plug your card reader into one of the unused USB ports on your computer. Windows should recognize it and state:

New hardware found

Then Windows should announce:

New hardware is installed and ready to use

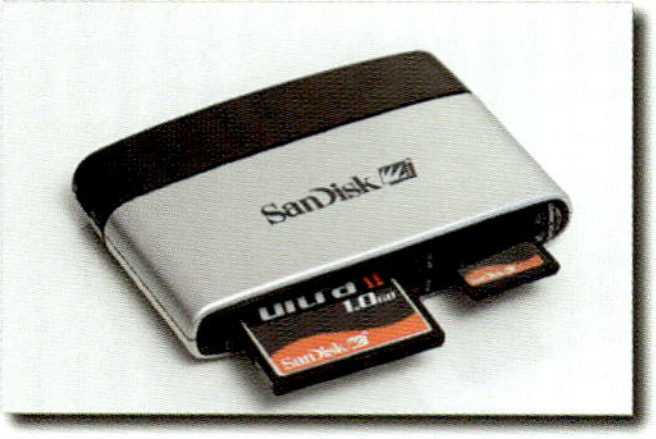

Using the Card Reader

Insert your full memory card into the card reader.

There are two ways to download photos:

1. The Adobe Downloader will pop up and offer to download your images. **<u>Or</u>**

2. From the Main menu, choose:

Get Photos

From Camera or Card Reader

Click **OK** to load the images.

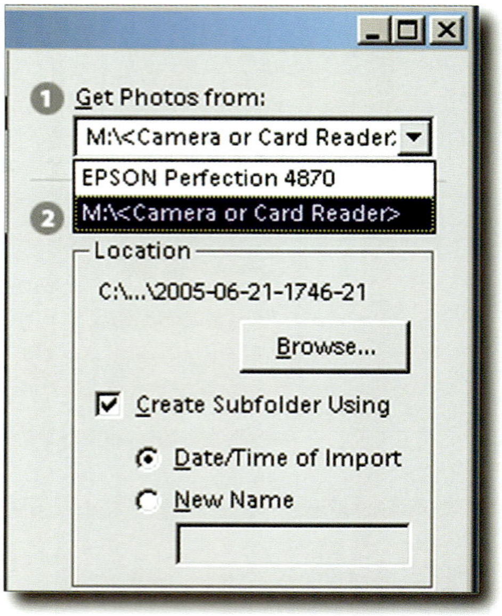

Unplugging the Card Reader

You may then remove your memory card. We recommend that you don't unplug your card reader. However, if you wish to unplug it to free up USB ports, you should click on the **green arrow** on the lower right part of the Window screen to do so.

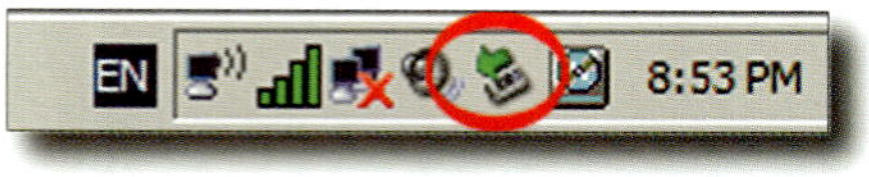

Elements Advanced - Setup

Adobe Elements is a very versatile program. It is essentially two programs in one.

It can be used in its basic form to make quick fixes to photos, or in its advanced form to make high-powered photo edits.

In this chapter we will deal with the ***advanced form*** and more ***advanced & powerful fixes.***

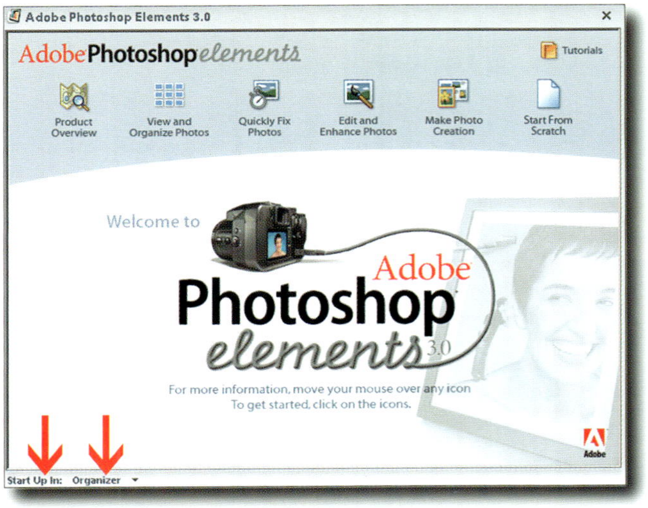

The Welcome Screen

The Welcome Screen appears as shown on the right. This is fine for our first time in the program, but we don't want it to appear every time we open the program. We have to get rid of it. If you look at the bottom left of the Welcome Screen, it should read: **Start Up In:**

Click the **Drop Down menu** button.

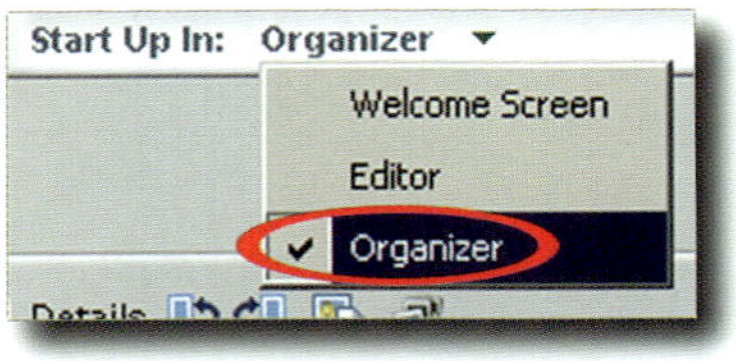

No More Welcome

Now we want to get rid of the check mark beside "Welcome Screen". You can do this by checking something else. That something else is **Organizer**.

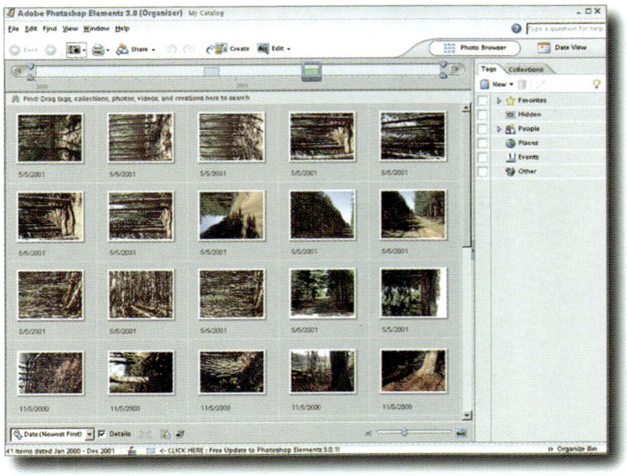

The Organizer

The Organizer is new for Elements 3.0. It was not present in Elements 2.

It is a major step forward and the way of the future for Elements.

Elements previously used the **File Browser**. You can still use this in Elements 3.0, but we do not advise it.

Selecting a Photo

Once your images have been downloaded from your memory card reader, the Organizer will display them for you in the Photo Well.

The Photo Well

All your downloaded images will be added to the **Photo Well.**

The **Photo Well** is the thumbnail representation of all your images. It appears in the center part of the screen.

If you do not see any of your images displayed, click the **Show All** button.

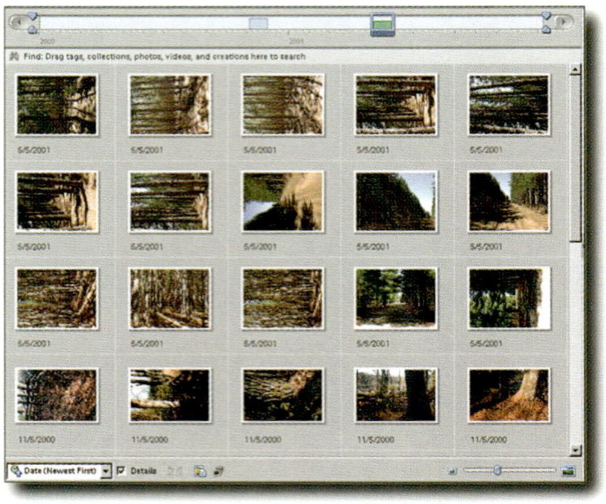

Thumbnail View Size

Use the **Thumbnail Views** slider at the bottom right corner of the screen to resize the images in the **Photo Well** as desired.

As the slider is moved to the right, the images get bigger and fewer images fit on the screen.

As the slider is moved to the left, the images get smaller and more images fit on the screen.

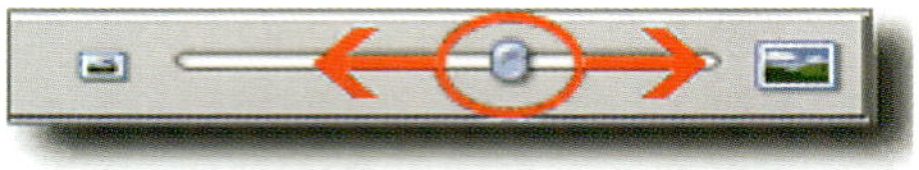

The Selected Photo

When you find the photo that you want in the **Photo Well**, click on it.

A box will appear around this image to indicate that you have selected it to work on.

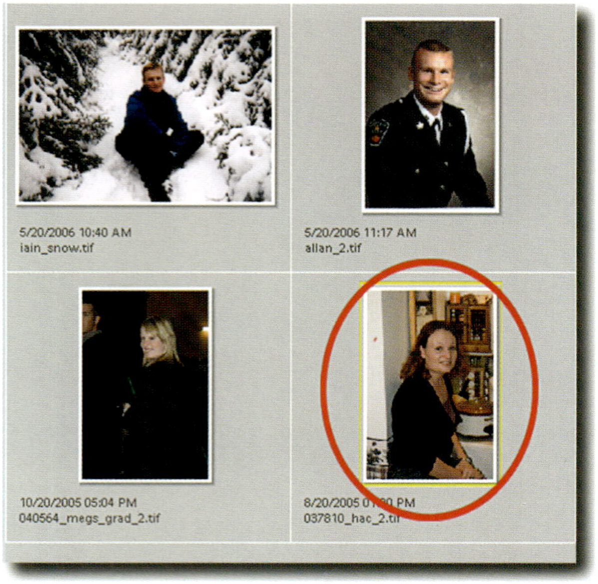

Standard Edit - Rotating

In this section we will deal with rotating your images to the correct orientation and we will discuss automatic horizon leveling. This either works very well or not at all. If it doesn't work, refer to the web site for instruction.

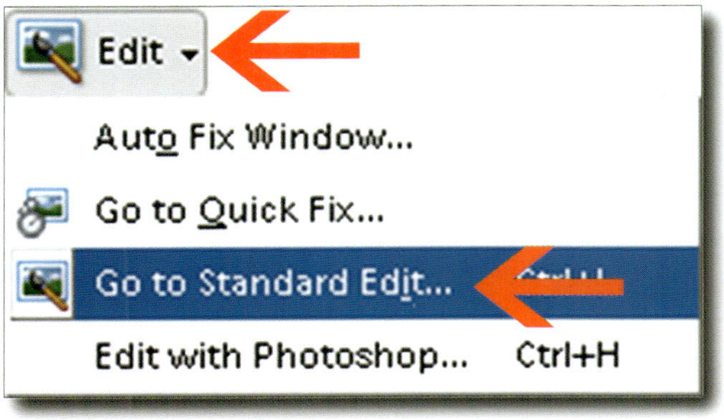

The Standard Edit Screen

Once you have selected the image you wish to work on, you should select the following from the Main menu:

Edit > Go to Standard Edit

This action will bring up the Standard Edit Screen interface where you will make all of your repairs.

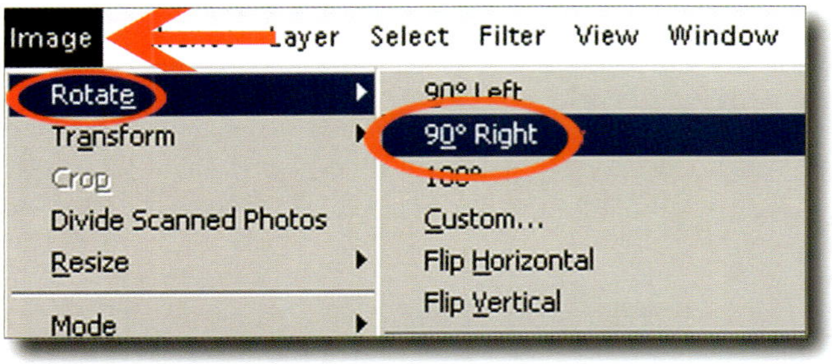

Rotate Image

To rotate your image, you go to the Main menu and click the **Image** button, then choose **Rotate**.

Then click the appropriate **Rotation direction**.

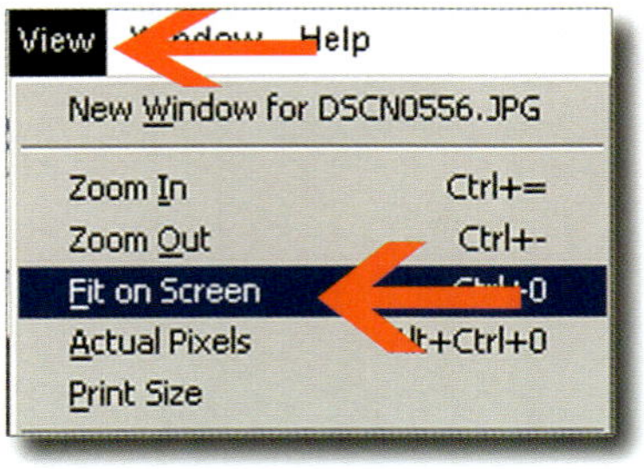

Fit on Screen

To make your image fit on the screen, choose **View**.

From the drop down menu, click the **Fit on Screen** button.

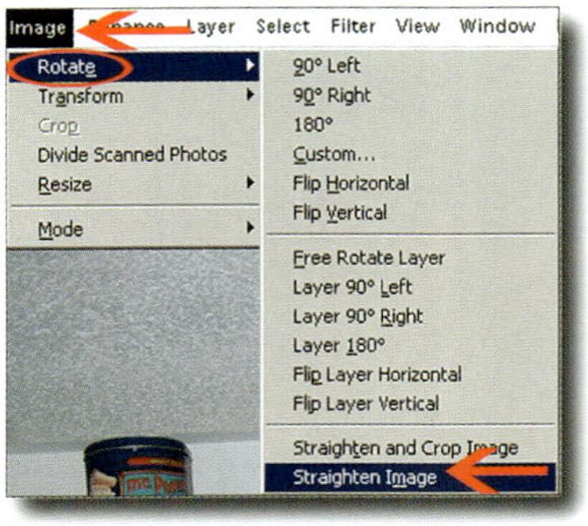

Auto Straighten Horizon

In the Main menu, choose **Image**.

From the first drop down menu, choose **Rotate**.

From the next drop down menu, choose **Straighten Image**.

Fixing a Photo - Cropping

In this chapter we will deal with cropping your image to any size and/or shape as to any specific size and/or shape.

The Crop button

Once you have selected the image that you wish to work on and clicked on the **Fix** button and **Go to Standard Edit**, you will be taken to the **Fix** section of the program.

To crop, you must select the **Crop** tool from the toolbox.

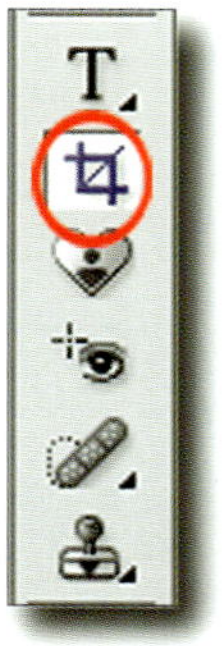

Unrestricted Crop

If you leave the **Width, Height,** and **Resolution boxes** empty, you can crop to any desired shape or size.

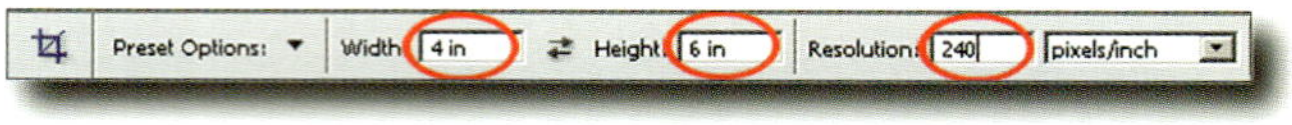

You will notice a dark square showing up at the top of your image. Click your cursor at one corner of the square and drag it over the image as desired.

Sometimes you will want to crop the image to any shape – whatever you deem makes the best photograph. Set the following on the Tool Option Bar: **Width**, **Height** and **Resolution** (240 for print 72 or 96 for emailing).

Cropping to Preset Dimension

Other times you will want to crop the image to a specific shape, or aspect ratio.

There are a number of **Preset Options** that contain the most common aspect ratios.

You can select one of these to use

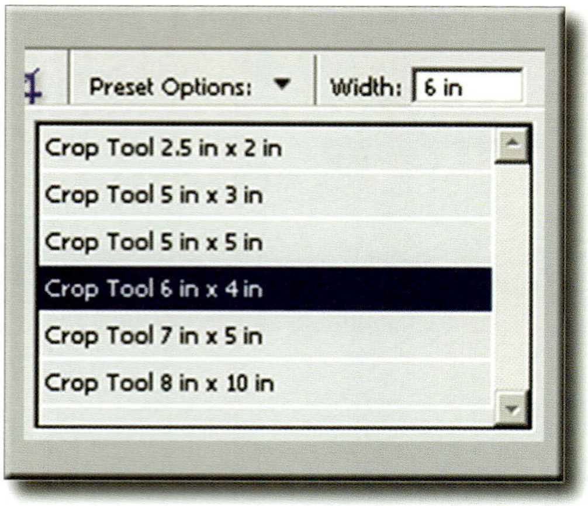

Resizing Images

In this lesson, you will learn how to resize images to the size that you desire. This is ***not cropping***, which cuts out a part of your image. When you resize, the resolution and dimensions are changed to alter the size of the entire image.

The Resize Function

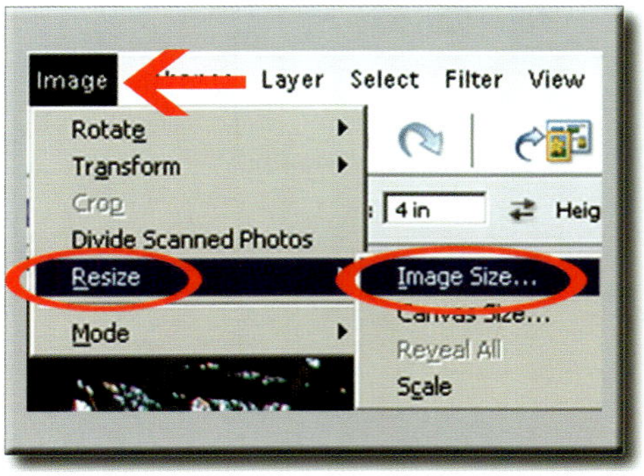

Once you have selected the image you wish to work on and clicked **Edit > Go to Standard Edit,** you will be taken to the Standard Edit section of the program.

To resize your image, choose **Image** from the Main menu.

Then choose **Resize** and **Image Size…** from the drop down menu.

Initial Settings

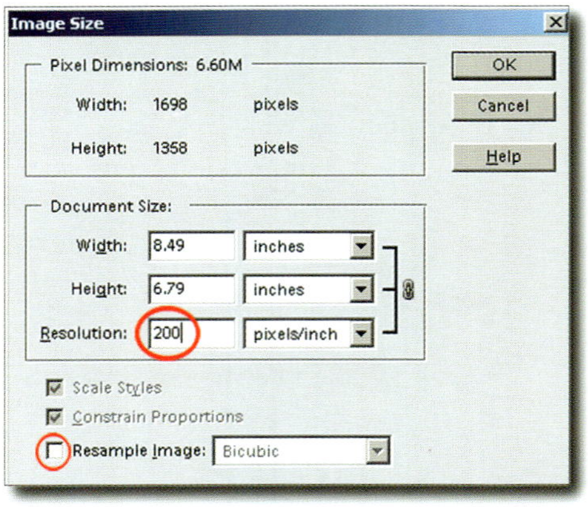

The **Image Size** screen will appear set exactly the way it was the last time that you used it. You need to change these settings:

Resolution

Set to 200 – 240 for prints or

Set to 72 -96 for email

Uncheck the **Resample Image:** button.

Correct Dimensions

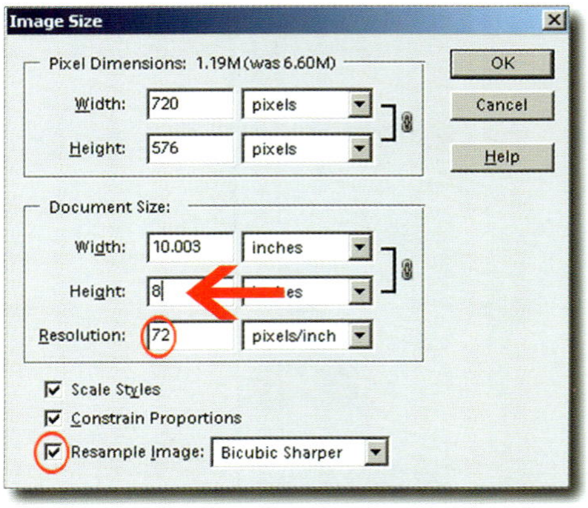

Now you need to set the dimensions that you want in your final image:

Choose **Resample = ON**

Choose **<u>one of the dimensions</u>** that you want.

The program will set the other dimension to match.

If you are making the image ***<u>larger</u>***, choose **Bicubic Smoother**.

If you are making the image ***<u>smaller</u>***, choose **Bicubic Sharper**.

Levels - Exposure Correction

In this lesson, we will show you a method of correcting images that are either overexposed or underexposed. You will use the **Levels** function to accomplish this.

Getting to the Levels Function

With your image selected, click the **Edit** button and **Go to Standard Edit**.

Choose **Enhance** from the Main menu.

Then choose **Adjust Lighting** and **Levels...** from the drop down menu.

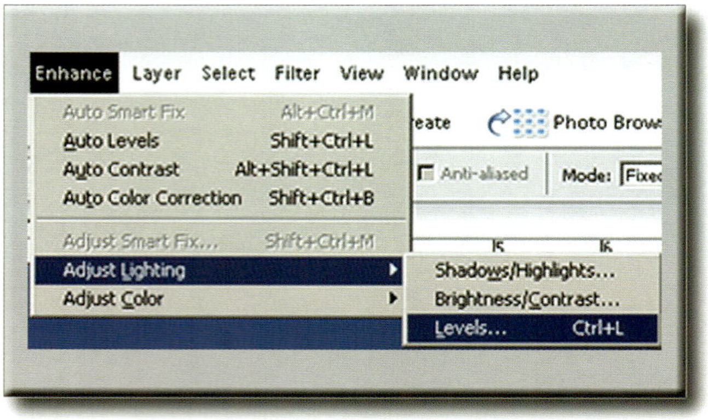

The Basics of Using Levels

<u>**Reclaim shadow area**</u> – if the left edge of the curve doesn't come to the **Black Point** – <u>**move the left slider**</u> to meet the left side of the graph, as shown.

<u>**Reclaim highlight area**</u> – if the right edge of the curve doesn't come to the **White Point** – <u>**move the right slider**</u> to meet the right side of the graph, as shown.

<u>**Move the Center Midtone slider**</u> to taste – by watching changes in the image itself.

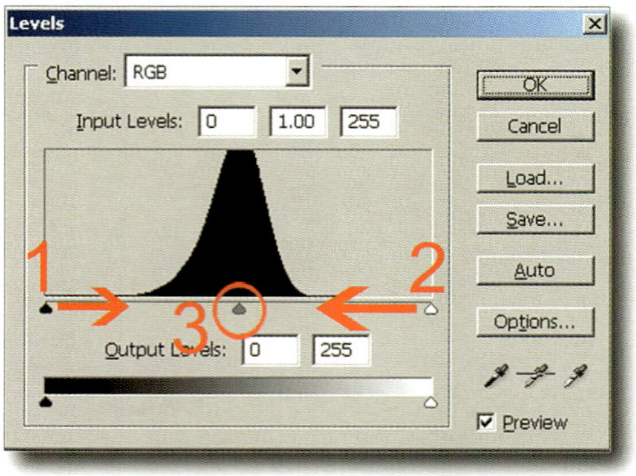

Sliders After Levels

This pane shows the sliders in their final positions.

The website now illustrates these principles with actual examples.

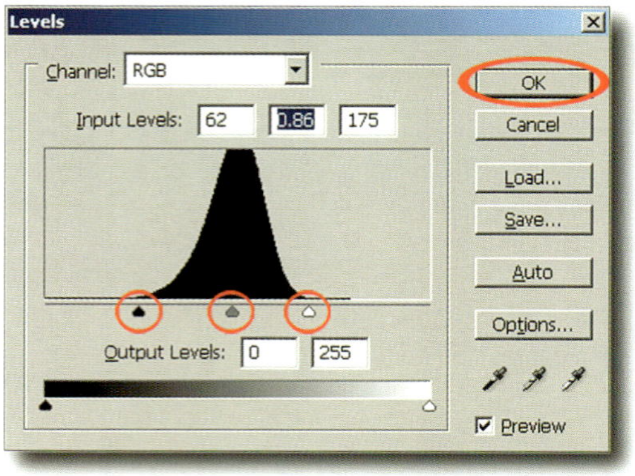

Shadows/Highlights Exposure Correction

Sometimes when we take photographs in difficult lighting, such as direct sunlight, the images have too much contrast. The shadows/highlights tool allows us to lighten the shadows and darken the highlights of an image to taste.

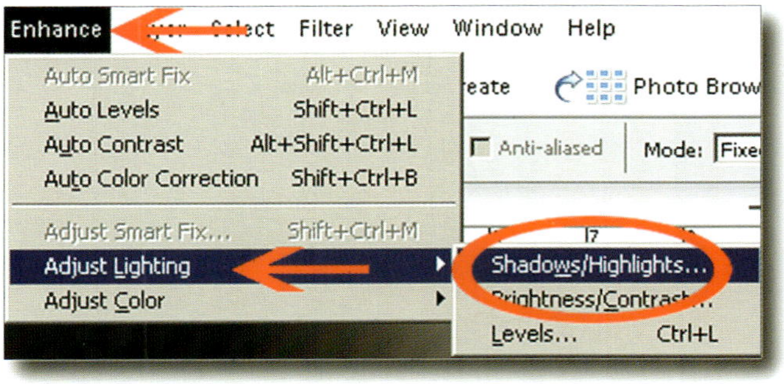

Shadow/Highlight Tool

Once you have selected the image you wish to work on, click **Edit** > **Go to Standard Edit**.

Choose **Enhance** from the main menu.

Choose **Adjust Lighting>Shadows /Highlights....**

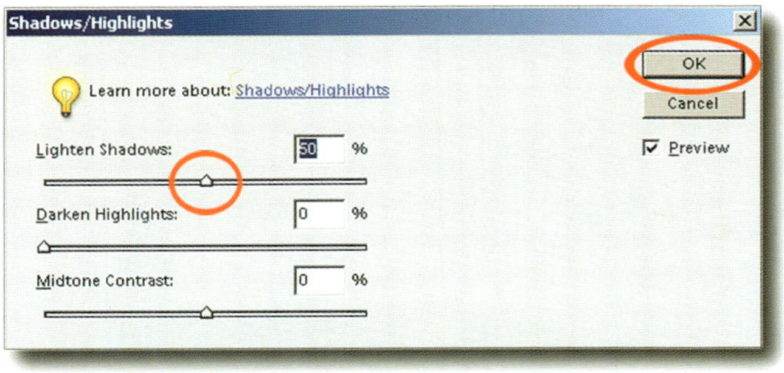

Lighten Shadows

Move the **Lighten Shadows** slider.

Watch the image for the desired effect.

Here, we set the slider at **50%**.

Click the **OK** button when all corrections are done.

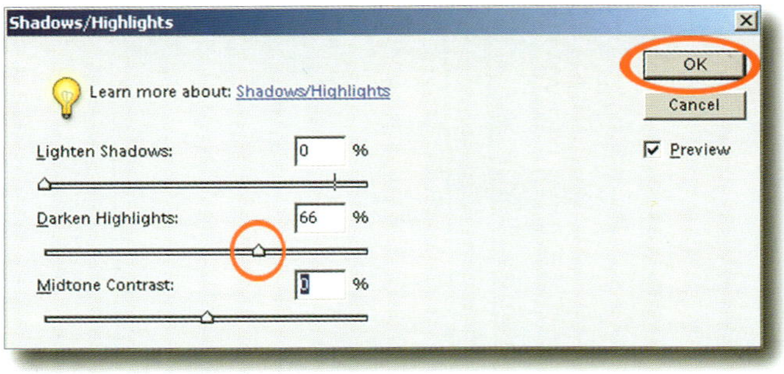

Darken Highlights

Move the **Darken Highlights** slider.

Watch the image for the desired effect:

Here, we set the slider at **66%**.

Click the **OK** button when all corrections are done.

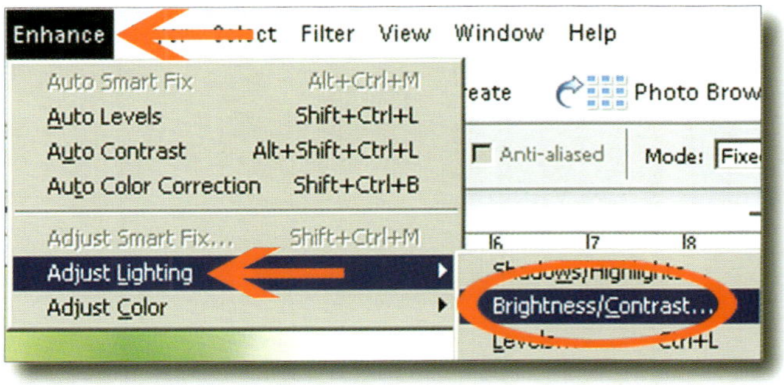

Shadow/Highlight Tool

Finally move the mid tone contrast to taste. We feel that it is better to use the **Brightness/Contrast...** tool for this part of the correction. This is explained on our website.

Color Hue/Saturation

The powerful Hue/Saturation tool gives us full control over correcting either all the colors together or any specific color. It also allows us alter the color saturation.

Hue/Saturation Tool

Select the image that you wish to work on and click the **Edit > Go to Standard Edit**.

Choose **Enhance** from the main menu.

Choose **Adjust Color** and **Adjust Hue/Saturation...** from the drop down menu.

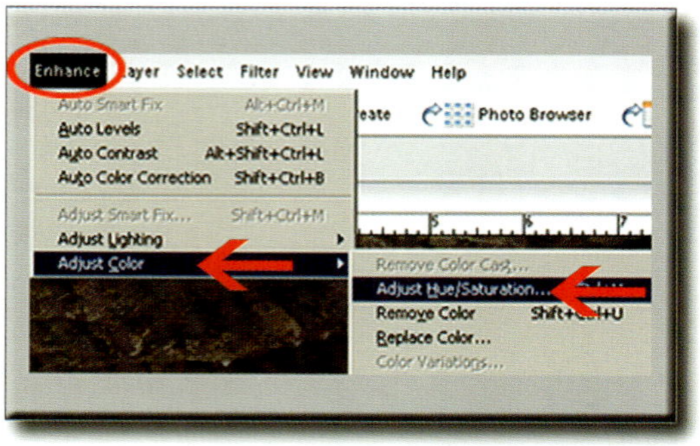

Adjust Master

From the **Edit window**, choose

Master.

We set the **Saturation** slider to **40%**.

We set the **Lightness** slider to **+2**.

These are example settings only. You can move any of these settings for your picture by observing the image as you make the adjustments.

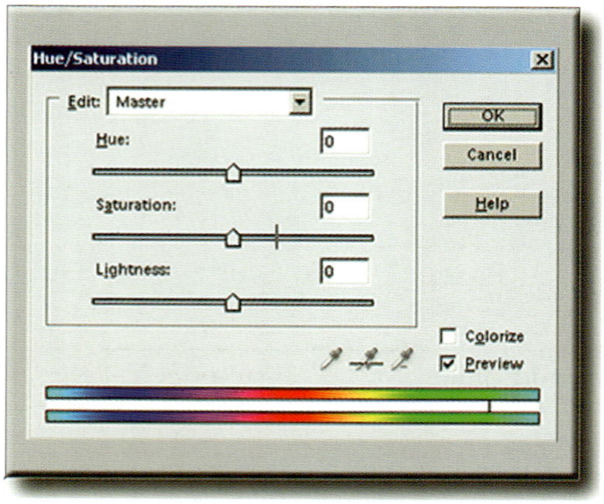

Edit Window

If we go to the **Edit Window** and click the **drop down menu**, we see that we can select ***any color for individual adjustment.***

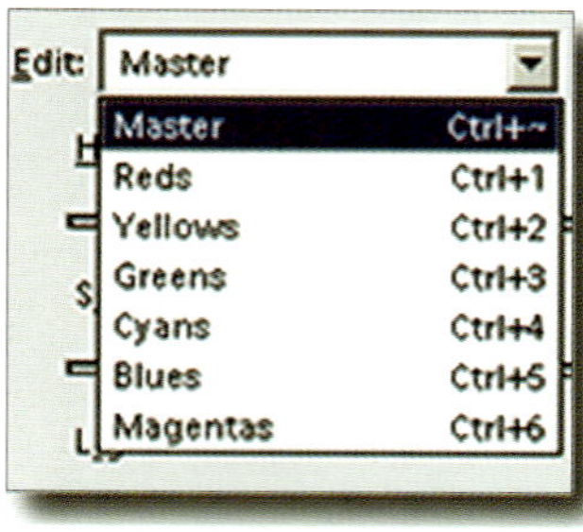

Adjusting Individual Colors

From the **Edit Window**, choose

Red:

We set the **Hue** slider to **–25**.

We set the **Saturation** slider to **27%**.

These are example settings only. You could move any of these settings

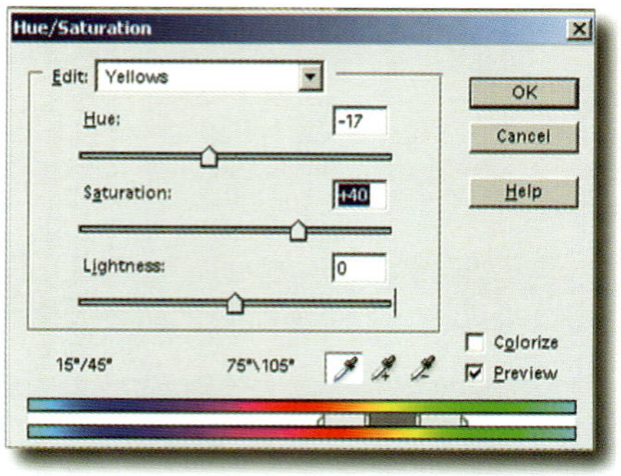

Color - Color Variations

Color can be further adjusted by increasing or decreasing the amount of any color in any tonal range.

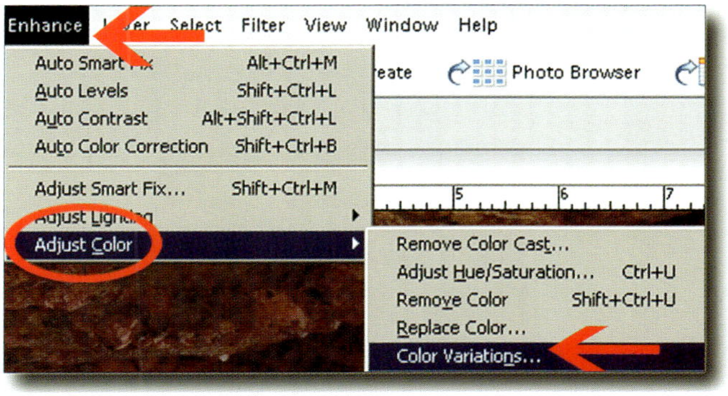

Color Variations Tool

Once you have selected the image you wish to work on and clicked **Edit > Go to Standard Edit,** you will be taken to the **Standard Edit** section of the program.

Choose **Enhance** on the main menu.

Choose **Adjust Color** and **Color Variations** from the drop down menu.

1	If you add Red	You Subtract Cyan
2	If you add Cyan	You subtract Red
3	If you add Green	You subtract Magenta
4	If you add Magenta	You subtract Green
5	If you add Blue	You subtract Yellow
6	If you add Yellow	You subtract Blue

Edit Window

The **Primary Colors** are:

Red, **Green** and **Blue**.

The **Secondary Colors** are:

Cyan, **Magenta** and **Yellow**.

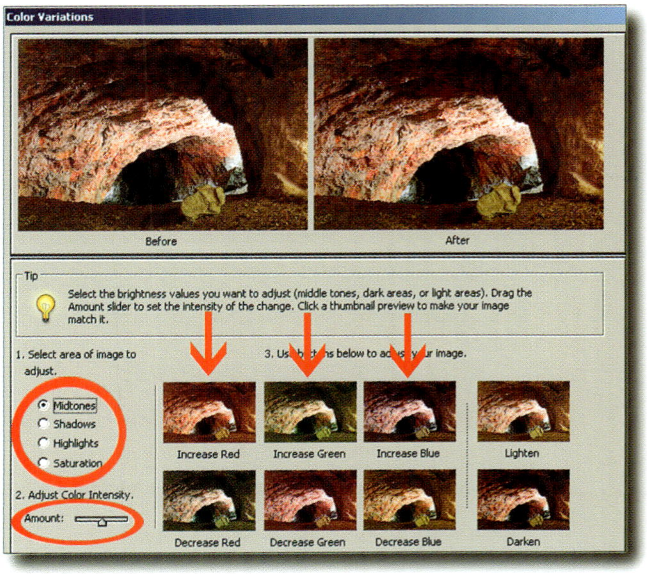

The Adjustments

There are 3 areas of adjustment:

The Tonal Zone,

The Amount of Adjustment, and

The Color to Adjust.

Click on the appropriate small thumbnail to increase or decrease any color.

Exit Standard Edit

To leave the **Quick Fix** screen, click the **X** button.

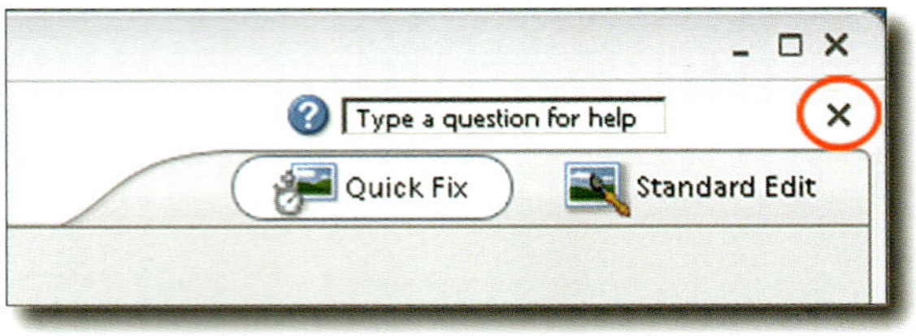

Save Format

The image from your camera was probably saved in a file format called **JPEG.** This format will recompress your image every time it saves it. This will result in a loss of quality.

We recommend that you convert your corrected image to Adobe's **PSD** file format. This is a lossless format that will not damage the quality of your image.

To accomplish this, click the down arrow beside **Format**.

Then choose **Photoshop PSD**.

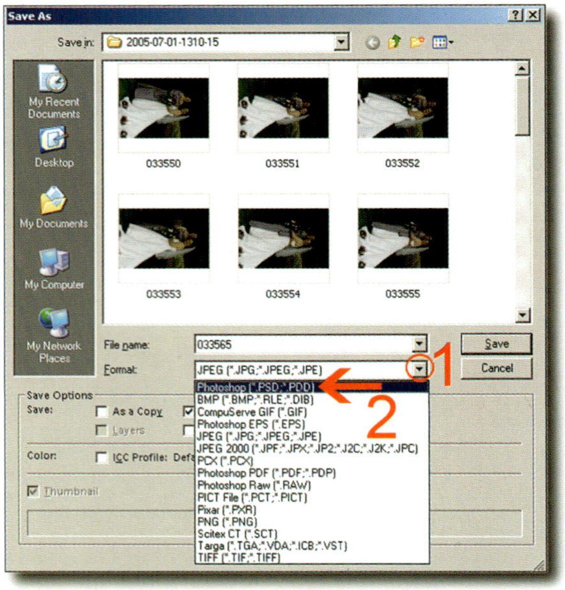

Where To Save It

Click in the indicated check boxes to save the image:

As a Copy

Include in the Organizer.

The corrected image will now appear to the right of the original image in the **Photo Well**.

Note: The original image still exists **untouched**.

There is now a **second image** with your **changes in effect**.

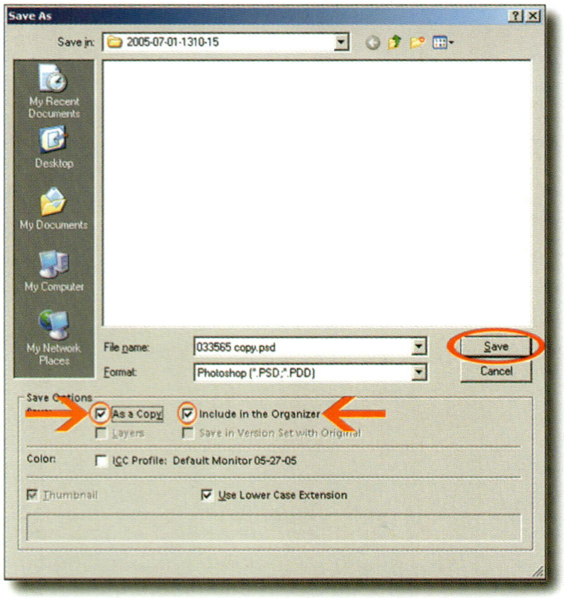

Fixing a Photo - Red Eye

Often after images are captured by digital flash photography, you will want to get rid of **Red Eye** - red pupils. **Red Eye** is a tool that allows you to do this.

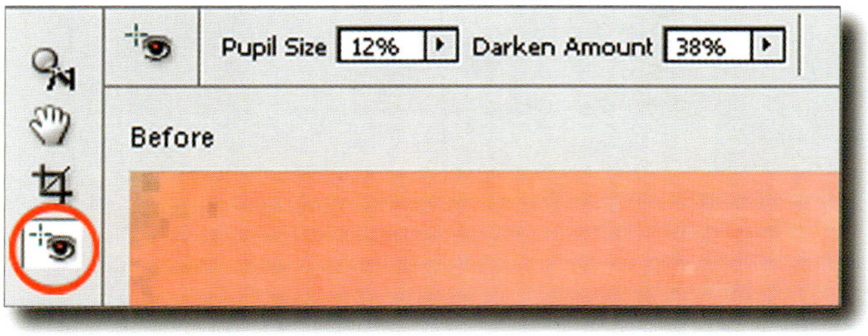

The Red Eye Button

Once you have selected the image you wish to work on and clicked the **Fix** button and **Go to Quick Fix**, you will be taken to the **Fix** section of the program.

To fix red eye, you must click the **Red Eye Correction** tool.

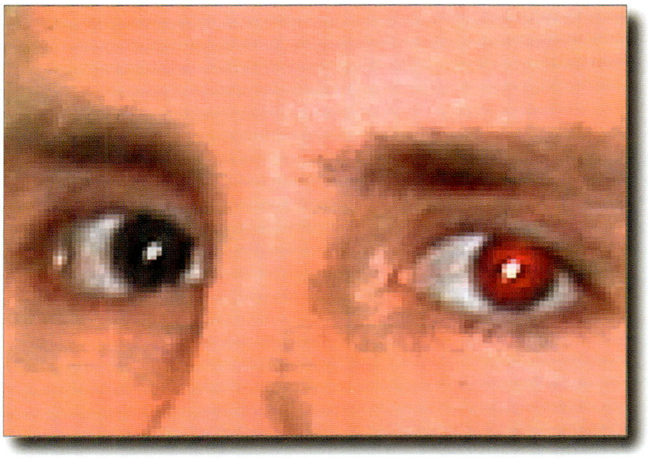

Applying Red Eye Correction

With the **Red Eye Removal** tool selected, drag it over one red eye area so there is a square selection around the entire eye.

The red will be replaced with a neutral color as shown.

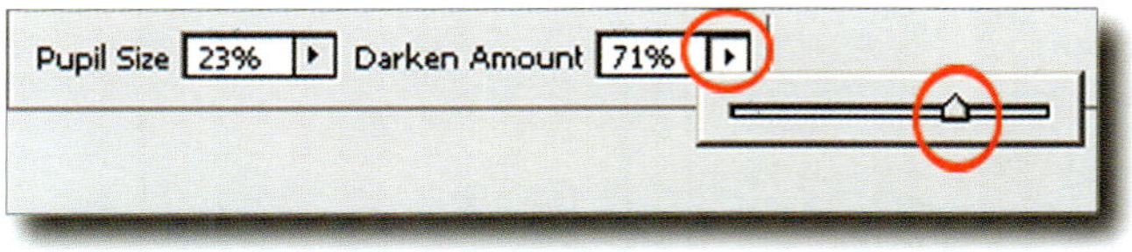

Fine-Tuning Correction

You can now fine-tune the size and darkness of the pupil.

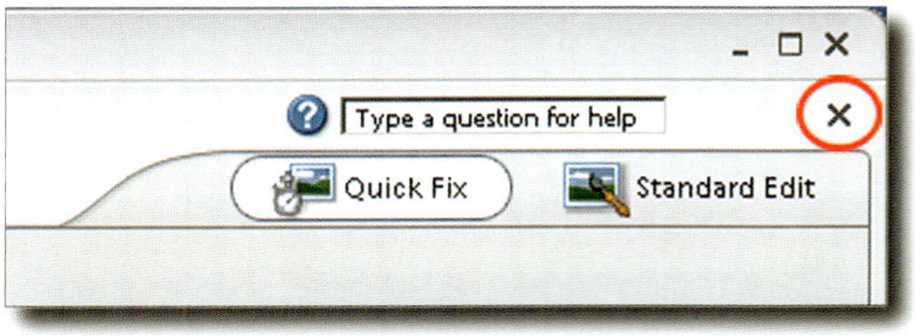

Finishing Red Eye Correction

Now you should exit the **Standard Edit** screen and save the changes to your image.

The methods for exiting and saving were outlined in chapter 7, page 107.

Printing Photos

In this lesson, we will use Adobe Elements Advanced to select an image, or several images, to print.

Selecting Photo(s) to Print

If you want to print one photo, just click on a photo in the **Photo Well**.

If you want to select several photos to print as a group, just hold down **Ctrl** and click on all the photos you want to print in the **Photo Well**.

A border will appear around each picture you have selected.

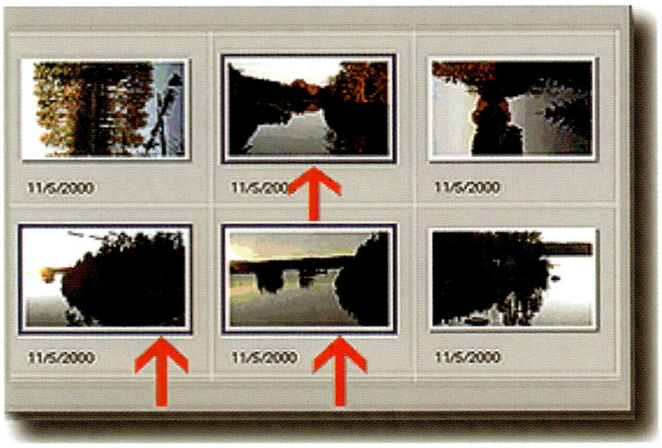

Select Print Function

From the Main menu, choose the **Print...** function.

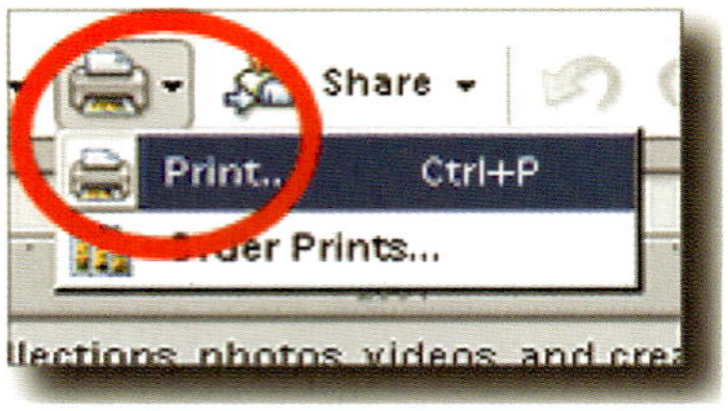

Selecting Printer & Layout

You must select the printer you wish to use as well as the number of copies.

Choose a layout:

1. Individual Print: use this to print one photo.

2. Contact Sheet: use this to print small prints of several different images on the same page in columns and rows.

3. Picture Package: use this to print several copies of the same image on one page.

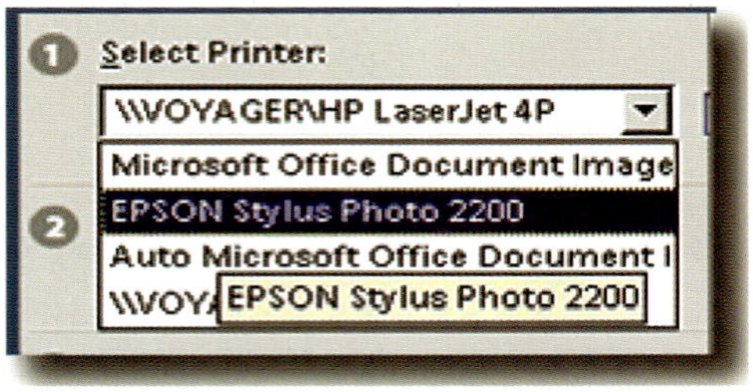

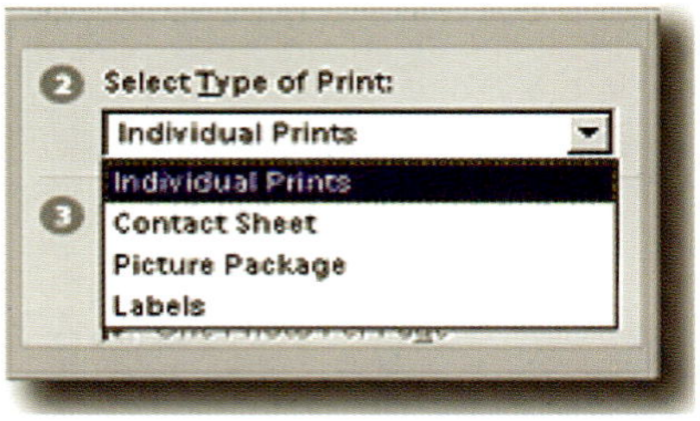

Print It

When you are ready to print, click the **Print** button.

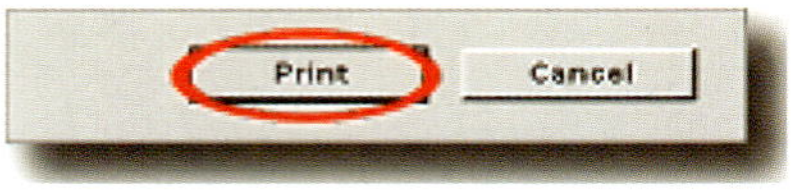

Emailing Photos

In this lesson, we will select a photo to email. The photo will then become an attachment in our email program.

Selecting Photo(s) To Email

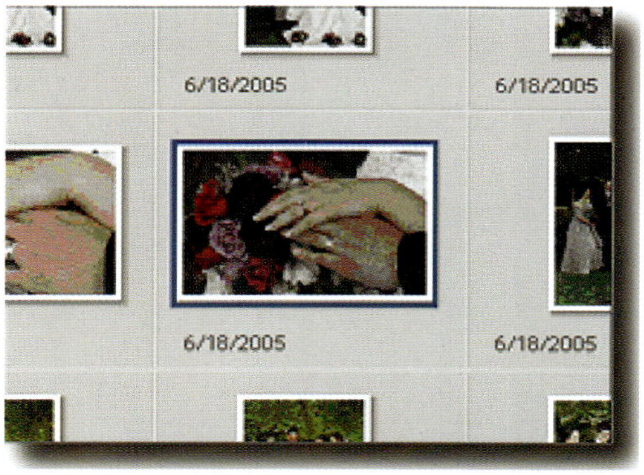

Click on the photo you wish to email.

A border will appear around the selected photo.

Select Email Function

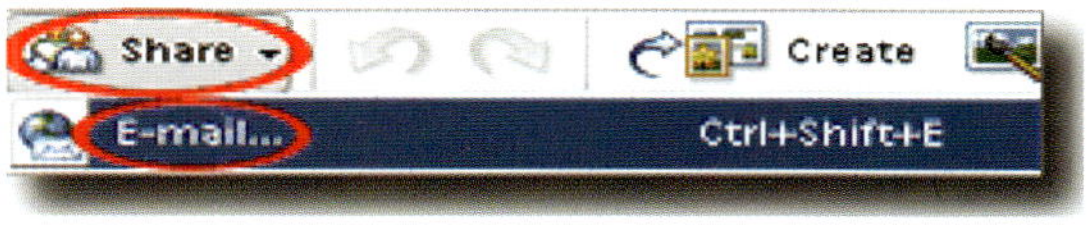

In the Icon menu, click the **Share** button.

In the drop down menu, click the **E-mail...** button.

Setting Size & Quality

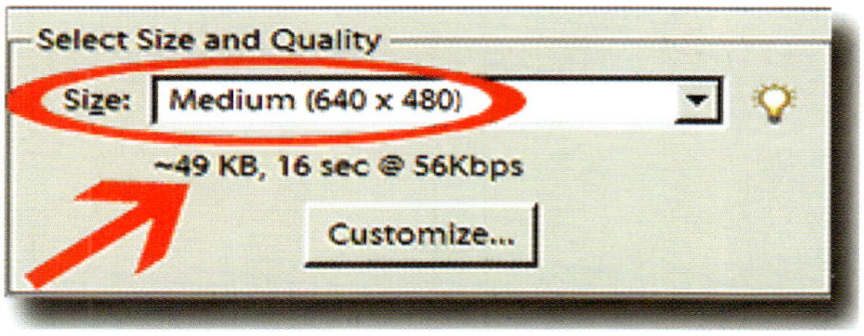

The transmission time for the image is 16 seconds @ speed of 56Kbps.

Send Email

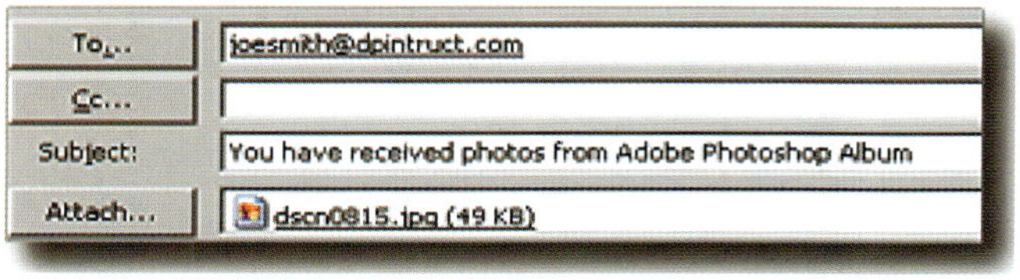

After this you will be dropped into your email program. The photo will automatically become an attachment.

Click the **Send** button.

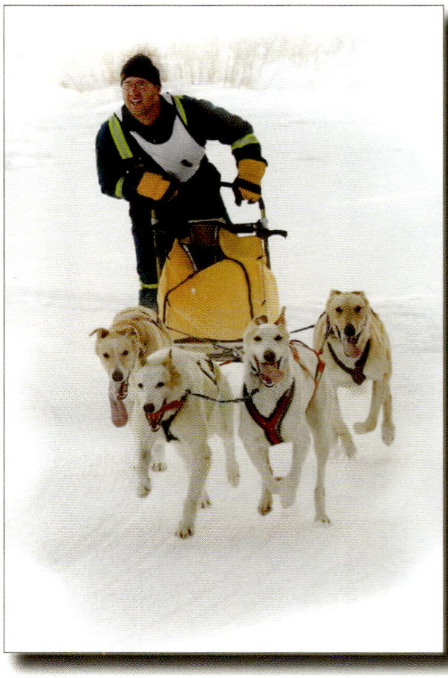

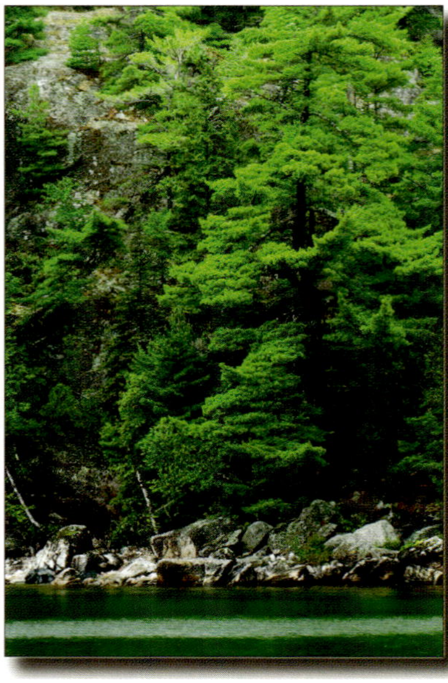

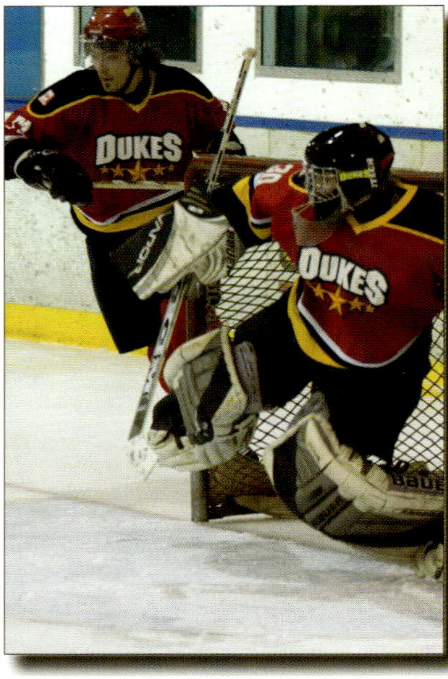

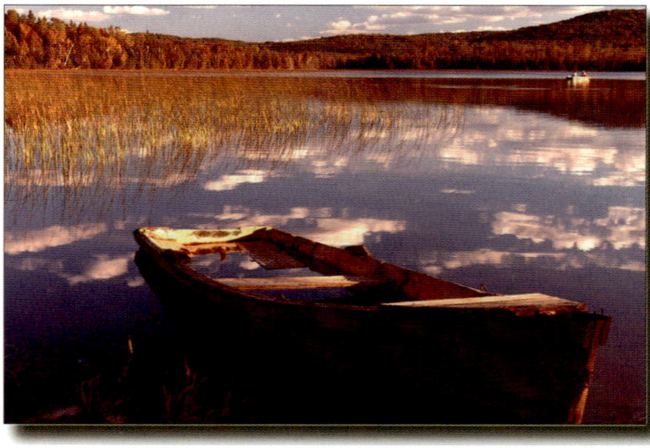

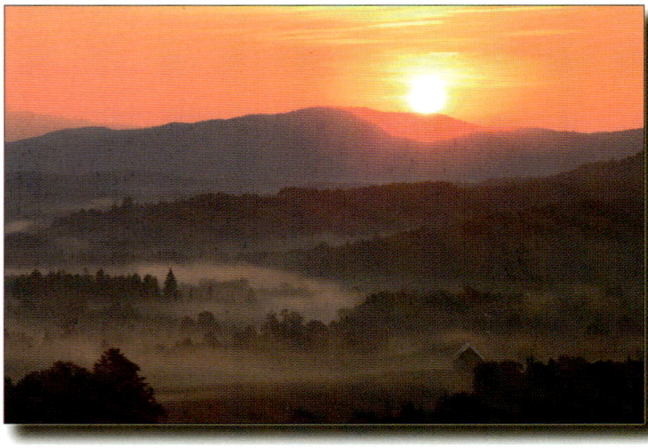

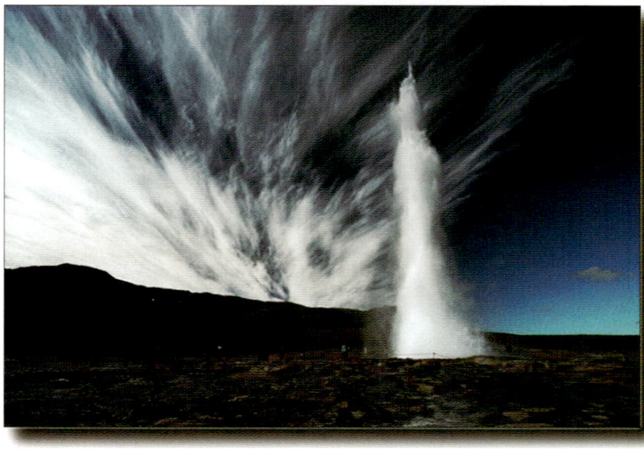

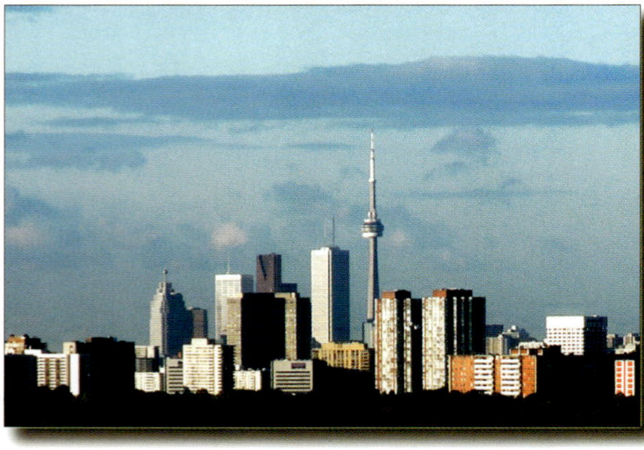

Photos by Henry Christiansen

Chapter 10 PHOTO EQUIPMENT

Photo Equipment

Buying the equipment necessary for digital photography can be a confusing process. In this chapter, we will break down every decision you will have to make when buying a digital camera, computer or photo printer into a series of simple steps. We will explain the complicated language that you will be confronted with by manufacturers and retailers in a way that you really will understand.

Buying a Digital Camera

In this section, we will give you a series of simple steps to follow when buying a digital camera.

Introduction

Selecting and buying a new digital camera is a daunting challenge. The number of new models that appear in the marketplace every day is staggering. Most sources of information line up camera features in a chart for comparison; buying a camera then becomes a process of checking features off a list. The weakness of this approach is no weight is given to the importance of any given feature. In fact, most people would probably feel more comfortable buying a car than selecting a camera.

Let's compare the similarities between buying a car and buying a digital camera.

Digital Camera Sales in the USA: 2nd Quarter 2005

	Company	Share	Change from previous year
1	Kodak	23.8%	Increase
2	Canon	21.9%	Increase
3	Sony	18.6%	Increase
4	Olympus	6.4%	Decrease
5	HP	6.2%	Decrease
6	Fuji	5.3%	Decrease
7	Nikon	4.5%	Decrease
	Other	11.3%	Decrease

Source: figures extracted from reports by news.com, forbes.com and zdnet.com.

Step One:

The Manufacturer

Some car manufacturers have better reputations than others. People usually have manufacturers they feel more comfortable with and trust more.

The same is true in the camera industry. People are usually eager to share their opinions of different manufacturers.

You will need to get your camera serviced just as you would a car. It's important to select a manufacturer that is a major player in the industry, and will be around for you when you need help.

Digital camera manufacturing is a competitive industry and a lot of players are falling by the wayside. The top three manufacturers on the list on the previous page are the most likely to be around in the future.

Considering the information in the chart will allow you to make a short list of camera manufacturers that you would consider purchasing from.

You can always return here and expand your list after doing more research.

Step Two:

Basic Camera Type & Budget

When you buy a car, you first need to decide what type of car you want and/or need. Do you want a sports car, a sedan, a minivan, a SUV or a truck?

You'll need to make the same basic decisions when purchasing a new camera.

Below are the basic types of cameras you will have to choose from:

1	Point & Shoot
2	Zoom Lens Reflex (ZLR)
3	Single Lens Reflex (SLR)

In cars – usually, the larger the car in the same basic category, the more expensive it will be.

In cameras – usually, the smaller the camera in the same basic category, the more expensive it will be.

Check the availability of local repair facilities as well as good web support for software updates, new information and manuals for your future camera.

The top three manufacturers in the table on the previous page offer comprehensive service and web support. After that, it gets a little spotty.

As mentioned previously, many camera selection guides just list the various features in different cameras in check-list fashion.

In this chapter, we take a different approach: the best camera for you is not the one with the most features; it is the one that serves your particular needs the best.

Point & Shoot:

These cameras are small and compact. They are easy to use and convenient to carry around. They often have many features, and are usually less expensive than cameras in other categories.

However, point & shoot cameras have limited lens capacity, fewer accessory add-ons, and suffer from "point & wait" syndrome (a time delay between when you press the shutter and when the camera finishes taking the picture).

Zoom Lens Reflex (ZLR):

These cameras are larger than point & shoot cameras. They cannot fit into pockets or purses but will fit into medium sized camera bags. They are usually intermediate in cost.

ZLR cameras have large lens zoom capacities but the lens cannot be changed, and they only have a few add-on accessories. They are still plagued by "point & wait" syndrome and delays in the viewfinder. However they are generally quicker than point & shoot cameras.

Single Lens Reflex (SLR):

These cameras are about the same size as ZLRs, but once you add in extra lenses and attachments, you will end up carrying around a lot more stuff.

SLRs are quick and there is no delay factor. They have larger and higher quality sensors, and give the greatest manual control over the camera.

However, SLRs are more expensive, especially when you factor in buying extra lenses and attachments.

Wide-Angle: A wide angle of view, with more in the picture. The subject appears smaller and further away.

28 mm or less	Very Wide
35 mm	Average Wide-Angle

Telephoto: a narrow angle of view with less in the picture. The subject appears larger and closer.

100 mm	Small Telephoto
110-150 mm	Moderate Telephoto
175 mm or more	Powerful Telephoto

Range:

28-100mm	Small Range
35-150mm	Moderate Range
35-300mm	Large Range

Note: We recommend that if your maximum telephoto range is 200mm or more, the camera have some form of image stabilization to prevent blurring.

Zoom Range:

Zoom Range can be expressed in different ways.

For example: a camera with a widest angle of 28mm and a maximum telephoto of 280mm can be expressed in two ways:

1. 28-280mm
2. 10 times (10X) – i.e. 280 divided by 28

Combined Zoom:

Combined Zoom is Optical Zoom + Digital Zoom.

You should ***not*** consider this combination when purchasing a camera.

You should consider **Optical Zoom** only.

Step Three (a):
Wide Angle & Telephoto

Most cameras have lenses that can be adjusted from a wide angle of view to a narrow angle of view. They are called zoom lenses for this reason.

Do you like wide-angle shots that allow you to get a lot of people and/or scenery in your pictures?

Do you like powerful telephoto lenses that let you zoom in from great distances and/or photograph small things?

Step Three (b): Zoom Range

After you have selected a basic type of car to purchase, you'll need to decide how big a car you want in that type. Do you want a large SUV or a small one?

In cameras, we can compare this to how big a zoom range you want. A large range can be an advantage, but is also means the camera itself will be larger.

Warning: The Real Zoom

There are two types of zoom.

Optical Zoom is real zoom. This is the true zoom range that your camera and lens system can deliver, and the only zoom you should consider.

Digital Zoom is not real. It sounds good, but is an electronic manipulation of your image to simulate greater telephoto power. You lose image quality with digital zoom. Never use it and never consider it in your selection process.

Step Four:

Megapixels (Engine Size)

When you select a car, you have to decide on the size of engine that you will need. Do you want a 4-cylinder or an 8-cylinder engine?

You don't always want the biggest, most powerful engine because you may not need all that power and you'll be paying for it in increased fuel costs. However, a little extra engine power is useful in case you need to tow something.

In cameras, you want enough megapixels to get the job done, with a little extra in case you need to crop something out of your images. If you get too many megapixels, you will pay with time delays when you store the images in your camera, as well as in memory card capacity costs.

We have been brainwashed into thinking that we need more and more megapixels. This is not always the case. Actually, many camera manufacturers have finally accepted this truth, and are making their new models into improved cameras with better lenses and more useful features instead of just more megapixels. Some new models actually have fewer megapixels than their predecessors.

Megapixels Myth:

The more megapixels, the better – this is ***wrong!***

Megapixels Reality:

We want as much image signal as possible.

We want as little digital noise as possible.

The more pixels you ram in a small sensor, the more noise and the less signal you get.

MP	Max Print Size @ 200dpi
1	4" x 6"
2	6" x 8"
3	8" x 10"
4	9" x 11"
5	10" x 13"

Most people do not print images any bigger than 8"x 10", but you should allow a little extra in case you need to crop out some of your image.

4-6 megapixels is all that most people will ever need. Any more will cost you in several ways. More megapixels slow down your camera because it takes more time to save each image. More megapixels fill up your memory cards quicker and reduce the number of images that you can get on a card.

Canon Line Up – Most Recent Releases Only

Model 2006	Size & Type	Opt Zoom	MP	US $ 2006
SD430	Subcompact P&S	35-105	5	467
SD600	Subcompact P&S	35-105	6	318
SD630	Subcompact P&S	35-105	6	382
SD700	Subcompact P&S	35-140	6	499
A430	Compact P&S	39-156	4	153
A530	Compact P&S	35-140	5	197
A540	Compact P&S	35-140	6	263
A700	Compact P&S	35-210	6	317
S80	Compact P&S	28-100	8	463
G6	LgCompact P&S	35-140	7	599
S31S	ZLR	36-432	6	499
Pro1	ZLR	28-200	8	699
350D	SLR	---------	8	699
30D	SLR	---------	8	1347

Source: dpreview.com, 2006

Note: Some cameras have extra features

SD430 has wireless capability

SD700 and S3IS have image stabilization

No professional level SLRs are listed above

Other Manufacturers
Kodak
Sony
Olympus
Hp
Fuji
Nikon
The Others

Step Five:

The Comparison Camera

Now you have made most of the major decisions that will allow you to narrow down your search for a camera.

Soon we will begin to look at specific features, but first we should select one camera manufacturer's lineup, in order to pick out a model to compare other cameras to.

We recommend that you select Canon as your comparison manufacturer. Canon is in the top three in sales, and in that group is the only manufacturer that offers a full range of cameras from point & shoot to SLRs.

Step Six:

Select Others to Compare

The next step is to go back to your short list of camera manufacturers from Step One and find camera models from those manufacturers that compare fairly closely to the one(s) you selected from Canon.

Step Seven:

Where to Compare

It may seem difficult to get all the specifications on these cameras in order to compare them effectively.

Fortunately, there is an easy source that will allow you to acquire the necessary information, presented neatly in a chart.

This information is in the website: www.dpreview.com

1. Go to www.dpreview.com
2. From the left menu, select: "Buying Guide".
3. From the drop down menu, select "Side-by-Side".
4. From the camera models listed on the left side, "Add" the models that you wish to compare.
5. Click on: "Compare Side-by-Side".

The models will be displayed across the page, with the important features listed down the side of the page.

Step Eight:

Major Features To Compare

There are so many features available in modern digital cameras. We will introduce only those we consider most important to your decision.

Eight (a)	Exposure Control
Eight (b)	Viewfinder Type
Eight (c)	LCD Screen
Eight (d)	Flash Considerations
Eight (e)	Focus
Eight (f)	ISO
Eight (g)	Cards, Batteries & Output Exposure Control

Step Eight (a):

Exposure Control

Cars come with either automatic or manual transmissions.

In cameras, it is different. They all come with automatic exposure control. However, some cameras allow you to control the exposure manually as well.

Some cameras allow you partial manual override while others allow you complete manual control. Others even allow you to accept the automatic exposure, but then adjust it by what's called exposure compensation. Some have histograms to help compensate.

We recommend that your camera have at least auto exposure, exposure compensation and histogram features.

Automatic Exposure Control
Fully Automatic - Light is measured and the camera set automatically.
Program - The exposure is set by a computer program in the camera
Preset Scenes – The user tells the camera what kind of scene is being photographed and the camera sets itself.
Semi-Automatic Exposure Control
1. Shutter Preferred – You set the shutter speed and the camera sets an aperture that gives you the correct exposure.
2. Aperture Preferred – You set the aperture and the camera adjusts the shutter speed for a correct exposure.
Manual Exposure Control
The camera provides a light reading and the user sets the aperture and shutter speed
Histogram and **Exposure Compensation**
A histogram is a graphic representation of the exposure information shown on the LCD screen on the back of some cameras after the exposure has been taken. It can be a useful feature to have if you want to do a lot of manual exposures or use exposure compensation.

Histograms are explained in detail on page 20-23.

Step Eight (b):
Viewfinder Type

The viewfinder is what you use to view the image that you want to photograph. In most film cameras you look through a window called an optical viewfinder.

In digital cameras, many people compose their photographs using the small screen on the back of the camera, called the LCD screen. This is why digital photographers often hold the camera away from their eye when taking pictures.

No Optical Viewfinder: Some digital cameras have no optical viewfinder and rely only on an LCD screen on the back of the camera. This works well most of the time except in bright sunshine when the LCD screen can be hard to see.

Optical and **LCD Viewfinder:** In these cameras, the LCD screen on the back of the camera can be used most of the time. When there is bright sunlight, the user can switch to the optical viewfinder.

EVF (Electronic Viewfinder): In these cameras, there are really two LCD screens. There is the regular LCD on the back of the camera. There is also a smaller LCD viewfinder in place of the optical viewfinder. It is not affected by sunshine.

SLR (Single Lens Reflex): Both film and digital Single Lens Reflex (SLR) cameras view scenes through the lens system. This is considered the most ideal viewing system.

Step Eight (c):
LCD Screen

With more people relying on the LCD screen on the back of the camera to compose their pictures, as well as to view their finished images, the characteristics and quality of the LCD screen become very important. These are the main considerations:

1. Size
2. Number of Pixels
3. Anti-Glare Properties

Size: The actual physical size of the LCD screen.

Bigger screens are better for visibility

Small	Less than 2"
Medium	2" to 2.5"
Large	Bigger than 2.5"

Number of Pixels: The more pixels there are on the LCD, the more detail that can be seen

Less than 100,000	Less Detail
100,000 to 125,000	Moderate
More than 150,000	Amazing Detail

Sun Glare: LCD screens can be hard to see in bright sun; some have better anti-glare properties, and others flip and twist so you can adjust them to compensate for glare.

Step Eight (d):

Flash Considerations

If you want to be able to take pictures indoors or in low light situations, you will need a flash.

Some of the lower range cameras do not come with a flash.

For the majority of cameras that do come with a flash, there are some considerations that can determine their practical usefulness.

1. **Flash or No Flash**: Some digital cameras do not have a built-in flash. This limits their usefulness in low light situations and indoors.
2. **Pop-up vs. Integrated Flash:** Most digital cameras do come with a built-in flash for indoor and low light situations. If the flash is "Integrated", it is built into the body of the camera. These flashes are prone to causing "red eye". Cameras with a "pop-up" flash are less likely to cause this problem.
3. **Extra Flash Features:** Some cameras have extra features that help to overcome some of the limitations of flashes. Pre-flash is an example of this. A small pre-flash is sent out to constrict the pupil and reduce the risk of "red eye".

Hot Shoe: Most built-in flashes are small and weak. They have a limited range of about 10'-12'. If a camera has a "Hot Shoe", a more powerful flash can be attached to the camera to allow photographs to be taken at a greater distance.

Step Eight (e):

Focus

All modern digital cameras offer auto-focus.

Some offer manual focus and some don't. There may be times, such as when shooting in dark areas, where you can't get a focus lock and you will need manual focus.

Some cameras have a focus assist light that can help you attain focus in the dark, or with difficult subjects.

Some cameras have a focus lock that lets you lock onto the subject you wish to focus on, and then move the camera to re-compose your picture while maintaining your original focus.

Step Eight (f):

ISO

ISO relates to film speed or film sensitivity in film photography.

ISO relates to sensor speed or sensor sensitivity in digital photography.

High ISO settings allow pictures to be exposed in dark, low light situations. However, the cost of high ISO settings is more "electronic visual noise" and a poorer quality image.

One should always use the lowest ISO possible for the amount of light available.

Cameras with a higher maximum ISO allow photography in lower light and darker situations. A maximum ISO of 400 or more is advantageous for low light photography.

Step Eight (g):

Cards, Batteries & Output

Secure Digital (SD) cards and **Compact Flash (CF)** cards are universal and preferable to proprietary cards such as **XD** cards and **Memory Stick** cards. They are usually cheaper and more available. You will need extra memory cards for effective camera use.

Lithium-Ion batteries are better than NiMH which are better than NiCAD. Lithium batteries do not lose memory in the recharging process and therefore maintain their charging capacity over time.

You should use rechargeable batteries only. Non-rechargeable batteries are more expensive to use.

For output, USB 2.0 is far preferable to a USB 1.1 or a Serial connection. Firewire is also fast, but not as common.

Step Nine:

Comparing Minor Features

There are too many minor features to cover here. Examples are: movie modes, remote control shutters, filter threads, video-out, orientation sensors, panoramic stitches, etc…

These are less important features. However, some of these features may be important to individuals with special photographic needs.

Step Ten:

Read Reviews

Read the conclusions of reviews first. If the camera seems interesting, you may wish to read more details, or the whole article

Use various review web sites:

For example: www.dpreview.com

We feel that dpreview.com has many thorough and complete reviews.

Step Eleven:

Read Owner's Comments

We feel these are more useful than reviews, since they reflect the experiences of actual users.

Use various review web sites:

For example: www.dpreview.com

In the user's comments section, actual owners relate their impressions of the cameras they have purchased and used.

Step Twelve:

Test Drive

You should approach this as you would test driving a vehicle. You should confirm the camera performs to your expectations. Don't skip this step. Get the camera out of the salesperson's hands and into your own. Compare cameras while they are in your hands.

1. How does camera feel in your hand? Check the fit and quality.
2. Location of main controls – Are they easy to manipulate? Check the following:
    a. On/Off
    b. Shutter
    c. Zoom
    d. Record / Replay
    e. Other important controls, such as exposure compensation.
3. Is the camera menu or button driven? Is it easy to change settings or is it a multi-step time consuming procedure.
4. Lens cap – Is it integrated or stick on?
5. Viewfinder – Does it work with extra lenses and filters? Is there an EVF lag, where you see a delay between what the electronic viewfinder shows and what the camera is pointed at when it is in motion?
6. LCD – Check the size, resolution and visibility. Is there glare in bright sunlight? Does it flip and twist? Is there a histogram?
7. Zoom range – Check to see if it is to your liking. Zoom in and out fully.
8. Is there a time lag when taking a picture? Are you clicking and then waiting too long?
9. Focus hunting – Check it, especially in dark areas. Does it take a long time for the camera to focus or to change focus?
10. Picture to picture time – How long do you have to wait between taking pictures? How many pictures can you take in succession before you are forced to wait?
11. Info feedback on the LCD – In addition to the image, does the camera display useful details such as the shutter speed, aperture or exposure compensation on the back of the camera? In the histogram feature, can the LCD be set to show over the exposure?
12. Flash – Is it pop up? Is there a hot shoe?
13. Battery – what type is it? Is it easy to insert and remove?
14. Memory Card – What type is it? Is it easy to insert and remove?
15. Tripod socket – Will a tripod block access to anything?
16. Picture quality – Are samples available?

Conclusion

In this chapter we have compared selecting a new digital camera to selecting a car. These are the basic steps that we recommend before buying a new digital camera:

1	Assess the various manufacturers.
2	Decide on a basic camera type and budget.
3	Decide on the zoom range that is important to you.
4	Decide how many megapixels you want (4-6 is plenty).
5	Select a comparison camera.
6	Select other cameras to compare to the camera in step five.
7	Go to www.dpreview.com and compare camera models.
8	Compare major features.
9	Compare minor features.
10	Read reviews.
11	Read owner's comments.
12	Test drive the camera(s).

Digital Printers

In this section, we'll give you an introduction to digital printers and printing considerations.

Introduction

When printing your images, you will have to decide whether you wish to print them yourself or have them printed for you.

We will outline some of the options that exist in retail printing.

We will also discuss some of the issues that you should consider if you decide to acquire a printer of your own.

The No-Printer Solution

There are several ways that you can get prints from your digital camera without owning a printer or doing the printing.

We have listed some of these methods on the right.

1. In-Store Photo Printing Services: You bring your memory card or CD into an appropriate store. They will process your pictures, just as they would do with film. You will pick up your professionally printed pictures and memory card, or CD, when they are ready.
2. In-Store Photo Kiosk: You bring your memory card or CD to a self-service kiosk and follow the simple instructions to print your own images in the store.
3. On-line Photo Printing Services: You find a web-site that offers this service, upload your images to the site and edit them as needed. You then select the size, paper and number of prints. You pay on-line and your prints arrive at your door in about one week.

The No-Computer Solution

There are several ways that you can print your own pictures without using a computer. Some printers are capable of printing in this manner.

You can use this approach for printing, but we recommend that you use a computer to back up your images onto CDs.

The no-computer printing solution is discussed in chapter 13 page 169-174.

1. Printing from a Memory Card: Some printers have slots that accept common memory cards. These printers usually have a small LCD screen built-in to allow you to make choices. You simply place your memory card in the printer and select which images you wish to print.
2. Printing from a Digital Camera using "PictBridge": If your camera and printer both have "PictBridge" capability, you can print very easily. Just connect your camera directly to your printer with a USB cable, make your selections and print.

Type of Printer

There are three basic types of printers that can be used to print your images at home.

These types are compared in the table on the left.

We recommend that you use a Photo Quality Ink Jet Printer.

Printer Type	Advantages	Negatives	Cost US $ 2006
Ink Jet	High Quality	Output not Waterproof	80-450
Dye Sublimation	Water Resistant	Slow Speed, High Print Cost	400-800
Color Laser	Low Print Cost	Lower Quality	900-5000

Printer Size

When we speak of printer size, we are basically referring to the width of the printer carriage. This size determines the maximum size of print that you can print.

Therefore, you should determine the largest size print that you will ever want to print with the printer before buying it.

1. Narrow Carriage: Largest print = 4" x 6"
2. Normal Carriage: Largest print = 8" x 10"
3. Wide Carriage: Starts at 13" x 19"

Wide carriage printers come in various sizes, from 13" up to 96".

The most popular printer carriage size is "Normal".

The Print Fade Problem

One of the problems that has occurred in digital printing is the fading of the printed images after only a few years. There are now choices to be made in printer selection that can help to solve this problem.

There is a respected company that researches and tests various printers and inks, publishing the results on their website.

This website can help you assess various manufacturer's product's resistance to fading.

Their web address is: www.wilhelm-research.com.

Inks and Fading

Some printers use inks that are more resistant to fading. Selecting one of these printers will help overcome this problem.

Originally, Photo Quality Ink jet printers all used dye based inks that faded within a few years.

Newer printers from Epson, Canon & HP use pigment based inks that are resistant to fading for more than 40 years.

Their web address is: www.wilhelm-research.com.

Photo Paper and Fading

Every printer can use various types of paper. Some papers are more resistant to fading than others.

Glossy	Quickest to Fade
Semi-Gloss	Intermediate Fading
Matte	Resistant to Fading

Matching Ink and Paper

Once you have selected a printer from a given manufacturer, it is always advisable to use the paper and ink from the same manufacturer for that particular printer.

One of the major challenges in digital printing is securing a print that matches the colors displayed on the monitor.

There are methods of calibrating monitors and printers so they correspond. These are complex and can be considered later.

However, it is always advisable to use the matching photo paper and ink intended for your printer. This will help secure a better match.

Conclusion

The issues we covered in this chapter were:

1. Decide if you are going to print your own images or purchase prints from a retail outlet.
2. Do you wish to print with or without using a computer?
3. Which type of printer should you select? We recommend a Photo Quality Ink Jet.
4. What is the largest size print that you would like to make?
5. Consider buying a printer that uses fade-resistant inks.
6. Consider using photo papers that are less likely to fade.
7. Use papers and inks that match your printer.

Choosing a Desktop Computer

In this section we will discuss what you should consider when purchasing a desktop computer for the purposes of digital photography.

Introduction

The Central Processing Unit (known as the CPU) and Random Access Memory (known as RAM) are the two most important factors in determining computer performance.

The video card and the monitor are the two most important factors in determining how well you will be able to view your photographs – this is especially important if you plan to do a lot of photo editing.

CPU: "The brain of the computer"

Buy the fastest CPU you can afford

Minimum Intel CPU: Pentium 4, 2.0 GHz

Minimum AMD CPU: Athlon 2600, 1.8 GHz

The CPU determines how fast your computer runs. The faster the CPU, the faster the computer. A CPU's speed is expressed in GHz, with a higher number indicating a faster CPU. A 2.0 GHz CPU is faster than a 1.0 GHz CPU. You can also improve performance by using more than one CPU. A computer that uses two CPUs (known as a Dual Core) is faster than a computer that only uses one CPU.

CPUs are manufactured by two main companies: Intel and AMD. AMD and Intel have each designed their CPUs differently. This makes comparing an AMD CPU with an Intel CPU a little difficult. However, CPUs manufactured by AMD are usually less expensive than those manufactured by Intel. Below is a chart that shows equivalent CPUs manufactured by Intel and AMD:

AMD	Intel
Athlon 2600: 1.8 GHz	Pentium 4: 2.8 GHz
Athlon 3000: 1.8: GHz	Pentium 4: 3.0 GHz
Athlon 3200: 2.0 GHz	Pentium 4: 3.2 GHz
Athlon X2 3800: 2.0 GHz	Pentium D 820: 2.8 GHz
Athlon X2 4400: 2.2 GHz	Pentium D 940: 3.2 GHz
Athlon X2 4800: 2.4 GHz	Pentium D 950: 3.4 GHz

RAM

RAM is more important than processor speed and should be given preference in your buying decision.

Minimum: 512 MB.

Recommend: 1 GB.

After the speed of your CPU, RAM is the most important factor in determining how fast your computer will run. Programs and files have to be copied from your hard disk to memory before the CPU is able to use them. The more RAM memory you have, the more programs and files you can have in memory, the better the performance of your computer.

Hard Disk

Minimum Capacity: 80 GB

The hard disk should have a capacity of at least 80 GB. A 80GB hard disk can hold approximately 1,800 photographs in TIFF format.

While RAM memory relates to how much memory space you have to work in, hard disk capacity refers to how much space you will have for storing images and software programs.

Video Card

Minimum Memory: 64 MB

The video card determines the quality with which you will be able to see photographs on your monitor. The higher the maximum resolution, the better the quality. A good maximum resolution is 1600 x 1200 pixels. Likewise, the more memory on the card, the better it will be and the faster it will display your images on the screen. The minimum memory size should be at least 64 MB.

Monitor

LCD

The bigger the monitor, the better it is. The monitor should be at least 17 inches. There are two types of monitors available: CRT and LCD.

LCD monitors are smaller in size than CRT monitors. In the past, LCD monitors did not display colors as accurately as CRT is, but this is changing. Get a higher quality LCD.

CD/DVD Burner

Recommend: DVD Burner

A CD or DVD burner does not affect a computer's performance. However, while a CD can hold up to 700 MB of data, a DVD can hold 4.8 GB of data, more than 6 times the capacity of a CD. Because of the immense difference in memory capacity, we recommend you choose a DVD burner over a CD burner even if it costs a little more. CD burners can only burn CDs. However, DVD burners can burn CDs and DVDs

USB

USB 2.0

Your digital camera will be connected to your computer via a USB connection. Make sure you have a USB 2.0 connection and not the older USB 1.1. Firewire is just as fast as USB 2.0, but not as universal.

Conclusion

Although there seem to be a lot of different factors involved, buying a computer is actually quite simple: the speed of the CPU and the amount of RAM are the most important factors that will affect performance.

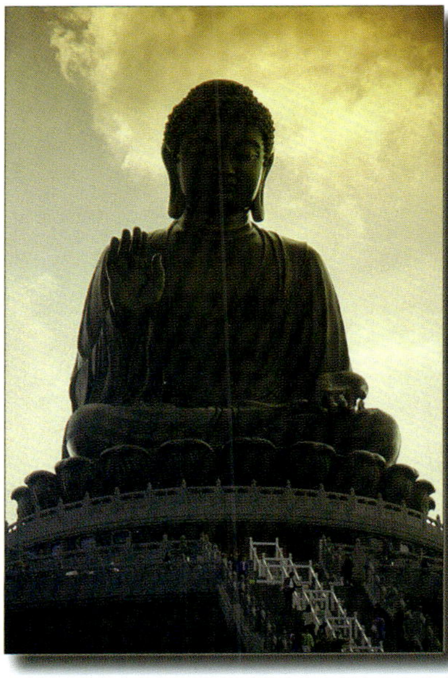

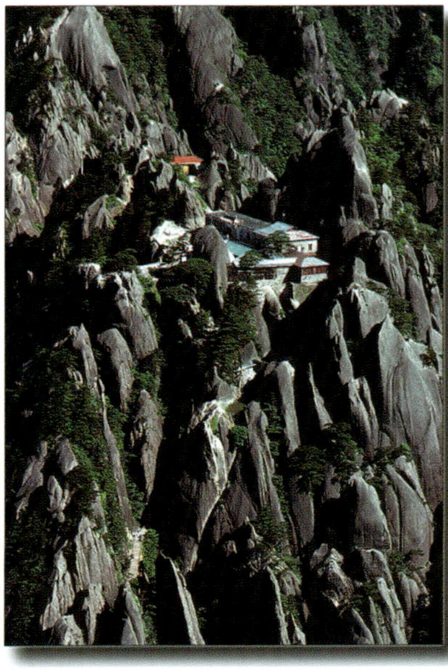

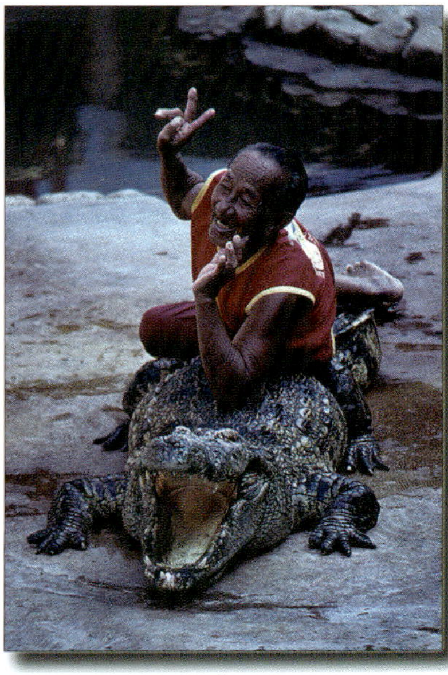

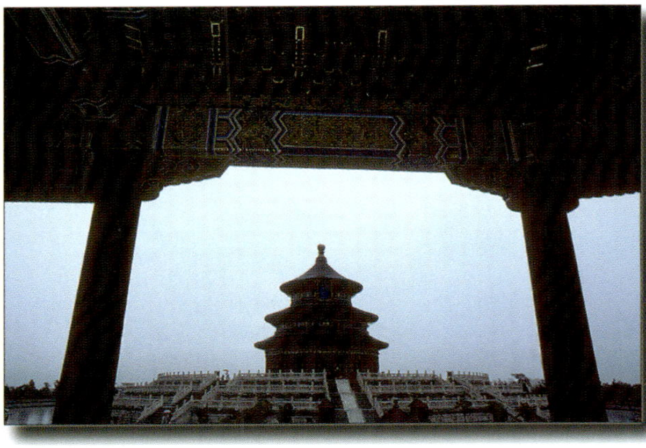

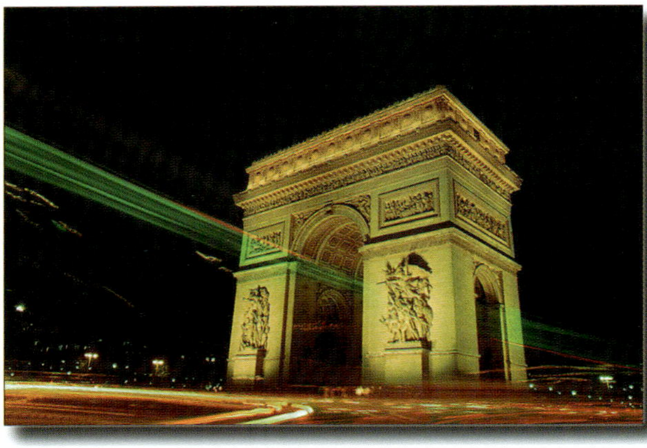

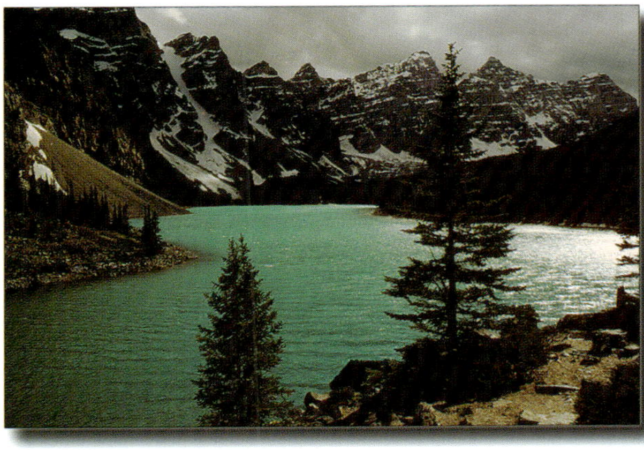

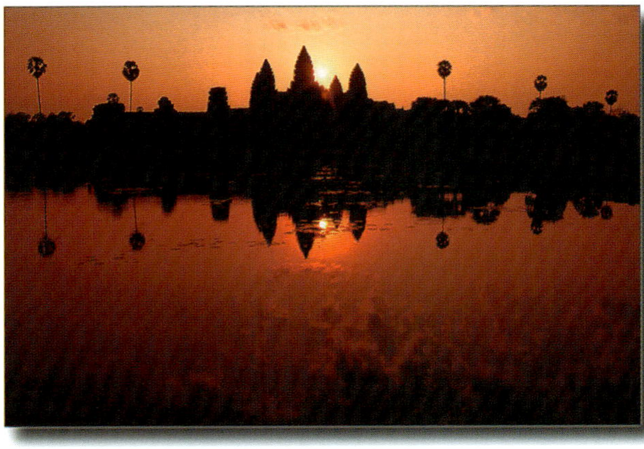

Photos by Antony Chow

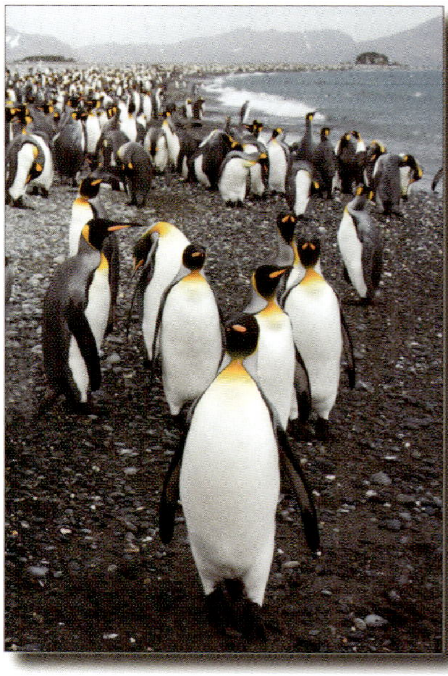
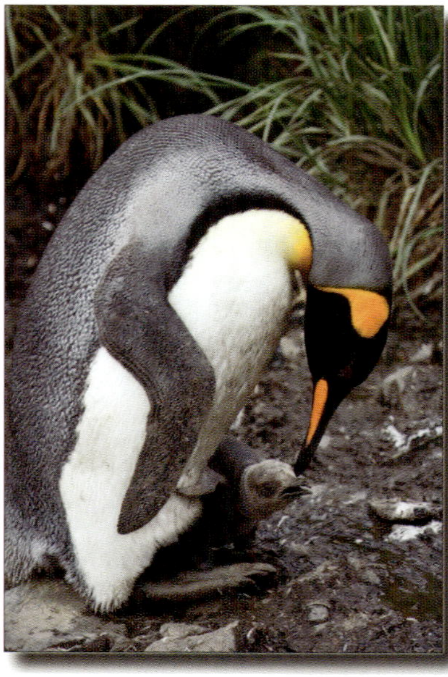
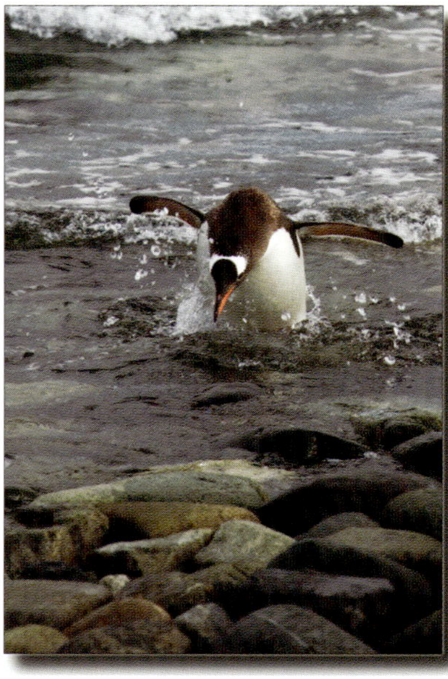
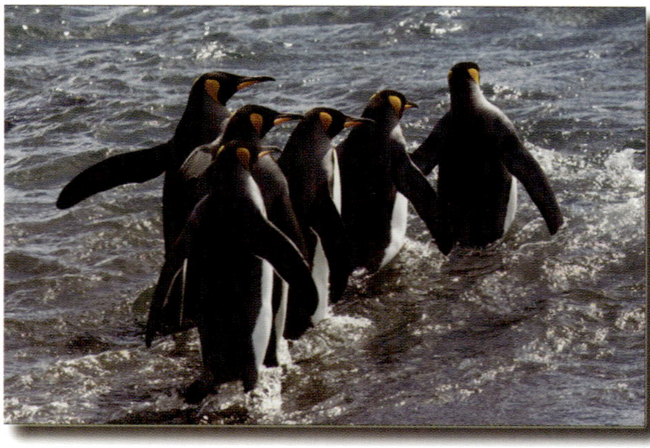
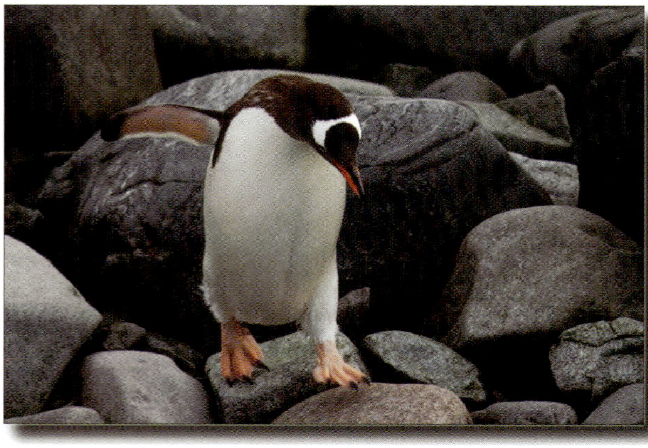
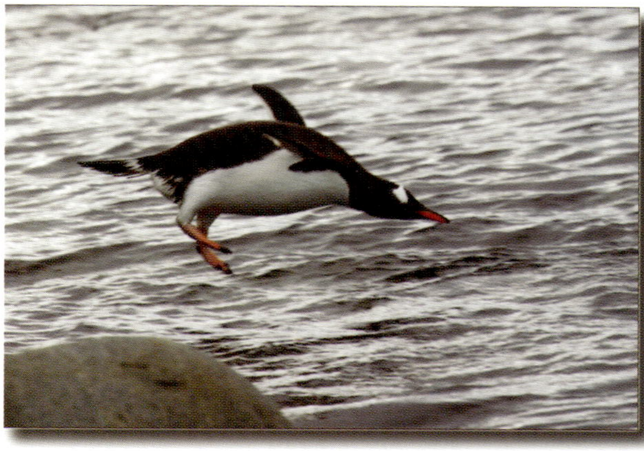
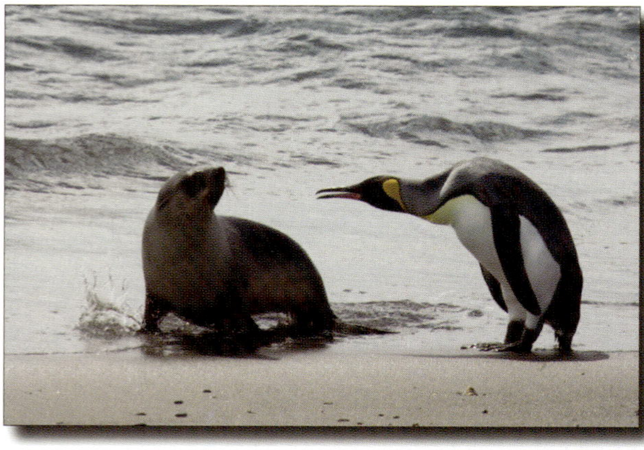

Photos by Phil Kwan

Chapter 11 MAKING YOUR OWN PRINTS

Introduction

Making your own prints can be a simple and rewarding experience. Selecting an appropriate printer will allow you to print at home at a good level of performance with the option for further growth.

Printing Services

Most people would like to have prints made of many of their images.

In the days of film, you handed in your exposed roll and prints were returned to you in an envelope without any fuss.

In the digital world, you can achieve the same level of simplicity by taking your memory card into an appropriate retail outlet and getting your prints back in an envelope without any fuss.

We discussed this printing option in Chapter 10 page 154 on Digital Printers – The No Printer Solution.

Home Printing

Another alternative is to make your own prints. You can also do this with a memory card.

Many beginners avoid this option because they are afraid they will have to learn to use complicated editing software. This is no longer true.

Today, you can print your own images without using a computer. You need a printer, of course, but no computer is necessary. We call this **"Easy Printing"**.

At first: If you select your printer carefully, you will be able to print without a computer using: **"Easy Printing"**. Using that same printer, you will later be able to connect that printer to a computer and reprint. We call this **"Printing with computer"**.

Selecting a Printer: Chapter 12

It is important that the beginner select an appropriate printer. The best option is to select one that will allow them to start with **"Easy Printing"**, but still offer the opportunity to move up to **"Printing With Computer"** at a later point.

In chapter 12, we will roll up our sleeves and get down to the specifics of selecting a printer for the beginner. In a previous chapter on Digital Printers, we provided an overview of printers. In chapter 12, we will discuss the types of printers and printer features that are relevant to the beginner. We will specifically discuss some of the printers from various manufacturers, outlining pros and cons. Finally, we will select one manufacturer to demonstrate the selection process in detail.

Chapter 12, **"Selecting a printer"**, is a must read for you if you want to purchase your first printer.

Easy Printing: Chapter 13

In Chapter 13, we will deal with the easiest and most straightforward way to print: printing with a printer and no computer.

We will use a stand-alone printer, the Canon IP6600D, for illustrative purposes. Similar printers from other manufacturers will perform in the same way.

We will cover:

1. Setting up the printer.
2. Initial printing directly from a Memory Card.
3. Initial Printing directly from a camera.
4. Storing your pictures and erasing the Memory Card.

Printing with Computer Chapter 14

In Chapter 14, we will discuss using the same printer as in chapter 13. However, this time we will explore how to use it when it is attached to your computer to print and reprint your desired images. We will cover:

1. Setting up your printer in Windows.
2. Reprinting your images from a Memory Card.
3. (Re)printing your images from the computer.

Conclusion

It is important that you select an appropriate printer that will allow you to print easily at home and also give you the option for growth.

Chapter 12 SELECTING A PRINTER

Introduction

There are a multitude of printers on offer in today's marketplace. Selecting a simple printer can be a mind boggling experience for the beginner.

We feel there is a type of printer ideally suited for the beginner. It is utterly simple. It allows you to print without a computer.

We will outline the unique characteristics of this type of printer in this chapter. We will then consider its significant features with specific examples from four of the major manufacturers. Finally, we will select one manufacturer's model to demonstrate the selection process in more detail.

The Necessary Features

1	Print Without a Computer
2	Specialize in 4"x 6" Prints
3	Fade Resistant Prints
4	Color LCD Screen
5	Memory Card Slots
6	"PictBridge" Capable

We particularly like Epson's name for this type of printer: "Photo Lab". That is exactly what this type of printer should be. A stand-alone unit that doesn't require a computer. An easy printing machine.

This type of printer should have the following features to be considered.

It should be a stand-alone machine and be able to print without a computer.

It should specialize in printing 4" x 6" prints. This is the most common size of print. Other sizes are a luxury.

It should make fade resistant prints. As we discussed in the previous chapter on Digital Printers, this is a major problem in the industry. The printer you select should have this feature, no questions asked.

It should have a large color LCD screen to allow you to select which images that you wish to print.

It should have card slots for all the major memory card types. This will allow you to plug your memory cards directly into the printer.

It should have "PictBridge" capability. This will allow you to connect your camera directly to the printer and print images easily and directly from your camera.

Useful Features

1	Computer Attachment
2	Print Larger Sizes
3	Wireless Communication
4	Editing Features
5	Extra Printing Features

Previously, we listed the features a printer must have to be considered in this category.

Here we will list other features that make a printer more desirable and give it more potential for future growth. You may never want to go beyond **"Easy Printing"**, and that's perfectly understandable. However, if you want to spread your wings and **"Print with Computer"** later, it would be nice to be able to do so without having to buy another printer.

Here are some features that allow for the flexibility of future growth without compromising the simplicity of **"Easy Printing"**.

Although the printer must be able to work without a computer, it is useful if it can be connected later.

Although the printer should specialize in 4"x6" prints, it will have more future potential if it can print larger sizes.

Wireless communication is a useful feature that allows images to be transferred from cameras, camera phones and other wireless devices to the printer.

Integrated editing features such as cropping and red eye reduction can also be useful.

Some printers come with special printing capabilities such as two sided printing and printing on card stock.

It should be stressed that none of these useful features should in any way impair or restrict any of the necessary features we listed directly above.

Printing System Choice

There are two competing technologies for this type of printer:

1. Inkjet
2. Dye-Sublimation

Choosing between them is a matter of taste. You should have a look at prints from both.

Personally, we prefer Inkjet, but both systems are acceptable.

Advantages of Inkjet:

1	Less Expensive
2	No Dust Problems
3	More Paper Surface Choices
4	More Paper Sizes Choices
5	Not Sensitive to Skin Oil

Advantages of Dye Sublimation:

1	Superior Range of Colors
2	Laminate Coating – Water Resistant
3	No Drying Time Needed
4	No Chance of Clogged Ink

Ink Considerations

1. Number Of Colors
2. Number Of Ink Tanks

As stated above, we prefer the Inkjet system because of the greater choice of paper surfaces (e.g. Matte, semi gloss and glossy) and the greater choice of paper sizes.

If you select an Inkjet system, there are two other ink related considerations that are important.

1. Number Of Colors – more is better
2. Number Of Ink Tanks – more is better

Generally, the more colors of inks there are, the higher the quality of the color output.

Generally, the more ink tanks there are, the less ink that is wasted when whole tanks are replaced when only one color has run out. One ink tank for each ink color is the ultimate option.

Card Slots

Memory cards are listed in order of descending significance in our estimation.

1	SD (Secure Digital)
2	MMC (Multi Media)
3	CF (Compact Flash)
4	MS (Memory Stick & Pro)
5	XD (Fuji & Olympus)
6	USB Flash
7	SM (Smart Media) *

We actually prefer using Memory Cards to transfer your images to your stand-alone printer as opposed to connecting your camera directly to the printer. However, your printer should be able to do both.

It is important that the printer you select be able to accept the specific card used by your camera.

However, we feel that the printer should be able to accept every major type of Memory Card. You may change cameras and thus Memory Card in the future. You may also wish to print from other people's cards. There is no reason to limit flexibility in this regard.

* Note: We do not consider SM (Smart Media) to be a good choice for the future.

PictBridge

PictBridge gives you complete inter-brand connectivity between any PictBridge camera and any PictBridge printer without using a computer.

PictBridge is a worldwide Direct Print Standard that allows digital cameras and other image capture devices to connect and print directly to photo printers and other output devices – no computer is required.

You can connect any PictBridge compatible digital camera to any PictBridge compatible printer regardless of the manufacturer to enjoy direct printing without using of a computer.

Major Manufacturers

The major manufacturers, in our estimation, listed alphabetically:

1. Canon
2. Epson
3. Kodak
4. Sony

As stated in a previous chapter on Digital Camera Selection, we suggest limiting your initial choice to the major manufacturers. You can look at other manufacturers later if desired.

According to the camera sales figure, previously listed on page 143, Canon, Sony and Kodak are the major players in the digital imaging industry at the present time.

We feel one other manufacturer should also be taken into consideration. Epson has specialized in digital printers and has become an industry leader and innovator in digital printing.

We will now consider an appropriate example product from each of these four manufacturers.

The Product List

We have selected one representative product from each of these four manufacturers:

1	Canon	PIXMA iP6600D
2	Epson	Picture Mate Deluxe – Viewer Edition
3	Kodak	Easy Share Photo Printer 500
4	Sony	DPPFP55 Picture Station

Product Comparison

Manufacturers	Canon	Epson	Kodak	Sony
Functional Type	Alone + Computer	Alone + Computer	Alone + Computer	Alone + Computer
Printing System	Inkjet	Inkjet	Dye Sub	Dye Sub
Print Size Available	4” x 6” up to 8”x10”	4” x 6” max	4” x 6” max	4” x 6” max
Fade Resistance	Yes	Yes	Yes	Yes
Color LCD	3.5” flip	2.4” flip	3.5” flip	2”
# of Ink Colors / Cartridges	6 / 6	6 / 1	n / a	n / a
Card Slots	SD,MMC, CF, MS, xD, SM,	SD,MMC, CF, MS, xD, SM,	SD,MMC, CF, MS, xD, USbFlash	SD, MS
PictBridge	Yes	Yes	Yes	Yes
Wireless	Yes	Yes	Yes	Yes

Product Comments

Canon: PIXMA iP6600D

This product uses an inkjet printing system. It distinguishes itself by have 6 ink colors with 6 separate ink cartridges, one for each color. It prints 4"x6" prints with ease, but it also can print up to 8"x10".

Epson: Picture Mate Deluxe – Viewer Edition

This product uses an inkjet printing system. It has 6 colors but only one ink cartridge. It is very compact with a small footprint and therefore quite portable. However, it is restricted to a maximum print size of 4"x6".

Epson also makes a product called the R300 which accepts memory cards and print up to 8"x10". However, it lacks fade resistant inks.

Kodak: Easy Share Photo Printer 500

This product uses a dye-sublimation printing system. It has a small footprint and is very compact, but is restricted to a maximum print size of 4"x6".

Sony: DPPFP55 Picture Station

This product uses a dye-sublimation printing system. It has a small footprint and is very compact, but is restricted to a maximum print size of 4"x6".

This product also suffers from a lack of Memory Card slot availability.

Canon For Illustration

This selection process would be easier if every manufacturer only made one printer in this category. Unfortunately, it's not that simple. But, of course, more models mean more choices when it comes to selecting a ideal printer.

Fortunately, we can use the same considerations listed above to assess the various models available from one manufacturer.

We will now illustrate this process using Canon as they have a good variety of models. We will not consider all the Canon printers in this class, there are too many. But, once you understand this process, you can easily apply it to other Canon models and other models from other manufacturers.

Cannon Models	iP6600D	iP6220D	Sephy DS810	Sephy CP710
Functional Type	Alone + Computer	Alone + Computer	Alone + Computer	Alone + Computer
Printing System	Inkjet	Inkjet	Inkjet	Dye Sub
Print Sizes Available	4" x 6" up to 8"x 10"	4" x 6" up to 8"x 10"	4" x 6" max	4" x 6" max
Fade Resistance	Yes	Yes	Yes	Yes
Color LCD	3.5" flip	2.5" flip	2.5" flip	1.5"
# of Ink Colors / Cartriges	6 / 6	6 /2	3 /1	n/a
Card Slots	SD,MMC CF, MS, xD, SM	SD,MMC CF, MS, xD, SM	SD,MMC CF, MS, xD, SM	SD,MMC CF, MS,
PictBridge	Yes	Yes	Yes	Yes
Wireless	Yes	Yes	Yes	Yes

Model Comments

Canon: PIXMA iP6600D & iP6220D

These products use an inkjet printing system. Both have 6 ink colors. The former has 6 ink cartridges, one for each color. The latter has only 2 cartridges. Both print 4"x6" prints with ease, but can also print up to 8"x10".

Canon: Sephy DS 810

This printer uses an inkjet system. It has a smaller footprint and is more portable, but cannot print any larger than 4"x6".

Canon: Sephy DS 710

This printer uses a dye sublimation system. It has a smaller footprint and is more portable but cannot print any larger than 4"x6". It has a smaller non-flip LCD screen and fewer Memory Card options.

Conclusion

We feel that this class of printer best meets the needs of the beginner who want to print at home. These printers allow **"Easy Printing"** without a computer, but allow you to print with a computer later.

Chapter 13 EASY PRINTING

Introduction

In this chapter, we will deal with the easiest and most straight-forward way to print: printing with a printer but no computer.

We will use a stand alone printer, the Canon iP6600D, for illustrative purposes. Other similar printers from other manufacturers will perform similarly.

We will cover:

1. Setting up the printer.
2. Printing directly from your Memory Card.
3. Printing directly from your camera with PictBridge.
4. Moving your images to your computer.

Printer Supplies

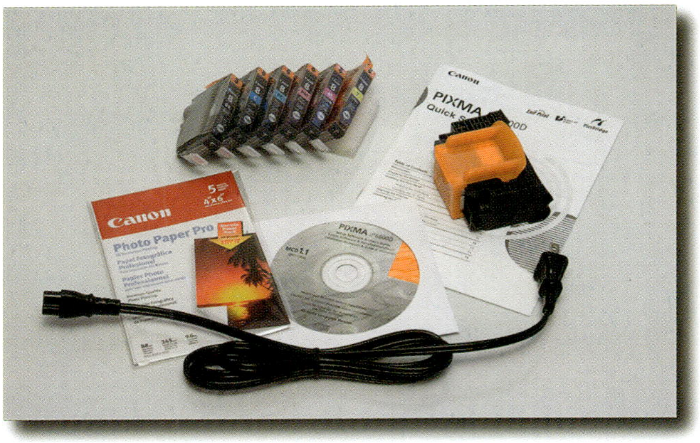

Open the printer's box and check that the contents are all there.

You will receive only a small amount of photo paper with the printer. You should purchase more paper when you pick up your printer. We recommend you purchase only photo paper and ink made by the manufacturer of your printer specifically for your printer.

Printer Setup

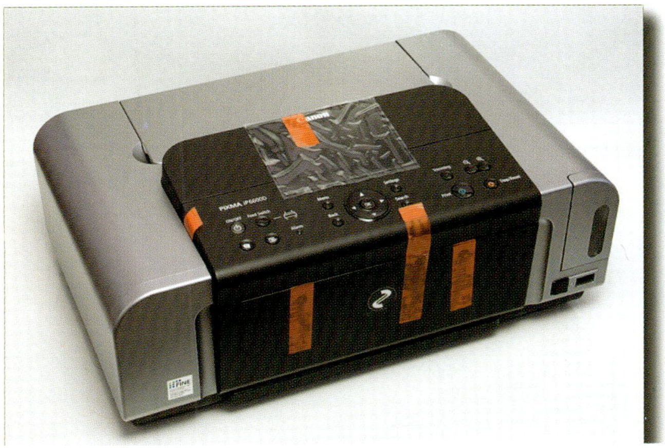

Remove the tape and packing materials according to your instruction manual.

Follow the printer manufacturer's instructions to install the print head and ink cartridges.

DO NOT install the printer drivers and software that came with your printer if you want **"Easy Printing"** without a computer.

The next chapter will deal with this in **"Printing with Computer"**.

Printer Controls

We are only going to deal with a few of the printer controls in this chapter, because we are just doing **"Easy Printing"**.

If you haven't already done so, press the **ON** button.

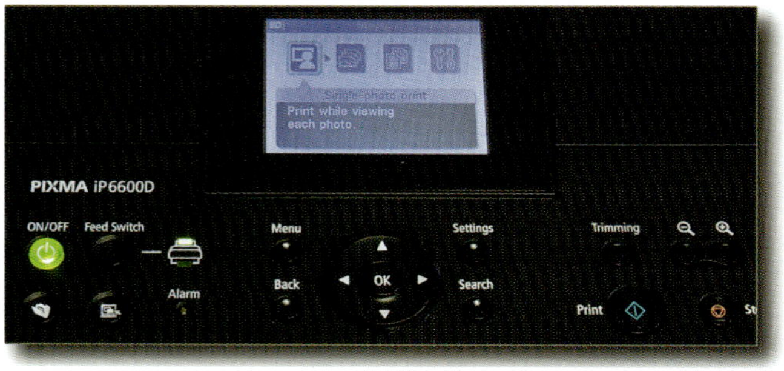

Settings Button

Before printing, we must be sure that our basic settings are correct.

Press the **Settings** button.

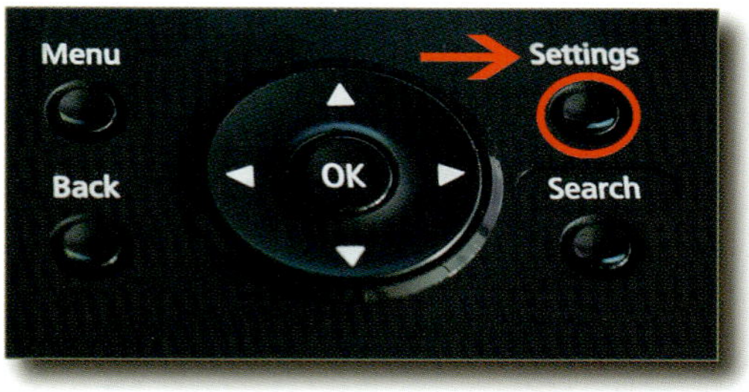

Basic Settings

1. Set the size to 4" x 6"
2. Set to match the type of paper you put in your printer
3. The printer profile should be "Standard"
4. Set your printer to "Borderless"

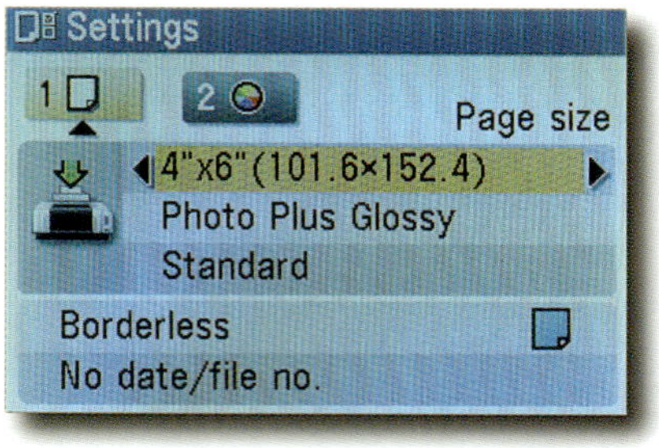

Menu Button

Bring up the main menu on the printer LCD by pressing the **Menu** button.

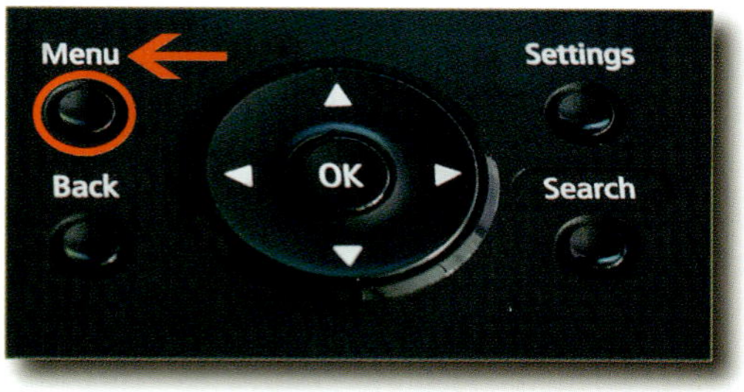

Menu Settings

In this chapter, we are only going to deal with Single-photo print, so you don't have to change that setting.

If you want to explore other features later, the menu selections will take you there.

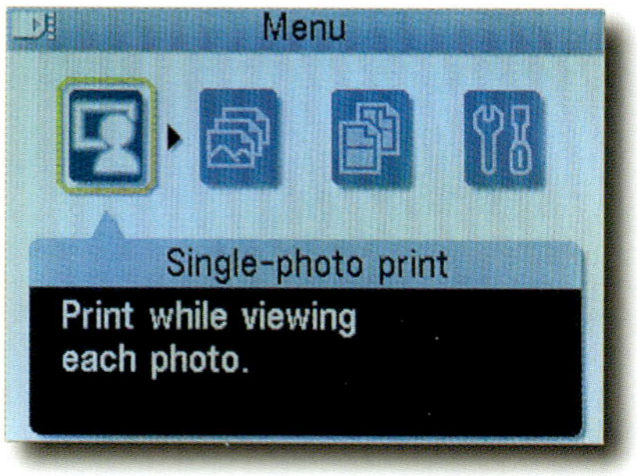

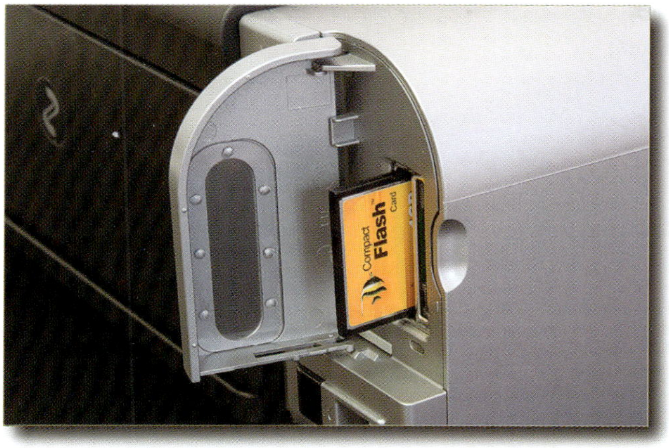

Printing From A Memory Card: Step 1

Put your full Memory Card from your camera into the appropriate card slot in your printer.

Make sure the contacts are facing in, and the card is facing the correct way

The card should slip in easily and smoothly.

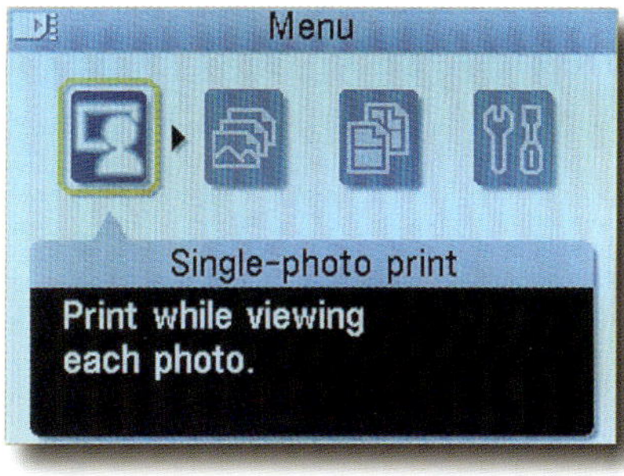

Card Printing: Step 2

As stated above, do not change the default menu selection.

We want **Single-photo print**.

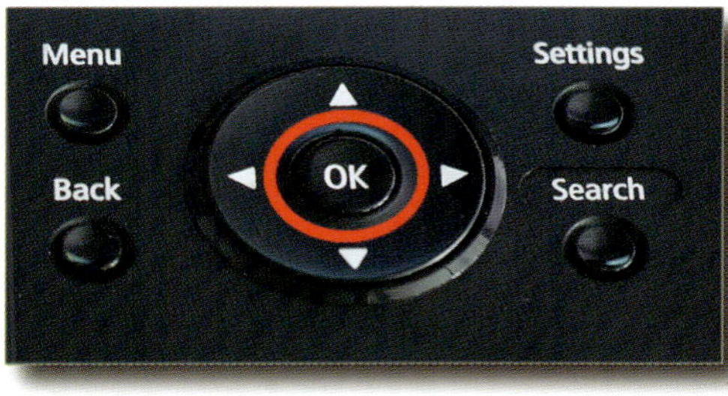

Card Printing: Step 3

To proceed,

Press the **OK** button.

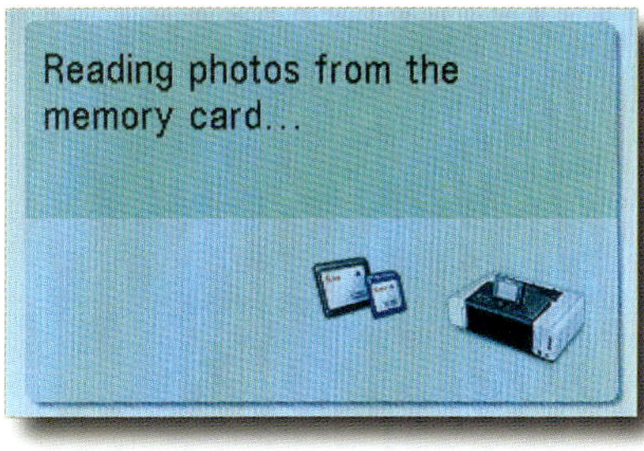

Card Printing: Step 4

The printer will now automatically read all the photos that are on your Memory Card.

Card Printing: Step 5

Your images can now be displayed on the LCD screen of your printer.

The first image will appear on the LCD screen.

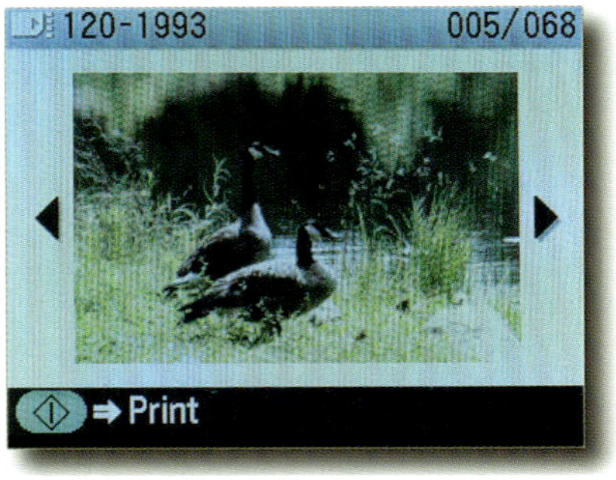

Card Printing: Step 6

You can use the horizontal rocker switch to move through all the images on your Memory Card.

When the image that you want to print appears on the screen, you are ready to print.

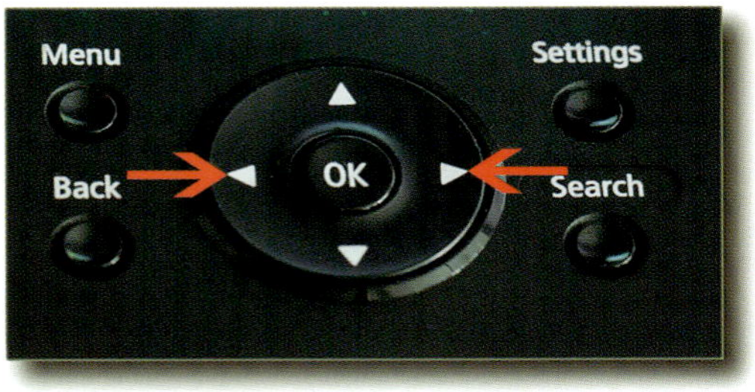

Card Printing Step: 7

Press the **Print** button.

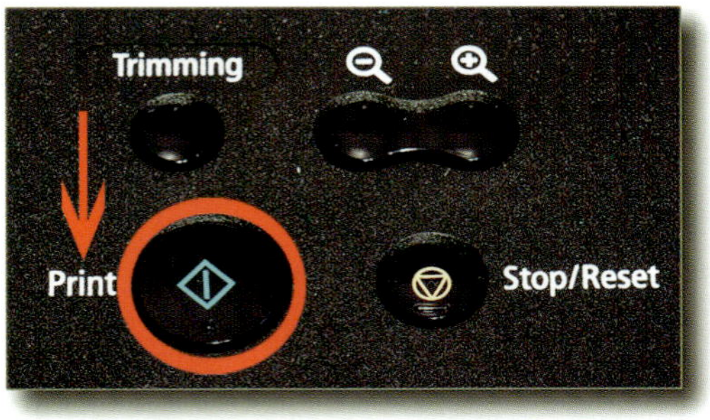

Card Printing: Step 8

As long as you have photo paper and ink in the printer, your image should print.

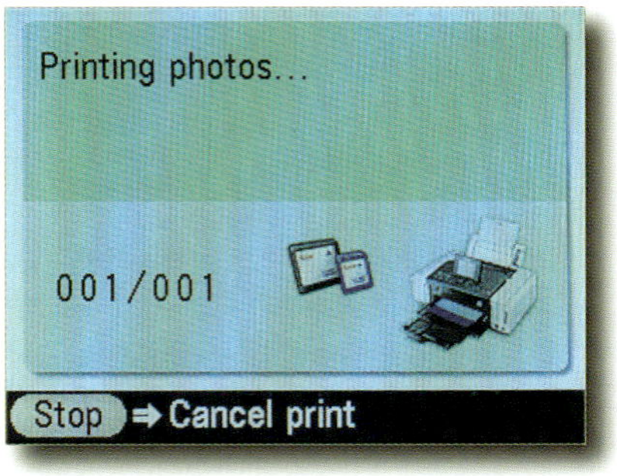

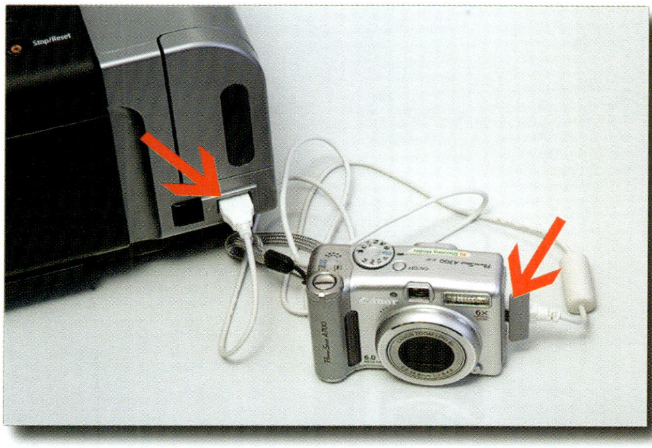

Printing From Your Camera With PictBridge:

Step 1

Attach your PictBridge compliant camera to your PictBridge compliant printer.

You must use the special cable that came with your camera.

Make sure printer and camera are turned on. The camera should be in **Play** mode, not the **Record** mode.

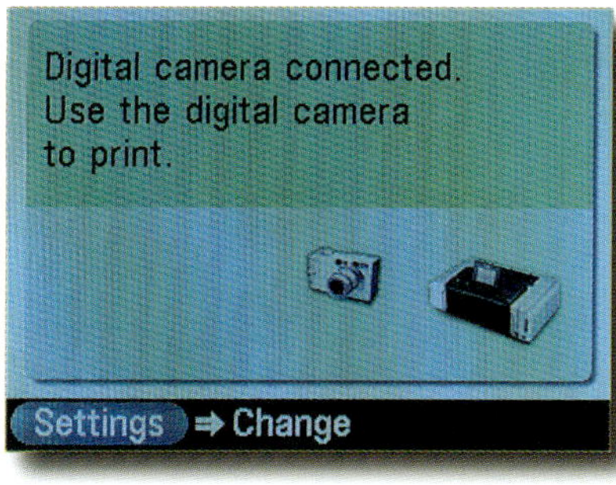

Step 2

The LCD screen on the printer will tell you that the printer is turning over control of this printing session to the camera.

You print from the camera through the printer when using PictBridge.

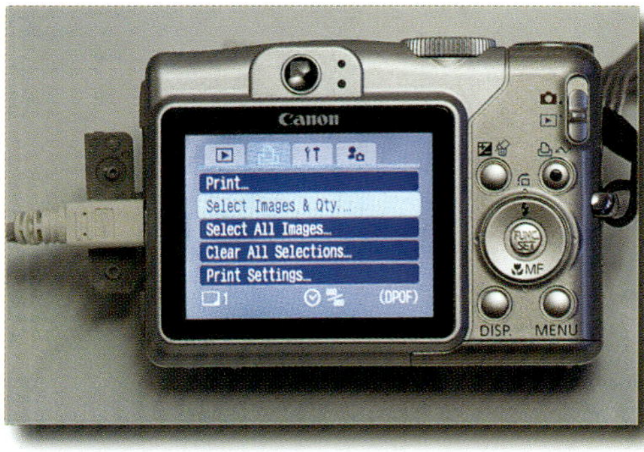

Step 3

Use the camera's menu system to select the image(s) that you want to print.

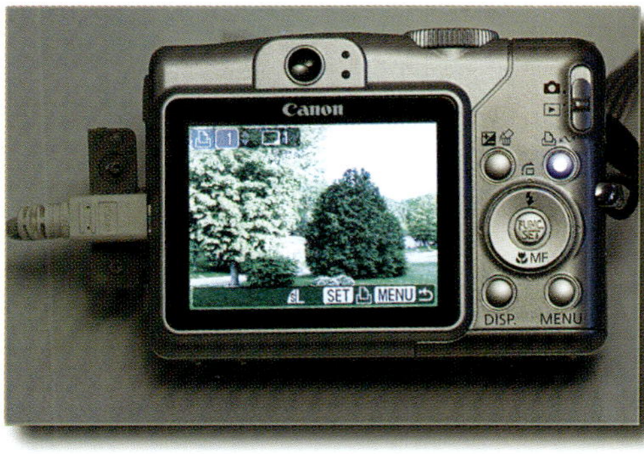

Step 4

Use the LCD on the back of the camera, not the printer's LCD, to view and select the images you want to print.

Step 5

Once the image(s) are selected, the camera will direct the printer to print.

You can repeat this process to print other images.

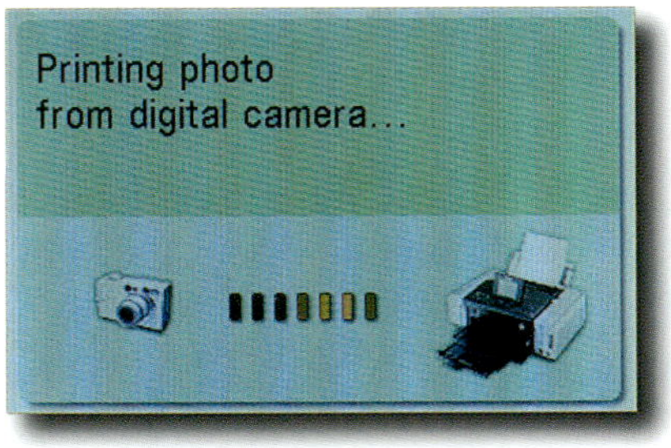

Storing your Pictures

Once you have printed all the images that you want printed, you should copy all your images onto the hard drive of your computer.

We recommend that you do this with a Memory Card Reader. You will need some software as well. We recommend any of the Adobe products detailed earlier in this book. Please refer to the appropriate chapter for instructions on storing your pictures.

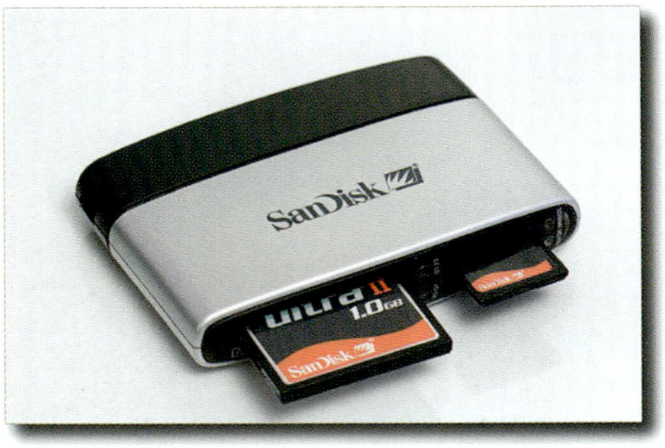

Reformatting your Card

When the desired images are printed and all your images are safely stored on the hard drive of your computer, you will have to erase the images from your Memory Card. This will allow you to reuse the Memory Card.

We strongly recommend that you do this by (re)formatting the card in your camera using it's menu system.

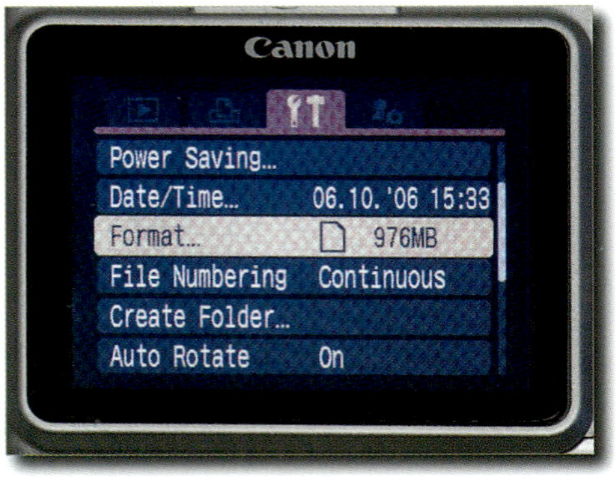

Conclusion

In this chapter, we used the Canon iP6600D to illustrate two ways to print without using a computer. Other similar printers will perform in the same way. We then copied our images to a computer and erased the Memory Card.

Chapter 14 PRINTING WITH COMPUTER

Introduction

In this chapter, we will discuss using a printer to reprint your images after your Memory Cards have been erased, as well as the recommended software you will need to allow this to happen.

We will cover:

1. Setting up your printer (drivers) in Windows.
2. (Re)printing your images from the computer.
3. Reprinting images from your Memory Card.

Printing with Computer

There are three considerations you need to take into account for printing with computer:

1. Extra Printer Functions: such as cropping, red eye reduction and multi printing – we will not cover these since there is too much inter-printer variation.
2. Reprinting Images from the Computer: this requires a computer attached to your printer and editing software – we will cover this.
3. Reprinting Images from a Memory Card: this requires a computer, not necessarily attached to your printer and editing software – we will cover this.

Why Connect Printer and Computer?

It's not difficult to connect a computer and the printer together. If you connect them, you will have more printing options available to you. Also, just because they are connected, doesn't mean you have to use them that way.

It is not mandatory that you connect them, but we recommend it.

To connect your computer and your printer, you will need an appropriate USB cable, (USB 2.0), as shown below.

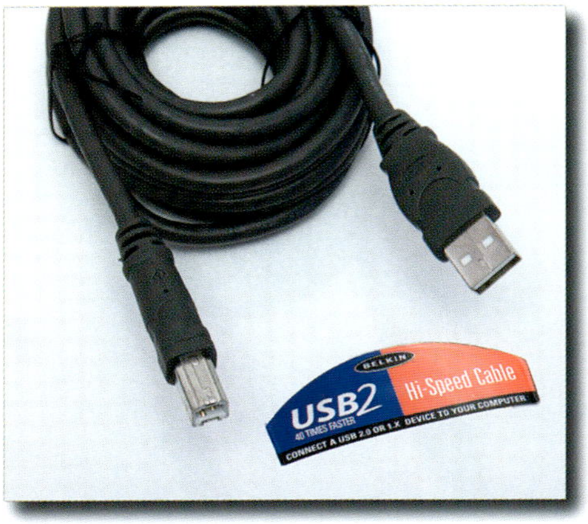

Software Selection

All Adobe products allow you to reprint your images with your printer connected to a computer.

Album Starter does not allow you to export images to a Memory Card for reprinting. (page 178)

Album Starter does not allow you to backup images onto CDs or DVDs (covered in next chapter).

We recommend upgrading from Album Starter to one of the other products.

Printer Drivers From CD

To connect your printer to your computer, you must install the Printer Software Drivers from CD that came with your printer. This will let Windows get to know your printer.

It is preferable to <u>**not**</u> let Windows do the installation by itself. If you see the screen similar to the one shown on the right, it is advisable to **Cancel**, turn off the printer and start over again.

Printer Driver Installation

Follow the instructions for software installation in your printer manual. It is important that you do not turn on either the computer or the printer until instructed to do so. It is also important that you do not physically connect the printer and computer until instructed to do so. We have shown the usual order of steps on the right, but follow the printer manual if there are any differences.

Adobe Products	Export Option	Backup Option
Album Starter	No	No
Album Full	Yes	Yes
Elements (All)	Yes	Yes
Photoshop CS2	Yes	Yes

Album Full is the most affordable and basic of the recommended products. It is covered earlier in this book in Chapter 7, page 101-112.

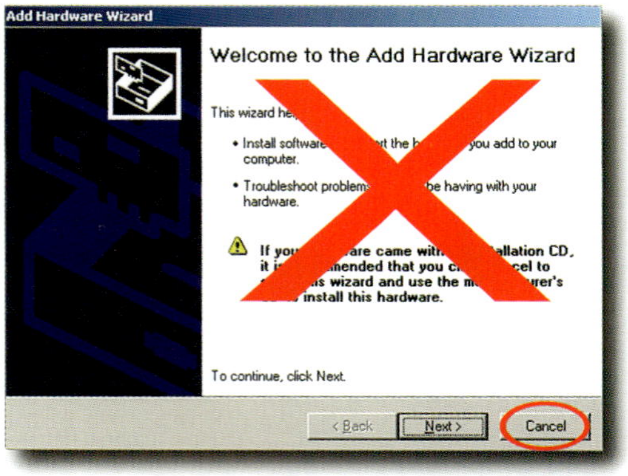

Normal Installation Steps for Printer Software Drivers.

1. Turn off printer and computer.
2. Turn on computer.
3. Put printer software CD in the CD drive.
4. The CD should auto-start.
5. Follow the screen prompts to install the software.
6. When instructed to do so, connect printer and computer with a USB cable (shown previously).
7. Turn on the printer.
8. Windows should display a message that it has found new hardware, and that the new hardware is ready to use.
9. We recommend that you reboot your computer.

Methods of Printing from your Hard Drive:

1. Print through the computer to the printer using editing software.
2. Copy images from your hard drive to an empty Memory Card using editing software. Then, using the "Easy Printing" technique discussed in the previous chapter, print the desired images.

Printing in Adobe Software:

Software	Chapter	Page
Album Starter	6	98
Album Full	7	110
Element Basic	8	124
Element Advanced	9	140

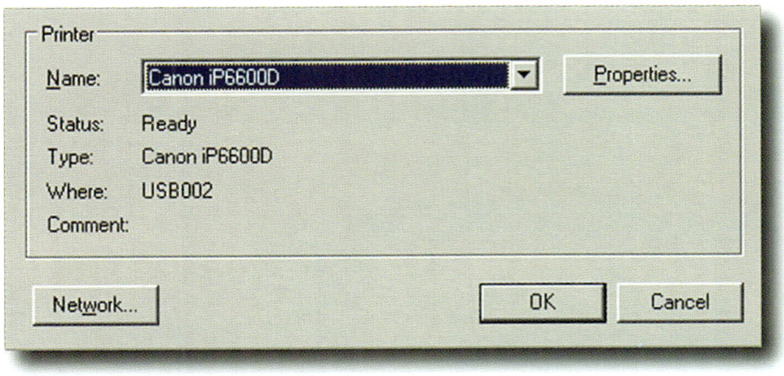

Which Method to Use

There are two ways to print images after they have been copied onto the hard drive of your computer and erased from your Memory Card.

These two methods are shown on the left.

We recommend the first method since it is more straight forward.

Method #1:

Printing from a Computer

If you wish to print images from your computer, you will need to use some editing software. We recommend you use Adobe Album, Adobe Elements or Adobe Photoshop.

Therefore, to print images from your computer, please refer to the appropriate page in this book for the Adobe product that you wish to use.

Printing From Computer Caution

One word of caution, if you have more than one printer attached, make sure you select the correct printer as shown on the left.

In our example, we have made sure that the "Canon iP6600D" is selected as our printer.

Method #2

The Memory Card Option

There is another option for printing. You can copy images from your computer onto an empty Memory Card. You can then insert the Memory Card into your printer and print using the **"Easy Printing"** method detailed in the last chapter.

Adobe Products	Export Option
Album Starter	No
* Album Full	Yes
* Elements (All)	Yes
* Photoshop CS2	Yes

Note: Only the products with a "*" beside them can be used for the Export Option.

Memory Card (Re)Printing:

Step 1 – Selecting Images

Select any image that you wish to copy onto the Memory Card by clicking on that image in the Photo Well. A colored box will appear around that image.

If you want to select several images to copy to the Memory Card, hold **Ctrl** while you click on the desired images.

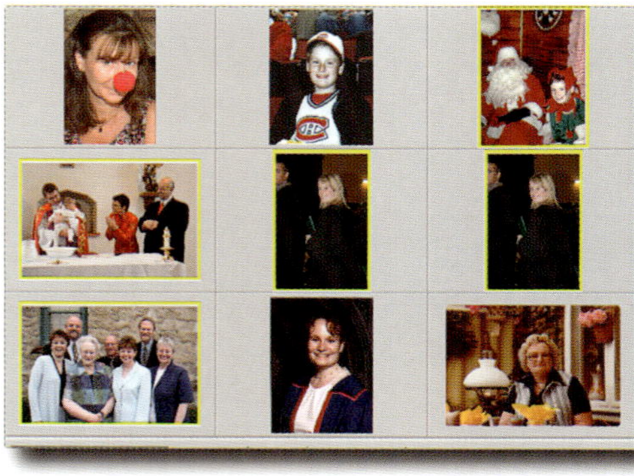

Memory Card (Re)Printing:

Step 2 – Export Function

From the Main Menu, click on the **File** button.

From the Drop Down Menu, click on the **Export** button.

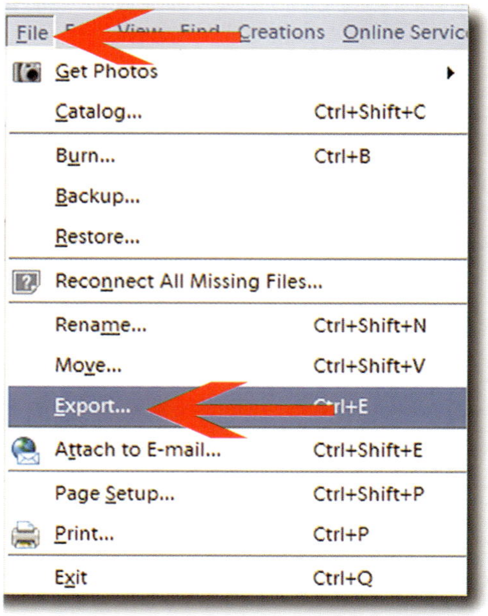

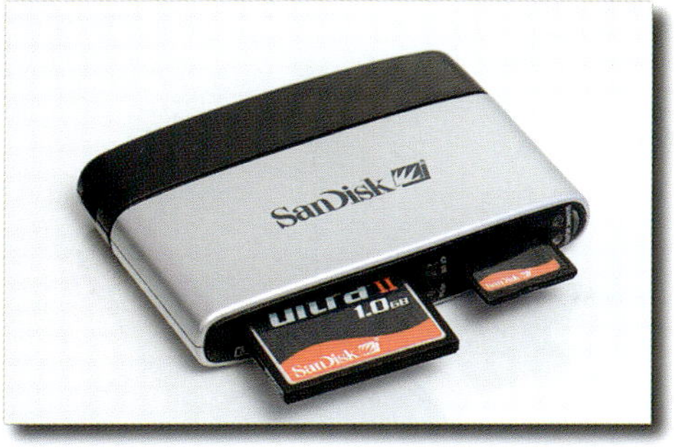

Memory Card (Re)Printing:

Step 3 – Insert Card

Insert your Memory Card into the Memory Card Reader.

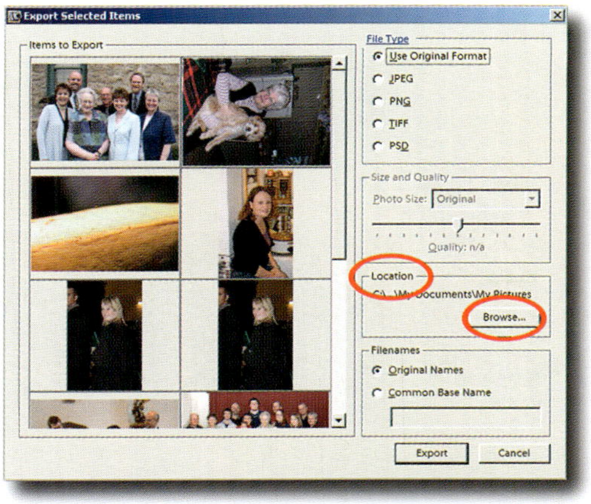

Memory Card (Re)Printing:

Step 4 – Browse

With the **Export** dialog box on the screen, find the area of the screen labeled: **Location**.

In this area, click the **Browse** button.

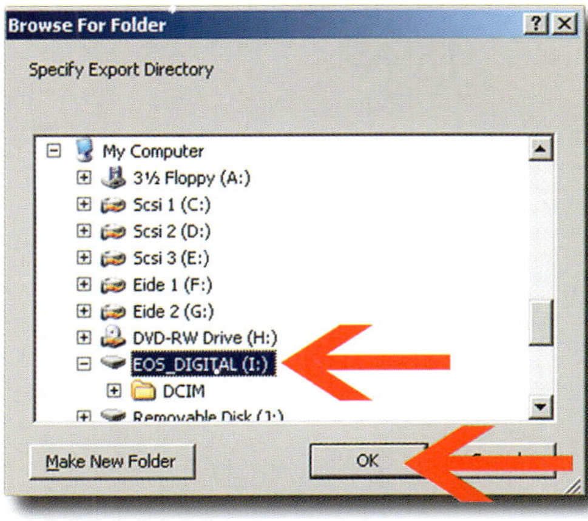

Memory Card (Re)Printing:

Step 5 – Direct to Card

Find the **Drive Letter** that represents your Memory Card and Reader. Click on this Drive. In this example our card in the card Reader is represented as Drive **I**.

Here we have clicked on Drive **I** and it has been highlighted in blue.

Then click the **OK** button.

The images will transfer to your Memory Card.

Memory Card (Re)Printing:

Step 6 – Copy to Card

To begin the copy process, click on the **Export** button.

The images will now be copied to your Memory Card. When the copying is complete, you can remove the Memory Card from the Reader.

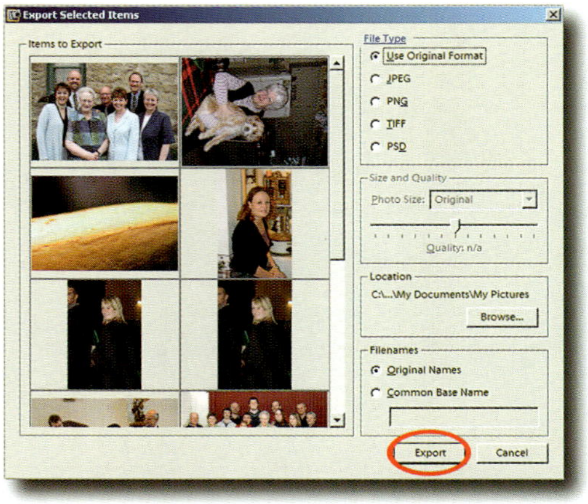

Memory Card (Re)Printing:

Step 7 – Easy Printing

Please refer to the chapter on "**Easy Printing**" and follow the instructions for printing images from a Memory Card.

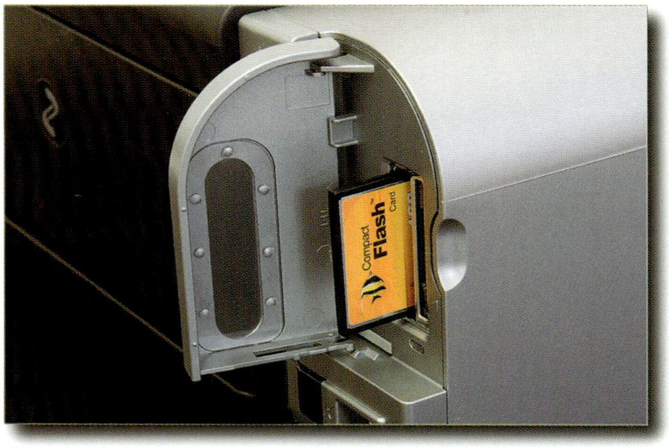

Conclusion

In this chapter, we discussed using the printer to reprint your images after your Memory Cards have been erased. We recommended software that you will need to accomplish this.

We covered

1. Setting up your printer in Windows.
2. (Re)printing your images from the computer.
3. Reprinting images from your Memory Card.

Chapter 15 BACKING UP

Introduction

As you take more pictures and transfer them to your computer's hard drive, the need to back them up increases. Every hard drive will eventually fail and when this happens, you could lose some if not all of your images. You must back up and have at least two copies of each image.

You need software to be able to back up images. We recommend that you use Adobe Album Full or Adobe Elements to do this since there is a backup routine seamlessly built into these programs. You must also have a CD/DVD burner in your computer.

Accessing Backup

In this chapter, we will use Album Full to illustrate the backup process.

In the Main Menu, click the **File** button.

From the Drop Down Menu, select either one of these two: **Burn** or **Backup** button.

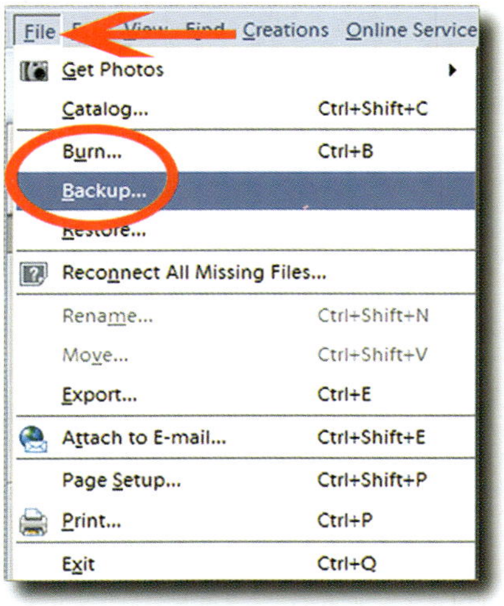

Catalog Backup

We need to backup the images in our Image Catalogue, so click beside:

Backup the Catalog

Then, click on the **Next** button.

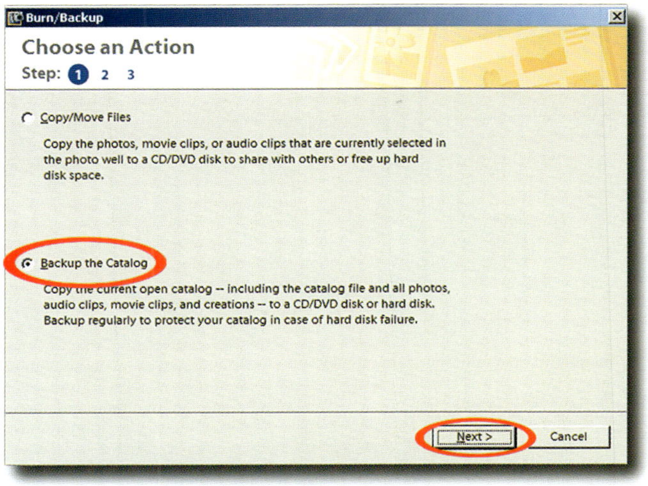

Reconnect

We recommend that you click on the **Reconnect** button.

This will insure that no images are missed during backup.

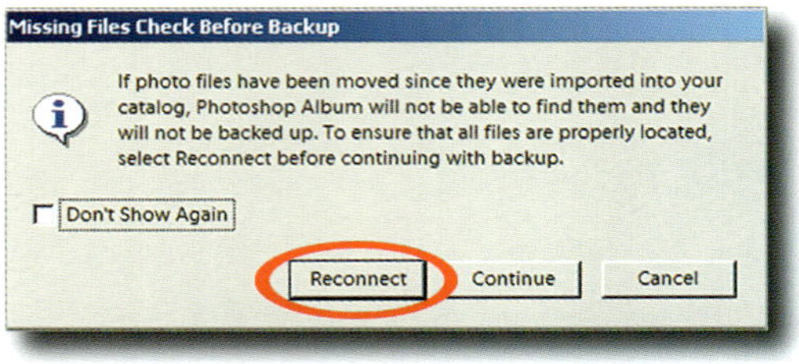

First and Complete Backup

The first time you want to perform a backup and any time you wish to make another copy of the complete backup, we suggest that you click beside the **Full Backup** button.

Then, click on the **Next** button.

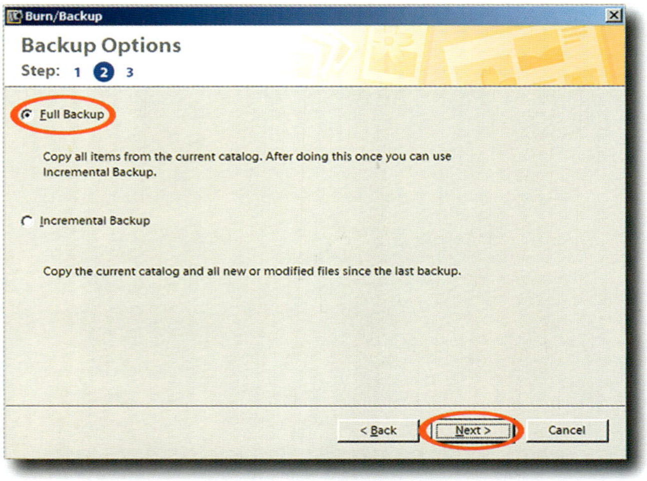

Subsequent Backups

After the first backup has been performed, you should use the Incremental Backup.

This will backup only the images that have been added since the last time you backed up.

For subsequent backups, click on the **Incremental Backup** button.

Then, click on the **Next** button.

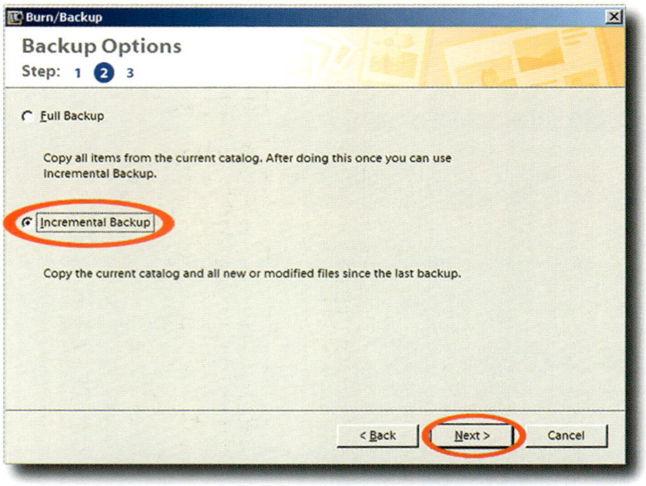

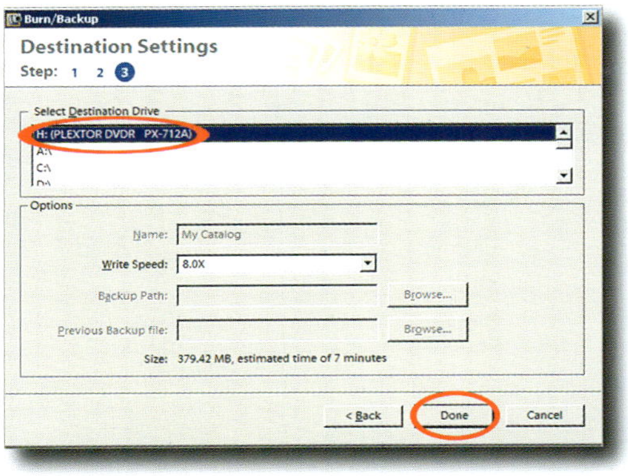

CD/DVD Drive:

The program should be able to find your CD/DVD recording drive. If you have more than one CD/DVD drive, you may have to direct the program to the appropriate one. Here, we have indicated Drive "I" as our CD/DVD drive.

Place a blank CD or DVD in the appropriate slot and click the **Done** button.

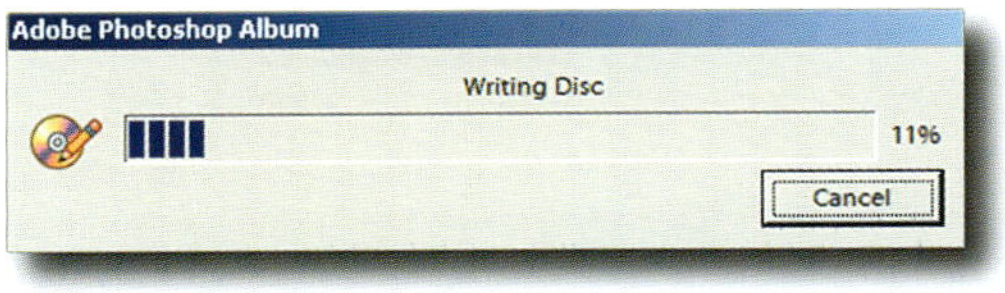

Writing To Disc

The Program will now copy your images to the blank CD or DVD in the drive.

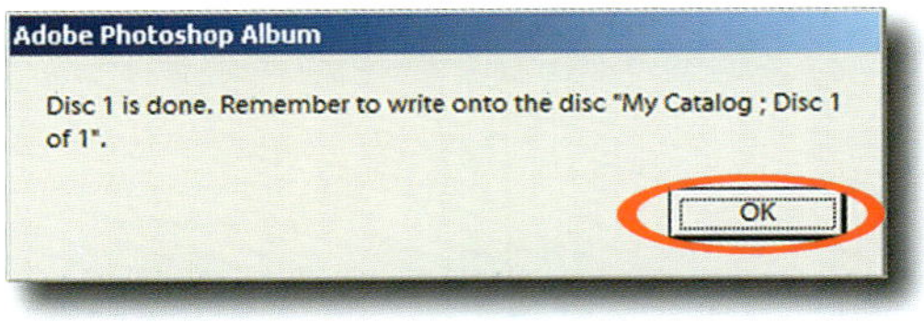

Label the CD or DVD

Once you have backed up a few times, it can be difficult to keep track of things. It is important to keep well organized and label your CDs or DVDs.

Click on the **OK** button.

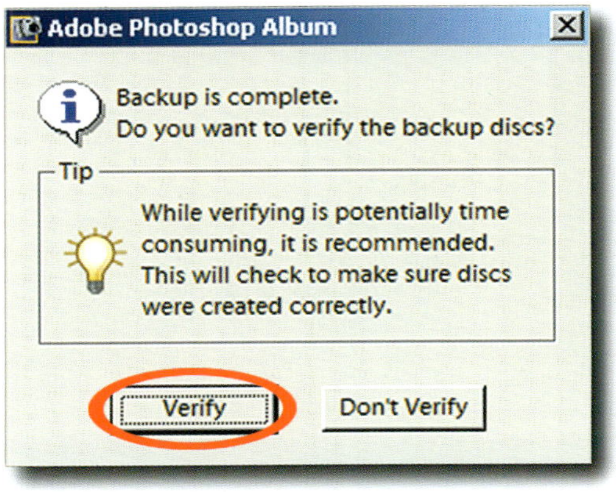

Verification Recommended

Computers can make mistakes and you can purchase CDs & DVDs that are defective. It's strongly recommended that you allow the software to confirm that the images on the CD or DVD are identical copies of the original on the hard drive.

Click on the **Verify** button.

Start Verification

Your disc should still be in the computer, so just click on the **Verify Disc** button.

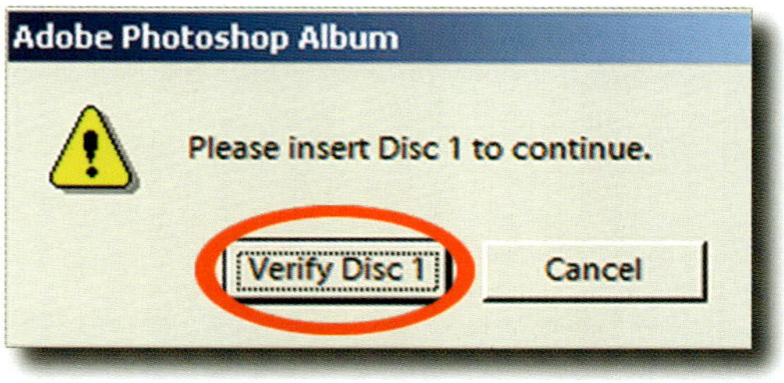

Verification Process

The verification process will then take place.

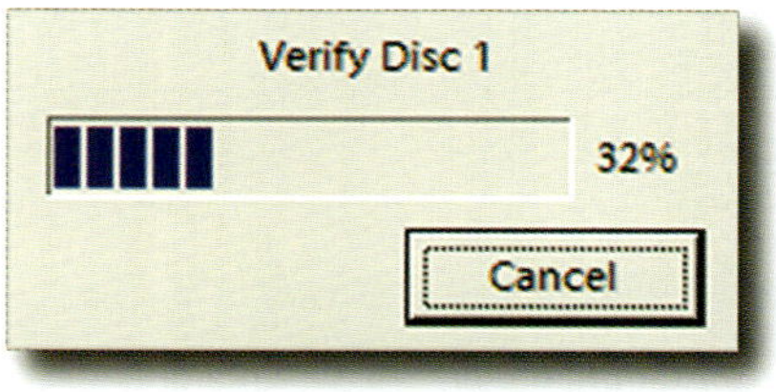

Backup Complete

When the backup has been confirmed as complete and successful, click on the **OK** button.

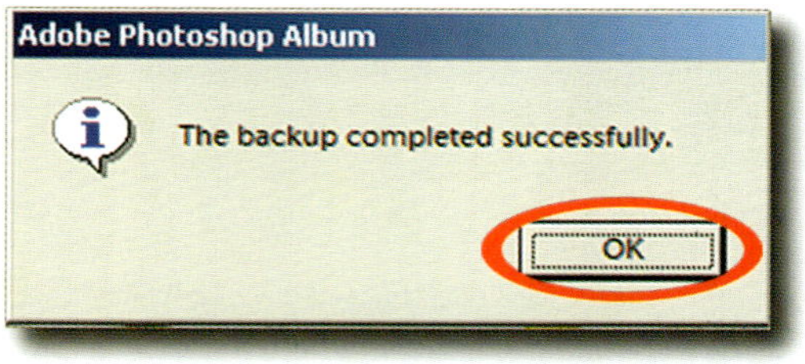

Conclusion

You must backup and have at least two copies of each image that you own.

We recommend that you use Album Full or Elements to backup since there is a backup routine seamlessly built into these programs. You must also have a CD/DVD burner in your computer.

This chapter illustrated, using Adobe Album Full, the complete backup procedure needed to make and maintain backup copies of all your images.

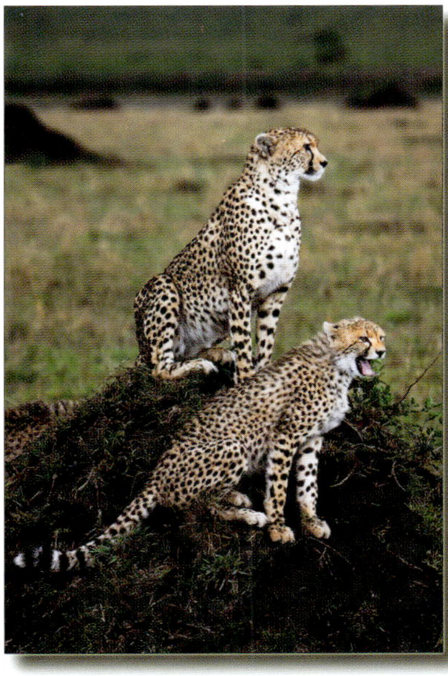
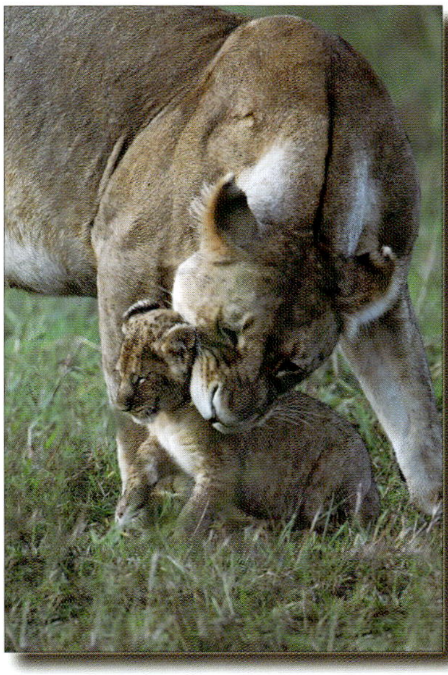
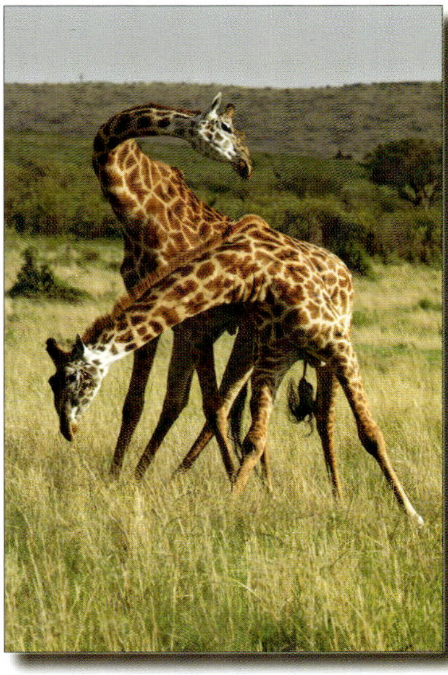
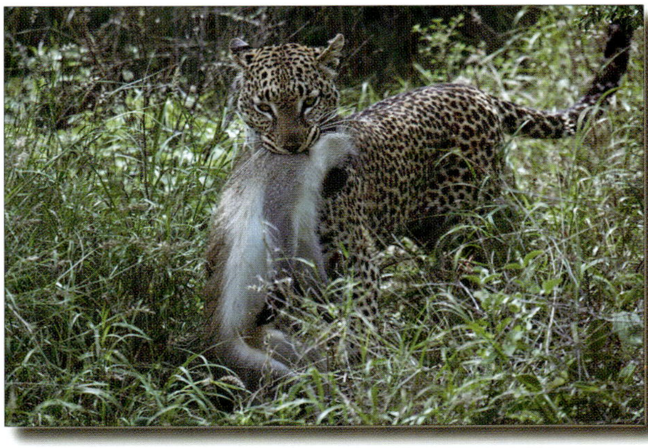
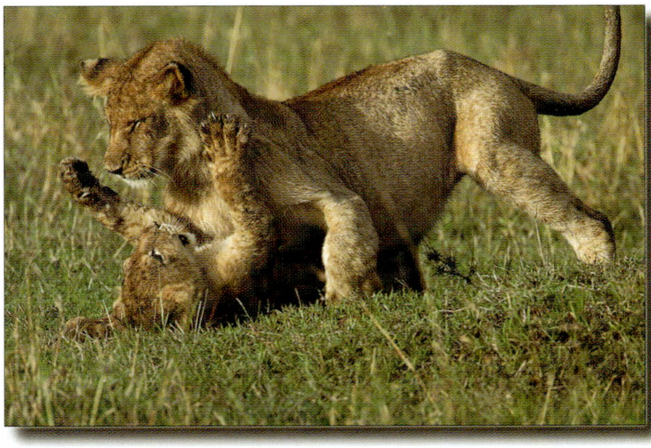
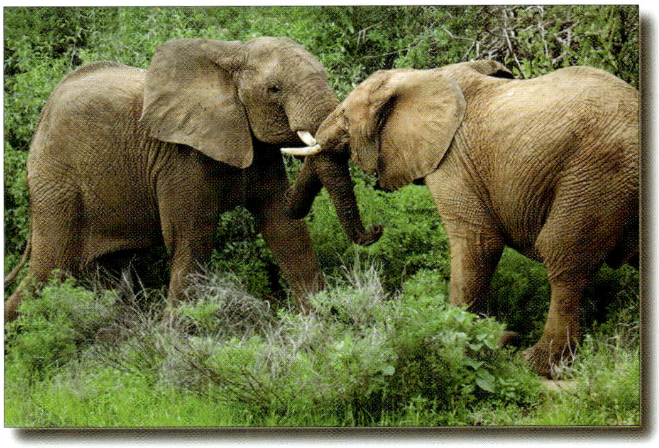
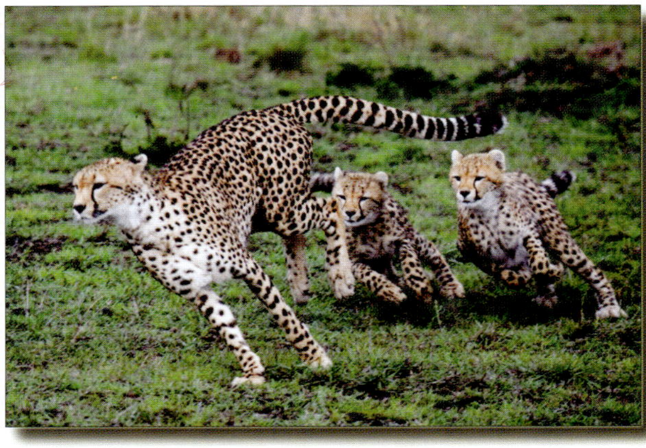

Photos by Phil Kwan

INDEX

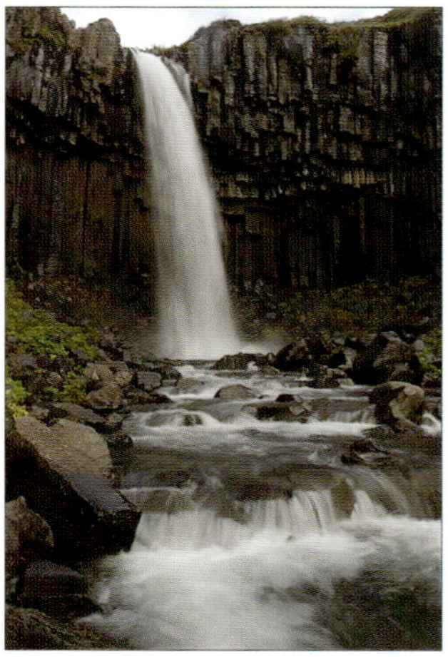

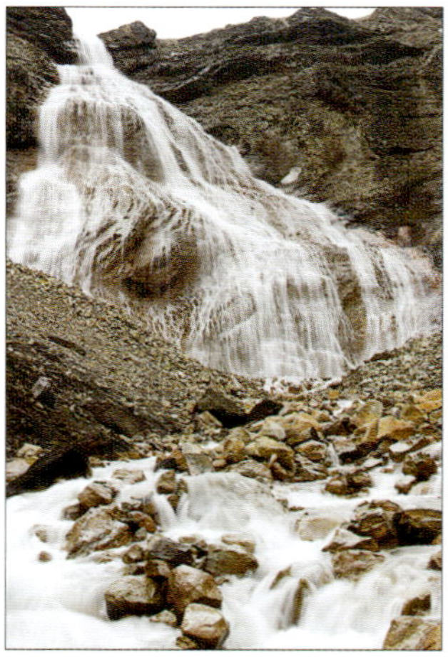

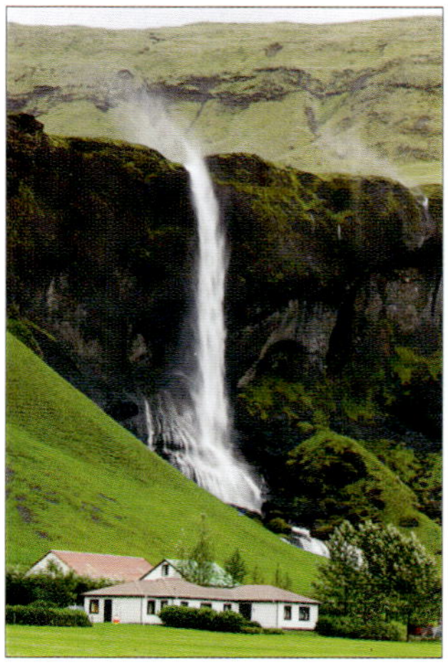

A

B

C

INDEX

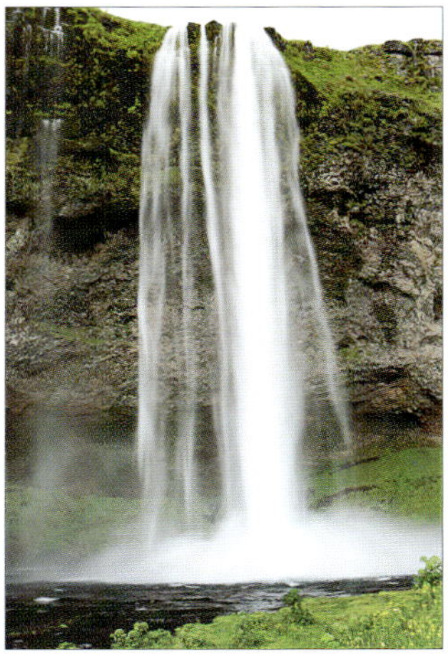

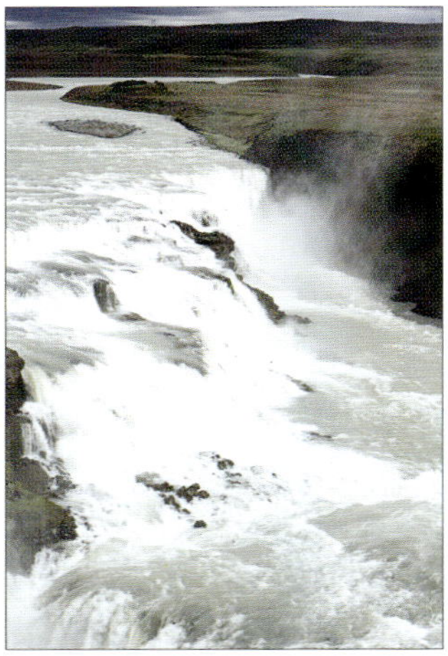

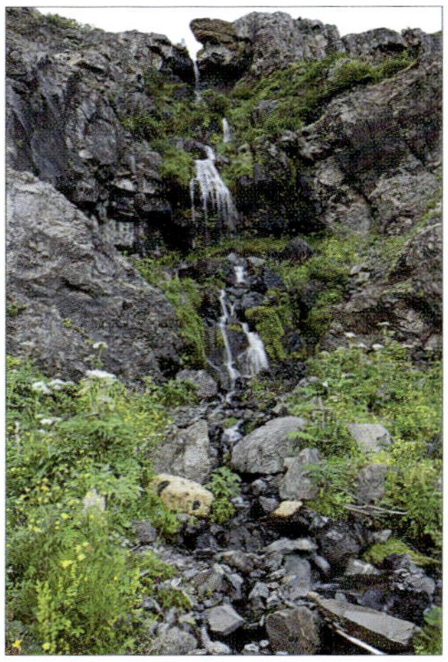

INDEX

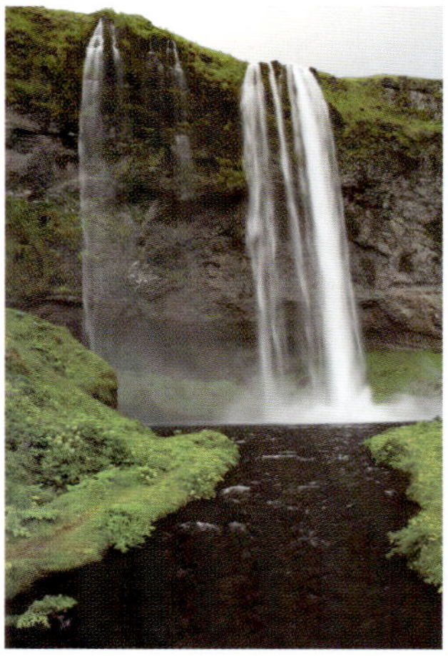

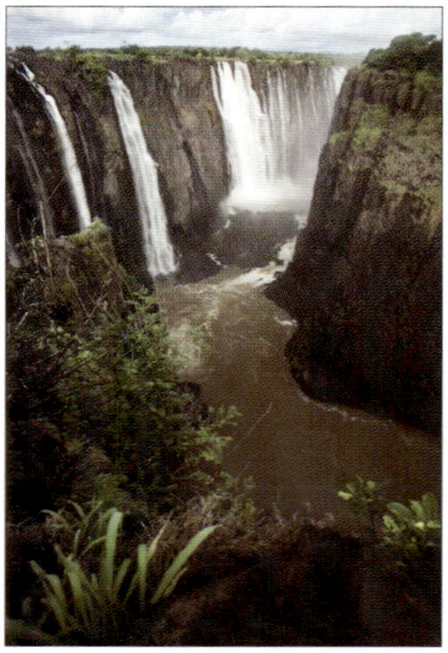

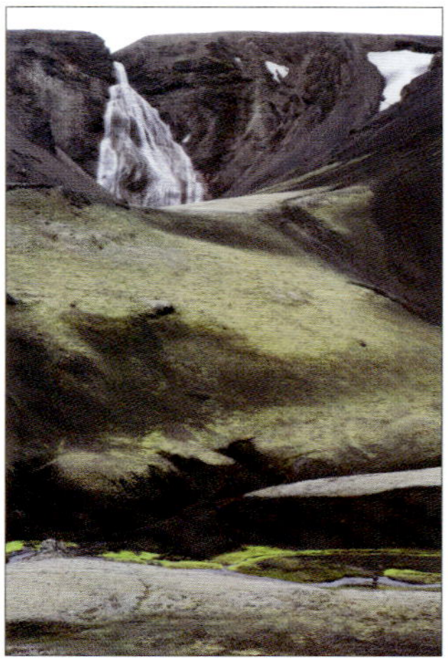

INDEX

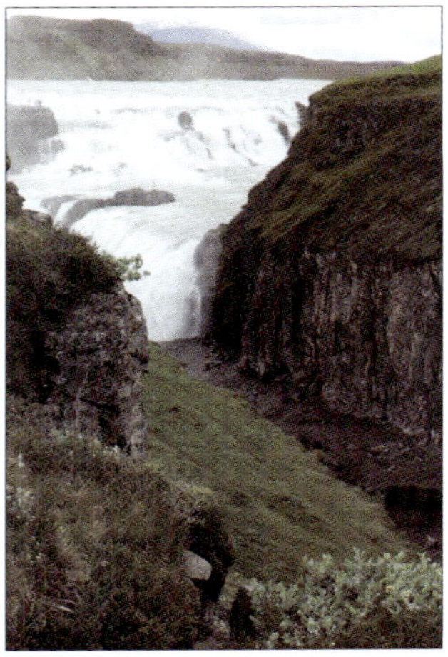

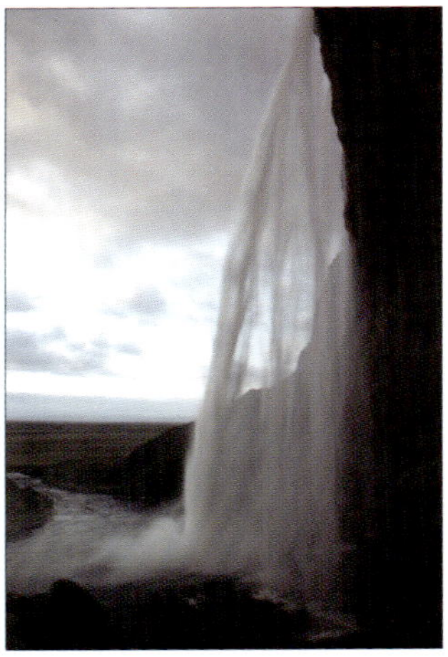

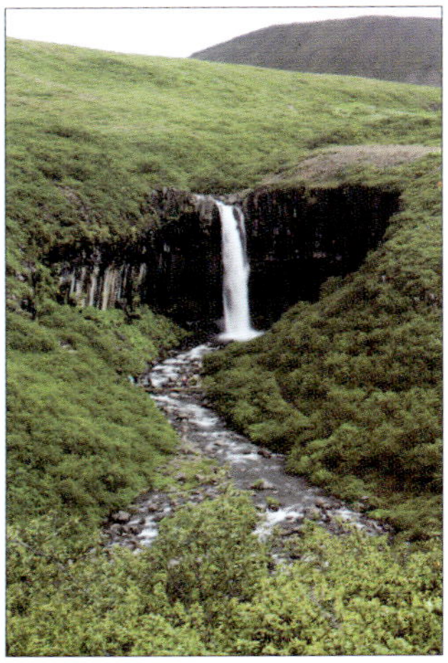